R.I.P.
G.O.P.

R.I.P.

G.O.P.

HOW THE NEW AMERICA IS
DOOMING THE REPUBLICANS

STANLEY B. GREENBERG

THOMAS DUNNE BOOKS
NEW YORK

First published in the United States by Thomas Dunne Books, an imprint of St. Martin's Publishing Group.

www.thomasdunnebooks.com

Library of Congress Cataloging-in-Publication Data

Names: Greenberg, Stanley B., 1945– author.
Title: RIP GOP : how the new America is dooming the Republicans / Stanley B.
    Greenberg.
Other titles: How the new America is dooming the Republicans
Description: First edition. | New York : Thomas Dunne Books/St. Martin's Press
    2019. | Includes bibliographical references and index.
Identifiers: LCCN 2019021289 | ISBN 9781250311757 (hardcover) |
    ISBN 9781250311764 (ebook)
Subjects: LCSH: Republican Party (U.S. : 1854–) | Political culture—United States. |
    United States—Politics and government—2009–2017. | United States—Politics and
    government—2017–
Classification: LCC JK2356 .G728 2019 | DDC 324.2734—dc23
LC record available at https://lccn.loc.gov/2019021289

Our books may be purchased in bulk for promotional, educational, or business use. Please contact your local bookseller or the Macmillan Corporate and Premium Sales Department at 1-800-221-7945, extension 5442, or by email at MacmillanSpecialMarkets@macmillan.com.

First Edition: September 2019

10 9 8 7 6 5 4 3 2 1

Dedicated
to
The Women's March
and
The Resistance

TABLE OF CONTENTS

INTRODUCTION

THIS BOOK TELLS AN AMAZING STORY, and if you hadn't seen what happened to America over the last four years, you wouldn't believe it. It even has a happy ending, and that's none too soon for all of us who've had enough fighting, enough division, enough politics. This time the end of politics portends a country united and finally liberated from gridlock to address the nation's most serious problems.

It ends with the death of the Republican Party as we've known it, while the survivors work to re-create the party of Lincoln relevant for our times. It ends with a Democratic Party liberated from the nation's suffocating polarization to use government to advance the public good, as the country used to expect.

You see, our country is hurtling toward a New America that is ever more racially and culturally diverse, younger, millennial, more secular, and unmarried, with fewer traditional families and male breadwinners, more immigrant and foreign born who are more concentrated in the growing metropolitan areas, which are magnets for investment and people. The New America encompasses a vast array of family types and working families in which both the men and women face growing challenges. The New America is ever more racially blended and multinational, more secular and religiously pluralistic. The New America embraces the country's immigrant and foreign character. It now includes the college-educated and suburban women who want respect and equality in a multicultural America.

America was shaped by major social movements, civic unrest, political battles, and government action at historic junctures, and by the choices the two national political parties took that created a more modern America. Each moved America away from traditional strictures on blacks, women, and immigrants. Each juncture made America freer, more equal, and more democratic. Those choices put the Democratic Party on a trajectory that aligned Democrats with the country's emerging civic norms and alienated the Republican Party from the country and itself.

America was changed profoundly by the battle to pass the civil rights laws that ended racial segregation and ensured blacks had the right to vote. Bipartisan immigration laws reopened the country to non–Anglo Saxon immigration in 1965 and greatly expanded it in the late 1980s. The Supreme Court put women on a path to greater independence and equality when it declared in 1965 that women have a right to privacy and birth control and in 1973, when it made abortion legal.

And these different choices came to fruition with the election and re-election of Barack Obama, the first African-American president whose activist government produced a Tea Party movement and revolt that accelerated the polarization of the country and made attitudes about race and immigration matter as never before. The Tea Party and Donald Trump battled to stop history and stop government.

At each juncture, the Democrats were deeply divided, sometimes more than the Republicans. That was true on matters of civil rights, immigration, and abortion. Nonetheless, after these defining social issues were settled in law or by the U.S. Supreme Court, national Democratic leaders embraced and defended the social changes and new freedoms that aligned the party with a modernizing America and its values. After more than five decades of such choices, the Democratic Party is associated with equal rights, equality, gender equality, tolerance, openness to diversity, and more.

The Republicans' electoral base was in the South and later in the Appalachian Valley and rural states across the country, so at each juncture, they escalated their battle against these national changes. The party's national leaders ignored their own deep divisions and worked inventively to show they were champions of white people during the battle over civil rights and affirmative action. Its leaders scorned the sexual revolution and champion to this day a constitutional amendment to make abortion illegal. They were opposed to women breaking free of the patriarchal family and winning equality. They mobilized against illegal immigration in the states and nationally, fueled by Patrick Buchanan's three campaigns for president.

Newt Gingrich led a revolution in the early 1990s that put the GOP into a total war footing against a Democratic Party determined to expand the "liberal" welfare state and marginalize "conservatism," but those forces defeated him.

The Tea Party led the GOP's life-and-death battle against President Obama and his Affordable Care Act, fueled by Tea Party protests that elevated white racial resentment and hostility to immigrants. Defeating and delegitimating President Obama was the last chance to stop the New America from winning.

Obama's 2008 election, the Wall Street bailout, and the searing battle to pass "Obamacare" produced the Tea Party revolt and the Tea Party wave election of 2010, the most consequential election of our lifetime. It gave the Tea Party–fueled Republican Party effective control of the U.S. House and Senate, two thirds of the governorships, and more than 60 percent of the state legislator chambers, which rushed to radically redraw the legislative and congressional maps to ensure big GOP majorities for a decade.

The Tea Party–led GOP pushed the country into fiscal austerity and to deconstruct government—to stop Democrats from using government for positive ends or "paying off" its growing coalition with new entitlements. Limiting the right to vote and allowing unlimited, secret campaign spending, both sanctioned by the U.S. Supreme Court, hardly needed to be justified.

The Tea Party–wave election put the country into a decade of suffocating polarization and gridlock, led by Donald Trump since 2016.

Trump got vital help from the Russians and the FBI, but he is president because he seized the leadership of the Republican counterrevolution and waged an all-out, take-no-prisoners war against New America and the Democrats, which won him the undying loyalty of his Tea Party and Evangelical base. He sent racist, misogynist, and nationalist signals that branded the GOP an anti-immigrant, white, and patriarchal party.

Donald Trump auditioned for the job as a "birther." Comfortable with the most off-putting of attacks, he denied the citizenship and legitimacy of the first African-American president. President Obama was everything conservative voters hated. Figuratively and symbolically, he represented America's multiculturalism and its political triumph.[1]

Trump got the job of leading the GOP because he hated Obama and Clinton so viscerally, and he promised to repeal Obamacare and build a wall against Mexican immigrants. He was so determined to wipe out Obama's legacy that maybe conservatives finally had a leader who would push back against the modernizing trends that were making the country more racially diverse, immigrant, millennial, secular, metropolitan, and unmarried, where working women stood over the faltering male breadwinners and their faltering traditional families.

Repealing Obamacare formed the core motivating agenda of the Republican Party in the elections of 2010, 2012, 2014, and 2016. That impassioned call contributed to two off-year wave elections, a diminished Obama reelection, and Trump's Electoral College victory in the Rust Belt.

Donald Trump based his candidacy from the first moment on winning Tea Party support and then forming a tight alliance with Evangelicals and the most religious conservatives—and together they formed a clear majority of those who identified with the party and voted in GOP primaries.

After his Trump Tower announcement, Trump moved to the top of my polls with Republican primary voters, but that was produced by his insurmountable margin with Tea Party supporters who formed a quarter of the GOP base in my surveys at the time. I conducted surveys and face-to-face focus groups, for Democracy Corps and Citizen Opinion, organizations I founded together with James Carville. We partnered with different progressive groups who charged us with conducting representative surveys with registered voters and self-identified Republicans.[2]

Trump won Tea Party support because he was the most anti-Obama and anti-Obamacare, most hostile to Islam, and most anti-immigrant.

Trump won Evangelicals because they trusted the Tea Party since its revolt in 2010 to fight with most bravery against President Obama. And with the prospect of a feminist and culturally liberal president in

Hillary Clinton, they became Trump's most loyal supporters. Donald Trump was the only way to defeat Clinton and forestall Armageddon.

Trump won the white working-class base of both because he was angry that the elites didn't respect working people and those living outside the metropolitan centers.

Steve Bannon became the chief strategist in the campaign and the White House, and he embedded the base's aversion to social modernity and new freedoms into a bigger call to put America first and promote Christianity over Islam. The president embraced an economic nationalism and scorned the "globalists" who head up the establishment parties everywhere.[3]

That Tea Party strategy would badly divide the GOP and energize Democrats and the New America to resist, but it worked for Trump.

I had been long critical of center-left parties for not showing that managing immigration was a first principle and not showing they would prioritize citizens over non-citizens. John Judis was right that a failure to adapt to these global pressures would create opportunities for "Brexit" and the election of Donald Trump.

The contrasting choices of the Democratic and Republican parties produced a hugely more polarized and politicized country where partisan identity became everything, yet don't assume the current madness produces an America that is even more polarized. That history is over. In statistical terms, the line can't get any steeper.

A shrinking coalition of voters who must do everything to stop a modernizing America identifies with the Republican Party. A growing coalition that values a modernizing America identifies with the Democratic Party. A shrinking coalition of voters that is determined to stop government identifies with the Republican Party. A growing coalition that wants government liberated from the gridlock identifies with the Democratic Party.

That won't be sustained.

The coming elections may well look like prior periods in our history—the Whigs during the 1850s when it could not resolve its deep divisions over slavery, or the Republican Party during the 1930s and 1940s with its deep divisions over the welfare state. The anti-slavery Whigs broke and formed a new party, today's Republican Party, led by Abraham Lincoln. After two decades of electoral defeats, the Republican Party under Eisenhower, Nixon, and Reagan accepted and expanded the welfare state.

Before Trump's takeover, the GOP was already becoming the party of the oldest, most married, most religious, whitest, and most rural voters while the country was becoming much younger, immigrant, unmarried, secular, and urban—and it had won the popular vote only once in thirty years. But the Trump-Tea Party-Evangelical–dominated GOP horrified women most of all. It impelled college-educated and affluent women, millennials, and people of color to vote in record numbers against Trump's GOP.

What so surprised the country since Trump's election and inauguration as president was his decision to govern nationally as he had before, as a militant Tea Party and Evangelical conservative, like the ones that got elected to the House and Senate in the Tea Party wave of 2010 and have made life miserable for the GOP establishment.

President-elect Trump appointed the former leader of the House Freedom Caucus, Congressman Mick Mulvaney, to acting head of the Office of Management and Budget and, later, as acting chief of staff. The president's first budget shockingly proposed to cut the State Department by one third, the Environmental Protection Agency by more than a quarter, and the Department of Health and Human Services by nearly a fifth. He proposed abolishing Meals on Wheels for seniors and slashing federal cancer research as not cost-effective enough to justify the tax burden it placed on hardworking Americans. The president's 2019 budget required food stamp recipients take a job, not caring that two thirds of the beneficiaries are children, disabled, or the elderly. And his radical plan for reorganizing the federal government proposed to pull food stamps, Temporary Assistance for Needy Families (TANF), and the Education Department and create a new "Department of Welfare."

In President Trump's budget for the 2020 election year, he cut the big three—Social Security, Medicare, and Medicaid. He targeted $25 billion from Social Security's disability benefits, $845 billion from Medicare, and $777 billion from Medicaid. The Medicaid cuts were breathtaking. It would abolish the Affordable Care Act's Medicaid expansion and slash subsidies to purchase health insurance, introduce work requirements, and turn the whole program into state block grants that would not rise with rising costs.[4]

Trump filled his cabinet with secretaries who fought and sued those departments in the past and promised to undermine them at every opportunity. This was a Tea Party administration intent on destroying government, something the country has never seen before. Betsy DeVos quickly became the most hated member of the administration, as she expressed such contempt for public education. The Environmental Protection Agency administrator Scott Pruitt turned to energy and chemical industry to run the EPA and blacklisted climate science and scientists, before the stench of corruption forced him out in favor of a former coal industry lobbyist. Trump's secretary of state Rex Tillerson froze hiring for a year, and broad swaths of the earth were left without anyone there representing the United States of America.

Adam Schiff tweeted on April 9, 2019, his "update on our national security leadership":

> Defense Secretary: Vacant.
> DHS Secretary: Vacant.
> UN Ambassador: Vacant.
> FEMA Director: Vacant.
> Secret Service Director: Vacant.
> ICE Director: Vacant.

The Trump administration had confirmed and filled just 54 percent of its civilian executive branch positions at the beginning, far below the 77 percent for President Obama and below that for all prior presidents. That is not a pretty picture, but what the hell is happening at the Department of Labor, Department of Justice, and Department of Interior where barely 40 percent of the positions are filled?[5]

Trump repaid Evangelicals for their loyalty by choosing Neil Gorsuch to take the U.S. Supreme Court seat denied President Obama's selection, Merrick Garland, and by replacing swing justice Anthony Kennedy with Brett Kavanaugh, thereby giving conservatives control of the highest court for generations.

It was a bargain with the devil that paid off. The president announced a return to Reagan Era policies on contraception and abortion. And the Trump administration every year has found new ways to defund Planned Parenthood, the highest priority of the Trump–Tea Party–Evangelical pact.

If you wonder why the Trump administration has sought to abolish climate science and purge the government of anyone working on the issue, or why the U.S. withdrew from the Paris climate accord, look no further than Trump's base. Evangelicals and Tea Party supporters are the ones most opposed to recognizing the human role in global warming, the religious conservatives because they oppose anyone who questions God's role, and the Tea Party because they viewed it all as an elite hoax to expand government.

If you wonder why President Trump will never act to address the epidemic of gun violence, you need look no further than the Tea Party bloc that is so passionate about the NRA and most opposed to regulating guns in any way.

If you wonder why President Trump closed down the federal government and declared a national emergency to build his wall, remember again the Tea Party base. They were the voters most angry about immigration. If you want to scare mothers in Central America into contemplating the hard trip north, with the prospects of long jail time and long separation from their children, then look no further than the Evangelicals who believed it was the right thing to do.

President Trump and the congressional Republicans viewed repealing Obamacare as priority number one of the Trump–Tea Party–Evangelical GOP. With the Tea Party's instinctive demand to slash government and Paul Ryan's unfulfilled plans to reform "entitlement programs," Trump's GOP embarked on the most radical curtailment of federal health care spending for the vulnerable, the low-income, and retirees. That was precisely the kind of conservative agenda Trump promised voters he would never support.

President Trump, visibly frustrated by his failure to repeal the Affordable Care Act, did everything possible in the next three years to destroy it, with immense cost to ordinary people struggling to afford health insurance. Each day, life became more uncertain.

Donald Trump's election moved the New America to defend itself and become conscious of what it really believed, including a bigger role for government to reform the country. It struck back and badly bloodied the GOP in 2018 and will finally crash it in 2020.

And the members of the New America asked one another, am I alone? Do I know my own country? Is this what Americans really believe? Will President Trump be reelected?

Their shock deepened once they realized that the GOP had total control of the federal government, and Donald Trump doubled down on his determination to form a Tea Party and Evangelical government that would give conservatives control of the U.S. Supreme Court, repeal the Affordable Care Act, slash taxes and regulations for corporations and the rich, ban Muslim immigration and build a wall with Mexico, pit race against race, ban abortion, and end the battle against climate change.

The New America believes in their country's diversity. They think immigration enriches. They believe in women's aspirations. They want a fairer country that reins in corporate control of government. They hate the corruption. Every day, however, they came to realize that the GOP was rushing to enact an extreme mandate, the polar opposite of what most Americans believe and want from government.

Neighborhoods and offices became battlegrounds, friends defriended friends, and families were split: parents from children, siblings from siblings, cousins from cousins, as dining room table gatherings were broken into the United States and the Confederacy.

For a time the New America was unsure who spoke for the country, but the Women's Marches on January 21, 2017, reminded them that they did. More than 2 million people protested across the country in what may have been the largest single-day demonstration in U.S. history. It's no wonder that the more than 500,000 people who jammed downtown Washington gnawed at President Trump, whose inauguration crowd a day earlier had paled in proportion to President Obama's eight years earlier. This massive resistance began with a Facebook post, and brought 250,000 to Grant Park in Chicago, 400,000 in New York City, 175,000 in Boston, and 500,000 in Los Angeles. The official website reported 673 marches in all 50 states plus 32 countries. The marchers chanted, "Tell me what America looks like! This is what America looks like." "We are the popular vote!" "Don't take away our ACA."

The millions who joined the Women's Marches that dwarfed President Trump's inauguration signaled to the New America: You are not powerless. You stand with the majority. President Trump may crash and burn, along with his political party.

Commentators asked whether this was a one-day event, or even "a little temper tantrum,"[6] but a sign at a Boston protest declared otherwise: WE CAN DO THIS EVERY WEEKEND, ASSHOLE. The resistance to Trump and the GOP was followed by the wave of women candidates and their victories in the Democratic primaries. That was followed by Republican congressmen having to defend their votes to repeal Obamacare and its protections against preexisting conditions and demonstrations in Congress before the GOP failed to repeal. That was followed by the student walkouts after Congress did nothing after the shooting at Marjory Stoneman Douglas High School in Parkland and the March on Washington. That was followed by teacher strikes in GOP-controlled states where the party had slashed education spending only to suddenly find new money for books, salaries, and additional teaching time. And then, the New America asserted itself fully in the 2018 election, which shattered voting records and in which women voters and candidates shocked Trump's GOP.

These cascading shocks were a singular period of intense polarization and politicization that sharply divided America and produced civil war in families across the country. Across the spectrum, people became immediately engaged because the stakes were so high. They became politicized because they understood that politics now matters. They became newly conscious of their rights, having perhaps taken them for granted and now understanding that they were genuinely at risk. Every time President Trump took an even more outrageous step, public sentiment shifted even more strongly in favor of liberal democratic values and reform. Every time President Trump's GOP sought to deconstruct the government, the majority that wanted to use government for a public purpose grew.

With pretty stunning speed, the New America became newly conscious of its values, what it truly believed. In a surprising punch back at President Trump, they began to feel more positively about immigrants and immigration. They became more concerned about inequality and the unfinished work of addressing discrimination against women and

African Americans. As the president moved aggressively to dismantle the government, the New America pushed back and said, "We want more."

The New America watched the president divide the country, setting group against group.

They watched the president's attacks on immigrants.

They watched the president indulging his violent supporters and white nationalists.

They watched his sympathy for misogyny and disrespect of women.

They watched the president polarize the country.

They watched his assault on government, his attempt to destroy the Affordable Care Act and the Obama legacy.

A not insignificant number of Republicans were shocked, too.

Donald Trump's winning the presidency accelerated the pressure for reform and movement toward a new progressive era in which Democrats are hegemonic. There is now a growing demand to attack corruption, raise taxes on the rich, achieve universal health care, boldly address climate change, and invest in education, infrastructure, and a Green New Deal and confront America's inherited racial disparities. Against the Trump backdrop, America has embraced its multicultural identity and a reformed government that will address the country's growing problems and forge an America that works for all.

The New America's story and politics will soon be the ones that matter.

1 THE NEW AMERICA

THE REPUBLICANS' COUNTERREVOLUTION HAS BEEN animated by deep worries about America's rapidly changing demography. Well, it turns out, they were not imagining or exaggerating. They have good reason to believe revolutionary changes are reshaping the country irretrievably.

The most important change is immigration. The globe has witnessed a massive, growing international migration over the last ten years. Migrants in the aftermath of the Syrian civil war ended up primarily in Europe in the most recent count, but before that fully one in five ended up in America, most coming from Mexico, China, India, and the Philippines.[1] At the end of the Obama presidency in 2016, the growing numbers of foreign born in the United States was very real, and considered part of America's dynamism. Immigrants fill many of the engineering positions in Silicon Valley and are overrepresented in construction, professional and scientific occupations, and recreation and food-service jobs. The number of foreign graduate students getting authorization to work in STEM fields surged in 2016.

Looking to the states, over a quarter of California's population is now foreign born, as is over or near 20 percent in New York, New Jersey, Florida, and Nevada. Foreign-born people now comprise about 40 percent of the residents in New York City and Los Angeles and a majority in Miami; at over 20 percent they are a strong presence in Chicago and Seattle.

For myself, who struggles with any foreign languages, I am impressed that half of the foreign born speak English at home or very well, but half do not. Prior generations of immigrants, like my foreign-born grandparents and mother, were more insistent English be the first language at home. In the diverse metropolitan areas, most hardly notice the change, but not so in many rural counties. The slowest-growing with the biggest rise in foreign-born residents gave Trump some of his biggest gains in 2016.

Immigration is where globalization makes itself felt most directly, impacting the labor markets, demand on public services, and the meaning of citizenship. That is why Trump made immigration issue number one in his campaign, resisted any calls to help Dreamers or refugees, and proposed reducing legal immigration quotas. That is why the GOP has chosen to go into battle armed with warnings about immigrant gangs, U.S. citizens killed by illegal immigrants, and the need to stall the "infection" from uncontrolled immigration. "Zero tolerance" means the U.S. government will stop what seems inexorable.

Nonetheless, after Trump's first year in office, the percentage of foreign born rose to its highest level since 2010, over 40 percent now from Asia.[2] The number of undocumented immigrants dropped and net migration from Mexico was negative, yet the growing foreignness was just as important to his war on immigrants.

The Republican counterrevolution was also grounded in the decline of rural America and the growing dynamism of the metropolitan areas. Trump's 2016 vote surged in rural and smaller manufacturing communities where people rightly demanded respect and policies that viewed them as more than collateral damage in the trade and skills debates. The elites of both parties supported the global disruption that made the growing metropolitan areas more dynamic. In the Rust Belt, 4.5 million people have lost jobs since the passage of NAFTA and China's full integration into the global economy.[3] A flood of articles and books sought to help elites and liberals understand the "twin convulsions" of 2016, Trump and Brexit.[4]

Well, Trump's surprising vote got their attention. Many books were published by the big New York publishers in an attempt to understand the white working class and their plight. One, J. D. Vance's *Hillbilly Elegy*, was on the *New York Times* bestseller list for two years.

Later Vance moved to Columbus, Ohio, and an array of entrepreneurs have focused on how to bring new investment to the area he grew up in.[5]

But no number of presidential trips to West Virginia, Montana, and Indiana will stall for a millisecond the growing movement of populations and the younger generations to the metropolitan areas across the country. The suburbs have grown 16 percent since 2000 and the cities by 13 percent, the rural areas by just 3 percent.[6] Contributing significantly to the metropolitan growth was the moving in of foreign-born migrants, 5 million to the suburbs and 7 million to the urban areas.[7]

The economies of the fifty largest cities are responsible for two thirds of the growth of the GDP. They are the most integrated into the global trading economy, and they account for nearly all of America's job growth. Major businesses and people are moving into metropolitan areas and even into the inner cities, attracted by the urbanism, universities and research institutions, culture, and the growing immigrant and racial diversity—all the ingredients that stir the GOP's counter-revolution.

President Trump embraced every emotive policy priority of the GOP's Evangelical base, but none of it would slow America's growing secularism.

Every religious denomination is coping with drops in the number who are religiously observant, with the exception of the Evangelicals. "No religion" is now the faster growing faith in the religious census. More than one in five Americans identify as secular; they outnumber the mainline Protestants. The traditional family at the heart of the social conservative vision is giving way in the face of profound changes in marriage, child-rearing, and women working to produce a growing pluralism of family types. Younger people are delaying marriage, having fewer children, and fewer are getting married at all. Barely half of American adults are married.[8]

Getting back to having more men in breadwinner roles and a strong patriarchal family structure is pretty fundamental for many social conservatives and for many working-class women who wouldn't mind being married to a husband who could really provide a family with some security. But the Women's March, #MeToo, and the surge of women political candidates have put the spotlight on working women and their suppressed public agenda.

Three quarters of women are now in the labor force, and two thirds are the principal or co-breadwinner. Without much help from government for childcare, health care, or parental leave, working women put in a lot more hours than men doing childcare and household work. To make it that much more stressful, half of working women and a third of mothers are unmarried and on their own. More than 60 percent of unmarried mothers earn less than $30,000 a year.[9]

White working-class men over the last three decades have struggled to get the jobs that would get them into the middle class, which previous generations could count on. They marry later, some not at all, or get divorced. Their incomes have gone down and many have withdrawn from the labor force—and that is before we get to those who succumb to drugs and have other issues.[10]

As I point out in chapter 7, "Is This All They Have to Offer Working People?," the only thing Republicans and President Trump have had to offer the struggling working class is all government benefits being subject to "work requirements." They think food stamps and Medicaid for the working poor are a "hammock" that leads to indolence.[11]

Working women are not confused by this conservative fog. They know they are on their own despite seismic changes in work life. A large majority of women (62 percent) believe that men earn more than women for the same job, but fewer than half of men believe that (47 percent).[12] They believe the playing field is tilted against women, and that is even more true when they move further up the job and status ladder.[13] Their views are politically explosive.

So when Fox News commentators ask what family issue tops the public agenda, it is how you ensure pay equity for working women, not how you get back to a patriarchal family.

The triumph of the millennials is the last straw for the conservative agenda, and why it is so urgent the GOP stop the New America from governing. After all, millennials have displaced the baby boomers as the largest generation and will form 36 percent of the eligible voter population in 2020, 45 percent in 2024.[14] And Generation Z, who were born after 1996 and were 13 to 21 years old in 2018, will be larger still, sealing the generational revolution.

If you want to see the changing face of America, look to the millennials. About 40 percent of millennials are racial minorities, and now 17 percent of their new marriages are interracial.[15] Most describe President Obama as mixed race, not African-American or black. They just take for granted America's multiculturalism. That attitude extends to gay marriage, supported by something near 80 percent of millennials.[16]

And they are the reason Republicans will lose the battle over rural and urban America. Millennials have not followed the path of other maturing young people to the suburbs. More than three quarters want to live in an urban area and a majority have no driver's license. And they are acting on that worldview. Two thirds of millennials with a four-year college degree have already moved to one of the fifty-one largest cities.[17]

That millennials have won and consumers and business remain committed to a multicultural America is evident in Nike building a major ad campaign around former San Francisco 49ers quarterback Colin Kaepernick. He began sitting, then taking a knee during the national anthem before games in order to protest racial injustice in America. President Trump vilified him and NFL team owners by claiming falsely that he was protesting the national anthem, and when he opted out of his contract in March 2017, NFL team owners allegedly blackballed him, thereby proving his point.[18] "Believe in something," Kaepernick said in the Nike ad. "Even if it means sacrificing everything." President Trump tweeted, "What was Nike thinking?"

Old people didn't approve of the ad, but two thirds of millennials did, and they mattered. Nike's stock hit an all-time high and its direct digital sales jumped 36 percent during the game's quarter the ad was aired.[19]

So Republican congressman and white nationalist sympathizer Steve King could have been describing America at large when the new Congress convened in January 2019, the Democratic side of the House including a record number of women, African Americans, and the first Native American and Muslim women, and he observed, "You look over there and think the Democratic Party is no country for white men."[20]

THE NEW AMERICA RESPONDS

As the GOP's intensifying battle to keep the New America from governing became unabashedly anti-immigrant, racist, and sexist under President Trump's leadership, the New America responded in real time.

Soon after Trump's election, I discovered I could not put Clinton and Trump voters in the same room, because the Clinton, anti-Trump voter had become more vocal and assertive, sometimes disbelieving and rude. The same must have been happening across the country.

After one Trump voter in a focus group agreed with the president, the Clinton supporter turned to her and said, "So, I see. You are the face of those ugly things I hear being said on TV every day." The project director for Democracy Corps Nancy Zdunkewicz and I were stunned, and we both thought, "Is she going to apologize?" She didn't.

By the 70-day mark, the anti-Trump women pushed back against Trump voters in conversation, even when outnumbered in the room. The moderator had to make an effort to bring Trump voters into the conversation to ensure the outnumbered Clinton voters did not dominate the discussion and so the Trump voters could be heard. This turned out to be an unintended test of the strength of their views and resolve to resist.

Amazingly, at the seventy-day mark into the Trump presidency, the anti-Trump voters in these groups were bringing up the off-year elections to be held in 2018. Their doubts about Trump dominated their outlook, and they used words like "flabbergasted," "devastated," and "terrified" to describe how they felt about the country right now.

> In my eyes, the biggest issue is going to be this president. He's going to drive this country into a shithole.
> —WHITE UNMARRIED WOMAN, UNDER 45, CLEVELAND

> Every time Trump opens his mouth I want to scream.
> —WHITE MILLENNIAL WOMAN, CLEVELAND

And that people were organizing and marching made them feel more optimistic about how this will all turn out for the country:

> There are people organizing and finally getting their heads out of the sand and paying attention to what's going on in politics.
> —WHITE WORKING-CLASS WOMAN, AKRON

> I think maybe people are bonding over their hate for certain things, like protesting and a lot of people are bonding in groups. I mean, people have a voice now with social media and everything. They're really getting it out there. A lot of people are being heard.
> —WHITE UNMARRIED WOMAN, UNDER 45, CLEVELAND

The Trump context changed the formula for political engagement in this so-called off-year election when a lot of presidential-year voters go to the sidelines. The anti-Trump, women college graduates were consolidated and motivated to resist the Trump presidency. They turned a simple "fact sheet" passed around a focus group into an organizing weapon. They were seeking out tools and information to win arguments and maximize their engagement and were increasingly intent to vote. The college-educated women seemed as much an anti-Trump base as African Americans who were discovering they too must be involved.

The Trump presidency so invaded the public's consciousness that it was hard to talk to previously disengaged and unregistered unmarried women, people of color, and millennials without them going right to Trump. How is it going with your family and community? No, they *wanted* to talk about what was going wrong with the *country*. When asked how often they think about national issues, they said, "every day." "Donald Trump's everywhere . . . all over the news" and the big conflicts he stirs up were inescapable (African-American man, Detroit). Even the white unmarried women who were most likely to "try not to watch the news" said they "don't have a choice," including one bartender who said she hears "Trump all day long" at work (white unmarried woman, Cleveland).

They were being pulled into the political debate by members of their families who wanted them to pick a side. These were people who said they "are not interested in politics" and in the past, some avoided political decisions they didn't feel informed enough to defend before their more passionate family members. Others, particularly the African-American men and women were "more likely to vote, now, because I hear my mom on my head about voting" (African-American woman, Detroit). The Hispanic women were most likely to say they were sharing information with their families and friends because "we don't want to make the same mistake twice" (Hispanic millennial woman, Orlando).

These groups were very conscious that their parents' generation and the country had sacrificed for their rights and lives. And here we have a president of the United States who was "dividing our country." He was forcing us to fight again for the gains our parents won for us:

> Just the way he talks it allows you to—it incites something. He incites some type of crazy feeling, like, oh no, all these criminal aliens are coming. It just sounds like something you hear a crazy dude on the side of the street saying.
> —AFRICAN-AMERICAN WOMAN, DETROIT

> I don't want him to be the example for my daughter, like the president of our country being accused of sexual harassment.
> —WHITE UNMARRIED WOMAN, CLEVELAND

> I remember a line in the movie *Remember the Titans*, where the guy told his teammate that attitude reflects leadership, and I just think right now America's attitude is not good because of our leadership.
> —AFRICAN-AMERICAN MAN, DETROIT

Trump produced a similar transformative shift in the consciousness of unregistered voters. They saw people who suffer from Trump's new policies and saw "protections" that "were written in place," and suddenly "they go." You can't change that "if we did not vote." That double negative was now part of the new formula to get people mobilized:

We all have to do something. Can't just sit and watch.
                    —HISPANIC MILLENNIAL WOMAN, ORLANDO

We already lost our health care, a bunch of rights and laws,
it's been racist, all in the white Congress, if you don't vote,
your just handing over America to the KKK.
                    —AFRICAN-AMERICAN WOMAN, DETROIT

A white unmarried woman from Cleveland wondered, "Where are we going to be in the next 4 years if we are so miserable right now?"

Nobody struggled anymore to explain the risks of the wrong person winning an election. Donald Trump transformed our politics by showing people they must resist this horror-show representation of America.

AND WITH NEW CLARITY OF CONSCIOUSNESS

This new engagement made itself felt first on immigration, where every Trump outrage increased the proportion of Americans who said, We are an immigrant country.

America was created by more than a century of virtually unregulated, open immigration from Europe until after World War I, after which America closed its doors. The Chinese were barred after 1882. But the civil rights period in the 1950s and 1960s saw major immigration reforms that reopened the doors and got rid of national quotas. Legal immigrants were mostly Hispanic and Asian, the numbers accelerated by Republican presidents who granted asylum to undocumented immigrants and expanded legal immigration. The most recent decade saw a surge in foreign-born people living in the United States, and Trump was able to exploit it to get the election to break for him.

Voters do want the country to better manage immigration, but this stoking the anti-immigrant fires will end badly for Trump's GOP. The proportion believing immigrants "strengthen the country with their hard work and talents" surged to 65 percent. Just as Trump was charging that immigrants fueled gangs and included murderers and rapists, the proportion who said immigrants "burden the country by taking jobs, housing, and health care" plummeted to just 26 percent in mid-2017. Three quarters in mid-2018 favored granting permanent legal status to immigrants who came to the U.S. illegally as children.[21] The country settled these issues. They are not contested.

More say immigrants strengthen U.S. as the partisan divide grows

% who say immigrants

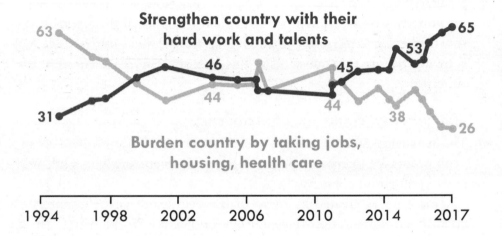

Strengthen country with their hard work and talents

63 · · 46 · 44 · 45 · 53 · 65

31 · 44 · 38 · 26

Burden country by taking jobs, housing, health care

1994 · 1998 · 2002 · 2006 · 2010 · 2014 · 2017

America believes it is an immigrant country, but Trump's election as an anti-immigrant candidate and his daily anti-immigrant provocations, unchallenged by his own party, made us all uncertain what Americans really believe. Well, individually, Americans recognize in larger numbers the benefits of immigration and, collectively, they have rushed to airports to protest the Muslim travel ban, to welcome refugees, and to protest babies being separated from their mothers at the Mexican border.

For most of the past decade, the public was evenly split on whether the country "needs to continue making changes to give blacks equal rights with whites" or whether it has made the changes that were needed. But by being blind to discrimination and by disinviting black athletes to the White House, Trump changed all that. Suddenly, over 60 percent of Americans believe the battle for equal rights is unfinished.[22] In 2014,

63 percent supported affirmative action programs to help blacks and minorities get to a university, but that grew to 71 percent in 2017.[23] Trump's counterrevolution is producing a counter-clarity for the changed America.

Acceptance of homosexuality and gay marriage has reached the level of a norm, surging to 70 percent for homosexuality and 62 percent for gay marriage.[24] Just a quarter of the country believes homosexuality should be "discouraged"—the core conviction of Evangelical Republicans.[25]

Three in five Americans consistently believe that stricter environmental regulations are worth the cost, and four in five believe there is "solid evidence that the average temperature on Earth has gotten warmer."[26] Since the issue of climate change was broached at the beginning of the 2016 presidential election, that belief has jumped 13 points to 92 percent.[27] A majority of 53 percent said that there is solid evidence that climate change is caused by human activity.[28] Only a quarter of Republicans believe that, which is why they will be sidelined.

President Trump withdrew America from the Paris climate accord and joined a battle royal with the G-7, while 60 percent of Americans believed the "U.S. should take into account the interests of its allies even if it means making compromises with them"—the opposite of the posture President Trump offered to the world.[29]

President Trump's one great legislative accomplishment before he lost control of the Congress was his $2.2 trillion tax cut for corporations and the richest 1 percent. It was supported by huge majorities of House Republicans and every Republican senator. His tax cut plans always favored the rich and big business, despite his promise to the working-class voter, but this corrupt tax scam was breathtaking in its benefits for Wall Street and billionaire donors. That massive tax cut was right out of the Tea Party playbook in the states where huge tax cuts for corporations, the oil companies, and the millionaires were followed by huge cuts in education spending.

Republicans didn't notice or care that two thirds of Americans believed "the economic system in this country unfairly favors powerful interests" and "economic inequality in the U.S." is a very big or moderately big problem.[30] Nearly 60 percent thought "business corporations make too much profit."[31] The tax cut was the opposite of what most Americans wanted to see happen, which is part of why President Trump's election and Tea Party–Evangelical agenda has produced such rage and determination to reverse it.

So, just as the Republicans and President Trump dramatically freed up business from regulation, they lost the favor of the voting public on government and markets, nearly 60 percent of whom said the government "should do more to solve problems and help meet the needs of the people," rather than leave more things to business and individuals.[32] That is hardly a country hospitable to a businessman president doing his radical work.

Most telling was that at the beginning of 2018, as the Tea Party–dominated GOP made stopping government in its tracks its first mission, the proportion of people who wanted more government surged to its highest point in the twenty years of polling on this question by *The Wall Street Journal/NBC.*

The GOP campaign against government has met its match in the New America.

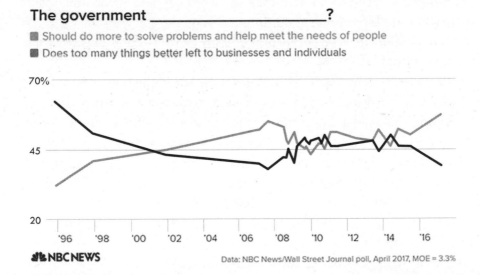

The government _____?
■ Should do more to solve problems and help meet the needs of people
■ Does too many things better left to businesses and individuals

Data: NBC News/Wall Street Journal poll, April 2017, MOE = 3.3%

2 THE GOP COUNTERREVOLUTION AGAINST THE NEW AMERICA

THE REPUBLICAN PARTY IS TRAPPED in an ever more desperate counterrevolution against the cumulative and accelerating trends that are producing a New America. It is a party defined and divided by its leaders' unrepentant struggle against an America that is more and more racially diverse. It is also a battle to slow the growing secularism, the decline of the traditional family, and the growing independence of women and their sexual freedom. It is a fight against the rising immigration and foreign presence. And in its Tea Party and Donald Trump stage, it is a party pitted against the growing millennial generation, the young, and against the growing metropolitan centers where very different values are taken for granted and now defended.

THE GOP BATTLE AGAINST CIVIL RIGHTS AND SHADES OF BLACK AND WHITE

America passed the Civil Rights Act in 1964 and the Voting Rights Act in 1965 after a huge upheaval in the country, and both political parties and their leaders faced a historic choice on whether to accept the end of legal segregation and civic inequality. The GOP's national leaders not only opposed the laws at the time, they visibly resisted the government playing any role in protecting black Americans in the face of enduring discrimination.

Since the passage of the civil rights laws, every Republican presidential nominee has made clear that they would resist these changes and that white voters could trust them to look out for their interests. Barry Goldwater voted against the Civil Rights Act and Ronald Reagan strongly opposed it, saying it was "humiliating to the South."[1] Pointedly, Reagan gave his first post-convention speech in Philadelphia, Mississippi, where civil rights workers were murdered by the KKK, and he called out the "welfare queens" who lived lavishly off the public dole.[2] Richard Nixon promised to restore "law and order" and called on the "silent majority" to make itself heard.[3] Nixon also railed against affirmative action. And George H. W. Bush put Lee Atwater at the head of his 1988 campaign and ran a flood of "Willie Horton" ads that depicted a convicted black murderer on weekend parole killing people again.[4] John McCain selected Sarah Palin as his vice presidential nominee, the Tea Party favorite who wanted to take down Barack Hussein Obama, the "community organizer" whose pastor Reverend Jeremiah Wright said such hateful things about America's "white government."[5] And President Trump threw off all the subtlety and indirection and declared there were "good people on both sides" after the white nationalists' violent marches in Charlottesville, Virginia.[6]

So, the national GOP presidential campaigns always made clear that white people concerned about their status in America could depend on them.

Successive GOP national presidential campaigns starting in 2000 did everything legally possible to suppress the black vote. They were unbothered by the dramatic television coverage of black voters forced to wait in long queues to cast their ballots in the critical swing states of Florida and Ohio, where Republican governors and secretaries of state created shortages of voting machines, limited early voting, and challenged ballots at voting locations.[7] Republican state leaders were even accused of blocking traffic to make it difficult for blacks to get to their polling stations. With Republican secretaries of state battling with the U.S. Department of Justice and the federal courts to bar early voting and to purge voter rolls close to the election, the GOP sent a defining signal that it wouldn't be governing for black people.[8]

But despite the GOP's top leaders' efforts to nationalize and politicize the racial divides and gain from white fear of blacks in the 1960s,

1970s, and 1980s, the full racial polarization of the parties would have to wait at least another three decades for the election of an African-American president in 2008 and of Donald Trump in 2016.

In 1964, both the Democratic and Republican parties considered equal rights part of their legacy and both genuinely competed for the growing black vote. They were able to pass new civil rights laws only after President Lyndon Johnson broke the longest-ever filibuster by the southern Democratic senators and the gridlock created by southern committee chairs in the House. It took both Democratic and Republican votes in Congress to pass the Civil Rights Act of 1964, which deepened the country's commitment to equality and barred racial discrimination in public accommodations and government facilities and by employers and government agencies.[9]

After the passage of the Voting Rights Act in 1965, President Johnson told his close adviser and speechwriter, Bill Moyers, "I think we just delivered the South to the Republican Party for a long time to come."[10]

President Johnson did deliver a red-hot racial baton that would have a deep, enduring impact on the Republican Party's core values and identity. Barry Goldwater carried only his home state of Arizona and the five Deep South states of Louisiana, Arkansas, Mississippi, Alabama, and Georgia, where slavery, plantations, tenant farming, racial segregation, and opposition to black equality and the voting franchise ran deep. Richard Nixon's Southern Strategy four years later added the rest of the South to the GOP's national Electoral College base.

The GOP won its strongest support in the Black Belt counties with the highest proportion of slaves prior to the Civil War.[11] These were the voters with the most attenuated democratic sensibilities who had struggled to preserve white status and were conscious of their region's history of being willing to do everything to hold on to political power.

This GOP base of twelve southern states explains why GOP presidential campaigns let white southern voters know they still get it and why the Republican Party has had so much trouble transcending its racially charged history. This was the original sin of the GOP, when it first chose to fight America's historic steps toward modernity.

Moreover, the federal system gives states their own elected leaders, and a U.S. Senate and Electoral College where the GOP's base of southern and more rural states could have disproportionate, prolonged influence on national affairs.

But President Johnson's prediction about the shift in voter identification with the parties did not turn out to be true for at least another three decades. For sure, the Democratic vote for president among white southerners collapsed after Johnson signed the civil rights laws, but only to be pushed back up a few percentage points by the next two southern Democratic presidential nominees, Jimmy Carter and Bill Clinton.

Professor Larry Bartels thought identification with the Democratic Party should have crashed, too, if reasonably rational southern white voters had taken out their anger with a Democratic Party that backed civil rights, desegregation, and integration and had begun identifying with the GOP.[12] But Bartels gets that wrong, because he assumes that the black-white divide was all that mattered for those voters and that the black-white divide defined the parties. Many of these white southern voters were New Deal Democrats who continued to identify with the party. Democrats won the support of many white Evangelical voters and elected progressive governors in the South for four decades after the signing of the 1964 Civil Rights Act.

And critically, prominent Republican leaders outside the South continued to be strong supporters of civil rights, leaving the fuller black-white polarization to wait until the elections of Barack Obama and Donald Trump.[13]

THE GOP BATTLE AGAINST THE SEXUAL REVOLUTION AND WOMEN'S EQUALITY

The U.S. Supreme Court ruled in 1965 that women had a right to privacy and a right to use birth control to plan whether and when to become pregnant.[14] In 1973, the high court extended that right to privacy to legalization of abortion and gave women the right to terminate a pregnancy.[15] Those decisions would profoundly change the role of women in society and the workplace and threaten the traditional family and male breadwinner role. In time, accepting the autonomy of women in these areas was intimately linked to supporting equality for women.

In retrospect, the Supreme Court in 1973 threw a hand grenade into a country where half the public attended church every week and families were just coming to terms with the sexual freedom made possible by birth control and mothers bearing fewer children. It landed in a country where socially conservative Evangelicals dominated the political culture in the South and Appalachia, and socially conservative Catholics dominated in the industrial Midwest. It landed in a country where the major political parties and major denominations were divided on the issue.

While a majority of the public has always believed abortion should remain legal in all or most cases, a significant and intense minority resisted this change. The right of a woman to end a pregnancy and not be forced by government to carry a baby to term came to symbolize the freedom of women from the traditional social strictures.

The national Democratic Party and its candidates formally accepted the Supreme Court decision and its larger implications for women, even though many elected Catholic Democrats in the Midwest remained pro-life. The Democratic Party platform in 1980 said, "The Democratic Party supports the 1973 Supreme Court decision on abortion rights as the law of the land and opposes any constitutional amendment to restrict or overturn that decision."[16]

The GOP, by contrast, nationalized and politicized their voters' opposition to the sexual revolution and abortion, affirmed by President Ronald Reagan's executive orders on the "squeal rule," which prohibited government-funded family planning clinics serving low-income communities from counseling on abortion, and the Mexico City protocol, or "gag rule," which prohibited U.S. aid to international clinics that used their own funds to provide counseling or referrals for abortions. He responded to lobbying from pro-life groups and the Catholic bishops and reflected a 1980 party platform that said, "We affirm our support of a constitutional amendment to restore protection of the right to life for unborn children."[17]

Within hours of being sworn in as president in 1993, Bill Clinton reversed five executive orders regarding abortion, family planning, and stem cell research.[18] This included reversing both the squeal rule and the "Mexico City policy."[19] He commented at the time, "As a result of today's action, every woman will be able to receive medical advice and referrals that will not be censored or distorted by ideological arguments that should not be a part of medicine." Shortly after taking the oath of office, President Clinton also tried to change the long-standing prohibition against gays in the military, ordering the secretary of defense to draft legislation to overturn existing policies.[20]

Religious conservatives reacted with horror. Focus on the Family president James Dobson told his followers that Bill Clinton had "debase[d] the presidency" with his "homosexual agenda" and his "hands are stained with the blood of countless innocent babies." Pat Robertson warned of the stark choice this created: "Either we will return to the moral integrity and original dreams of the founders of this nation . . . or we will give ourselves over more and more to hedonism, to all forms of destructive anti-social behavior." A Christian Voice pamphlet commanded its followers to "make sure government is . . . punishing what is wrong and rewarding what is right." And homosexuality was the ultimate wrong, Rev. Jerry Falwell declared, a sin "so grievous, so abominable in the sight of God that he destroyed the cities of Sodom and Gomorrah because of [it]."[21]

The battle of religion and politics was joined, and the parties became newly polarized over the traditional family, sexuality, and freedom of women.

Large numbers of pro-choice Republican women changed their party affiliations in these two decades. By the estimate of one group that followed a panel of voters, only half of those who were pro-choice in 1982 continued to identify as Republicans in 1997.[22] At the same time, one half of pro-life Democrats changed their position on abortion. Everyone knew *Roe v. Wade* was about more than abortion; it was about sexual freedom and equality for women.

In the Senate, 80 percent of Democratic senators were casting pro-choice votes by 1987. Interestingly, almost 40 percent of Republicans were still casting pro-choice votes then, too, but that plummeted to virtually zero by 2005 as the culture war was fully joined. The House was fully polarized by 2008: about 90 percent of House Democrats but only 10 percent of House Republicans were pro-choice.[23]

When the Massachusetts Supreme Court legalized gay marriage in 2004, GOP strategist Karl Rove saw his opportunity to push party polarization even further. Gay marriage and abortion became the incendiary material in President Bush's divisive 2004 reelection campaign that escalated the culture war.

What Rove saw in 2004 was an evenly divided country and a declining bloc of genuine swing voters, and he decided the GOP could win by raising the turnout of the base rather than by working to persuade swing voters across the electorate. His own campaign team described the plan as a radical departure, but Rove was intently focused on the millions of missing Evangelicals who did not turn out for the 2000 national election.

President Bush invited expressions of faith during his time in the White House, including prayer, and said in debates that the Bible was his favorite book, cautioning against the teaching of the theory of evolution, saying, "Religion has been around a lot longer than Darwinism." He hired Ralph Reed, the former head of the Christian Coalition, and reached deeply into the religious communities to fuel his campaign: 350,000 of his 1.4 million campaign volunteers were "pro-family" Evangelicals. President Bush promised a constitutional amendment to nullify the Massachusetts Supreme Court decision to legalize same-sex marriage and supported the thirteen states that held referendums to define marriage as a union between a man and a woman. Evangelical minister Rick Warren wrote to the 136,000 subscribers of his weekly newsletter for pastors urging them to use the pulpit to compare the presidential candidates on five nonnegotiable issues: abortion, stem cell research, cloning, gay marriage, and euthanasia.[24]

On Election Day, Bush voters pushed "moral values" as their biggest issue—the first time that had topped the list. Gay marriage and abortion also topped the list of doubts about John Kerry. A whopping 6 million new Evangelical voters came out for Bush.[25]

When contemplating the GOP's suicidal decisions, historians will look back on 2004 as the year the legions crossed the Rubicon.

When President Obama proposed the Affordable Care Act, abortion and contraception of all things became the main points of attack that nearly defeated the law. The Republicans allied with the U.S. Catholic bishops, who worked to defeat the introduction of universal health care.[26] They declared inaccurately that Obamacare would require insurance companies to cover abortion, subsidized by U.S. taxpayers.[27] Former Arkansas governor Michael Huckabee was derisive: "If the Democrats want to insult the women of America by making them believe that they are helpless without Uncle Sugar coming in and providing for them a prescription each month for birth control, because they cannot control their libido or their reproductive system without the help of the government, then so be it."[28]

Conservatives prevailed in the U.S. Supreme Court when they won the *Burwell v. Hobby Lobby* case, which ensured the right of religiously conservative employers to refuse to include contraceptive coverage in health insurance policies for their employees.[29]

During this battle against the Affordable Care Act, almost half of Evangelicals believed it is "always wrong" to have sex before marriage. Half. When at the time just one in five of all Americans believed premarital sex is "always wrong."[30] And in case you were not paying attention, the Republicans in Congress during the 2018 budget battle sought to abolish sex education and expand abstinence programs in the public schools.[31]

Every election in America now is just the next iteration of Presidents Reagan and Bush's culture war that the GOP chose to join.

Battling abortion as a life-and-death, moral issue is the other original sin of the GOP, whose base expanded under President Reagan and afterward among Evangelicals and religious conservatives in the Deep South, border states, Appalachian Valley, Plains states, and Mountain West. That bloc of up to twenty states gave all the reason GOP leaders needed to maintain an absolutist position on abortion and fight a losing battle against the sexual revolution and against women.

This cultural war is also quite exceptional for the United States. Everywhere else in the world when citizens have voted in referenda or where the highest court has legalized abortion or gay marriage, the issue has been settled and depoliticized. These social issues disappear from partisan politics. But not in the United States, where the Republican leaders used those U.S. Supreme Court decisions to launch a culture war, made electorally possible by its Evangelical and rural religious base in the states where the U.S. Constitution gives them inordinate influence.

The nation's civic, business, agricultural, and religious leaders and both political parties under President Ronald Reagan and President George Herbert Walker Bush rallied to pass bold reforms of the immigration system, namely the Immigration Reform and Control Act of 1986 and the Immigration Act of 1990. They dramatically changed the country's approach to legal and illegal immigration, both of which expanded greatly during the 1990s. But the political revolt in the GOP to reverse it was just as stark. Insurgent, antiestablishment leaders quickly upended the complicit Republican leaders, and the GOP would own a determined three-decade campaign against immigration. The years 1994, 1995, and 1996 were ground zero for a Republican Party that committed its third original sin that made it an anti-immigration party.

President Reagan had supported the effort to pass reform legislation that would grant asylum to millions who had come here illegally to work. The new Immigration Reform and Control Act of 1986 created a process for legalizing undocumented immigrants while strengthening border enforcement to discourage future migrants from crossing illegally. The "keystone" of the bill was new sanctions to be imposed against employers who knowingly hired undocumented workers and a 50 percent increase in border staffing. The new law created a two-step process for the undocumented people who had lived here peaceably and continuously since 1982 to gain permanent status. The result was 3 million undocumented immigrants getting amnesty, including 2.3 million Mexicans.[32]

President Reagan supported expanded immigration for the country, if not his party, when he signed the new law at the Statue of Liberty, observing, "We have a statue in New York Harbor [of] a woman holding a torch of welcome to those who enter our country to become Americans. [She] represents our open door." The diversity of those entering the country "became American. And this diversity has more than enriched us; it has literally shaped us."[33]

President H. W. Bush welcomed and signed the Immigration Act of 1990, which dramatically changed the character and scale of immigration to the country, and unabashedly embraced immigration as a powerful and positive vehicle to enrich America.

The system of immigration up to this point had prioritized family reunification—or "chain migration," in Donald Trump's words—but the reforms in the 1990 law created a second-track, "employment-based immigration." It tripled the number of annual visas given for employment from 54,000 to 140,000. And it allotted visas for people with extraordinary ability in "the sciences, arts, education, business or athletics," for multinational executives, those with advanced degrees, skilled workers, and those who were investing in new ventures worth more than $1 million. The goal of the reforms was to make America more competitive, innovative, and diverse.[34]

"What we are really talking about is how all of us basically arrived here," Senator Ted Kennedy observed. "Whether it was three hundred years ago or one hundred years ago, it was immigration and immigration policy that really defined how America became America." The Immigration Act of 1990 was meant to change the face of America, and it did.

Legal immigration grew from 16 million people in 1990 to 19 million in 1994 and 22.5 million by 2000.[35] The foreign-born population jumped by 12.5 million to 31.1 million by 2000.[36] They were now 11.1 percent of the population, with dramatically more coming from Mexico and Central America.[37] And despite the heavier border security and employer penalties, the number of undocumented immigrants ("illegals") grew from 3.5 million to 8.6 million by 2000.[38]

Initially, the public became more concerned about the changes in immigration. Before the enactment of the new immigration reform laws, about half thought the country should be reducing immigration, but in 1994, that had spiked to two thirds.

Steve Kornacki in *The Red and the Blue* posits rightly that Newt Gingrich's "revolt against establishment power" shaped all our polarized politics thereafter, but he also highlighted the role played by Pat Buchanan, the conservative "brawler" on CNN's *Crossfire*. Buchanan was the first to warn against the country's changing immigrant character and attack the elite's embrace of expanded immigration. He ran to win the GOP nomination in 1992 and 1996 and surprised the GOP establishment and traditional conservatives by over-performing, tying, or winning early primary and caucus states, like Iowa and New Hampshire. He ultimately won 35 percent of the

Super Tuesday states in 1992 and a quarter in 1996, but he never went away quietly.[39]

Buchanan ran so strongly the first time that the national party was forced to give him a prime-time speaking spot at the Republican National Convention in Houston, where he promptly attacked the Clintons as "Mr. and Mrs. Mao of the culture war," Hillary Clinton as a radical feminist, and declared, "There is a religious war going in our country for the soul of America," and it will be "as critical to the kind of nation we will one day be as the Cold War itself." That campaign and speech, Timothy Stanley wrote, "fired the first shot in the American culture war."[40]

Other GOP leaders carried the banner against abortion, "liberal permissiveness," taxes, and big government, but Buchanan alone among the national leaders attacked the elites on immigration and foreign trade. And he was not shy about using examples that betrayed his real worries about the nation's demographic changes: "If we had to take a million immigrants in, say Zulus, next year, or Englishmen, and put them in Virginia, what group would be easier to assimilate and would cause less problems for the people of Virginia?"[41] When responding to a student question in Arizona about how hard Mexicans work, he retorted, "But they've got no right to break our laws and break into our country and go on welfare, and some commit crimes."

He decried the fact that "one in five felons in a federal prison is an illegal alien" and that in California "immigrants are coming in such numbers that they're swamping the schools, and you have to raise taxes." To address this "mass immigration," he proposed building "an impenetrable wall on the Mexican border" and a five-year moratorium on legal immigration.[42]

And Buchanan's culture war also included an attack on the international alliances and trade deals that "sold out" the American worker. In 1991, he drew a stark contrast with George Bush: "He is a globalist and we are nationalists. He believes in some Pax Universalis. We believe in the Old Republic. He would put America's wealth and power at the service of some vague New World Order. We will put America First."[43] In 1996, he lamented that South American flowers were putting Iowa farmers out of business and labeled Senator Bob Dole "Mr. NAFTA, Mr. WTO, and Mr. Mexican bailout."[44]

And the result was a surge of anti-immigrant, nativist hate groups that "proliferated since the late 1990s, when anti-immigrant xenophobia began to rise to levels not seen in the United States since the 1920s," according to the Southern Poverty Law Center.[45]

Newt Gingrich eschewed Pat Buchanan's anti-establishment populism because his conservative revolution did not include an aversion to America's military alliances and indeed, he led the fight to pass NAFTA and other trade agreements. His 1994 "Contract with America" included no steps to roll back the immigration laws. So, others would ultimately lead the fight to make the GOP an "America first" Party.

But Newt Gingrich led a Republican Party that would strike a dramatically different course on immigration. In the titanic battle to reform welfare in 1996, the Republicans' bill barred both legal and undocumented immigrants from receiving cash assistance, food stamps, and Medicaid benefits.[46] President Clinton vetoed the first plans, because they went too far on denying government benefits to legal immigrants, but he reluctantly agreed in order to win passage of these major reforms. The new law, for the first time, barred legal immigrants from receiving government benefits for five years.[47]

California Governor Pete Wilson in 1994 led the party's anti-immigration effort in the states by getting Proposition 187 on the ballot: it would bar illegal immigrants from using public services, including education and health care, and required all state and local officials to report undocumented immigrants to law enforcement. Nearly 60 percent of the voters supported it, though federal courts ultimately declared the referendum unconstitutional and kept the law from ever being implemented. GOP state leaders also moved to bar illegal immigrants from getting driver's licenses, which became the next hot issue in California, Georgia, New York, and other states.[48]

The Democratic Party did not join the battle because it was divided on the issue. Even though President Clinton campaigned in California against Prop 187, Democrats nationally had not settled on how to handle the undocumented population or how to create a path to legalization or citizenship.

The fading GOP establishment tried periodically to put comprehensive immigration reform back on the table to be passed by a bipartisan majority in the Congress, but those efforts were marginalized within a GOP that was now virulently anti-immigration. President George W. Bush pushed for reform before it died in the U.S. Senate. After President Obama won reelection in 2012 and the GOP lost ignominiously among both Hispanics and Asians and lost more states in the Southwest, the Republican Party leaders pressed the pause button. Their official postmortem declared, "If Hispanic Americans perceive that a GOP nominee or candidate does not want them in the United States (i.e. self-deportation), they will not pay attention to our next sentence."[49]

Comprehensive immigration reform passed in the U.S. Senate, but Republican senators knew their party. Two thirds of the Republican senators had voted to kill it. House Republicans hated the reforms, and the party leaders never even considered bringing it to the floor for a vote. House and Senate GOP leaders knew their caucuses and committed to reversing President Obama's executive order legalizing the DACA "Dreamers" and 5 million additional undocumented immigrants. After a member of the House leadership lost in a primary for seeming to be open to immigration reform, the House GOP would never give in to the pleadings of the GOP establishment.[50]

In the states after the 2010 Tea Party wave elections, party leaders put even more pressure on undocumented immigrants. They sought to transfer enforcement of immigration laws from the federal government to the states, which would be more vigilant in chasing down undocumented immigrants and denying them access to schools, employment, and housing. These efforts were initially overturned by the federal courts, but more conservative justices would soon allow the Republicans more latitude to lead the fight state by state.[51]

When the House leadership was forced to debate immigration in 2018, a big majority of the House Republicans voted to reduce legal immigration. Remember, 1994.

THE GOP–TEA PARTY BATTLE AGAINST PRESIDENT BARACK OBAMA

The election of Barack Obama as president of the United States was celebrated across the country and the globe, but his election brought to fruition the successive, escalating battles of the GOP against civil rights, abortion, and immigration. He embodied the political triumph of the New America and the Democratic Party that controlled all branches of government. This activism was resisted by the Tea Party that carried the GOP's social mission into battle.

Newt Gingrich meant for the Gingrich Revolution to be as incendiary. Steve Kornacki writes of Gingrich's unique contribution to our polarized politics: the GOP must embrace confrontation, fight back with every weapon, eschew bipartisan compromise, and expose the cozy corruption of Washington if they are to win control in Congress. They must expose the profound dangers that the country will face if New America gets to govern.[52]

The Kennedy School had to cancel its bipartisan orientation for new members because the Gingrich Republicans were more interested in crashing convention and learning about policy from the conservative Heritage Foundation.

The Gingrich Republicans insisted on passing a budget that balanced the federal budget in seven years that cut $270 billion out of spending on Medicare and pushed seniors into HMOS, while cutting the capital tax rate in half. The House Republicans were not shy about their intentions: making the program so unattractive it would "wither on the vine."

President Clinton vetoed the Republican budget and for the first time in the country's history, the federal government was shut down for a sustained time, thirty days in all. Essential services continued and people got their Social Security checks, but all government agencies were shuttered.

And the Republicans got slaughtered. The public predictably blamed the congressional Republicans by about a three-to-one ratio in some polls. They were forced to cave without winning anything. President Clinton's job approval ratings began rising immediately thereafter, and Bob Dole, the Senate majority leader, won just 39 percent of the vote in the 1996 presidential election and Newt Gingrich was forced out as speaker after the disappointing 1998 off-year elections.

Newt Gingrich created the precedent for raising the stakes and shutting down the government, but he didn't slow government or the growth of liberalism. Vice President Al Gore won a plurality of the vote in 2000 and probably a majority of the Electoral College as well. The New American Majority had won.[53]

That contrasts with the tsunami produced by the election of President Obama and the Tea Party revolt. They produced an explosive growth of racial and partisan polarization that put a Tea Party–dominated GOP in charge of most of the country for a decade. The GOP was angrily determined to stop Obama and the Democrats, big government, Obamacare, and immigration at all costs. The explosion produced the 2010 Tea Party wave election that gave Republicans control of the House and, in 2014, control of the U.S. Senate and half of the state governments, where the GOP was able to prevent government from performing its normal functions. The GOP worked to marginalize President Barack Obama, whom they hated. They were determined to stop everything the Democrats were trying to do. They tried to snuff out Democratic governance.

This put the GOP's counterrevolution into a virtual war with multiculturalism and the New America.

Immigration was incendiary, as in 1994. The number of "illegal immigrants" grew every year under President Bush until it reached 8.3 million in 2010, when both the state crackdowns on undocumented immigrants and financial collapse stopped the rise. None of that stopped the proportion of Americans who were foreign born, which reached 13.9 percent and 40 million in 2010.[54]

Do not underestimate how important that change was and how much it disrupted traditional immigration patterns: fully 37 percent of the foreign-born population came from Central America; 30 percent from Mexico. In 2010, when the Tea Party wave hit, only 28 percent of those from Mexico spoke English well and only 24 percent had become citizens, one half the rate of prior generations. America was sounding much more foreign and that was not just a racist imagining. The Republican base resented that the elites did not mind the change or even notice.

The bailout of the Wall Street banks could not have been more incendiary. Wall Street excess took the economy off a cliff, and Democrats rightly came to the nation's rescue by passing TARP. But the bailout of the banks was a searing event in America's consciousness—and Democrats owned it. While President Bush and his Treasury secretary proposed the bailout, it was embraced by then-candidate Obama and passed with Democratic votes in the House and Senate. The bank executives got their bonuses and no bank official was prosecuted, while those facing home foreclosure got no relief whatsoever. That is why a year into the Obama administration, 57 percent of the public thought it was the "wrong thing for the government to do."[55] In fact, one year after the passage of the president's own economic recovery plan, the majority of voters conflated TARP and the Economic Recovery and Reinvestment Act and thought the big banks, not the middle class, were the main beneficiaries—and the middle class was seething.

The crash in income and wealth was incendiary. In 2011, well into President Obama's first term, "the real incomes of the middle class and working families was 8 to 10 percent lower than they had been in 2007," Bartels writes.[56] Their incomes did not get back to pre–financial crisis levels until 2016.[57] And perhaps "the most shocking economic fallout" was the "massive collapse of ordinary Americans' net wealth."[58] The median household's net worth crashed immediately and by 2013, it was 36 percent lower than it had been years earlier before the crisis.[59] Those on the bottom quarter of the income ladder lost over half their net wealth in 2013.[60]

In President Obama's first term, the incomes of the top 1 percent grew by 31.4 percent while all the rest grew by only .4 percent.[61] People were stuck, struggling, and angry.

The economists Alan Blinder and Mark Zandi concluded that the administration and Federal Reserve's "stunning range of initiatives" averted "a Great Depression 2.0" and created 2.7 million additional jobs.[62] Paul Krugman credits President Obama's unique and brave response compared to those of the rest of the Organization for Economic Co-operation and Development (OECD) countries, where belief in austerity restrained the government response. Other developed countries struggled to lower unemployment, but in the U.S. Obama was able to get unemployment down to 4.5 percent by 2015.[63] President Obama proposed more steps when the recovery slowed, but they were all blocked by the Tea Party Congress that embraced deficit reduction and austerity as the overriding priority.

President Obama never used his charisma and great communication skills to educate or mobilize the country around these unprecedented steps. That was incendiary, too. He did not define this extraordinary moment for the country or demand accountability and responsibility. He did not identify those who had done wrong and insist they pay a price. Instead, he told the country starting just one year after the crash that millions of jobs were being created and "the recession has been transformed into a dependable recovery" and the country is "on the right track." The Republicans who created this mess were doing "everything possible to obstruct our progress." That made Republicans even angrier, if that was possible, but those supporting the president wanted much more accountability, too.

That failure of a Democratic president to build the case for his own bold policies and demand accountability diminished enthusiasm among people of color, unmarried women, and millennials, who were suffering profoundly, and pushed away the white working class, who could not believe what they were watching.

President Obama's job approval rating fell abruptly by double digits in Maine, Michigan, Minnesota, New Hampshire, and Pennsylvania by the beginning of 2010. The president's disapproval rating with the Democratic base of African Americans, Hispanics, millennials, and single women rose to 40 percent in 2010, so it was a volatile moment.

The Democrats' party identification advantage in President Obama's first year fell off a cliff with white working-class voters—defined as those with some college, a high school education or less. In 2008, the Democrats had battled back to near parity with white working-class voters, but the Republicans' party advantage soared to thirty points in 2010 and grew further in 2012.[64] This realignment of white working-class partisan identity had a profound impact on the composition and attitudes in both parties, but particularly the Republicans because the white working class was so frustrated and angry with the choices elites made in this financial crisis.[65]

But President Barack Hussein Obama was perhaps the most incendiary element of all, bringing to fruition the building resentments.

In reality, his election represented nationally the triumph of a new diverse, educated, metropolitan, and younger America, and his reelection confirmed their ascendancy and the country's acceptance of an African American as president of the United States. President Obama himself embodied everything that was happening at this explosive moment.

Whites had every reason to believe they were losing standing and power, perhaps moving to fear when they listened to Fox News, which widely reported the "end of white America" when the U.S. census projected America would be a minority majority nation by 2045. After President Obama's reelection, Fox News glitterati hardly celebrated. "I went to bed last night thinking we're outnumbered," Rush Limbaugh lamented. "[All] of this discussion we'd had about this election being the election that will tell us whether or not we've lost the country. I went to bed last night thinking we've lost the country." Bill O'Reilly focused on the changing demographics and that this victory meant, "It's not a traditional America anymore." That 50 percent not only won, "they want stuff. They want things. And who is going to give them things?" He concluded, "The white establishment is now the minority."[66]

Not surprisingly, the importance of race, attitudes toward blacks and immigrants, and racial resentment hit the levels they had in the 1964, 1968, and 1972 elections when the country was on fire, literally.[67] And that fiery shift became the new normal in this period.

The growth of immigration and foreign-born populations and the acceptance of multiculturalism had transformed the GOP's counterrevolution. Up until 2012, a not inconsiderable 30 percent of Republicans in a survey said being white was "very important" to them, but that rose to 40 percent after Obama's reelection.[68] And when they were asked what aspects of American identity were important to them, being "able to speak English" and having "American citizenship" stood out from the other possible responses.[69]

Republicans, white conservatives, and born-again Evangelicals watched the growth and acceptance of multiculturalism, and they believed increasing racial diversity was shifting the political balance against whites, according to Pew.[70] About 60 percent of Republicans, white conservatives, Evangelicals, and seniors (65+) believed that racial minorities were using their hold over government to discriminate against whites. But just a third of college graduates and millennials agreed with that at the end of Obama's term.[71] At the base of the GOP's anger was the fear that the new electoral majority would use its political power to expand government and spending on behalf of racial minorities.[72]

But of course, Barack Obama was African American, and racial resentment was a huge factor in both of his elections. In 2008, those whites most resentful gave Obama only 20 percent of their vote, compared to 80 percent among those least resentful.[73] And racial resentment was now as strong a factor in predicting Obama's vote as party identification and George Bush's job disapproval. President Obama changed what mattered.

The GOP was more impacted by the jump in white and racial resentment and strongly opposed Obama's expansive use of government, which sent his job approval rating with Republicans plummeting.

The Tea Party movement was a big factor, as it was the organizational heart of the GOP. The Tea Party movement supporters scored very high on racial resentment measures and more than a few of their marchers and demonstrators sported signs saying OBAMA'S PLAN: WHITE SLAVERY and THE AMERICAN TAXPAYERS ARE THE JEWS FOR OBAMA'S OVENS.[74] They helped produce an "extraordinary . . . hemorrhaging of Republicans," Don Kinder wrote.[75] Obama's approval rating with them fell at three times the rate of his predecessors, finishing at only 9 percent on the eve of the midterms.[76]

The Tea Party 2010 wave gave the GOP the ability to stop President Obama from doing any further damage. No more initiatives, period. But at the state level, it was the GOP that could take the initiative. And immigration was the flashpoint. Governor Jan Brewer of Arizona signed S.B. 1070 during the summer of 2010, which required state law enforcement officials to detain suspects if there was reasonable suspicion that they were illegal immigrants. The law imposed penalties on those sheltering, hiring, or transporting "unregistered aliens," and the stated intent was to achieve "attrition through enforcement." Arizona passed the toughest immigration law in the country, and the Republican-controlled states of Georgia, Indiana, South Carolina, and Alabama were moved to act, too. Two years later, the Supreme Court overturned the Arizona law as an infringement of federal constitutional prerogatives regarding immigration, but the parties' polarization on immigration was advancing.[77]

The Republican candidates in the lead up to the 2012 presidential election competed to be toughest on immigration. Mitt Romney won the 2012 nomination, promising harsh enforcement to get undocumented immigrants to "self-deport."

President Obama was the only president in over a century to win reelection with a reduced margin from his original election. He won only 39 percent of the white vote in 2012, down from 43 percent in 2008. Racial resentment suppressed his job approval rate, according to the analysis by John Sides and Lynn Vavreck in their book *The Gamble*, and reduced his popular vote margin against Romney by up to four points.[78]

Those worrying about the demographic implications of 2012 accurately described the increased role of racial resentment and white identity, particularly for the Tea Party base who thought they were in a zero-sum competition for jobs and political influence.

They probably did not notice the Gallup poll in 2012, which showed the proportion wanting to *decrease* immigration had dropped to 40 percent, nearly its lowest, and the proportion wanting to "increase" immigration had visibly moved up to a new high at 33 percent.[79] The conservative pundits' fear that President Obama's reelection in 2012 really did reflect a growing acceptance of a very different America was right. That is why GOP voters were at their wits' end. How could they stop it?

That response foretold 2018, when more Americans wanted to increase rather than decrease immigration and the big majority that viewed President Trump's handling of immigration as "too harsh."[80] The GOP's battle against President Obama was backfiring as more and more people supported a multicultural America.

THE GOP AFTER PRESIDENT OBAMA'S REELECTION

After President Obama's reelection, I conducted focus group discussions with people from different parts of the GOP base. They felt conservatives had lost control of the country and were increasingly powerless to change its course. They watched Obama impose his agenda, and Republicans in Washington roll over. The GOP saw a president who had lied, fooled, and manipulated the public to pass a secret socialist agenda.[81]

How do you feel about the direction of the country?

In President Obama's second term, the GOP base thought they faced a victorious Democratic Party intent on expanding government to increase dependence and therefore electoral support. It started with food stamps and unemployment benefits; expanded further to legalize the undocumented immigrants; and finally, insured the uninsured through the Affordable Care Act, which would dramatically expand the number of those dependent on government. The GOP believed these policies were part of the Democrats' electoral strategy—not just a political ideology or an economic philosophy. If Obamacare was fully implemented, they feared the Republican Party would be lost forever.

While few explicitly talked about Obama in racial terms, the base supporters were very conscious of being white in a country with a growing minority population. Their party was losing to a Democratic Party whose goal was to expand government programs that mainly benefitted minorities. Race remained very much alive in the politics of the GOP.

The Evangelicals and the Tea Party were the heart of the GOP base during President Obama's second term. They were nearly 90 percent white in a country growing ever more racially diverse, and two thirds were married in a country where the types of families were growing ever more pluralistic. Nearly two thirds were working class at a time of gathering alienation from the elites, who embraced globalization and trade agreements.[82]

The religiously devout were the biggest bloc and encompassed nearly half of the GOP base voters in 2013, dominated by the Evangelicals, who comprised 29 percent of the base.

The Tea Party was powerful, too, comprising 25 percent of the base at the time, though their influence was multiplied by the intense support they won with Evangelicals. Evangelicals embraced the Tea Party because they fought the hardest against the trends in the country and against President Obama's agenda.

Composition of the Republican base

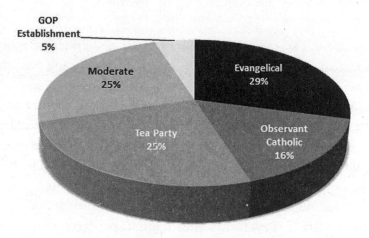

For all the energy motivating its base, the GOP was a very divided party, split by its battle against the sexual revolution and against any government role. Fully one in four of the base were moderates who were fiscal conservatives, patriots, and those concerned with immigration who felt isolated in their own party. Their alienation from dominant GOP thinking began on social issues such as gay marriage, abortion, and whether homosexuality should be discouraged by society, but it was also evident on issues such as climate change and the Second Amendment.

The country would hit a tipping point within two years, according to the Gallup Poll, when 60 to 70 percent said gay and lesbian relations, having a baby outside of marriage, sex between an unmarried man and woman, and divorce were "morally acceptable." Acceptance had jumped fifteen to twenty-three points, depending on the issue, since 2001, when the GOP culture war was being escalated. It was in 2015 that a majority of Americans said gays and lesbians are born, not made. That pretty much put to bed the issue as a moral question, and, as a result, many moderate women in the GOP would be pushed out of the party before long, as Evangelicals became even more central.

Evangelicals felt most threatened by the ascendant demographic and cultural trends in America and brought unique intensity to their opposition to what was happening with homosexuals. Abortion was one of the issues on which Evangelicals and the Tea Party base were equally aligned and intense—and they had led the charge in that battle against the trends in marriage and independence for women. The observant Catholic bloc was strongly opposed to the growing public acceptance of homosexuality and gay marriage but less strongly than Evangelicals.

The Evangelicals talked about how the dominant politics and culture encroached on their small towns, schools, and churches. They were troubled by these trends and talked with friends, family, and fellow believers about Obamacare, guns, government intrusion, gay marriage, and "culture rot." It used to be different and very white in their towns:

> It's a little bubble. So everybody—it's like a Lake Wobegon. Everybody is above average. Everybody is happy. Everybody is white. Everybody is middle class, whether or not they really are. Everybody looks that way. Everybody goes to the same pool. Everybody goes—there's one library, one post office. Very homogenous.
>
> —EVANGELICAL MAN, ROANOKE

In Roanoke, participants remarked that it was refreshing and unusual to be in a room where everyone shared their beliefs—which gave them an opportunity to speak openly about guns, gay marriage, church, and their values. In Colorado Springs, participants remarked that Colorado used to be a conservative state where they could expect that their values and rights would be protected. This seems to be slipping away, one noted: "We're having to realize that we're going to be in a very politically incorrect minority pretty soon" (Evangelical man, Roanoke).

The Evangelicals felt besieged and wondered why their own party had not stood up, battled, and won. Republican establishment politicians had lost their way, and there were too many "RINOs" (Republicans in name only) who could not stop what was happening.

For the GOP, Barack Obama was the starting point for everything that was wrong with the country. For the GOP base, President Obama was a "liar" and "manipulator" who fooled the country, and when he was reelected, they were frustrated with a country that believed him. When some were asked to write open-endedly what comes to mind when they heard the name Barack Obama, this was the result.

How would you describe President Barack Obama?

The Tea Party participants described him as a "spin doctor," "misleading," "slick," "slimy," "untrustworthy," "condescending," and "an SOB."

When they watched a TV video of the president speaking on the Affordable Care Act, the Evangelical women in Colorado Springs wrote some pretty harsh and dismissive things: "Spin Dr." and "chronic liar"; "fake"; "lies"; "just a speech"; "liar"; "bullshit." The comments from the moderate men there were almost indistinguishable: "lies, lies, lies, lies, lies!!!!!!!"; "lies"; "disregards real facts"; "socialism"; "lies, lies, lies"; "health care lies."

The private doubts they wrote on a piece of paper before discussion with the group betrayed a much deeper suspicion of the president as a person. Many had questions about him being foreign, not a citizen, non-Christian, secretly Muslim, or a socialist.

These questions on character and legitimacy mattered so much because the Republican base thought President Obama, Nancy Pelosi, and the Democratic Party were conspiring to push for bigger government and more spending to control the people. The GOP base was united in its opposition to big government programs and wasteful government spending, including the new health care reform law. Evangelical and Tea Party group participants also thought he was trying to fool the middle class with a more palatable patina while pursuing a darker, secret, socialist agenda. The Democratic Party existed to create programs and dependence—the food stamp hammock and entitlements—for the "47 percent," a critique of government that Mitt Romney took on.

The GOP believed President Obama was on the verge of using his powers to pursue his agenda without limits. When asked what was going right in the country, a Tea Party woman in Roanoke joked, "Well, we're not a communist nation . . . yet." This fear was evident in the frequent discussions about executive orders and action: "When Congress is gone . . . he just does an Executive Order. He's going to get anything he wants. And there's nobody there that will have the guts enough to stand up to him"; "There's so many secret things that go on—that are—bills are passed and regulations are passed—we never know about" (Evangelical man, Roanoke).[83]

What united the base of the GOP then was a deep hostility to Obamacare. That was why it would become the unifying issue in the 2014 off-year elections, and why it became the litmus test for Republicans in 2016.

And critically, they viewed undocumented and illegal immigration as negatively as Obamacare, underscoring how central a role immigration and the growing Hispanic presence played in their vote. The Tea Party bloc led the opposition to both Obamacare and "undocumented" immigrants. On immigration, Republicans spoke literally and in graphic terms of being invaded, and the immigrants' failure to speak English made them pretty crazy. This was a party ready for an anti-immigrant and nativist leader.

The Tea Party bloc was the most anti-immigration, anti-Islam, pro-NRA, anti–food stamp, and anti–Obama and Obamacare, and they led the GOP into its total war against the New America. The explosion produced two parties now fully polarized on race and civil rights, and immigration; indeed, on rejecting or embracing America's multiculturalism.

3 THE TRUMP GOP BATTLE AGAINST MULTICULTURALISM

WHEN DONALD TRUMP CAME DEFIANTLY DOWN the long escalator in Trump Tower in July 2015 to announce his candidacy for the presidency, he understood that the Tea Party was the heart of the GOP fight against Obama's America, and he set out to make them his base.

In his announcement speech, Trump focused with great discipline on trade agreements, immigration, Obamacare, and the useless politicians who had sold out the country to foreigners. His speech was a nationalist cry of anger against the elites and GOP politicians who had betrayed America, its working people, and their hopes of realizing the American dream. It sounded as if Trump had read the research I had conducted two years earlier. He targeted the Tea Party voters like a laser, giving full voice to their contempt for "the politicians."

He assured the Tea Party voters, as well as moderates and Catholics, that he and the GOP would "save Medicare, Medicaid and Social Security without cuts."[1]

Trump made no mention of abortion, the social conservative issues, or the moral rot that was so motivating for the Evangelicals. His focus was the Tea Party.

"Our country is in serious trouble," Trump began, because "we don't have victories anymore." And, he asked, when was the "last time anybody saw us beating" China or Japan? Answering his own question, he continued: "They kill us. They send cars by the millions," and "when was the last time you saw a Chevrolet in Tokyo? They beat us all the time."[2]

And then he went to the primary threat: "When do we beat Mexico at the border?" They're "laughing at us, our stupidity." America "has become a dumping ground for everybody else's problems." And that was Trump's vehicle for sending his anti-immigration message in the most racist form possible. "Mexico is not sending their best." Lest anyone look for nuance, "They're not sending you. They are not sending you"—i.e., they are not sending white people. They are sending people that "have lots of problems. . . . They're bringing drugs. They're bringing crime. They're rapists."[3]

Foreign political leaders in Mexico, South and Latin America, and the Middle East are sending their worst, while our "politicians are all talk, no action." Trump almost spits out the "p": "How stupid are these politicians to allow this to happen? The politicians negotiating on our behalf are clueless and treasonous."[4]

The result of the politicians' collective perfidy, according to Trump, is an economy at near zero growth and unemployment at 18 to 20 percent. America's workers struggle to get jobs "because China has our jobs and Mexico has our jobs," but he will bring them back. "Bring back our manufacturing" and "rebuild the country's infrastructure." He declared modestly, "I will be the greatest jobs president that God ever created."[5]

He also made clear his priority on Obamacare. Right up front he declared, "We have a disaster called the big lie: Obamacare. Obamacare." Premiums and deductibles were unimaginable. "You have to be hit by a tractor, literally, a tractor, to use it, because the deductibles are so high." And this is before Obamacare becomes fully operational: "Obamacare kicks in in 2016. Really big league." That is why he promised "to repeal and replace Obamacare" with "something much better for everybody."[6]

And then, as if almost aggressively ticking off a Tea Party checklist, "I will immediately terminate President Obama's illegal executive orders on immigration, immediately."

"Fully support and back up the Second Amendment."

"Renegotiate our foreign trade deals."

"Put a General Patton to lead our war on ISIS."

He won't be a corrupted politician because "I'm not using my own money. I'm not using the lobbyists. I'm not using the donors."[7]

And "so I've watched the politicians," he concluded. "They will never make America great again." They are "talk, no action," and, sorrowfully, "they will not bring us . . . to the promised land."[8]

But Donald Trump will.

Donald Trump surged into the lead with 32 percent of the primary vote when I conducted my first poll in February 2016. He pushed the former Tea Party favorites, senators Ted Cruz and Marco Rubio, far back in the pack with 17 and 18 percent support, respectively.[9] He had a real base that wanted to put out lawn signs and let people know.

Trump spoke directly to the Tea Party bloc that was the most working class and most male and formed a quarter of the GOP base. Trump immediately won half their votes and surged into an unassailable lead with them. Trump was competitive with another candidate in all the other factions (with Cruz among Evangelicals, with John Kasich among observant Catholics, with Rubio among moderates), but no other candidate had a base that gathered support from them with this intense audition. Trump rode the Tea Party base to the nomination.

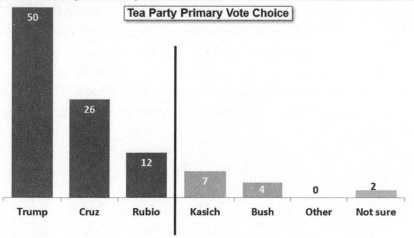

Trump's base Is In the Tea Party bloc

Thinking about the Republican presidential primary election or caucus in your state, if the primary or caucus for the Republican nominee for President were held today, for whom would you vote?

Tea Party Primary Vote Choice

Trump	Cruz	Rubio	Kasich	Bush	Other	Not sure
50	26	12	7	4	0	2

Trump rode the dominant attitudinal dimension that reflected the deep hostility to President Obama, attacks on the Constitution, the Democratic Party, Hillary Clinton, and Obamacare. Trump was the candidate who was demonstrably the most hostile to Obama and Clinton, which was motivating the growing anger of the GOP base. That one dimension explained more than twice as much of the variation in GOP thinking as the next strongest dimension.[10]

Dominant underlying dimension is anti-Obama, Clinton, Democrats, Obamacare, and Constitutional threat

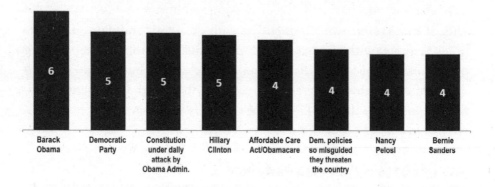

Opposition to Democratic leaders & Democrats in general explains 24% of responses

Barack Obama	Democratic Party	Constitution under dally attack by Obama Admin.	Hillary Clinton	Affordable Care Act/Obamacare	Dem. policies so misguided they threaten the country	Nancy Pelosi	Bernie Sanders
6	5	5	5	4	4	4	4

Trump spoke to a GOP base where four in five believed there is "no real difference between the Democratic Party and socialism" and nine in ten believed "the Democratic Party's policies are so misguided that they threaten the nation's well-being."[11] Yet it was the Tea Party element of the base that believed that with the most intensity, followed by the Evangelicals. That set the foundation for Trump building support with them, too.

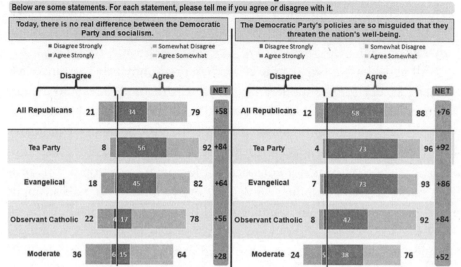

Donald Trump understood that the GOP was defined by its battle against the New America, making race and immigration central to why people identify with the GOP. It does not matter what faction you look at; Republican voters were uncomfortable with immigrant diversity: they thought illegal immigration was out of control and wanted their leaders to fight it. Furthermore, two thirds of the Republican base said, "It bothers me when I come in contact with immigrants who speak little or no English," and that included almost 60 percent of the moderates.[12] A stunning 87 percent of the GOP, including 70 percent of moderates, said they wanted their party's nominee to fight the acceptance of the 12 million undocumented immigrants living in the country and the growing proportion of foreign born in our major cities.[13]

The GOP base broadly wanted their leaders to battle to get illegal immigration under control. That was what Donald Trump understood and what helped him to grow support among all of the parts of the base. Trump's nationalist campaign united the Tea Party, which allowed him to lock up the party and the convention.

But the GOP was profoundly divided on the sexual revolution and on whether government should tackle major problems, like child care or climate change. Abortion became the issue that most defined the party, but moderates formed a surprising 31 percent of the GOP base in 2016, and they were solidly pro-choice on abortion and hostile to pro-life groups. About one in five were poised to defect from the party. The party was divided down the middle on gay marriage and climate change.[14]

All of the base groups of the GOP were predominantly working-class voters, except for the moderates: two thirds of moderates had a four-year college degree and were socially liberal. Two thirds said abortion should be legal in all or most cases. All the GOP primary candidates were pro-life, and they declined to target the moderates because support for abortion was not considered a legitimate position in this pro-life party. A pretty stunning 86 percent of the moderates, half strongly, said that the Republican nominee should accept that "women and men feel free to have sex without any interest in getting married, forming a family or a long-term relationship" and move on to other issues. Half of the Tea Party base agreed, but not the Evangelicals and observant Catholics. About 70 percent of them said the GOP should fight this trend.[15]

Moderates accept sexual revolution and pre-marital sex

Many Republicans think the county is off on the wrong track. Below are some changes taking place in America. For each, please indicate if you want a Republican nominee who will fight to stop it or one who will accept it and move on to other issues.

Women and men feel free to have sex without any interest in getting married, forming a family or a long-term relationship.

	Accept it		Fight it	NET
All Republicans	56	30	18	44	-12
Tea Party	50	27	19	50	--
Evangelical	27	12	32	72	+45
Observant Catholic	33	17	23	67	+34
Moderate	86	47	5	14	-72

The moderates also accepted gay marriage but that set them apart from the rest of the GOP base. Over 74 percent of the observant Catholics and 83 percent of the Evangelicals were intensely hostile to accepting this change in the definition of marriage.[16]

The moderates were also in a different place than the rest of their party on the environment and climate change, though with less intensity. Over 60 percent said that global warming is real, produced by human activity, and now required serious measures to address it. On this issue, observant Catholics too were prepared to accept that 2015 was the hottest year on record.[17]

But Trump understood the Tea Party believed climate change was the work of the liberal media, and it would provide the pretext for much bigger government and regulation.

Trump topped the primary polls and was poised to lead a GOP that had waged the counterrevolution against the New America, but that produced a fractured party. One quarter of the moderates said they might split off and vote for a Democrat for president.

Donald Trump went to the Republican Convention in Cleveland determined to crush his opponents and consolidate the base that had gotten him the nomination. That meant putting the GOP 180 degrees in opposition to the new multicultural America. The party started by putting Phil Robertson, the male leader in *Duck Dynasty*, as the first speaker on the first night of the convention. He represented a conservative return to the traditional family in which men and women played their traditional roles. When faith mattered. And he was an entertainer, who had observed that the blacks he knew growing up in Louisiana, "pre-entitlement, pre-welfare," were "happy" and "godly" and "no one was singing the blues," unlike today, when self-reliance was in short supply.[18] And most prominently, Robertson had warned that homosexuals commit "indecent acts" and "perversion" that are an insult to God: "They are insolent, arrogant God haters. They are heartless. They are faithless. They are senseless. They are ruthless. They invent ways of doing evil."[19]

The first night's speakers included the three parents, Donald Trump said two days later, "whose children were killed by illegal immigrants—Mary Ann Mendoza, Sabine Durden, and Jamiel Shaw"—three parents who saw "no demonstrations to protest on their behalf."[20]

Donald Trump accepted the nomination "at a moment of crisis for our nation." These "attacks on our police, and the terrorism in our cities, threaten our very way of life." And he reassured the country: "Beginning on January 20th, 2017, safety will be restored." Donald Trump will be "the law and order President."[21]

Trump catalogued the violence and homicides that plagued American city after city and assured his audience the country "cannot afford to be so politically correct anymore." And that meant being honest about the cause: "Nearly 180,000 illegal immigrants with criminal records, ordered deported from our country, are tonight roaming free to threaten peaceful citizens." They were "being released by the tens of thousands into our communities." And the murder of "an innocent young girl named Sarah Root" was the sorry result.[22]

Trump pointed out that President Obama wanted to increase massively the number of Syrian refugees, while Hillary Clinton wanted to allow sanctuary cities, despite that "decades of record immigration have produced lower wages and higher unemployment for our citizens, especially African-American and Latino workers." So, Trump's plan was the exact opposite of what Clinton offered: "Americans want relief from uncontrolled immigration. . . . Clinton is proposing mass amnesty, mass immigration, and mass lawlessness." That was the choice for voters in the election.[23]

This has played out in a country with a disastrous economy, Trump said, that has been "edited out of your nightly news and your morning newspaper." He seemed sorrowful about the numbers of African Americans and Latinos trapped in poverty, the 14 million who had left the labor force totally, and the trade deficit that had grown to $800 billion. And then he offered an extended critique of what trade agreements had done to this country: "America has lost nearly one-third of its manufacturing jobs since 1997 following the enactment of disastrous trade deals supported by Bill and Hillary Clinton."[24] These agreements included NAFTA, China being admitted to the World Trade Organization, the South Korea deal on paying for U.S. military protection, and the Trans-Pacific Partnership Agreement.

"I have visited the laid-off factory workers, and the communities crushed by our horrible and unfair trade deals," Trump told the convention and country. "These are the forgotten men and women in our country. People who work hard but no longer have a voice."[25]

Then Trump pledged, "never again." He would never "sign any trade agreement that hurts our workers." As president, he would "turn our bad trade agreements into great trade agreements."[26]

He summarized the break with conventional wisdom: "Americanism, not globalism, will be our credo." We must have leaders "who will put America First."[27]

He concluded with his promise to make America strong, proud, and safe again. And, of course, "we will Make America Great Again."[28]

Few in the GOP establishment thought he would get that chance as president. None of the party's living presidential nominees appeared in Cleveland to attend or speak at the convention. The primary opponents who had most closely contested the nomination did not endorse Trump for president. After the release of the *Access Hollywood* tape of Trump's lewdness in speaking with Billy Bush, many prominent senators and House members announced they would not vote for Trump or campaign with him. After all, just 56 percent of Republicans had voted for Trump in the primaries and caucuses. And after all the fanfare of winning the nomination, which usually leads those who supported the opponent to forget the past battle and think they supported the winner, Trump's recalled primary vote did not rise. Those who voted for Cruz or Kasich recalled their vote accurately right through to the election.

The GOP establishment believed Donald Trump had the national party on loan for three months, after which they would reclaim it.

They didn't realize the FBI and Russians would push him across the finish line in key battleground states.

They didn't expect that Hillary Clinton would run such an inept campaign.

They watched the Democrats attack Mitt Romney early for running an investment firm that callously pushed out so many working people, which testified to his rich indifference. An ad run by the Obama-supporting super Pac Priorities USA Action featured a Kansas City steelworker: "When Mitt Romney and Bain closed the plant, I lost my health care, and my family lost their health care," and he lost his wife to cancer in just twenty-two days. "I do not think Mitt Romney realizes what he's done to anyone, and furthermore I do not think Mitt Romney is concerned."[29]

That attack disqualified Romney in Ohio and Michigan. So, in 2016, the GOP thought the Democrats would readily disqualify Trump because of his even greater vulnerability from his bankrupt companies that left small businesses, contractors, and employees holding the bag. They thought the Democrats would disqualify Trump because of his use of undocumented and foreign workers rather than Americans. The Clinton campaign, extraordinarily enough, did not attack Trump for forgetting his "forgotten Americans."

The GOP establishment did not understand how deeply the Tea Party and Evangelical base of the party were committed to Trump as the only leader who could forestall Armageddon. They were going to vote for an antiestablishment nominee, and they were not going to readily give the GOP back.

Donald Trump showed that campaigns matter. Candidate Trump and chief strategist Steve Bannon ran a national campaign focused on Mexican immigrant violence, Muslim terrorists, a bad economy, and bad trade agreements that failed working people—all of which communicated that this Republican Party, unlike the elites of the past, would put America first and its hardworking white and Christian citizenry who were losing out in this new, multicultural America first. The powerful argument was this nationalist claim against the globalists, who couldn't care less about the working stiff.

President Obama closed the campaign for Hillary Clinton with rallies in Philadelphia, Raleigh, Miami, and Cleveland. Joined by Clinton and bedecked by big posters proclaiming "Choose Hope" and "Stronger Together," the president on every occasion declared the country was headed in the right direction, with 15 million jobs, rising incomes, and falling poverty. He called on citizens "to build on the progress." He told the base voters attending the rallies and the voters watching on their TV or phone, if you want to have another Obama term, Hillary is your man.

In her book *What Happened*, Hillary Clinton noted that "Stan also thought my campaign was too upbeat on the economy, too liberal on immigration, and not vocal enough about trade."[30] She accepted "that, despite the heroic work President Obama did to get our economy back on the right track after the financial crisis, many Americans didn't feel the recovery in their own lives and didn't give Democrats credit."[31]

So, Clinton struggled to offer a clear economic break from Obama, which meant the change voters broke for Trump, particularly in the battleground states.

For the first time in our post–World War II history, one major party's stand on trade agreements played a contributory role in the election of a president, Donald Trump. He just brazenly cut through all of the fractures that divided both parties on trade and globalization and set the GOP against the Trans-Pacific Partnership (TPP) and NAFTA, the World Trade Organization (WTO), China, the EU, and the whole global trade regime.

President Obama played a big role in aligning Democrats with these agreements and thus in legitimating Trump's claim that only he would be able to bring back American jobs. Obama was proud to build on Bill Clinton's legacy, which included passage of NAFTA and China's entry into the WTO. He successfully completed the Panama, Colombia, and South Korea treaties and got them confirmed by the Congress.[32] And he negotiated the Trans-Pacific Partnership Agreement and battled to have it pass through Congress as his final legacy, including personally lobbying the Democratic platform committee to make sure it included no language hostile to the agreement and sending cabinet members to advocate for the agreement in key states in the lead-up to the election. His plan was to bring up the treaty in the lame-duck session after Hillary Clinton was elected and before she took office.

That meant Hillary Clinton was virtually silent or tongue-tied on trade agreements, even as Trump campaigned against TPP and NAFTA to show he was focused on American jobs. The result was trade mattered for the first time. The Diana C. Mutz study interviewed more than three thousand respondents in both 2012 and 2016, and you can see whether voters changed their positions on some issues and their perception of where the presidential candidates stood on them. Well, in 2016, the voters shifted to Trump's position, wanting fewer trade agreements with other countries, and, ironically, voters came to believe that Clinton was pushing even harder for more trade agreements than Obama had in 2012. Then, the parties were seen as indistinguishable on wanting more trade agreements, but in 2016, voters saw the candidates as far apart, and it hurt Clinton in the election. Trump the candidate had set the agenda at Clinton's expense.

Issue positions of self (average voter) and perceptions of Republican and Democratic presidential candidates, 2012–2016. Note that change over time in opinion (self) is significant for own opinions on trade and immigration but not for own opinions on China. Change over time in perceived candidate positions is significant for all three issues for placement of both Republican and Democratic candidates (P<0.001).[33]

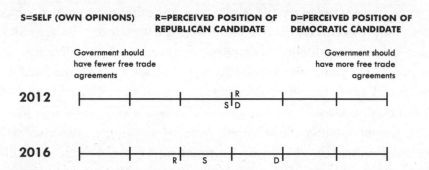

The president was pressing the trade agenda against the will of all the presidential candidates and the national Democratic political class: 75 percent of Democratic senators and 85 percent of Democratic House members voted against it.

President Obama publicly attacked opponents Senator Elizabeth Warren, Congressman Sander Levin, and Congresswoman Rosa DeLauro, my wife, and suggested they needed to do their homework. Congresswoman DeLauro, who led the House and outside opposition to the TPP, described the contentious meeting with President Obama during a small group dinner at an off-site Democratic issues retreat.[34] The exchange wasn't angry but it was contentious. She observed, "I haven't been invited to dinner with the president again."[35]

Democrats opposed the trade agreements, not because of union pressure, as President Obama charged, but because corporate lobbyists crafted it in secret, with special protections for foreign corporations and the outsourcing of jobs that undercut U.S. wages. It also weakened food and environmental standards.

At the heart of Trump's attack was the accusation that U.S. leaders had sold out the citizenry because American interests had to supersede the interests of all others. Trump did not think it was possible to have a trade agreement with reciprocity and that was mutually beneficial. He reflected Steve Bannon's contempt for globalization that "derided the nation."

In the final weeks of the election, Trump declared that he would renegotiate NAFTA if elected and withdraw from the TPP.[36]

The Trump-led effort to put trade agreements front and center shifted attitudes in a dramatic way. In June before the 2016 election, a majority of voters thought "past trade agreements have been a good thing" for the United States, and that view exceeded the opinion of those who thought them a bad thing by fifteen points in polls. By October and the weeks before the election, a plurality of 45 percent said past trade deals had been a bad thing. In June, strongly held opinions were equally split between their being a good and a bad thing, but in October, intense opposition was double that for those who thought them a good thing.

The presidential campaign, on the other hand, turned Republicans dramatically against TPP, NAFTA, and just trade agreements in principle. This reflected pre-Trump long-term trends in the GOP base, which is heavily working class. Opposition in 2016 reached an intensity that would be hard to match on many issues after candidate Trump made it so central to his case against the failed elites. In June, 50 percent of registered voters opposed the TPP, but that jumped to 61 percent in October. The GOP base's intense opposition jumped from 29 to 40 percent. So, if voters were looking for a party that hated the trade status quo, Trump gave it to them.[37]

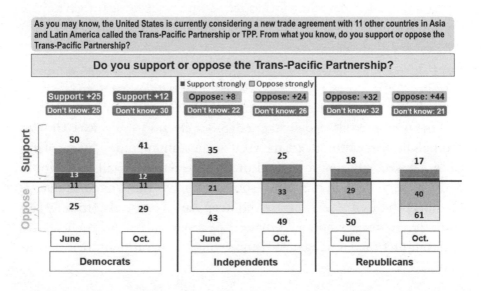

As you may know, the United States is currently considering a new trade agreement with 11 other countries in Asia and Latin America called the Trans-Pacific Partnership or TPP. From what you know, do you support or oppose the Trans-Pacific Partnership?

Do you support or oppose the Trans-Pacific Partnership?

■ Support strongly ☐ Oppose strongly

	Democrats		Independents		Republicans	
	June	Oct.	June	Oct.	June	Oct.
	Support: +25	Support: +12	Oppose: +8	Oppose: +24	Oppose: +32	Oppose: +44
	Don't know: 25	Don't know: 30	Don't know: 22	Don't know: 26	Don't know: 32	Don't know: 21
Support	50	41	35	25	18	17
(strongly)	13	12				
(strongly oppose)	11	11	21	33	29	40
Oppose	25	29	43	49	50	61

In October 2016, when the Trump-led GOP turned against NAFTA, even the GOP base had never been as enthusiastic as the party's congressional leaders, who had provided most of the votes for its passage. Republican support went off a cliff in October when NAFTA sank to a mean score of 30.8 degrees (17 percent warm and 58 percent cool). Half gave it the most negative response possible.[38]

Donald Trump made the GOP an America-first party in 2016 that was going to stand up for the American worker, unlike the elites of both parties, who had failed them. Public sentiment on trade moved closer to Trump's position between 2012 and 2016, in part because both parties had grown substantially more doubtful about the agreements. The trade debate in the future is likely to be fought in very different ways.[39]

The GOP and NAFTA

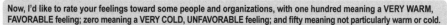

Now, I'd like to rate your feelings toward some people and organizations, with one hundred meaning a VERY WARM, FAVORABLE feeling; zero meaning a VERY COLD, UNFAVORABLE feeling; and fifty meaning not particularly warm or cold.

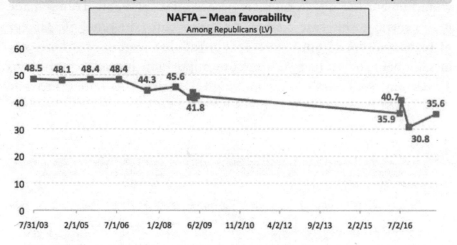

Just as unprecedented in the 2015–16 election cycle was Donald Trump's determination to set the GOP against immigration, particularly from Mexico, offering a "beautiful . . . impenetrable wall that would deter these violent immigrants from coming to the United States."[40] He also promised a Muslim ban to keep Americans safe from Syrian and other refugees who might make it to America.[41]

Trump set the GOP against the growing immigration, foreign diversity, and growth of Islam in the West—all part of the growing multicultural diversity in the country.

Hillary Clinton's campaign was tongue-tied on economic change and trade agreements that favored Trump, but she communicated widely and with conviction her belief in America's diversity.

The campaign settled on "breaking barriers" as her authentic story and purpose and that a Clinton government would prioritize women and people of color. She personally flew to Flint, Michigan, to champion the African-American community there and aired her breakthrough ad in Nevada in which she hugged a Dreamer. As had President Obama, Clinton said she would build "ladders of opportunity" for each racial and ethnic group and close the gender gap for women.

Her silence on how to manage immigration and almost exclusive focus on "a path to citizenship for the undocumented" left her vulnerable to attacks from Donald Trump.

Nonetheless, Hillary Clinton communicated in a bigger sense that the Democratic Party was comfortable with growing immigration and foreignness, unapologetic about promoting immigration, and identified America proudly as an immigrant and multicultural country.

The full realization of the GOP as an anti-immigrant party and the Democrats as a pro-immigration party completely polarized the parties and set their future course. It set the GOP against the multicultural America that could not be reversed—and put the GOP into a civil war against millennials and the dynamic metropolitan centers.

But this was a Pyrrhic victory for the GOP in a country that was changing dramatically and welcoming it.

Donald Trump played the race card in the most unapologetic way and it worked to get him across the finish line with working-class whites and in battleground Electoral College states. A study of eight thousand respondents who were polled in December 2016 and originally interviewed in 2011 and 2012 rightly put the spotlight on the Obama-Trump voters who comprised one in ten Trump voters. Sadly, the probability of switching to Trump was primarily a result of attitudes toward immigration, black people, and Muslims. Those were much more powerful than any other issues examined.[42]

The success in using attitudes toward immigrants and blacks was critical to putting the pieces together for Trump in 2016. Immigration uniquely allowed Trump to unite a GOP divided on so many other issues. But immigration was also an important factor in why some of the independents and Democrats broke for Trump at the election's close. The non–Republican Trump voters that helped him win in Pennsylvania, Michigan, and Wisconsin thought it was true that millions of undocumented immigrants voted illegally to elect Hillary Clinton. Their greatest hope for Trump was that he keep his promise to get immigration under control and deport those here illegally.[43]

Clearly, some Democrats were looking for more from the Democrats on immigration, and that impacted Trump's ability to shift voters with his racial ugliness in 2016.[44]

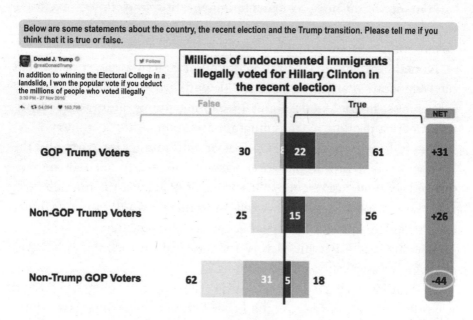

The impressive research by Diana Mutz that included interviews with the same voters in 2011–12 and 2016 confirms the bigger story that unfolded on immigration. Trump had won votes because of immigration, but the electorate had shifted to be more pro-immigration, not less. More had shifted to support a "pathway to citizenship for illegal immigrants" and to oppose returning "illegal immigrants to their native countries."[45] Structurally, the country was moving toward greater acceptance of immigration, even as the parties were more polarized on this issue than any other.[46]

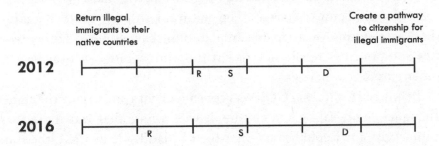

Issue positions of self (average voter) and perceptions of Republican and Democratic presidential candidates, 2012–2016. Note that change over time in opinion (self) is significant for own opinions on trade and immigration but not for own opinions on China. Change over time in perceived candidate positions is significant for all three issues for placement of both Republican and Democratic candidates (P<0.001). S=Self (Own Opinions), R=Perceived position of the Republican Candidate, D=Perceived position of the Democratic Candidate.[47]

As the country became more visibly multicultural and accepting of the change, President Trump forced the GOP to resist even harder, pushing the GOP closer to the precipice.

Think of that next time President Trump trashes a black NFL athlete, attacks refugees as "savages," tries to investigate land seizures from white farmers in South Africa, describes African nations as those "shithole countries," or describes his handling of Hurricane Maria in Puerto Rico as "one of the great untold success stories." He is telling the country in the starkest and ugliest way that the GOP is a party for white people, just as the majority of the country who welcomes a multicultural America grows year on year.

THE CALIFORNIZATION OF THE GOP

Two decades earlier, California Republicans had watched their state grow steadily more Hispanic, and they reacted by putting Proposition 187 on the ballot in 1994. It barred undocumented immigrants from attending public schools or being treated in hospitals and required their names be reported to the authorities or to Immigration and Customs Enforcement (ICE), though the federal courts later blocked the law from ever being implemented. Governor Pete Wilson campaigned in favor of Prop 187, and that proved a defining and branding moment for the GOP in California and, increasingly, in the Southwest, where other Republican governors led similar fights to toughen enforcement of immigration laws.

In California, the Republican Party had always been a low-tax, small-government party in the Ronald Reagan tradition, but worries about the growing demographic threat from Hispanics and the battle over immigration drove out other issues. The party's candidates included many who were pro-environment and pro-choice on abortion or who wanted to regulate guns, including Pete Wilson, for one, as well as Governor Arnold Schwarzenegger. The cultural battle for survival against these accelerating, unstoppable immigration changes pushed other worries and priorities to the side or left those moderate constituencies to other parties to win over.

Before the California GOP was consumed with addressing the state's changing demography and culture, it was a state that was more than competitive for Republicans. After the LBJ landslide in 1964, the state voted Republican in every presidential race until 1992. Californians were as likely to elect Republican as Democratic governors until the battle over Prop 187 in 1994. In the decade up until 2000, California's House delegation was fairly evenly split between the parties.

Republicans watched their strong position deteriorate after Governor Wilson left office. They lost every statewide office in 2010 and saw the Democrats win growing majorities in the State Assembly. Yet at no point did the threat of political annihilation move them to adapt politically. In fact, they doubled down on immigration and became more socially conservative, as abortion came to define the two parties nationally.

California conservatives believed they were the canary in the coal mine for the country. And they had to mobilize to save the Republic. California was already 32 percent Hispanic and 11 percent Asian in 2000.[48] In the most recent decade before President Trump's election, California's white population dropped by 700,000, while the Hispanic segment surged by more than 2 million and the Asian by a million.[49] Currently, Hispanics are 40 percent of California's population.

Republican leaders like Ronald Reagan in California and George Bush in Texas, the states with the biggest Hispanic presence, welcomed Hispanics in their conservative vision. Both governed permissively in their states and both supported legalizing the undocumented and expanding immigration. Well, the California conservatives had no patience for elites' comfort with immigration and the changing country. The stakes were much higher, and they started the GOP's counterrevolution against immigration in 1994.

And California would have the final say.

Breitbart News was launched in Los Angeles. Its founder, Andrew Breitbart, met Steve Bannon there, and they began a long working relationship that put Bannon at its head and ultimately as chief strategist for Donald Trump. Breitbart News mentored Ben Shapiro, and he founded Daily Wire, which operates out of California and is one of the most widely used ultra-right sites in the conservative network. The *Claremont Review* published a widely discussed piece by Michael Anton on the urgent need to elect Donald Trump, and Anton would be hired to work along Stephen Miller in the White House. Miller grew up in Santa Monica. And President Trump's trade adviser was Peter Navarro, who taught at University of California, Irvine.

So, the "intellectual engine" of today's Tea Party–dominated Trump party is all grounded in California, and all "view themselves as philosophically, culturally, and demographically under siege," as Jane Coaston observed in *Vox*. They created a political movement with such an "apocalyptic approach to politics" because they see both the country and the GOP as truly endangered. They are conservatives "that fight" and "have the mentality, and the unanimity, of people under threat." They have lived this "nightmare scenario: an America in which they are powerless, demographically swamped, where the particular virtues and ideas that made America great for so long are uprooted by a surging left."[50]

That is why, Coaston writes, these conservatives have "a laser focus on culture, immigration, and race."

The California conservatives were disdainful of what they call "the *National Review* conservatives" and the Republican leaders in other states who had the luxury of offering "considered views on immigration." Non-California Republicans didn't live with the consequences of demographic change. Before there was a Donald Trump, California conservatives battled for Prop 187, in a campaign they branded "Save Our State." They embraced Donald Trump, who called out the "national emergency." He alone understood that the Republican base felt "isolated" and was "holding on for dear life against an endless attack from a culture and a demography."

New analysis of the 2016 election and its aftermath by an academic team showed how central the California conservatives were.[51]

Donald Trump and Fox News joined Breitbart News and the Daily

Wire to create a powerful ecosystem that reached about a third of the country.[52] The intense reenforcement of the top conservative social media sites, Facebook, Fox News, and Donald Trump and his tweets confirmed what Coaston concluded: "California conservatism is simply conservatism writ large."

The country entered a new world, which is brilliantly described by Yochai Benkler, Robert Faris, and Hal Roberts in *Network Propaganda,* of "epochal change" in how news is shaped, what is deemed accurate and fake, and how the new forces contaminate public discourse and standing of elected leaders.[53] While the main media right-wing players changed over the course of the election, Fox News ultimately allied and amplified Breitbart News and Robert Mercer's other opinion sites to create a right-wing media ecosystem. The authors show how the right, using hyperlinks, Twitter retweeting, and Facebook sharing, radicalized "roughly a third of the American media system." They built distrust, hyper-partisanship, and belief in conspiracies and emerged victorious in their "sustained attacks on core pillars of the Party of Reagan—free trade and relatively open immigration policy, and more directly, the national security establishment and law enforcement when these threatened President Trump himself."[54]

They delegitimized the military and intelligence agencies, but also the bureaucracy that with them formed the "deep state." The right-wing ecosystem waged a war on the government that they believed was carrying forward President Obama's socialist agenda, intent on President Trump's failing.[55]

Breitbart News was "clearly the most effective media actor promoting immigration as the core agenda of the election and framing it in terms of anti-Muslim fears," according to the authors. It was sometimes more effective than Fox News in driving the conservative discourse, elevating concerns about "personal security" and "fear of Muslims" to animate worries about immigration. The most shared stories from Breitbart News were about Muslims, Islam, and terrorism.[56]

"The major agenda-setting success of the Donald Trump campaign and Breitbart," the authors write, "was to make immigration the core substantive agenda in the 2016 election." That was clearly what both candidate Donald Trump and strategist Steve Bannon hoped to achieve when they constructed the "Make America Great Again" campaign that warned of a dark future without leaders fighting back against the "foreign" forces. President Trump and White House Chief Strategist Bannon would work to withdraw from trade deals and NATO and build the wall.[57]

THE GOP'S TOTAL POLARIZATION OF AMERICA

The leaders of the Republican Party fought an ever more determined counterrevolution against each successive, disruptive change that moved America toward greater racial equality, secularism, and sexual freedom that put the traditional family, patriarchy, and the male breadwinner role at risk and that required greater independence and equality for women, and the dramatic growth in immigration that made America more foreign and multicultural. The metropolitan elites, businesses, and the Democratic Party accepted legal equality for blacks, the legalization of abortion, the growth of legal and illegal immigration, and relished the election of African-American Barack Obama as president, but not the GOP leaders. They become even more alienated and determined to fight this changing country.

They could sustain this long battle because of the GOP's base in the politically reactionary Black Belt, South, and states where Evangelicals were dominant, which put this high-stakes explosive battle forward and pushed the polarization of the political parties to greater extremes. They made partisan identity everything.

What made it so explosive was the growing recognition of conservatives after the Tea Party wave and President Obama's reelection that the country was not only reelecting Barack Obama, but was accepting increased immigration as good for the country, tolerating foreignness, and embracing multiculturalism.

Conservatives were on the defensive; in fact, the proportion in the country identifying as "conservative" abruptly dropped from about 45 percent to 37 percent in 2015 and has remained there. That is why they had to turn to an antiestablishment leader like Donald Trump, who had no limits. That is why Donald Trump told a group of pastors and Christian leaders in the State Dining Room before the 2018 blue wave that the election was a "referendum on your religion," the First Amendment, because "they will overturn everything that we've done and they will do it quickly and violently." He warned, "You're one election away from losing everything that you've gotten."[58]

Donald Trump did his part, relentlessly attacking NFL football players who took a knee or stayed in the locker room during the national anthem. He was suitably indifferent to the refugee children from Central America separated from their parents at the border. But so did Nike. By running ads featuring Colin Kaepernick, the NFL quarterback blackballed from the league because he knelt to protest police brutality, it aligned big business with a multicultural America. This was in the tradition of Coca-Cola, which ran an ad during the Super Bowl in 2014 and again in 2017 with "America the Beautiful" sung in eight different languages. They knew the New America, as well as the generation of millennials who would set the future.

The GOP's desperate counterrevolution produced two political parties that were increasingly defined by their ideology and values and polarized on what really mattered. And those values and ideology were now highly correlated with who won the presidential vote in each state, according to important academic studies.[59]

Liberals now prioritized "harm to the vulnerable" and "fairness," and their secularism or "moral color-blindness" devalued faith-based conclusions; they minimized the role of "sacredness" and "authority"—central for conservatives. Liberals cannot grant that conservatives have moral reasons to oppose gay marriage.[60] By contrast, the strongly conservative rated all values dimensions very high, but they viewed "authority" and "purity" as most important.[61]

The GOP-led counterrevolution produced a thoroughgoing ideological polarization of the two parties in 2017 that was certainly accelerating, if that were statistically possible. The median Republican is more conservative than 97 percent of Democrats; and the median Democrat more liberal than 95 percent of Republicans.[62]

This battle raised the importance of party identity dramatically, turned independents into partisans, and nearly eliminated ticket splitting. In 2016, all thirty-four states with a Senate contest voted for the same party for president and the U.S. Senate—the first time that has happened in about one hundred years. Since the 1990s, about a quarter of voters split their tickets in Senate races, but only 20 percent did in 2010 and a mere 10 percent in 2014—at the height of the Tea Party revolt against President Obama and the Democrats.[63]

The GOP battles against government, help for the poor, immigration, black rights, gay marriage, and environmental protections have created two dramatically polarized parties whose identities accompany the values that matter to people—and which party one identifies with is now dramatically more important than your gender, your class, your generation, your religious attendance, or your race. In 2017, the average gap on these measures between Democrats and Republicans was 36 points, compared to just +14 for race, about +11 for religion, education, and age, and +7 for the gap between men and women. Your party has become the identity that matters more than all other, and people use it to filter their perception of events and motivate their political engagement.[64]

As partisan divides over political values widen, other gaps remain more modest

Average gap in the share taking a conservative position across 10 political values, by key demographics

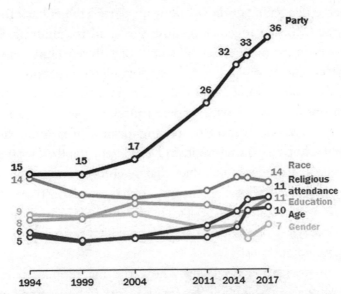

Notes: Indicates average gap between the share of two groups taking the conservative position across 10 values items. Party=difference between Rep/Lean Rep and Dem/Lean Dem. Race=white non-Hispanic/black non-Hispanic. Education=college grad/non-college grad. Age=18-49/50+. Religion=weekly+ religious service attenders/less often. Source: Survey conducted June 8-18 and June 27-July 9, 2017.

PEW RESEARCH CENTER

In 1994, when Pew asked these ten questions about values for the first time, the GOP battle against legalized abortion had already made partisan identities more important than others, except for religious attendance. The two parties were sorting into religious and nonreligious camps and pro-life and pro-choice voters were shifting parties or their positions on abortion. Then, in 1996, the GOP nationalized its battle against immigration that would push the average difference to 17 points in 2004, already visibly bigger than the difference for all other identities. Then, Karl Rove launched George Bush's culture war on abortion and homosexuality, and the partisan gap reached an unimaginable 26 points in 2011, right after the Tea Party takeover. The Tea Party effort to stop Obama and the Democrats from governing produced the steepest rise yet, to an average of 32 points. Donald Trump's victory took the average gap between Democrats and Republicans to 36 points when the next most important identity, race, moved up to a modest 14 points. The gap with men and women was half that.

This GOP-driven polarization has flummoxed Americans who want to escape the deadening gridlock and want parties to get back to the days when parties worked together because they had to. Shutting down the federal government or threatening default or failure to fund simple highway projects is not normal. The polarization, ideological consistency, new consciousness about values, and politicization also demolishes the work of patronizing academics who studied this same period and pointed to "the sheer magnitude of most people's ignorance of politics."[65] Christopher Achen and Larry Bartels write in *Democracy for Realists* that people "adopt beliefs, attitudes, and values that re-enforce and rationalize their partisan loyalties."[66] They are bemused that these partisans "misconstrue" their parties' signature policies or the state of the economy to align with their party loyalty. They label these so-called rational voters as "the rationalizing voter."[67]

Their ahistorical accounts miss how the meaning of partisanship has been shaped by the choices national leaders have made and what issues and values are contested in presidential elections. The Republicans' choice to contest black equality, abortion, the sexual revolution, immigration, and multiculturalism has produced a new ideological coherence and political consciousness. Given how urgent people believe it is to push back against the GOP's rejectionism and the GOP's belief that their way of life is at risk, their aligning of the facts is completely reasonable. The evolving political battle has raised the stakes in politics and the voters' determination to elect leaders who will advance their priorities.

BEYOND POLARIZATION

What's next for America could be unimaginable if you assume that the past predicts the future and life is linear. That the line somehow just keeps getting steeper without some dramatic change. That line represents the escalating counterrevolution of the GOP against a country that is increasingly diverse and that increasingly embraces its multiculturalism. That battle has completely shaped party identification, so that a smaller and smaller coalition of voters identifies with the Republican Party and a larger and larger coalition identifies with the Democratic Party.

The Trump takeover of a Tea Party–dominated GOP accelerated every trend, and accelerated the sorting of voters who have been politicized, like never before.

They are intent on the Republican Party facing a shattering defeat, because there is no room for a party at war with a modernizing America. But what happens after it is humiliated and fractured? Is it California, where the Republican Party simply lives with its total marginality without any movement for renewal?

What happens if a shattered GOP can no longer impact what is happening in America on immigration, abortion, the sexual revolution, and the role of working women? What if it can't stop government from functioning anymore? What if the GOP is focused on its own renewal, not fighting the New America?

4 THE TEA PARTY–TRUMP DECADE

IN THE 2010 OFF-YEAR ELECTIONS, the Republican Party achieved a once-in-a-century electoral triumph. They picked up sixty-three House seats, the biggest midterm gain since 1938, and six senators, which allowed them to filibuster all Democratic initiatives. They gained six governorships and occupied the executive branches of government in 60 percent of the states. The Republicans gained 675 state legislative seats and won control of both legislative chambers in twenty-nine states. After the 2014 off-year sweep, the GOP picked up more than three hundred legislative seats and had total partisan control of nearly half the states.[1]

President Obama described the 2010 defeat as a "shellacking," but he surely would have used even more graphic terms had he realized the defeat was just the sound of the starter's pistol for a decade of anti-government fervor, national gridlock, and Tea Party–Evangelical rule in most of the states.

Academics and pundits wrote of the scale of the 2010 electoral victories and the conservative swing in Congress, but they did not realize then that this sweep would lock in a decade of an escalating conservative war against Democrats and democratic governance that would allow Donald Trump to become president of the United States without winning the popular vote or a conservative mandate. That was before they realized this Tea Party–Evangelical domination was inspired to stomp out any effort by the Democrats to use the government for any public purpose.

Jonathan Chait understood that the GOP was waging a "guerrilla war" against President Obama that justified a "procedural extremism."[2] And Thomas Mann and Norman Ornstein described in *It's Even Worse Than It Looks* how an ideological party fearful of its opponent winning would exploit every nook of our constitutional system to produce a "willful obstruction."[3] But even they did not realize that a GOP, moved by an anti-government evangelism, tinged with fear of foreigners, would get to deconstruct government nationally and in the states and produce a harrowing gridlock worse than anything they had expected.

A victorious GOP stopped in their tracks the Democrats' efforts to expand public investment to grow the economy, to give a government guarantee that all have health insurance, and to regulate the energy industry and address climate change. And that was before any of us realized the GOP would extinguish for a decade any effort to expand government investment, mitigate inequality, raise incomes of the poor and middle class, regulate corporate governance, expand access to health care, and do anything about climate change. That relentless and successful battle against governmental activism produced a country so polarized it defied measurement.

Even the leaders of the Tea Party groups did not realize what they had accomplished. After all, President Barack Obama would be re-elected by the American people with an Electoral College landslide in 2012. But that landslide obscured the escalating erosion of white and white working-class voters' support for Democrats and the Democrats' own voters' disillusionment with the economic recovery. Both allowed Republicans to gain from a second off-year wave in 2014 and Donald Trump to win the presidency in 2016.

This historic but deep and prolonged political moment was produced by the rebellion of the conservative, antiestablishment wing of the Republican Party, which deeply feared a socialist Obama presidency, fueled by a genuine grassroots resistance that brought 250,000 into membership and organized rallies and marches, the work of the Koch brothers, far-right billionaire allies, and Fox News, which devoted itself to promoting the Tea Party resistance. Academics Vanessa

Williamson and Theda Skocpol rightly describe it as "a mix of local networks, resource-deploying-national organizations, and conservative media outlets [that] constitute Tea Partyism and give a great deal of dynamism and flexibility at a pivotal juncture of US politics."[4]

It began with Rick Santelli's rant on CNBC from the floor of the Chicago Mercantile Exchange and his call for a "Chicago Tea Party" that went viral, pushed by conservative activists skilled in using the web. "This is America! How many of you people want to pay for your neighbor's mortgage that has an extra bathroom and can't pay their bills? Raise their hands! President Obama, are you listening?"[5] He situated his rebellion against the government plan to help people facing foreclosure to refinance their homes; in reality, he was outraged that African Americans and Hispanics, who had been targeted for subprime loans packaged by the very derivative traders who were now being offered government help, were now in desperate need of help.[6] It made it easy for conservatives to elide white and black, instead targeting "hardworking taxpayers" and "freeloaders."[7]

The couple dozen protests on February 27 were sparsely attended, despite Rush Limbaugh's branding the economic stimulus as "Porkulus" and organizational help from the Koch brothers' Americans for Prosperity and FreedomWorks, headed by former Congressman Dick Armey.[8]

Ultimately, 400,000 to 810,000 people joined 542 rallies across the country and 250,000 would join one of the Tea Party groups—Tea Party Patriots, ResistNet, Tea Party Express, Tea Party Nation, FreedomWorks Tea Party, and 1776 Tea Party. Some of the groups were genuinely local and decentralized, and the Tea Party Patriots led the membership growth after the Tax Day rallies in 2009.[9] The average congressional district had 402 Tea Party members. At the core were the 250,000 activists and 150,000 who posted personal profiles on Tea Party sites in 2010.[10]

None of this mobilization would have been possible without Fox News. Three in five Tea Party supporters watched Fox News, and its coverage of the Tea Party grew in the month leading up to Tax Day and continued at a respectable level in the month afterward. CNN covered the Tea Party during the April 15 rallies. Fox's most popular hosts Glenn Beck, Sean Hannity, Greta Van Susteren, and Neil Cavuto broadcast from Tea Party events. Glenn Beck received $1 million a year to read embedded content provided by FreedomWorks, and he cosponsored a September 12 rally as the Democratic Congress was taking up the Affordable Care Act.[11] That rally was a turning point for the movement, as all the groups worked together and met in the street: "Before the last port-a-potties were removed from the Capitol Mall, the Tea parties had turned from periodic protests into a full-fledged social movement."[12] Tea Party members tried to dominate when questions were asked at Democratic congressional members' town halls and their jostling and shouting at Democrats going to vote at the Capitol made them a disruptive presence.[13]

The size of the Tea Party as a social movement was not that large by historical standards nor as large as the Women's March that would follow the inauguration of Donald Trump as president. "But the professionalization of the underground infrastructure," Jane Mayer writes, "the growth of sympathetic and in some cases subsidized media outlets, and the concentrated money pushing the message from the fringe to center stage were truly consequential."[14]

This social movement gained force and momentum, to be frank, because President Obama was "at the vortex." The Tea Party was dominated by a "freewheeling anti-Obama paranoia."[15]

Of course, all the Tea Party groups said their biggest concerns were budget deficits, taxes, and the overreach of the federal government, but the Institute for Research and Education on Human Rights report, *Tea Party Nationalism,* said the Tea Party gave "a platform to anti-Semites, racists, and bigots." Hardcore white nationalists and militias were attracted to some of the rallies of the 1776 Tea Party, a group with fewer members than I have Twitter followers. The leader of the Tea Party Express was forced to resign because of his racist rants, referring to President Obama as "a half-white racist, a half-black racist and an Indonesian Muslim turned welfare fraud."[16]

But racial resentment and hostility to immigration were front and center for the principal groups, which is why they had such an impact. The leaders of the two largest groups, Tea Party Patriots and Resist-Net, were strongly anti-immigration and wanted repeal of the Fifteenth Amendment, which ensured citizenship by birthright. Their keynote speaker was Congressman Steve King, who led the GOP caucus pushing for stronger enforcement of immigration laws. All but the Freedom-Works Tea Party had "birthers" in their leadership and described the president as not an American, probably a Muslim, creating a compelling rationale for the call "Take it back, Take your country back."[17]

As Barack Obama was being inaugurated as president of the United States, Charles Koch, the CEO of Koch Industries and longtime funder of far-right and libertarian groups, gathered a small group of billionaire allies at a small desert down outside Palm Springs. The mood could not have been more grim. Koch had written to his employees that America faced "the greatest loss of liberty and prosperity since the 1930s."

The participants at Koch's annual retreat invited donors who funded the most conservative initiatives for decades: Richard Mellon Scaife, Harry and Lynde Bradley, John Coors, Betsy DeVos, Robert Mercer, and Sheldon Adelson. They included more than a few who faced legal or regulatory jeopardy. And they included the owners of energy and coal companies who shared the Koch brothers' worry about what an Obama administration might do in addressing climate change.[18]

They determined, in Jane Mayer's description, "to nullify the results of the election." They were determined "to stop the Obama administration from implementing the Democratic policies that the American public had voted for but that [the Kochs] regarded as catastrophic."[19] Senator James DeMint of South Carolina, who spoke at the meeting, set the tone: "Compromise is surrender." DeMint would soon have a whole coterie of Senate and House Tea Party allies who were determined to stop the Democrats from governing or doing anything they had been elected to achieve.[20] DeMint also did not realize yet that stopping the Democrats cold was a tactic that would be extended through four elections. Indeed, during the fight over the Affordable Care Act, DeMint said, "If we're able to stop Obama on this [ACA], it will be his Waterloo. It will break him."[21]

The GOP leadership in Congress never gave the president a honeymoon and tried to ensure his failure, even at the middle of the financial crash. Every Republican House member voted against the president's economic recovery program and all but three in the U.S. Senate voted against it in early 2009.[22] The determination of Republican base voters to stop the Democrats was growing, and by 2012, GOP establishment candidates lost their primaries, were forced off the party's line, or were forced out of the party in Utah, Alaska, Kentucky, Colorado, Delaware, Pennsylvania, and, most spectacularly, Florida, where Tea Party–backed candidate Marco Rubio defeated the incumbent governor Charlie Crist.[23]

On January 21, 2010, right at the outset of the off-year election, the U.S. Supreme Court in *Citizens United v. Federal Election Commission* overturned the ban on corporations and unions giving to political campaigns. Justice Anthony Kennedy, the swing vote on the highest court, wrote, "By suppressing the speech of manifold corporations, both for-profit and nonprofit, the Government prevents their voices and viewpoints from reaching the public and advising voters on which persons or entities are hostile to their interests. Factions will necessarily form in our Republic," citing Federalist Paper No. 10, "but the remedy of 'destroying the liberty' of some factions is 'worse than the disease.'"[24] That ruling liberated billionaires to become oligarchs and spend their wealth seeking control of the U.S. government. It was already legal to donate secretly to 501(c)(3)s that engaged in nonpartisan charitable activities and 501(c)(4)s that did some political work related to their social welfare purpose. In 2006, just 2 percent of campaign spending was "dark money" channeled through these vehicles or super PACs, but in 2010, it would be 40 percent. Koch and his allies spent $130.7 million to stop the Democrats.[25]

The Tea Party wave election created a Republican Congress and the freshmen class was determined to disrupt regular order in the House and President Obama's plans on increased government spending, above all else. As the economy stalled short of a recovery and unemployment was still near 10 percent, President Obama sought modest new spending and tax cuts, but the determined House Republicans pressed for big short- and long-term cuts in federal spending that would give America its own period of austerity.

The 2010 Tea Party wave election produced an unprecedented and enduring ideological shift in the Congress. The new class of Republicans into the 112th Congress was dramatically more conservative than the Republicans in the prior one, but indeed, the extent of the shift to the right was greater than witnessed in any prior wave election—including that produced by the Newt Gingrich Revolution in 1994. Over three quarters of the new members were Tea Party freshmen, and they were committed conservatives.[26] The GOP Tea Party triumph produced an immediate polarization of the Congress that only worsened with time.

With such an ideological wave, Theda Skocpol wrote, the Tea Party freshmen had a mandate "to demand immediate measures to slash public spending and taxes," "go nuclear," and "refuse compromises with Democrats over the funding of government." They were acutely conscious of the Tea Party protests to stop the Democrats from moving their agenda on the economy, health care, and climate change.[27] They had a mandate to repeal Obamacare, slash government spending, and block "cap and trade." Sent by the Tea Party and Evangelical base, the legislators were determined to stop immigration and abortion, too.

Half of Republican identifiers supported the Tea Party, and their views could not be clearer for the Tea Party freshmen: they viewed the government's rescue of the economy as "morally wrong" and their country as "going to be 'lost.'"[28] The Tea Party base and leaders almost universally opposed the economic stimulus (91 percent against), Obamacare (88 percent), and clean energy (81 percent), and wanted to end DACA, the program that legalized the status of the children of undocumented immigrants.[29] And the Evangelicals cheered on and joined the Tea Party protests against President Obama, making the Tea Party fully socially conservative: two thirds would ban abortion or permit it only in the case of rape, incest, or the health of the mother. Two thirds would ban gay marriage.[30]

The Tea Party class was acutely conscious of the Tea Party activism and rallies that drove the wave and produced a Congress that was dramatically more conservative than anything seen before. Sixty freshmen joined the Tea Party Caucus.

The strength and energy of these rallies in congressional districts, according to an impressive study by academics Michael Bailey, Jonathan Mummolo, and Hans Noel, elevated the image of the Tea Party and produced a bigger Republican vote.[31] And critically, increased Tea Party activism pushed members of Congress to join the Tea Party Caucus and even vote against the GOP House leadership on raising the debt ceiling and avoiding a government shutdown early in the new Congress.

The new Tea Party members were prepared "to go nuclear" almost immediately, and we now appreciate that this emboldened conservatism was produced by the Tea Party–Evangelical bloc that felt angry and threatened by the Obama presidency and expressed itself through a social movement of grounded opposition in their districts. They were determined to stand in front of this train of government activism.

FROM KEYNES TO AUSTERITY

The Tea Party mandate was to stop President Obama's efforts to address the financial crisis and deep recession.

President Obama took office in a maelstrom. The economy shed 650,000 jobs a month during his transition to the job and 780,000 a month after he was inaugurated.[32] People faced massive financial destruction in the devaluation of houses, stocks, and securities. The stock market lost over 50 percent of its value and shareholders lost $1.2 trillion. The burst housing bubble and deflation took away $16 trillion of net worth, and one in five had homes that were underwater. Consumer spending ground to a near halt. And "Watching wave after wave of foreclosure sweep across the American landscape," as Alan Blinder writes, "was like watching a slow motion train wreck take a human toll."[33]

President Bush, President Obama, the U.S. Treasury, and the Federal Reserve battled to enact and implement the bailout of the eight Wall Street banks. They were focused on restoring stability to the financial system, which was successful, though little was done to restrain executive bonuses or give the taxpayers ownership in the banks going forward. The Fed on its own bought $2 trillion worth of assets to further stabilize the financial system. The Democratic administration and Federal Reserve in the United States and the Labour government and Bank of England in the UK both virtually nationalized the banks, guaranteed personal savings accounts, and, for twelve months, got governments globally to cut interest rates and raise short-term spending to stimulate the economy.[34]

In unchartered territory, the Federal Reserve dropped interest rates from 3 to 2 percent and then to near zero, where they stayed for more than three years. The European Central Bank waited a year and momentarily raised them, but then cut interest rates sharply to 2 percent, ending at 1 percent.[35] And in a coordinated immediate turn to Keynesian stimulus, the United States passed an economic stimulus package worth 5.5 percent of our GDP, while China did more than double that, Spain

7 percent, and Germany 3 percent. These stimulus packages worked to avoid a global depression and stabilize most of the economies.

People were in pain, angry about the greed that had sunk the economy, though equally angry about the bailouts of the irresponsible and the lack of accountability. So, this whole structure was vulnerable to attack from conservatives and what economist Paul Krugman would call "the very serious people" in the room who frowned on unchecked spending.

President Obama went to the Congress to pass an economic recovery program costing $888 billion, which was unprecedented at the time, though liberal economists publicly and privately said it was not big enough to get the wrecked economy moving again. To muster Republican support in the Senate, the administration cut $100 billion slated to help state and local governments avoid job layoffs and made tax cuts 40 percent of the total package. Obviously, both changes came at the expense of a fuller jobs recovery.

Required to maintain a balanced budget, the states laid off 300,000 teachers. Republican governors did their part to block major infrastructure projects, including a planned tunnel under the Hudson River to increase train flow and high-speed rail construction in Florida and Wisconsin.[36]

The federal government increased spending, but most of it went to higher unemployment benefits, tax credits, and food stamps, which are expected to surge when the economy sinks.[37] They were helped by Congresswoman Rosa DeLauro, who won changes in the 2008 Farm Bill that greatly expanded eligibility for food stamps and added more funds for them in the recovery act.

The administration took only halfhearted steps to help the 3.1 million homes in foreclosure. "They had the power to do something about it," Blinder wrote, just as they had the authority to stabilize the banks, "and it just didn't [happen]." People, he concluded, "felt as though they were mugged. It's because they were."[38]

Government action did stabilize the financial system. It quickly slowed job losses and the economy began to add jobs in September. The elites could breathe again. However, this slow and incomplete recovery failed to get the economy back to full capacity and did not fix the underlying damage on the ground. The unemployment rate rose to a daunting 10 percent a year after Obama took office.

And as Blinder wrote, nobody on the economic team spoke to the country about their strategy and the president gave no speeches on what to expect, though he spoke to a joint session of Congress on health care in September. The public was on its own in a time of crisis and pain. Most pretty quickly came to see Obama's economic plan as a bailout of the banks.[39]

James Carville, John Podesta, and I met with White House Chief of Staff Rahm Emanuel and chief counselor David Axelrod repeatedly to discuss people's deep pain and anger about the bailout of those who had produced the crisis and the need for the president to let the country know where he was taking it. In March 2010, I warned that the recession and pessimism were "worsening for our new base voters" of people of color, those under age thirty, and unmarried women, and there wasn't much support for the idea that "Obama's policies helped avert an even worse crisis."[40] I became apoplectic when President Obama cheered each job report in the summer of 2010, as unemployment remained high and new jobs paid much less than before the crisis.

Unemployment was nearly 10 percent for much of 2010. All the seeming government activism left the economy well short of its capacity, and with 8.8 million people unemployed at the end of 2010—two and a half years after the financial crash. Clearly, America needed a federal government willing to spend and invest much more heavily in infrastructure and other job-creating programs that the private sector would and could not do. That is what Paul Krugman wrote at the time and later in his book: we cannot reduce unemployment and get out of this depression "without a burst of government spending."[41]

But because the first "economic stimulus" was much too small in scale and too limited in scope, the Obama administration undermined the legitimacy of government action. The president never proposed a second stimulus. In fact, his 2010 State of the Union address proposed spending cuts, as the president indicated that too big a federal deficit, which had reached 10.1 percent of the economy in his first year, could produce a double-dip recession.[42]

Conservative economists allied with the Republican Party argued that "public spending would be offset by a fall in private consumption and investment"—which was wrong theoretically, as the quick experiment of the economic stimulus demonstrated. They argued too that fiscal restraint gives private businesses the confidence to grow investment, something Krugman called "sheer ignorance" and political opportunism, as we wait for the "confidence fairy." Mark Blyth in *Austerity* called it "zombie economics." In fact, "everyone [who] cut their budgets as their economies shrank" saw "their debt loads get bigger, not smaller." Austerity had the perverse consequence of having "the poor paying for the mistakes of the rich."[43]

So, at this fragile juncture "the very serious people" talked about "growth-friendly consolidation," "cutting the welfare state in the name of producing more growth," and "preemptive tightening." The German elites believed wrongly that fiscal recklessness had produced the financial crisis, so "fiscal prudence" made this a morality play in which austerity is "penance," even if it made no economic sense.[44]

The "very serious people" in 2010 weighed in from the OECD: "The U.S. government should immediately move to slash the budget deficit," and "the Federal Reserve should raise short-term interest rates and dramatically by the end of the year."[45] The European Central Bank called for "confidence inspiring policies" that "will foster economic recovery."[46]

The Greek crash was a red flashing light for all those who thought this accumulating debt would not come with a price. The Greek story is longer and more complicated than that, but Ireland, Spain, and Portugal, each with 23 percent unemployment, would also pay a big price for this imposed austerity.[47]

The long-term unemployed and their pain would be the face of this pathetic recovery and failure to act boldly. Ultimately, U.S. unemployment would stay above 7.8 percent for forty-six months, the worst employment conditions since the Great Depression.[48]

Yet the failure of the government to act with greater boldness, the palpable unfairness, and the failure to educate the public allowed the elites to shift from "unemployment to a focus on debt and deficits." Elites gave "ominous warnings about the danger of excessive debt" and leaders of both parties believed rising debt represented "an existential threat."[49]

Congress created the National Commission on Fiscal Responsibility and Reform, chaired by former senator Alan Simpson and Erskine

Bowles, colloquially known as Simpson-Bowles, which met starting in April 2010 and issued its report on December 1, 2010. The commission had equal representation from both parties, including Congressman Paul Ryan, and its recommendations were never taken up by the Congress. Nonetheless, it strongly reenforced the elite conviction that reducing government deficits was the highest priority.[50] It legitimated the urgency of cutting government spending.

The new GOP House had their mandate to stop the spending and get to the budget austerity that America needed.

Unemployment was stuck at 7.8 percent at the end of 2010 and the economic stimulus of federal spending and tax cuts was set to expire in the coming months, yet the Tea Party candidates ran on a "Pledge to America" that committed them to cut federal spending by $100 billion. The Republican caucus and leadership agreed to press for $61 billion in cuts this year, which disappointed the Tea Party freshmen. And when that bold spending cut was passed by the House, it was quickly dispatched to the dustbin by a U.S. Senate controlled by the Democrats. Speaker of the House John Boehner was determined to get to the amount of $61 billion in increments of $6 billion with every budget extension and at every opportunity, but the freshmen viewed this incrementalism as a slap in the face. Each step of the budget process was taking the Congress toward a train wreck.[51]

South Carolina's four freshmen huddled in a basement conference room with Congressman ("You Lie") Joe Wilson to decide whether to vote against the speaker just two months into the new Congress. Each recited from scripture and Jeff Duncan read from Isaiah: "He gives power to the faint, and to him who has no might he increases strength."[52] The speaker proposed a one-week continuing resolution that included $10 billion in domestic cuts but funded the Defense Department for a year. However, a growing group of Tea Party members voted no, to the applause of outside Tea Party groups.

The U.S. Treasury announced that August 2, 2011, was the deadline when the United States would begin defaulting on its debts, unless the debt limit was raised. Even though threatening to not raise the debt limit and jeopardize America's credit rating has never been seen as permissible by either party, these times were different. The House passed its answer, "Cut, Cap and Balance": it cut the deficit in half immediately, capped future federal spending to 18 percent of GDP, and required passage of the Balanced Budget Amendment—if the debt ceiling was to be raised. It was tabled three days later in the Senate.

The near impasse created a super committee that would, by September 8, find $1.5 trillion in deficit-reducing measures. The Republicans would not accept any revenue-increasing measures and the Democrats would not accept steps to disproportionately cut domestic spending. The predictable impasse would mean a mandatory sequestering of the budget starting in 2013. The cuts would be made equally from defense and domestic spending that the conservatives tried unsuccessfully to undo.[53]

The GOP leadership turned to Democrats in the House and passed three appropriations bills on November 17. A stunning 101 House Republicans voted against the speaker, and the alienation of the Tea Party Republicans was now locked in.[54]

The Senate Minority Leader Mitch McConnell and Vice President Joe Biden reached a deal that ended the Bush tax cuts for those earning over $450,000 per year, but two thirds of House Republicans voted no. This Congress was set to be the most unproductive Congress in history, but that missed the real story. The Tea Party members and activists cut federal spending and pushed America into a period of austerity.[55]

When President Obama in a joint session address urged the Congress to support the American Jobs Bill, he repeatedly called out, "Pass the Jobs Bill." But it was dead on arrival, and the president would get no further economic stimulus out of the Congress.

The need to lift the debt ceiling was now the primary point of leverage for the House Republicans. Speaker Boehner's plan proposed $1.2 trillion in cuts and spending caps to raise the debt ceiling to the end of the year. It created a bipartisan super committee of twelve members of Congress to find another $1.8 trillion in savings that could not be amended by the Congress. The Tea Party members balked. The cuts were not big enough, and they would not support raising the debt ceiling. This time, the members went to the chapel and Mick Mulvaney read from Proverbs 22: "The rich rule over the poor, and the borrower is the slave to the lender."[56]

The White House and Congress were at an impasse with just days left before a potential default and government shutdown. Again Biden and McConnell reached an agreement. The president got the debt ceiling increase, but to get it, spending was cut by $1 trillion over the next decade, as Congress created annual spending caps on discretionary federal spending caps. If the caps were exceeded, the government would implement across-the-board cuts to both defense and nondefense spending. It created a super committee to find another $1.5 trillion in deficit reduction.

The Tea Party members voted against this deal. The cuts were not drastic enough. The cuts were not permanent, and there was no requirement that Congress pass a balanced budget amendment.[57] Yet they shifted the trajectory of federal spending toward deficit reduction and crowded out any debate about how to grow the economy with increased investment.

The budget caps and the acceptance of the virtues and value of austerity produced sustained yet constrained increases in domestic discretionary spending over the decade to follow. The percent of the budget devoted to domestic discretionary spending was 23.4 percent in 2008–2010, but dropped to 21.8 percent in 2012—the first budgets shaped by the Tea Party's battle—and averaged 20.3 percent between 2013 and 2017.[58] They successfully produced a decade of federal budget austerity, when the economy desperately needed investment spending.

The idea that America could make public investments just evaporated in this era. From 2010 to 2018, the American Society of Civil Engineers' rating of America's infrastructure dropped to D+, and for highways, the 2017 report stated that there was an $836 billion deficit in capital needs, meaning America couldn't even keep up with repairs of its own roads. For the first time ever, this Congress could not reauthorize the Highway Bill.

And do not lose track of the assault on spending in the states after 2010. All but four states in the country cut state spending and public services when the financial bubble burst, the economy contracted, and jobs disappeared. But the Tea Party came to power after the financial crisis was stabilized and the country was slowly gaining new jobs. So public sector employment had stabilized, but not in the states where the GOP had newly gained control: the twelve most solidly red states accounted for over 70 percent of the public-sector jobs eliminated in 2011.[59]

The Republican-controlled states led the way, slashing spending beyond what was needed and declining to use their "rainy day" funds to forestall cuts. In Texas, the Republican-controlled legislature, fueled by Tea Party supporters, passed a $172 billion two-year budget, an 8.1 percent decrease from prior spending levels. The budget cut $4 billion from public schools and $1 billion from higher education and financial aid to more than 40,000 students, and eliminated 5,600 state employee jobs. In the face of a $23 billion shortfall and a no-tax-increase budgetary policy, Governor Rick Perry and his allies in the legislature refused to avail themselves of more than $3.2 billion of the $9.7 billion rainy-day fund. GOP-controlled states oversaw a 22 percent decrease in education spending while state schools' tuition rose 31 percent on average.[60]

While education spending was cut almost everywhere to balance budgets, twelve states simultaneously cut corporate taxes and taxes on the wealthy, ensuring spending cuts would be larger than necessary. Accordingly, Louisiana, South Carolina, and Iowa joined Texas in refusing to use their massive rainy-day funds to avoid drastic cuts in state spending on vital public services. These GOP-controlled states have since gone a step further, seeking to lock in the new spending levels and legally bar future tax increases through constitutional amendment.[61]

In this brave new world, unemployment insurance—a state-administered, contributory program that provides workers up to twenty-six weeks of benefits if they lose their job without cause—was now seen as "welfare." That equation was only affirmed when millions were thrown out of work by the financial crisis and many remained unemployed through the Great Recession. Republicans determined that extended unemployment benefits removed the incentive to work. While the national unemployment rate stood at 9 percent at the worst of the Great Recession in 2009–2010, the U.S. Chamber of Commerce lobbied for unemployment insurance reform, "pressuring workers," in the Economic Policy Institute's words, "to take any job offered, no matter how low the wages or how poor the conditions."[62]

The GOP-controlled states enthusiastically stopped the countercyclical spending in time of economic downturn and assured the states affirmed the austerity the Tea Party imposed nationally.

DECONSTRUCTING GOVERNMENT

The Tea Party-Evangelical–dominated GOP disrupted and shifted the ideological posture of the House members to the right in unprecedented fashion, yet Democrats still controlled the White House and the U.S. Senate, though no longer with a filibuster-proof majority. So, the Tea Party elected leaders were left with the ugly tactic of going nuclear: threatening to close government, closing it—and using the gridlock to drive a polarization that stopped President Obama from doing more damage.

The states, however, were very different. After 2010, the GOP gained enough governors, executive branches, and legislatures to move the Tea Party's anti-Obama and anti-government agenda. They passed immediate sweeping tax cuts for corporations, the energy companies, and the wealthiest, which were paid for with major cuts to public services. They relished cutting the largest state expenditure, education and teacher salaries, which meant breaking the power of the education unions.

The GOP won a deeper wave in 2014 when President Obama tried again to convince working people and the Democratic base that his administration had created millions of jobs and the economy was moving in the right direction. That out-of-touch strategy gave the GOP control in half the states and enabled them to escalate their efforts to deconstruct government.

This effort got a lot of help from the American Legislative Exchange Council (ALEC), which was funded by the Koch brothers and other conservative philanthropists, like the Coors, Olin, Scaife, Milken, and Bradley families. It was supported by the U.S. Chamber of Commerce and the National Association of Manufacturers, tobacco and pharmaceutical companies, and the fossil fuel companies that evolved over time. They got policy support from the Cato Institute, Mercatus Center, the Heritage Foundation, and Grover Norquist's Americans for Tax Reform. And Americans for Prosperity helped mobilize in constituencies, buttressed by the Tea Party activists in 2010.[63]

After the 2010 wave election, the "troika" of ALEC, the State Policy Network, and Americans for Prosperity allied with the local Tea Party conservative activists to push "policy plagiarism" to a new level of success, as described by Alex Hertel-Fernandez's *State Capture*. One third of the state legislators belonged to ALEC, which kept their sessions secret, particularly when meeting with the host companies. The legislators used thousands of prototype bills created by ALEC, and two hundred of them became law after the Tea Party took control in the states.[64]

REFORM STATES

The Koch brothers and their allies prioritized deconstruction of the government in Wisconsin and North Carolina because those states were key to unpicking the Democrats' Electoral College majority, but, just as important, their leaders had once led efforts to reform politics and check corporate power, led in adapting to big social changes, and made deep investments in education and the university system.

Governor Robert La Follette of Wisconsin had achieved progressive reforms in the early 1900s that shaped the political culture of the state thereafter and the era of progressive reform nationally. La Follette believed government had to be a check on the railroads, utilities, and big businesses and the local party machine that they bought off. Wisconsin created a state minimum wage and unemployment insurance. It introduced the referendum to give voters' a bigger say. And Wisconsin raised the compulsory school age to sixteen in 1920 and launched an experimental university system in 1927.[65]

North Carolina stood out from other southern states as more tolerant and forward-looking in the 1960s. New South governors, beginning with Terry Sanford, urged racial reconciliation, not resistance, during the civil rights era. They welcomed an alliance with business that supported their approach on race and education. Governor Jim Hunt was elected four times as the "education governor" in the 1970s through the 1990s. And uniquely in the South, he introduced public funding for the election of judges, along with early voting and same-day registration to expand the electorate.

Well, just two months after his election in 2010, Governor Scott Walker of Wisconsin proposed across-the-board tax cuts, but they barely disguised the $2.3 billion in tax cuts for the wealthy. Those earning over $300,000 a year got an $1,800 cut, while those in the middle of the range got just $200. The top 1 percent got $420 million over five years, and the owners of the Milwaukee Bucks got $400 million in tax breaks to build their new stadium.[66]

The consequences became clear before very long. The Walker administration cut $1 billion in payment to local governments. Then it cut $1 billion in public school funding.

Walker embraced the ALEC playbook like few others, enacting 148 new laws from its templates. Act 10, passed on June 29, 2011, was the most important in destroying the public sector unions in Wisconsin. It prohibited collective bargaining over anything other than wages. It prohibited the collection of union dues and required a 51 percent majority of an annual vote for a union to maintain its certification.[67]

And on March 8, 2015, Governor Walker signed the legislation that made Wisconsin of all places a "right-to-work state." Within a short period, state and local union participation dropped from 50 to 31 percent. The National Education Association's share of all contributions to state and local campaigns dropped from more than 5 percent in 2012 to under 2 in 2014 and 1 in 2016. The Koch brothers must have been proud.

Governor Walker went after the teachers and their union. His legislature cut teacher pay on average by 2.6 percent and their benefits by almost 20 percent over five years. They put further pressure on the public schools at the same time by giving mostly Catholic parents an annual tax deduction of $10,000 for Catholic school tuition.[68]

Wisconsin cut funding for the state universities by $250 million, putting it in the ranks of an elite set of GOP-controlled states who went after the universities, led by Louisiana and Pennsylvania, with Kansas and Wisconsin cutting per-student funding by $3,000 a year between 2011 and 2017.[69] Governor Walker described the professors in the University of Wisconsin system as lazy and unwilling to work, and welcomed a culture war that empowered his assault on government.[70]

Walker would have to survive a recall election in 2012, but not surprisingly, got $11 million in help from Koch brother groups.

After voters threw out Governor Walker and took away the legislature's veto-proof majority in the 2018 off-year elections, Walker convened an unseemly and unhurried lame-duck session of the legislature to enact a law to limit the powers of the Wisconsin Democrats. It restricted their ability to pull out of the ACA lawsuit that was working its way through the courts, shortened absentee and early voting windows to two weeks before the election, allowed lawmakers to select their own attorneys to represent the state in cases over the attorney general, narrowed the number of roads eligible for federal repair money, and gave the legislature greater control over the economic development corporation to incentivize economic growth, among other provisions.[71]

The Koch brothers also backed the Tea Party protests and organization in North Carolina where Democrats had a strong hold on the state, yet won there in the 2012 national elections.[72] Retail magnate James Arthur Pope alone was responsible for 80 percent of the funding for conservative groups in the state that spent over $60 million to help produce the GOP sweep of the legislature in 2010.

They made North Carolina a laboratory for crony capitalism. After his election victory in 2012, Governor Pat McCrory made the retail magnate his budget director and they quickly made up for lost time. The North Carolina Republicans have proved themselves the most willing to break all conventions and the china.

In the summer of 2013, they enacted a flat tax of 5.75 percent, saving millionaires a cool $10,000 a year in state taxes. They abolished the estate tax and cut the corporate tax rate from 6.9 percent to 2.5 percent in 2018. In all, those in the top 1 percent got tax breaks of $21,780 a year. At the same time they eliminated the earned income tax credit for low-wage workers, as discussed at many ALEC conferences.[73]

And on schedule, "tax reform" produced an annual $3.5 billion deficit that had to be paid for from elsewhere in the budget and that elsewhere was education. In 2013, North Carolina moved immediately against the teachers, whose annual salaries have fallen 5 percent. They cut $66 million from the state university system and created a $4,200 voucher for children to attend private or religious schools. Over the past decade led by the state GOP, North Carolina cut K-12 funding by 7.9 percent and higher education by a stunning 15.9 percent. Tuition at the state's public universities was raised 44.5 percent.[74]

North Carolina voters elected Congressman Mark Meadows in 2012, who went to Washington and later led the Freedom Caucus and the government shutdown over health care.

Job well done.

Except voters turned out Governor Pat McCrory and elected Democratic Governor Roy Cooper and Attorney General Josh Stein in 2016; but North Carolina Republicans offered a new model on how to continue governing anyway. With the prospect of a Democratic governor, Governor McCrory signed a law that cut the number of governor-appointed positions in the state from 1,500 to 400, made cabinet appointments contingent on state senate confirmation, made partisan the state supreme court elections, and rigged county election boards to have Republicans in charge during election years.[75] America saw how important this last change was in the swirling controversy around the 2018 congressional election in North Carolina's 9th congressional district.

WHAT HAPPENED TO KANSAS?

The Koch brothers and Koch Industries made sure their home state was a model that would get the nation's attention, and Sam Brownback's 2010 election as governor of Kansas and the 2014 credit downgrade of the state by Moody and Standard & Poor did just that. The Koch family was the biggest contributor to this Tea Party favorite in Congress and uncompromising pro-life conservative.[76] "Our dependence is not on Big Government," Brownback declared, "but on a Big God that loves us and lives within us."[77]

In the home of the Koch brothers' Koch Industries, Brownback announced a goal of totally eliminating the personal income tax and the earned income tax credit for the working poor and capping spending increases at 2 percent a year, forcing immediate and major cuts in spending.[78]

Governor Brownback cut taxes by $1.1 billion and eliminated the income tax for small businesses while cutting welfare by nearly half. With trickle-down zeal, the plan cut the tax rate from 6.4 to 4.9 percent for those earning $150,000, but only a half a percentage for those earning less. Of course, it eliminated the earned income tax credit, too. Later, the GOP enacted changes that cut the top rate another percentage point by 2018 and required it to fall incrementally after that. The tax plan relieved owners of 200,000 small businesses paying any state income tax, among which were around twenty Koch Industries LLCs.[79]

The plan wiped out a budget surplus from before Brownback came to office and state revenue just evaporated as a result. His budget enacted, like other ALEC states, a 2.5 percent annual cap on spending increases and slashed education spending by $200 million, the largest cut in the state's history. The cut put education spending 16.5 percent below the pre–financial crisis level. This was the closest thing to assault. Abolishing teacher tenure put the teachers further back.[80]

When Kansas came slowly out of the recession, the GOP passed more tax cuts rather than fund education. That is why the state supreme court in 2013 found that school spending for poor districts was so low as to be unconstitutional and ordered that $129 million be restored. Despite that, the GOP proposed $44.5 million in further education cuts to fill a budget hole created by their accelerating income tax cuts.[81]

After the election, a prospective budget shortfall of $143 million in 2016 forced Governor Brownback and the Republican legislature to consider increasing sales and excise taxes and cigarette and liquor taxes and to slow the reduction of income taxes that were his signature conservative policy.[82]

THE RUST BELT STATES

The Kochs got their 2010 Rust Belt opportunity in Pennsylvania and Michigan—and with the latter, home of the progressive labor movement and the American labor movement and the United Auto Workers, becoming a right-to-work state.

Governor Tom Corbett of Pennsylvania was swept into office by the 2010 wave, and he cut corporate taxes by $1.2 billion and angrily opposed the Democrats' effort to impose a severance tax on the booming shale-gas industry. "It's the property owner's gas. I'm sorry. It's the mineral owner's gas," he declared.[83]

Corbett cut education spending by $841 million in his first budget, and twenty thousand teachers lost their jobs. The Republicans' education cuts, however, were not aimed solely at getting to a smaller government or a balanced budget. Their purpose was to reduce education spending for the poor, minorities, and immigrants. The governor scrapped the funding formula that took account of the number of students in poverty and those who needed English instruction. This guaranteed that the brunt of the education cuts would fall on the poorest and Hispanic populations.

Michigan was home of the UAW and progressive labor and Democratic leaders were powerful as well in education and the public sector. With 20.6 percent of the labor force belonging to unions, ranked first in the nation, Michigan had a history of supporting a strong state government, public education, and high environmental quality and regulation. So, the ALEC formula of corporate tax cuts, big corporate donations to the governor, and privatization took a dramatic toll here. The residents of Flint who paid with their lives stand as a testament to the withdrawal of effective government in this Tea Party period.

After the Tea Party wave, Michigan Governor Rick Snyder and the now GOP-dominated legislature passed $5.1 billion in tax cuts for corporations. They also eliminated the earned income tax credit, of course. They proceeded as the other Tea Party states had with cutting school funding by 9 percent until 2014. And when they needed to fund a business tax, they cut another $400 million from the education budget.[84]

To pay for the corporate tax cuts, Governor Snyder led the country's most widespread assault on public services, and in close alliance with his biggest corporate backers—Amway, Aramark, and Quicken Loans—spearheaded the widespread privatization of public services. He was constantly pressed to save money because of the massive corporate tax cuts at the outset of his term.

The governor unapologetically identified with the need to diminish the public sector and expand the role of the private sector. Companies like Amway and the dark money group Moving Michigan Forward funded public service campaigns in support of privatization. Betsy DeVos promoted doubling the number of charter schools and spent $5.6 billion lobbying for private school vouchers.[85]

In Flint, the governor's appointed emergency manager switched the source of the city's water to save money. That decision to divert water and reduce oversight led to the exposure of nearly one hundred thousand residents and their children to toxic levels of lead. In 2016, the Department of Environmental Quality, which supervised oversight of Detroit and Flint's water supply, was cut to meet the ongoing funding crisis.

During the special session 2012 election, Governor Snyder signed the bill that made Michigan a right-to-work state, which was shattering for the labor movement. Michigan unions suffered a net loss of 85,000 union members over a five-year period, or 137,000 members if one removes the United Auto Workers from the count, whose membership has rebounded with the auto industry. These unions also had to cut political spending by $26 million over those five years. State and local union membership also dropped 15 percent.[86]

When the voters ignominiously threw out the entire slate of Republican constitutional officers and elected Governor Gretchen Whitmer and Attorney General Dana Nessel, the Republicans rushed legislation in a lame-duck session to limit the damage.[87] It made it harder to get petitions on the ballot in future elections to discourage the use of these initiatives to boost state turnout. They also passed revised paid sick and minimum wage hikes that reduced paid sick leave from 72 hours to 36 hours per year and extended the timeline for raising the minimum wage by 8 more years.

DECONSTRUCTING GOVERNMENT NATIONALLY

In 2017, President Trump and the GOP were able to pass unanimously in the House and Senate precisely this kind of massive, unfunded tax cut for corporations and billionaires and specific industries—to set up, Paul Ryan assures us, the "entitlement reform" that must surely follow and blockage on any new investments in education and infrastructure. Trump nationalized the GOP effort to deconstruct the state, which is to destroy its capacity to do anything—completing the Tea Party decade's greatest work.

The determination to deconstruct government in the states and now nationally has produced a Republican base that devalues education. In America's modern history, it has educated each new generation of immigrants, but the GOP base does not want to educate the next.

This battle to deconstruct government and slash education spending has had a huge impact on Republican attitudes toward education, and it has set them apart. A remarkable 55 percent of Republicans believe a college education is not necessary for success in America, according to Ron Brownstein's national survey in October 2016.[88] And when asked which would do more for your local economy—"spending more money on education, including K through 12 schools and public colleges and universities" or "cutting taxes for individuals and businesses"—Republicans backed cutting taxes by a landslide margin, 55 to 38 percent.[89]

Deconstructing government has been deeply embraced by a party that has carried the spear for the Tea Party battle against big government and governmental activism.

STOPPED UNIVERSAL HEALTH INSURANCE IN GOP-CONTROLLED STATES

Congresswoman Rosa DeLauro reminds us that both parties contributed to the creation of America's safety net and, almost immediately after their passage, accepted Social Security and regularly raised benefits, accepted Medicare and Medicaid. Ronald Reagan never sought to change or reduce spending levels for social programs. George Bush introduced his plan to privatize Social Security, but promised not to reduce spending levels.[90]

But after the 2010 election, stopping the implementation of the Affordable Care Act became a litmus test for the Tea Party groups. Federally, the Tea Party bloc in the House and Senate would not entertain any "fixes." And in the states, they stopped it in its tracks, even though nationally, the ACA had dropped the proportion of uninsured from 16 to 11 percent between 2011 and 2017.[91]

The GOP governors were under pressure from state businesses and civic groups to participate in the health program and to accept the expansion of Medicaid in their states, but the Tea Party fought them for taking even a planning grant.[92] The Tea Party governors proudly announced their refusal to cooperate in any way.

Fully twenty-four states where the GOP had effective control refused to set up health care exchanges to allow people to select private health insurance plans and joined the suit to get the Supreme Court to rule that the ACA was unconstitutional. And I list them because it gives you some sense of the exceptional scale of the Tea Party resistance to President Obama and Obamacare. The state resisters included Alabama, Alaska, Arizona, Florida, Georgia, Idaho, Iowa, Kansas, Louisiana, Maine, Michigan, Mississippi, Nebraska, North Dakota, Ohio, Oklahoma, Pennsylvania, South Carolina, South Dakota, Texas, Utah, Virginia, Wisconsin, and Wyoming.[93] All but Arizona and Michigan refused to expand Medicaid, with huge consequences for public health. Most tried to introduce work requirements for receiving Medicaid, though that was blocked by the Obama administration until President Trump's election.[94]

In 2019, the Trump administration Justice Department decided to join the suit brought by thirteen Republican attorneys general contending the ACA mandate that health insurance policies must cover anyone, regardless of preexisting conditions. If they succeed, the ACA consumer protection guarantees, including the ban on using preexisting conditions as a factor in health insurance, will be history.

The results of boycott of the ACA were pretty evident and poignant: the first peer-reviewed study analyzing the effects of Medicaid expansion showed that two thirds of poor uninsured blacks in the country live in these "refusenik" states, where almost 6 million residents did not get health insurance.[95]

Medicaid expansion showed, more than any single act, that government can be effective in improving the well-being of Americans, if government weren't being suffocated by Tea Party governance. In Maine, voters by referendum forced their Tea Party governor to expand Medicaid but Paul LePage would not yield until forced to by the courts, while the voters elected a Democratic governor in 2018 to move forward. In Utah in 2018, one of the most Republican states in the country, 53 percent of the voters approved Proposition 3, forcing the elected leaders to expand Medicaid. Idaho and Nebraska, neither of them bastions of liberalism, passed an expansion of Medicaid by referendum, by 61 and 54 percent respectively.[96] Those broad mandates from the citizenry say voters welcome greater activism in health care.

When Donald Trump was elected, the GOP fought dramatically to repeal the Affordable Care Act, and the replacement version that almost became law, the Graham-Cassidy plan, would have turned the ACA into a state block grant and ended the essential benefits, like no penalty for preexisting conditions.[97] Having failed to repeal it, the

Trump administration has sought to sabotage it in every possible way and won the repeal of the individual mandate in the Tax Cuts and Jobs Act. The Tea Party–dominated GOP perversely increased the number of uninsured by 4 million in 2019 and an expected 12 million by 2021.[98]

America had been headed toward achieving universal health care. Government was demonstrably successful in achieving this public goal popular with the voters, but progress was stalled in the GOP-controlled states after 2010 and, now, the GOP owns Americans' having to face even more health care insecurity and rising costs, as a Tea Party–dominated government leads the retreat.

ACHIEVING AN END TO ABORTIONS IN GOP-CONTROLLED STATES

The Tea Party movement and activists in 2010 were vehemently hostile to government, but they were socially conservative as well, determined to end the murderous policies that legalized abortion. The Evangelicals were the largest bloc in the GOP base and they cheered the Tea Party groups that were brave enough to challenge the GOP establishment and gridlock the country.

So, fully half of the GOP members were determined to end legal abortion, and their pro-life elected leaders pressed for changes in law and regulations that would mean women could not get a legal abortion in GOP-controlled states.

The Supreme Court in *Planned Parenthood v. Casey* maintained the legal standards of *Roe v. Wade*, but allowed the states to regulate access to abortion, as long as no "undue burden" was placed on women.[99] Well, the Tea Party wave in 2010 was the firing of the starter pistol in the GOP-controlled states to push the limits of "undue burden."

Look how determined the most prominent pro-life governors and legislators were.

In Texas, Governor Rick Perry was a pro-life innovator. Texas was the first state to try to defund Planned Parenthood in 2010. The state mandated that a woman see a sonogram twenty-four hours in advance of an abortion, with no exception, and that there be a like waiting period for even a medically induced abortion in 2011. The pro-lifers set the state against family planning and women's health services for "spiritual reasons." In 2013, Texas pushed the limits. On one hand, it outlawed abortions after twenty weeks of pregnancy unless it would involve major physical risk to the woman and then embraced in 2013 requiring doctors to have admitting privileges at a hospital within thirty miles of a facility that performed abortions. In this vast state, Tea Party government brought the number of abortion clinics down from forty-two to five for a population of 26 million, all in urban areas and none in the western part of the state. In 2016, it required the burial or cremation of aborted fetuses. And to adapt to the passage of the ACA, in 2017 it banned insurance coverage for abortions.[100]

In Louisiana, Governor Bobby Jindal was inventive and determined, coming back each year to see how far he could push the boundaries of the law. In 2010, Louisiana mandated that women had to view an ultrasound two hours in advance of an abortion and barred abortion providers from being able to get malpractice insurance. Two years later, Jindal signed the Right to Know Act that required doctors notify patients of abortion alternatives and another law barring abortion after twenty weeks of pregnancy unless there was risk of bodily harm to the mother or congenital anomaly to the fetus. In June 2014, the government in Louisiana found a formula that would excite pro-life forces everywhere. A new law required doctors performing more than five abortions a year to register with the state, as well as requiring doctors to have admitting privileges at hospitals within thirty miles of their clinic. It dropped the number of clinics from five to two in the state. In 2015, they barred Planned Parenthood from performing women's health services.[101]

In Kansas, Governor Brownback led the pro-life legislative members, and he moved quickly after the 2010 wave. The state enacted a law that declared that life begins at conception, banned abortion after twenty-one weeks of pregnancy, and shared scientifically questionable information on fetal pain. They enacted building codes for abortion clinics that were so strict that they could have shut down all but one clinic in the state, if they were enforced.[102]

Governor Walker had to survive a recall election and the battle with the unions, but he was able to sign legislation that barred health care providers from giving abortions to government workers. Of course, Wisconsin would take up the plan of ALEC and the pro-life groups. In 2014, it required ultrasounds twenty-four hours before an abortion, and required doctors have admitting privileges at a hospital within thirty miles of an abortion clinic. In 2016, Wisconsin defunded Planned Parenthood. And in 2015, Walker signed a bill that banned nearly all abortions after twenty weeks.[103]

In Pennsylvania, the governor supported the "Women's Right to Know" Act. It required that women considering an abortion get an ultrasound and required that the abortion provider hand copies of it to the patient and let them hear the fetal heartbeat—"as long as it's not obtrusive." When asked whether the law goes too far, Governor Corbett offered, "You can't make anybody watch, okay? Because you just have to close your eyes."[104]

According to the Population Institute, eighteen states in total have a failing grade on access to abortion, maternal health care, and access to birth control.[105]

This strategy of what pro-life groups called "Targeted Regulation of Abortion Providers," or TRAP, laws, has radically changed the abortion landscape. Fully twenty-six states now require that clinics be turned into mini surgical centers at very high cost; four of the states require abortion providers have admitting privileges at a local hospital, which they never get. This process has left six states—North Dakota, South Dakota, Wyoming, Kentucky, Mississippi, and West Virginia—with one clinic.[106]

The GOP led a pincer movement nationally to impose a domestic "gag rule" that would effectively put Planned Parenthood out of business and to bar abortions in some states after the detection of a fetal heartbeat at six weeks, which would be as close as one can get to making abortion illegal. Georgia was the first to act, followed by South Carolina, Mississippi, and Ohio.[107]

Inventive women and doctors have turned to medically induced abortions and telemedicine, but inventive GOP states have limited the former and banned the latter.[108]

The federal courts paused some of the most dramatic steps, leaving it to the reconstituted U.S. Supreme Court to decide their fate. At the end of the Tea Party decade, the GOP is close to barring legal abortion in states where they govern.

SUPPRESSING THE VOTE

The GOP governors in the 1990s led the battle to bar undocumented immigrants from getting public services, particularly education. The

House Republicans in the Tea Party wave would follow that by focusing on preventing undocumented immigrants from getting welfare, food stamps, and access to federal health care programs. With Obama's election, the Arizona governor led the state effort to enforce America's immigration laws, but lost in the federal courts in 2012. President Obama was in charge of America's immigration laws for the time being.

But after the Tea Party wave elections in 2010, the governors moved to enact laws requiring voters show photo IDs at the polls, supposedly to discourage illegal voting, particularly by undocumented immigrants. Some added proof of citizenship requirements.

Immigration was the entry point, but there was no limit to how far the governors were willing to go. More than sixty voter ID laws were taken up by state legislatures in the 2011 and 2012 sessions, half introduced by ALEC members. The number of states that enacted stand-your-ground, right-to-work, and voter ID laws jumped from two to seven.[109] It is unlikely Donald Trump would have carried Wisconsin and Michigan, where the African-American vote was down sharply, and perhaps not North Carolina either.

In Kansas, Secretary of State Kris Kobach provided the model with the passage of the Safe Act in 2011. The act required a birth certificate, passport, or similar document in order to register to vote. Kobach tried to block voting by young people who were registered by the Department of Motor Vehicles under federal law.[110]

The Tea Party governors moved to reduce the participation of minority and younger voters by requiring a government-issued photo ID at the polls, ending same-day voter registration, reducing early voting by one week, and requiring university students to vote where they had registered their car.[111]

In North Carolina, the state no longer accepted consular documents as valid ID for registering and voting. It moved aggressively to keep African Americans from voting by cutting a week of early voting and a Sunday when many vote, and eliminated same-day registration. In 2013, North Carolina required specific IDs that students and others could not get, eliminated preregistration for sixteen- and seventeen-year-olds, and allowed "challengers" at the polling places who were meant to intimidate voters. The federal courts were impressed with "surgical precision" used by the GOP to reduce the African-American vote.[112]

In Wisconsin, the governor dismantled the board in charge of assuring nonpartisan oversight of elections. And the legislature passed a strict voter ID law that kept 17,000 people from voting in Milwaukee and Dane County alone, and up to 300,000 people statewide in a race decided by a mere 21,000 votes.[113] One report found that 11 percent of the population was deterred from voting in 2016.[114] And when the Republicans acted in the lame-duck session, at the top of their list was to shorten "early voting" to limit voting in the minority communities and at the universities.[115]

AMERICA GAGGED ON CLIMATE CHANGE

In May 2014, the National Climate Assessment concluded, "Climate change is already affecting the American people in far-reaching ways," including the "extreme weather events with links to climate change." The report said, expect "prolonged periods of heat, heavy downpours, and, in some regions, floods and droughts," which "have become more frequent and/or intense." Sea levels were rising, oceans becoming more acidic, and 2012 was the hottest year on record in the United States. These changes were "disrupting people's lives and damaging some sectors of our economy."[116]

Using sixteen climate models to analyze different emissions scenarios, the assessment said, the conclusion is "unambiguous": a half century of warming "has been driven primarily by human activity"—namely, "the burning of coal, oil, and gas and clearing of forests."[117]

President Obama accepted the findings and concluded after the American Clean Energy and Security Act died in the Senate that he could make progress only by executive action and by international agreements.

GOP leaders were silent or rejected the conclusions. They didn't need to be reminded that three quarters of Tea Party and Evangelical Republicans rejected any role for humans or fossil fuels in climate change. They didn't need to be reminded how big a role the Koch brothers and the oil and coal industry played in their campaigns.[118]

Almost immediately after the release of the National Climate Assessment, the House Republicans, with near unanimity, barred the Defense Department, against its wishes, from using any funds to implement the report's recommendations. And for good measure, the House

Republicans instructed the Defense Department to ignore any recommendations of the United Nations' Intergovernmental Panel on Climate Change.[119]

It is hard to remember that most Republicans supported the Clean Air Act and other landmark environmental laws. That included conservative U.S. senators such as James Buckley and Alfonse D'Amato, even Mitch McConnell, but today's Senate Republicans have largely embraced the new orthodoxy.[120] And a few weeks into the 114th Congress, all but two Republican senators in the new Republican-controlled Senate voted to limit President Obama's ability to negotiate at the U.N. Climate Conference in Paris in 2015 and quash his historic agreement with China on limiting greenhouse gas emissions.[121]

When candidates began auditioning for the 2016 presidential race, every one affirmed the new GOP orthodoxy on climate change: no human causation and therefore no reason for government action.

Senator Marco Rubio fell out with conservatives when he supported comprehensive immigration reform, but he tried to get back into the conservative mainstream by showing his scorn for all this PC climate change chatter right up front in his announcement speech: "I do not believe that human activity is causing these dramatic changes to our climate the way these scientists are portraying it," the senator from Florida declared. A reporter pointed to the report's conclusion that Florida was facing more damaging hurricanes. No, Rubio responded, "Climate is always evolving and natural disasters have always existed."

And most important, government activism is ineffective and counterproductive: "I don't agree with the notion that some are putting out there, including scientists, that somehow, there are actions we can take today that would actually have an impact on what's happening in our climate"—though they "will destroy our economy," with all the new regulations. Activist government is ineffective and counterproductive, so the country is powerless.[122]

The other 2016 hopefuls joined Rubio on the issue. Jeb Bush stayed in the GOP mix by denying the scientific consensus: "It is not unanimous among scientists that it is disproportionately manmade." Scott Walker signed the "no climate tax" pledge, and Bobby Jindal declared we "must put energy prices and energy independence ahead of zealous adherence to left-wing environmental theory." Rand Paul concluded that nobody "exactly knows why" the earth is warming, though Rick Santorum knew it went beyond the powers of scientists and humans: "The apostles of this pseudo-religion believe that America and its people are the source of the earth's temperature. I do not."[123]

Then on June 18, 2015, Pope Francis released his encyclical letter "On Care for Our Common Home," which chided humanity for the "harm we have inflicted" on this earth. After consulting with "scientists, philosophers, theologians and civic groups," Francis affirmed the "very solid scientific consensus" on the warming of the earth. He placed the blame not just on human behavior generally, but specifically on "a model of development based on the intensive use of fossil fuels."

Pope Francis did not endear himself with Republicans when he urged leaders and social movements to disrupt "the worldwide energy system" that is endangering the poor most of all.

Jeb Bush responded quickly, embracing Catholic candidate John F. Kennedy's formulation of the separation of church and state when Kennedy said, famously, he believed in an America "where no public official either requests or accepts instructions on public policy from the pope, the National Council of Churches or any other ecclesiastical source." Bush declared in a like vein, "I don't get economic policy from my bishops or my cardinals or my pope." The devout Catholic Rick Santorum just attacked the pope: "The church has gotten it wrong a few times on science," and "when we get involved with political and controversial scientific theories, then I think the church is probably not as forceful and credible."[124]

Appeals from the pope and world and business leaders did not stop President Trump from announcing America's withdrawal from the Paris climate accord in April 2017.

Then, it seemed America was hit with a biblical set of weather events, leading headline writers, commentators, governors, and meteorologists to search for language up to the scale of events: "NOAA: 2017 was Third Warmest Year on Record for the Globe," "Louisiana Flood: Worst U.S. Disaster Since Sandy," "Hurricane Harvey Projected to Be 2nd Costliest Storm in U.S. History," and "Extreme Hurricanes and Wildfires Made 2017 the Most Costly Disaster Year on Record," and the first Category 4 storm to hit in the Gulf Coast in October.[125]

Then, on October 6, 2018, the Intergovernmental Panel on Climate

Change warned that our earlier goal of containing warming to two degrees would be catastrophic, as summarized by *The Economist*: "Arctic summers could be ice-free once a decade," virtually all the ocean's coral might be "irreversibly wiped out," and "an extra 420m people exposed to record heat." The report called for greater partnering of government, nonstate actors, business, banking, and scientific institutions and accelerated investments in climate-driven innovation, the rapid adoption of disruptive technologies, and behavior changes that could slow the warming. In short, leaders had to embrace transformative changes to their economies to avoid calamity.[126]

Then, *The New York Times* displayed a graph across two thirds of the front page above the fold showing in as dramatic a way as possible that 2018 was the fourth hottest in 140 years. Those government scientists at NASA found "the five warmest years in recorded history have been the last five, and that 28 of the 19 warmest years have occurred since 2001." What was so striking and surprising to the scientists was "the relatively sudden rise in temperatures and its clear correlation with the increasing levels of greenhouse gases."[127]

Yet America was under the control of the Tea Party–dominated GOP that kept America gagged and powerless.

INEQUALITY AND MIDDLE-CLASS DECLINE: "THE CUPBOARD IS BARE"

In the spring of 2014, Thomas Piketty published the U.S. edition of *Capital in the Twenty-First Century,* which used global economic data over centuries to establish definitively America's soaring economic inequality, indeed, a "second Gilded Age," where, Paul Krugman writes, the "incomes of the now famous 'one percent,' and of even narrower groups, are actually the big story." Piketty argued, as well, that those with inherited wealth will dominate those who earned it, and both Europe and America are headed to a "patrimonial capitalism" where "the commanding heights of the economy are controlled not by talented individuals but by family dynasties."[128]

America's liberal economic circles were excited above all by the confirmation that the 1 percent was growing further apart from the whole country and taking all income gains. Liberals were also excited by the confirmation that America was in the second Gilded Age, because in America, the first Gilded Age had been followed by the New

Deal, which had mitigated the excess, built safety nets, and empowered workers. Politics mattered. Piketty missed what was exceptional in the American experience that could produce a very different economic trajectory.

America's exceptionalism begins with CEO income—which has played such a big role in the gains of the 1 percent and was pushed up by U.S. tax policies and changes in corporate governance.

Piketty demonstrated that American inequality today "is quantitatively as extreme as in old Europe in the first decade of the twentieth century," but he also acknowledged that "the structure of that inequality is rather clearly different." Two thirds of the top Americans' wealth was from current income, not capital accumulation. Today's economic titans are the CEOs and senior executives "earning" their "super salaries," not rentiers living off inherited wealth and capital gains. The wages of the American 1 percent are up 165 percent since the early 1970s, and that rises to 362 percent for the wages of the top 0.1 percent.[129]

The ratio between the compensation of the average worker and the CEOs of the top 350 American firms (ranked by sales) began to surge in the mid-1990s, interrupted dramatically by bursting bubbles, but headed to an unimaginable gap. The ratio in 2013 was 295.9 to 1.[130]

The pay of CEOs of the top firms increased 21.7 percent between 2010, when the recession ended for companies, and 2013. The CEOs of the 200 largest U.S. firms received a median pay package of $15.1 million, up 16 percent from 2011.[131]

In the period between 1940 and 1970, the average American CEO earned under $1 million. But changes in corporate governance and tax rates in the 1980s and 1990s produced an unseemly race to the top. The changes multiplied CEO compensation fifteen-fold, accompanied by surging pay in C-suites and on corporate boards. An analysis by *The Wall Street Journal* showed the median pay for CEOs reached $1 million a month in 2018.[132]

Wall Street bonuses totaled $27.5 billion and stock buybacks of $187 billion enriched CEOs, C-suites, and the richest 1 percent.[133]

CEO salaries jumped 17.6 percent in 2017 alone, and the ratio between CEO and average worker pay hit a staggering 312 to 1 ratio.[134]

The passage of President Trump's and Republicans' "tax reform" bill, which cut corporate tax rates from 35 percent to 21 percent and implemented other changes that favored particular kinds of investment, produced a surge in corporate profits in 2018.

Nobel economist Joseph Stiglitz strengthens further the liberal case that the scale of American inequality "didn't just happen"; "it was created." The amount seized by the upper 1 percent was "a distinctly American 'achievement.'"[135]

Under Franklin Roosevelt and the New Deal regime, the United States went much further than Europe in establishing the progressive taxation that Piketty prescribes. The top marginal tax rate fluctuated between 70 and 94 percent from the mid-1930s until 1981. But Ronald Reagan won a mandate for across-the-board tax cuts, and his tax reform cut the top tax rate to 50 percent in 1982, to 38.5 percent in 1987, and all the way down to 28 percent in 1988. The decrease in the top tax rate has proven to be "perfectly correlated" with the increase in the top earners' proportion of the national income. Before the 1980s, there was no financial incentive for a CEO to press for higher pay; but the dramatic drop in top rates "totally transformed the way executive salaries are determined" and "executives went to considerable lengths to persuade other interested parties (as in, the compensation committees that the executive often appoints) to grant them substantial raises."[136]

The liberals argued not just that this soaring inequality was created but also that those policies were increasingly the result of the soaring campaign spending of big corporations and billionaire donors.[137]

The campaigns for president and the U.S. Congress cost $6.3 billion in 2012, with a growing proportion spent by tax-exempt organizations that do not disclose their donors and by independent super PACs, now the vehicles of choice for corporations and America's billionaires. Four fifths of that outside money went to Republican-aligned conservative groups that, in turn, have taken advantage of Supreme Court decisions giving corporations a right to free speech—in particular, the "right to devote one's resources to whatever cause one supports." A decade ago, the GOP supported full disclosure of contributions and opposed the "soft money" that allowed special-interest groups to influence elections; but with increasing dependence on large undisclosed donations, the Republican Party now officially opposes any contribution limits and any disclosure.

What position will they take after grassroots resistance to President Trump put nearly every Democratic candidate at a financial advantage and the Democrats' billionaires outspent the Koch brothers and Sheldon Adelson?

Stiglitz concludes in *The Price of Inequality: How Today's Divided Society Endangers Our Future* that the 1 percent is able to use government to "write the rules of the economy" to benefit themselves, while middle-class incomes have stagnated.[138] They have stagnated because of the broken link between the rising productivity of American workers and wage gains.[139] That lack of connection symbolizes almost more than any other emerging fact about the economy the centrality of government policy. Legislative and regulatory actions at the national and state levels affect how many employees belong to unions and are empowered or disempowered to affect wage levels. Governments can raise the minimum wage—and did in eighteen of the fifty states in 2018. Government can raise the amounts of earned income tax credits and child tax credits and extend credits to young children. They can expand food programs, greatly expand health care subsidies, and raise Social Security benefits, as a start. The government's tool chest is so full.

Conservatives universally downplayed the worry about inequality, the top 1 percent, and middle-class decline, and argued, critically, there isn't much the country can do about them anyway. What we can do is address the most important economic problem, people pulling out of the labor force, which is produced by government policies that encourage idleness.

Conservative writers wrote breathlessly about Richard V. Burkhauser, Jeff Larrimore, and Kosali I. Simon's study for the National Bureau of Economic Research titled, "A 'Second Opinion' on the Economic Health of the American Middle Class." Their research inspired *The Washington Post* editorial page to run an op-ed piece by Ron Haskins under the headline THE MYTH OF THE DISAPPEARING MIDDLE CLASS. Scott Winthrop wrote a piece in the *The New Republic* headlined to get a response, STOP FEELING SORRY FOR THE MIDDLE CLASS! THEY'RE DOING JUST FINE. Fox News headlined its online contribution, SORRY, MR. BIDEN, MOST MIDDLE CLASS AMERICANS ARE BETTER OFF NOW THAN THEY WERE THIRTY YEARS AGO.[140]

Once the authors of the study factored in all the policies the Republicans wanted to cut—tax credits, food stamps, and health insurance—they found that the incomes of those in the middle of the income scale rose 37 percent over these three decades. That is about 1.1 percent a year and very close to the consensus calculations of progressive think tanks.

Perhaps most egregious is their lack of curiosity about what periods produced this 37 percent gain for the middle class over three decades. Well, it turns out that half the income growth came in the period dominated by Bill Clinton's economic and tax policies. During the Clinton period, it grew by 16.8 percent, double the average for the Republican presidents (8.3 percent).[141]

Moreover, after all of their calculations to factor in tax credits and food stamps, it is only during the Clinton period that the Gini coefficient—the standard measure of inequality—improved. The top 5 percent did okay, their income going up 15.1 percent, though that was a touch *less* than for the middle quintile, which gained 16.8 percent. The Reagan period brought a dramatic worsening of these numbers for the middle, second, and bottom quintile, and the George W. Bush years were just terrible for everybody.[142]

Had they paid attention to the political periodization, they might have at least speculated as to what policies made such a difference in mitigating the problem. Their own research showed incomes went up only under Clinton because of changes in the earned income tax credit and the value of all "public transfers," including food stamps, welfare, Pell grants, Social Security, and other government-provided cash assistance, as well as Medicare and Medicaid. They did not want to show that government activism can raise incomes and raise people out of poverty.[143]

The research also did not display data or talk about the top 1 percent. Those heralded top earners do not even get a line in Burkhauser's graphs, which pushes the problem of inequality out of sight in this Tea Party–dominated period.[144] Having no line for the 1 percent and blocking out the economic data for the Clinton presidency allowed Atlantic Council senior fellow Douglas Besharov to tell a sympathetic interviewer, "No one has the slightest idea what will work. The cupboard is bare."[145]

This is disingenuous, of course. These conservative economists are fully paid-up members of the conservative policy network. The Ryan budget would have decimated food stamps, eliminated or limited refundable tax credits, capped Pell grants, repealed the Medicaid expansion under the Affordable Care Act, and converted Medicare into a voucher program. The leading GOP governors competed to abolish the state versions of the earned income tax credit (EITC), slashed food stamps, refused to expand Medicaid, cut unemployment benefits, and shifted the cost of higher education onto students. The GOP did everything possible to make life harder for the middle class and the poor.

The truth is GOP leaders think the decline of the family and the growth of dependence on government are the real problems facing the country, not the decline of the middle class or growing inequality. Liberals grew "the welfare state" and created a growing "mass dependence on entitlements" that produced pathologies in so many areas. The answer is to provide less security and comfort, so people will become more self-reliant and seek out work. Working people and the poor benefit from a government that provides less, not more.

So, the debate over inequality and the middle class ended in this period of Tea Party dominance with governments shredding the social safety net and slashing tax cuts for the super rich and corporations. And it welcomed the 1 percent and corporations spending increasing millions to ensure that they would keep getting a government that writes the rules of the economy to work for them.

The Tea Party decade was forged in the firestorm created when government took over from business the job of rescuing a crashed economy and financial system, which it took up unevenly and unfairly, but also when government took on the unfinished job of ensuring all Americans have access to health care, and the formidable task of preventing catastrophic global warming. The anti-government Evangelical GOP reacted with horror and great urgency to government assuming such a superordinate role, particularly one led by President Barack Obama. The fear was not just of the public's acceptance of government activism in times of crisis, but, even greater, that this government overreach would succeed. Increased spending had slowed the loss of jobs, restored the banks' financial stability, and rescued the auto industry; the number of citizens without any health insurance fell dramatically; President

Obama's new regulations for coal and autos and higher fuel efficiency standards put America on track to shift the trajectory on global warming. Imagine how much the GOP might be on the defensive had President Obama been willing to explain why America had to meet these challenges and why government had to play this bigger role.

The Tea Party revolt against this Obama-led government activism gave the Tea Party control of the Congress and soon after, half the states. They immediately jammed the gears and gridlocked the federal government. They pushed a suffocating austerity where only deficits mattered. They deconstructed government with massive tax cuts for the richest, corporations, and special interests that required massive cuts in public spending, education, and the number of teachers and destruction of their unions. They stopped the Affordable Care Act in its tracks. They put abortion out of reach where they governed. They stoked fears of violent immigrants to push minority voters out of the electorate. And they just denied climate change, middle-class decline, and the 1 percent to suffocate any debate about what to do and thus what government can do. The War on Poverty failed, and people have withdrawn from the labor force because they got too much help from government.

This GOP party's policies were not beloved in the country, and its presidential candidates failed to win more votes than the Democratic nominee in any presidential election in this period. The country's founders created a constitutional system that favored rural voters, but the unabashed partisan gerrymandering raised public consciousness of the growing gap between popular support and popular control: the Democratic candidates won more votes than the Republican in every election for the U.S. Senate in 2016 and the Democrats won more than the Republicans in three of the five House elections in this Tea Party period.

Citizens United was the starter pistol in 2010 that gave the conservative billionaires and big corporations the green light to spend ever more dark money to take control of more and more states. Big money and corporate special interests turned government into a swamp of self-dealing and corruption that still hasn't been drained.

The Supreme Court eviscerated the Voting Rights Act in 2013 and the GOP then used photo IDs, reduced early voting and poll places, voter purges, and just legal scams to push millions of the poor, African

Americans, Mexican Americans, immigrants, college students, and Native Americans out of the electorate.

No one imagined that a Tea Party-Evangelical–dominated GOP would get a whole decade to suppress any consideration of the building problems facing the country and so much time to destroy the government's capacity to act. But America today looks like some kind of wind-up spring toy that has been turned and turned while someone uses all their strength to hold down the coil to keep the toy from suddenly spinning wildly and flying up to the ceiling. What happens now that the man holding it is gone, swept away by the elections of 2018 and, soon, 2020?

How long will it take Democrats to regain their innovative public spirit and willingness to use government to tackle problems that have only gotten dramatically worse?

Democratic state governments acted on raising the minimum wage, increasing early childhood education, expanding health care, and addressing climate change, so they will likely rush into a debate that has been repressed in this Tea Party period. Democrats know how to grow an economy that creates better paying jobs, how to make health care universal and dramatically reduce climate risk. They know greatly increased investment in education and infrastructure must no longer be stalled. They know very different trade agreements can set back the outsourcing of American jobs. They know higher taxes on the rich and CEOs, tax credits, social supports, empowered unions, regulations, and changes in corporate governance can raise middle-class incomes and reduce inequality. Just discussing the agenda and embracing government activism as a precondition for progress sounds like a country that may be liberated from the Tea Party decade.

Are people really ready to clean the swamp that this Tea Party period took to shameless levels?

Are people ready to restore democracy?

Do elites understand how desperate the country has been to address these collective problems? Are Democrats ready to use government after this decade of anti-government tyranny?

5 PRESIDENT TRUMP'S GOP IN BATTLE

AT THE BEGINNING OF EACH FOCUS GROUP, I ask people to finish this sentence: "I feel _____ about the way things are going in the country." Within months of Donald Trump becoming president, both Clinton and Trump voters began filling in words that almost united them: "terrified," "nervous," "depressed," and "distraught."

After Trump's inauguration, I went to listen to Trump voters in Macomb County, the Detroit suburb that I had helped make famous as the home of Reagan Democrats who Bill Clinton and Barack Obama had won back but who, in 2016, had given Trump his margin of victory in Michigan. They were shocked by how the country had reacted to Donald Trump's election.

I held these discussions with independents, Democrats, and Obama voters who had voted for Trump, and they had not regretted doing so. There was no "buyer's remorse." None of the thirty-five participants over the course of the focus group discussion or in their private post-group postcards to President Trump had pulled back from their vote, which is an impressive indication of the strength of Trump's support. They are were clear about why they voted for him and prayed he keeps his promises and succeeds.

They accepted Trump's version of the news and facts, and their reactions to videos of his press conferences and interviews reinforced that point. They said they "want to believe" him and described his demeanor as "very sincere. Like you could feel it from watching him.

You know it makes a difference to him." They felt hopeful watching their new president: "It's amazing to see him up there and go, wow, that's my president now, and those things are gonna happen. And he's gonna make things better."

They believed his opponents marching in the streets were "not satisfied with the results" of the election and "now they're trying [by] every means necessary . . . to change the outcome which is not going to happen." With tensions so heightened, some feared growing unrest and some even worried, "we're going to end up in a civil war." "If a Democrat won," they argued, "I wouldn't be sitting here doing a million man march because Hillary Clinton was in office, I'd have to deal with it because she's my president and move on." They hoped the protestors and the family members giving them a hard time would chill because if "he gets a chance, if they give him a minute here," they insisted, "he'll start doing some good things."

> More than half the people haven't come to terms with it. And they're still opposing it. We can't move on. And it seems like he tries to do things. They oppose it. Then everybody's out there protesting it.
>
> —NON-COLLEGE-EDUCATED
> WHITE WOMAN, AKRON

Stop "being a bunch of pussies" and "being so sensitive and let's get some stuff done."

My focus groups became group therapy sessions in today's polarized America where both sides speak about a virtual "civil war" in the country and within their own families. Trump and Clinton voters couldn't be placed in the same room, if you really wanted to learn something. The discussion became animated and revealing the moment when people realized they were together with only Trump or only Clinton voters. Ordinary people in focus groups now insisted on talking about politics, national issues, and the state of the country; they would not be distracted by our moderators, who attempted to open conversations with topics like popular culture and entertainment. They rushed to politics. Trump sucked all the oxygen out of the room.

My Trump focus groups were all white and working class; each group included only participants of the same sex and of a similar age. They were so relieved to discover they could express themselves freely without fear of being attacked. Nobody criticized them when they said something unflattering about immigrants, blacks, or Muslims.

They felt under attack at home—not only from younger generations in their own families but also from those in their communities. Some had been ostracized by close family members who criticized them for their vote, others confessed they had been "called racist, a xenophobe, homophobe, whatever phobe they could come up with." One woman's son was bullied after his first-grade class held a mock election: "My son hears us and he says, 'I'm going to vote for Trump,' and two of the kids in his class started yelling. Like, 'You're going to vote Trump? Are you crazy?' And just started yelling at him." This was personal.

A year into the Trump presidency, many Trump supporters found they had paid a high price for their vote choice in their own families. One white working-class man shared that he "lost contact with [his] own daughter because of the election." Others complained that their children and millennial friends challenged their views and suggested the media manipulates them.

> A lot of the young kids—I call them young, they're in their twenties, you know, late twenties—I see them as Democrats, they don't support the President on [bringing change], so they're latching on to everything in the fake news, about what he's done, what he's said, you know? What he's ruined, you know? What Obama did that was great, you know?
>
> —OLDER WORKING-CLASS
> WHITE WOMAN, MACOMB

> My girlfriend's little brother is ten years old and right away he is saying, "Oh, screw Trump." [. . .] it's like you don't even know anything about anything. It's like the mass media is brainwashing the younger generation and it's that serious.
>
> —WORKING-CLASS WHITE MAN, MACOMB

Two years into the Trump presidency, most rallied to protect him in this divided and polarized country, and were mobilized by the issues he raised, but not all, as we shall see.

President Trump's 2018 off-year, ugly campaign threw off all nuance as he slandered the caravan of immigrants and warned of an immigrant invasion and sent troops to the border to teargas any lingering refugees. Trump's GOP stood against the country's rising immigration, foreignness, and multiculturalism, and stood up as an American "nationalist" against the liberal globalists.

President Trump also stood up for the men who had been toppled from their breadwinner roles and had lost their security in American manufacturing. He and the Republicans in Congress battled for that "good man, Kavanaugh" and all the men who have been on the defensive at home and in the workplace. Men were being casually accused of rape, and President Trump alone stood up for them and their children, who were being victimized by the liberal orthodoxy.

Trump used his rallies and Fox News to wage war against the liberal media, "the enemy of the people," whom some of his supporters were motivated to stop with pipe bombs and guns. Cesar Sayoc's path to mailing pipe bombs to Trump's political enemies started in 2016 when he posted links to a YouTube video claiming "Satan Sent Obama to Destroy America" and a Sean Hannity clip exposing the "illegal immigrant Crime STATS." By the 2016 election, he was focused on Islamic terrorism, illegal immigration, and the Clinton Foundation. He later cheered on President Trump's tax cuts and added, "Happy Birthday to greatest gift from God President TrumpTrump Trump." His posts became more threatening and visually bloody in 2018.[1]

United States Coast Guard lieutenant Christopher Paul Hasson of Silver Spring, Maryland, worried about America's changing demographics and wrote in 2017 to an unnamed neo-Nazi, advocating a "white homeland." In 2018, he wrote of killing on a large scale and amassed an arsenal of fifteen firearms. He was readying a plan to kill prominent Democrats and members of the media.[2]

On March 15, 2019, fifty Muslim worshippers at two New Zealand mosques died at the hands of a white nationalist who worried about "white replacement" and referenced President Trump in his manifesto.

These violent acts were not isolated. In 2017, the Anti-Defamation League reported a 57 percent increase in anti-Semitic incidents, including "bomb threats, assaults, vandalism, and anti-Semitic posters and literature found on college campuses," before the murder of eleven Jews at a Pittsburgh synagogue in 2018 by a Trump supporter motivated by the refugee threat.[3] The Southern Poverty Law Center's 2018 annual census of hate groups showed a 50 percent increase in the sheer number of white nationalist groups, with 40 people killed in radical-right terrorist attacks in the United States.[4]

The president mobilized in the 2018 election his legions of ardent Tea Party supporters and the Evangelicals, who together formed 42 percent of registered Republicans, though importantly, 47 percent of those who vote in primaries. They cheered his abandon that led some on the fringe to turn to violent resistance. Trump's bragging and rallies were loved by the Tea Party supporters and Evangelicals, but they sent the Catholics into a brawl among themselves and pushed away most of the secular conservatives and nearly all of the moderates.

It turns out the Republican Party is more complicated than you imagine. The conservative and observant Catholics were more conflicted, but rallied to Donald Trump because he was pro-life, took on big corporations, and defended the border. Trump could stir and mobilize at least 60 percent of the party.

Composition of the GOP base

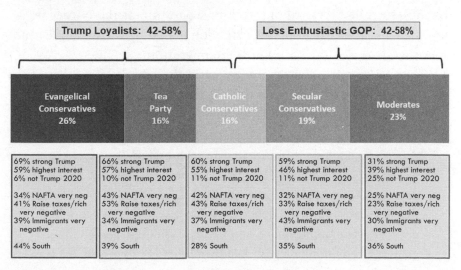

Trump Loyalists: 42-58%			Less Enthusiastic GOP: 42-58%	
Evangelical Conservatives 26%	Tea Party 16%	Catholic Conservatives 16%	Secular Conservatives 19%	Moderates 23%
69% strong Trump 59% highest interest 6% not Trump 2020	66% strong Trump 57% highest interest 10% not Trump 2020	60% strong Trump 55% highest interest 11% not Trump 2020	59% strong Trump 46% highest interest 11% not Trump 2020	31% strong Trump 39% highest interest 25% not Trump 2020
34% NAFTA very neg 41% Raise taxes/rich very negative 39% Immigrants very negative	43% NAFTA very neg 53% Raise taxes/rich very negative 34% Immigrants very negative	42% NAFTA very neg 43% Raise taxes/rich very negative 37% Immigrants very negative	32% NAFTA very neg 33% Raise taxes/rich very negative 43% Immigrants very negative	25% NAFTA very neg 23% Raise taxes/rich very negative 30% Immigrants very negative
44% South	39% South	28% South	35% South	36% South

I listened to these GOP base voters in the summer of 2018 as Trump turned up the heat on the country.

THE TEA PARTY

The Tea Party supporters proudly share the ethos and passions that have dominated the party since 2010.[5] These are the voters that Trump was speaking to in his campaign rallies, and they are the only group of Republicans who responded to videos of his rallies with uncompromising enthusiasm. The Tea Party GOP were sick of the "PC-police" and loved that Trump was speaking his mind and driving liberals crazy. They were glad someone wasn't scared of liberal name-calling and would roll up his sleeves and get tough on issues like immigration, the Second Amendment, and taxes. The Tea Party base were motivated to stop Democrats and defend Donald Trump in the 2018 off-year elections and are rallying to Trump to lead their party in 2020.

They loved that this businessman president was producing such a strong economy and some of the lowest unemployment rates—and those were the biggest validators of their vote when they faced pushback from their family or at work.

IMMIGRATION AND MULTICULTURALISM

Immigration was the first issue mentioned when we asked these Tea Party GOP what were the "hot topics" with their families and friends. These group sessions were held in the weeks following President Trump's so-called reversal of the child-separation-at-the-border policy and their social media feeds were still dominated by conservative headlines that defended the hard line on immigration.

When asked what comes to mind when they think of immigrants to the United States, they went straight to illegal immigration, the border, and the need to get tough on enforcement.

> And if you don't do it [the legal] way, then I think you should be kicked out of the country. I think you should be deported. And that goes back to the children, and I really was kind of in the middle on that one, cause I really didn't know—cause you see it, kind of like what we were talking about, you see these children, and you see your own, you think oh gosh. But then I thought to myself, If I was

standing at the border with my ten-year-old kid, and they said you
can come in but he can't, I'd say forget it, we're not coming.

What I got real annoyed about is you turn on TV, turn it on to see
what the local news is, and stuff like that. And they have a picture of
people walking with the little hobo things, with the family, with the
picture of the American flag in the back of it. They're not Americans.
They're people crossing the border illegally.

They liked Trump and appreciated his views on immigration and
border security because "it made everyone on the left decide that they
were against it suddenly."

The Tea Party were the base voters most uncomfortable with
the country's growing diversity and ready to say it. Portrayals of a
multicultural America were reminders of demographic changes and
they took them personally. They felt Black Lives Matter was out of
control.

I had the moderator play in each of the groups a Coca-Cola Super
Bowl ad featuring "America the Beautiful" sung in several languages.
The reactions to this celebration of a multicultural America were mixed
or positive elsewhere in the GOP base, but not here. The Tea Party voters called it "political propaganda" and, instead of bringing Americans
together, "it just causes more conflict."

I get offended by it. What it's telling me is that as Americans, we
don't include people. Whereas if something goes wrong in the rest
of the world, where do they come? The United States of America to
help them out. It just seems rather tacky.

It's every commercial these days, whether it's—it's always in the
sporting event, or some huge event where people are trying to have
fun and then it's political ads showing in our face.

I feel like inclusion of culture in American is a great thing. But it's
showing that ad produces conflict on both sides. Because the left is
saying the right is not inclusive, and then the right is saying the left
thinks we're not inclusive.

The Tea Party GOP were very bothered that the song was not sung in English and complained, "those lyrics were written in English. They were not written in—whatever the hell they were—Spanish, or Indian, or any other language."

The Tea Party base resented Black Lives Matter. They thought the media sided with the protestors and failed to defend the police officers who were being killed. They resented that concerts and music were being politicized with lyrics depicting blacks as victims and police as villains. "The last song for the encore was this song, was a poem composition by somebody that named all of the people, the Freddie Gray and the Michael Brown all of that," one of the men in Raleigh lamented.

> And they are all onstage and they are trying to get the whole crowd, 5,000 people to say, "Michael Brown, Michael Brown, say his name, say his name." And this is in Durham, North Carolina, and I'm sitting there looking like holy crap this is driving me crazy. And it's like I didn't hear one—they went through about fifteen different names of either black men or black women that had been killed by police officers recently. I did not hear them say one name of one police officer that had gotten killed.

Another man asked the others, "How many times does something happen at Waffle House in a week or two where some drunk girl wanders into Waffle House and spits in somebody's face?" And then somebody makes a video on their phone, and then the media is on it:

> They rushed some girl out because she was Black. And everybody is up in arms and there is protests and there is all these stuff. And oh it turns out she was drunk and belligerent, threw something at somebody and they called the cops and they asked her to leave, and she refused and punched someone. But by then it's too late.

> They make a correction, but nobody pays attention because if it's something that doesn't fit the narrative then it's not interesting and they're not going to put any kind of emphasis on it.

The Tea Party base is deeply socially conservative, starting with abortion, but to them, the threat to their guns is nearly as central.

When asked what words or phrases came to mind when they thought of Planned Parenthood, they said they were "terrible" and "murderers." "They advertise that they do a lot of good stuff," said one man, "but there's been a lot of information that came out that they make money off body parts and do all kinds of crazy stuff." Another one said that if more white women were having abortions, then society would call it genocide.

They were viscerally uncomfortable with gay marriage. Some said it was an "abomination" and complained it "turns to propagating the acts, the sexual acts and leniency in our communities." One of the men pushed back. Some gay relatives "changed my mind about that" and "that's fine if that's what makes them, those two people happy." But openness was pretty isolated.

Protecting guns produced the most animated defense of the Second Amendment. They felt that with all of the school shootings, their gun rights were even more at risk. "One thing I've seen a lot, I feel like it really is under threat. Every time there is a school shooting now—kids got shot, that's terrible and now we've got get to rid of all guns," said one Tea Party man. Another exclaimed, "People will walk all over you if you are not PC, if you are not politically correct."

That is why the open seat on the Supreme Court was so important for them. I listened to these Tea Party GOP the day after Brett Kavanaugh's nomination, as they reported "90 percent of the people on Facebook, that's what they're posting about." For many it was a reminder of one of the most important reasons for voting for Donald Trump. They stressed it was "very important" for this nomination to succeed "because the Supreme Court, really, in the last twenty years has become so much more politicized than it used to be" and they "realize that the major successes from the left have come from activist judges." The Tea Party voters wanted to see "more constitutional conservatives" and Brett Kavanaugh was their chance to appoint "someone who interprets the laws" and "not someone who thinks they can make the laws."

With his nomination they felt satisfied that the Supreme Court would now stand with them on abortion and the Second Amendment.

THE PC POLICE AND PRESIDENT TRUMP FIGHTS BACK

The Tea Party GOP were sick and tired of being told they are not politically correct. For them, it is the PC liberals and the media, not people like them, who are responsible for all the division in America. In my September 2018 poll for Women's Voices Women Vote Action Fund, 72 percent of Tea Party voters said the liberal media is the institution that most threatens their beliefs—higher than for all other GOP groups.[6]

They were thankful that President Trump has the backbone to say what they are all thinking, unlike typical politicians. When Donald Trump was on the campaign trail pumping up the audiences at his rallies, these were the Republicans cheering him on.

The Tea Party men in Raleigh felt under siege for their "politically incorrect" views. They complained that liberals were constantly changing the goalposts on them.

"Socialists attack the conservative viewpoints and find any area they can to say that conservatives" are constantly facing changing liberal standards, "and they can change their views any which way they want," one man complained. Many of them felt that on issues like race and sex, liberals had taken things so far they defy common sense. "Ten years ago people were bisexuals, now its six genders," said one Tea Party man. They were especially sensitive to being called racist. At the time of these groups, for example, they accused liberals of saying "all conservatives are racists for supporting the separation of the immigration stuff."

These Tea Party men complained that they were the victims of a double standard: it was okay for liberals who are "so worried about people's feelings" to harass people who disagree with them:

> It seems like we have very intolerant people in our society right now. People that consider themselves to be the most tolerant people, but yet, if you're anything conservative, anything on the right, they don't want to hear it.

I think that the left or the Democrats are always talking about . . . transgender acceptance. But they're only accepting if you believe what they believe. If you don't believe what they believe, then they don't want to hear that. They've always been the party that's talking about acceptance, and when you get somebody that's a conservative going to a college campus and then you see a riot by the people in the college campus, it just goes crazy.

Being a student at NC State, I don't post any political stuff on social media. My family doesn't either because of a lot of the hard core or liberals will make you feel ashamed to be conservative because of all the crazy things they say conservatives do.

I would say it's a cultural thing that's being promulgated by our leadership, whether it's in schools and government. Yeah. When you've got a sitting representative telling people to go and harass political opponents that you disagree with.

When I asked their reaction to the NFL protests, they quickly turned to how fearful they were of being punished for their political views. They felt they had to walk on eggshells and honestly worried that they could lose their jobs or leadership roles for their views, even in North Carolina.

We've now got the thought police and the word police out there. If you say the wrong thing, if someone looks on my Facebook account and sees that I post a view that, for some reason, irritates somebody, I can lose my livelihood. My daughter doesn't get fed. My wife doesn't get fed. That's just not right.

I'm in a student organization so I have a leadership position at school. So when somebody in my organization sees it and is not really fond of what I'm saying, they don't agree with it, then of course they can go to somebody in the office or whoever and say, "This guy is being racist because he is posting conservative viewpoints on Facebook."

Working at NC State, I mean, a lot of people I work with, most of the people I work with are very, very liberal and I'm very, very conservative and I have to really be careful what I say around the office. It's like in the office if I said, "Man, Trump is doing great," I can guarantee you I'd have three or four people on me. Not physically on me but verbally just coming after me.

It led many to censor themselves on social media.

The pushback against conservatives and Trump voters led them to map who in a certain group of friends or family members was "conservative" and who was "liberal." They filtered out non-conservative news outlets where their views were under attack. They were the biggest fans of Fox News. They said it was the "only option, right now, really" because "they at least give the [conservative] guy a chance to talk."

Maybe the single most appealing thing about President Trump to the Tea Party base was the way he unapologetically expresses what they all think but are too afraid to say. They enjoyed watching moments when he gives the media and liberals what they called "Trump derangement syndrome." The liberals are losing their heads on social media, spreading disinformation, and "calling him a Nazi." "He could literally cure cancer and they'd scream about it," but Trump has the backbone to take it.

"I finally since Ronald Reagan feel that there is somebody in there that is not going to take any crap and he's willing to take all the crap and have everybody left be all over him and every media outlet be all over him," said one man. Now "there is a large population of people that feel like their views are valid again. I mean people who have views that have been deemed unpopular," and it all started "the day Donald Trump went down that escalator."

This was the one group in which some of the men took up his disparaging remarks toward women during the presidential campaign. "You want equal everything, well, here's equal," said one man. "It's just dirty. Politics are dirty in general. I mean we used to duel over it."

They appreciated having a president projecting toughness on the world stage. Like the Evangelical conservatives, the Tea Party GOP thought that Obama was weak and other countries did not respect us, while Donald Trump was commanding respect on the world stage. Other countries were put "before America because of political correctness."

And now, I feel like Donald Trump puts America's values in security before the opinions of other countries.

Back in the Obama era, where, let's sit and drink a beer, we'll talk it over and you're all worked out. Where I think we need somebody like that, that is going to make somebody mad, like over at NATO, you're not paying your fair share, you need to pay your fair share, cause we're not footing the bill for everybody.

He demonstrates strength for our country.

TRUMP'S TEA PARTY RALLIES

President Trump spoke to the Tea Party base in his rallies, and those in my groups shouted repeatedly, "I love that." For them, it defined Trump and an urgent call to action.

"He speaks his mind, [is] not afraid of criticism, and drives liberals crazy." It reinforced their feeling that he is more trustworthy than other politicians. "He can afford to go out there and say exactly what he thinks and if it makes people mad, it just kind of bounces off of him," because "he's not so worried about, am I going to get reelected," because he is already so wealthy that he is not trying to "stay in politics to get a ton of money and get all the benefits of a retired politician."

A few wished he wouldn't tweet and had a smoother style, but they got to why they thought he had strong support:

Well, he's uplifting. He's definitely selling his brand to his base, and he's backing it up.

You can see that he actually believes what he's saying. He's not—it doesn't come off like he's saying something that he thinks he's supposed to say. Especially like it could be a little bit of his style, but he'll come off and he'll actually say something that obviously wasn't written on the paper, right?

The Tea Party base voters were desperate to keep Democrats from coming back in power. They said the Democratic Party had become socialist and too extreme and they can't imagine anything positive will happen if they were to regain power.

Well, if you want socialism and all of us other Americans to be equal while he lives in his big nice mansion. At least one.

[Nancy Pelosi] represents what's wrong, generally, with the Democratic Party and between her and Maxine Waters, it's just everything is no. If you like it, I don't. It doesn't matter what it is. If I liked it before, and you like it now? I don't like it anymore.

Congresswoman Maxine Waters was a focus for many of these Tea Party GOP, surely because she is African American and perhaps because she is the most vocal advocate for impeaching President Trump.

In 2018, the Tea Party GOP were motivated to turn out and to vote for Republicans, not because they supported the Republican Party or the GOP congressional leaders, but because they wanted to defend Donald Trump. They said it was more important than ever to vote in the off-year because they need "to maintain the momentum" of Donald Trump's election:

> Because for one, to maintain the momentum. Because I feel like that last election was an eye opener for a lot of people. Because a lot of people that probably would not have normally gone out and voted, voted because they were motivated to do so by Trump and by Hillary Clinton. And so if this same group of people aren't motivated equally to go out and do that same thing this year, then we lose all momentum and then it doesn't matter nearly as much what happens in 2020.

They did just that and helped President Trump defeat Red State Democrats, but the loss of control in the House more than slowed the momentum—as the government ground to an absolute halt over Trump's bizarre insistence that the Democratic House fund his border wall.

Post-session postcards to Donald Trump

Keep pushing for illegal immigration enforcement, tax reform, and an improved healthcare system. Always be yourself but maybe tone it down a bit.

Mr. Trump, Continue the good work. Keep your eye on the ball and please run for re-election in 2020. You will have Carl's vote.

Keep putting America's well being in front of the opinions of the other countries. Keep our border secure but also be accepting to other cultures.

President Trump, thank you for bringing real hope back to America. Obama sold us a false "hope" based on socialism. You have brought us a hope based on capitalism and love of country. Thank you for standing up for America.

President Trump, I would like you to know that Middle America really appreciates what you have done and are say to do for all of us.

Continue the good job, focus on jobs, trade, improve infrastructure, threat less and keep the majority in the Congress.

Thanks for helping our country get back to being America. Thanks for helping the vets.

Stay the course, we have your back.

THE EVANGELICALS

One in four of the base are Evangelicals, and they are the biggest faction. The women I talked to in North Carolina came from the smaller towns outside Raleigh.[7] They are the quintessential values voters at the core of the GOP who now look to President Donald Trump as a leader who is finally defending their values. Their conservatism is defined by their religious faith, which puts them on the defensive in a country that is increasingly liberal, secular, and politicized.

About 40 percent in my poll in September 2018 said they had to be cautious about people knowing their views. A third said atheists and people who don't share their faith are now the biggest challenge to their values.[8] So, not surprisingly, the moderator intervened to assure them they did not have to be apologetic about their social conservatism.

For all Trump's unchristian behavior and style, the Evangelical GOP thank President Trump for sticking to his guns, to their social agenda, and for appointing socially conservative judges. They welcome his pushing back against liberalism after eight years of Obama and the failure of the GOP establishment. That is why the stakes are so high in the off-year elections and why they will be cadres in the battle to defend the Trump presidency.

THE STAKES

The Evangelicals' conservatism is rooted in their religious faith, and half said they discussed policy issues like abortion with members of their congregation. They were unambiguous in their opposition to abortion. Several of these women said they could never vote for a candidate, even a Republican, who was pro-choice because it "went against my belief system." About half said that they were "torn" on the issue of gay marriage, but only because they questioned whether the government should "have their hands in" a religious institution like marriage in the first place. (Ironically, they pointed to how the government had criminalized interracial marriage as an example of why government should not interfere.) In any case, they always came back to gay marriage as "against my religious beliefs."

Being a conservative is a central part of their identity. These women came to understand that they were in our focus group to discuss politics, yet none called themselves Republicans. Instead, they defined themselves as conservatives many times throughout the evening and identified family members or friends as conservatives (or not) as well.

> My son shares similar views, conservative views. But my daughter is—she went to UNC Ashford. I don't need to say any more.

> My daughter lives in Pennsylvania and her husband—they're very conservative also.

> I have most of my friends and family on Facebook, they're all conservative and I think there's only about two cousins that aren't.

These Evangelical women believed they are now outnumbered by the secular-liberal younger generation and that their values are under attack from the mainstream media, educators, and Trump's opponents.

A recent local news story about a man assaulting a child for wearing a "Make America Great Again" hat was illustrative of the threat.

> It's the gentleman who yanked the hat off that sixteen-year-old boy and then dumped soda on it. I mean for what reason? He had on a MAGA hat. My child has a MAGA hat and he will not wear it out because, well, most of his friends are not conservative.

Because these Evangelical GOP base voters feel their values are under attack, they have made their worlds smaller by unfollowing those who disagree on social media, by making a rule of not discussing politics with some family members, and even by canceling cable. Their guards were up so much that the moderator eventually had to reassure them that they were in a room of like-minded people where they were free to speak their minds without apology.

DONALD TRUMP IS DEFENDING THEM AND THEY ARE DEFENDING HIM

The Evangelical GOP understood their values are out of fashion and increasingly outnumbered, yet most felt hopeful about the future of the country because conservatives are led by a "president that's a fighter, and the country hasn't seen that for a long, long, long time." The GOP establishment has disappointed them again and again.

Finally, they felt that conservatives are "on a good roll." Part of this is psychological: after eight years of "feeling lost" under President Obama, Donald Trump is unapologetically defending their values and vision of America, which gives them hope. Part of this is about their policy agenda: they felt that the country was "turning away" from conservative policies during the Obama presidency, but now their "issues are actually being addressed." For these reasons it was incredibly important for the Evangelical GOP to defend President Trump and to stop the Democrats in the November 2018 elections.

The Evangelical GOP women of Raleigh believe there has been a massive improvement in the country over the past year and a half. Just look at their postcards thanking Donald Trump at the end of the night! (See p. 137.) Some pointed to the economy as evidence:

More people are working. And my 401k is doing fabulous.

As far as economics, just how the country seems to be progressing towards more jobs and things like that.

I do think he's a smart, as far as business, good businessman and everything because I think that is something we needed at the time to help in our economic growth. Since Bush, since everybody, it's just the jobs just seem like there wasn't any, and then how much job growth we've gotten over the last few months.

Another mentioned progress on the border: "I feel like issues are actually being addressed. That stuff isn't being skirted around. Issues, whether it's agreed upon or not, about the border and immigration."

The greatest improvement in their minds was in America's standing on the world stage. They attributed this entirely to Donald Trump's "strength" and "patriotism."

Well, Obama took the apology tour and that was just bringing our country down across the board. So we really needed Trump to bring it back out from that. Our standing in the world has increased, whereas some people would say it has not but I believe that we are more respected because of the strength of Trump.

I think our country before Trump was almost a laughingstock and we'd never been that. So to have Trump be able to stand up to that image that was portrayed is completely opposite from what Hillary would've brought to the play.

He doesn't cave in to those that—I put down evildoers, those who make threats to him.

They believe that Donald Trump "cares about America truly" and once again, "patriotism's back."

Judicial appointments could not be more important and they could not be more satisfied with Trump's performance, or where the stakes were as high. The Supreme Court is so important because of their feelings about abortion: "I mean because of our religious beliefs,

Roe v. Wade is very important to me and, you know, having the people that are in place that feel as I do is a good thing for me." But that is just "one of many" issues in front of the court that they care about. Specifically, they also said they wanted to protect the Second Amendment.

Many in the base of the GOP held their noses and voted for Donald Trump because of the Supreme Court, including the husband of one of the women in the group. "My husband was unsure who he was voting for [. . .] and he didn't like either choice," she explained, "but he said, 'You don't know how this can affect our country down the road after he's out of the office' regarding nominating judges, and that was the—that's what convinced him to vote."

Their bargain paid off. They are thankful that Trump appointed a conservative like Neil Gorsuch to the Supreme Court and reacted enthusiastically to a video of Trump talking about his opportunity to fill a second vacancy.

> [Judges] are there to interpret the law and not make their own laws according to what the party in charge wants. That's what Donald Trump is doing, [that is who] he's picking.
>
> Really, instead of [the] Constitution in our country, there's a lot of activism going on. So sometimes it seems to me that politics are infused with these activist things. So, I think [Trump] was barking those sentiments at the conservatives he was speaking to there [at the rally] because those are the things that feel threatened and I think he was trying to say, had Hillary won, she might've put an activist judge rather than an institutional judge.

Ensuring Donald Trump's conservative nominees were appointed was more important than Republicans maintaining control of Congress in the midterms: "I think we have a lot on the line with, we talked about the Supreme Court justices and all those kind of things and I think these people that we move into position are part of that plan."

THE DEVIL AND DONALD TRUMP

These Evangelical Christians admitted that Donald Trump set a less than holy example. He is not a "good Christian man" like Mike Pence.

But they were willing to put up with those parts of the Trump package because he was appointing conservative justices to the Supreme Court, had the backbone to defend their conservative values and policy priorities, and had the patriotism to stand up for America on the world stage.

They were not as enthusiastic as you might have expected watching video clips of Donald Trump talking about his accomplishments because, like many other Republicans, these Evangelical conservatives had reservations about how Donald Trump expresses himself and his lack of self-control.

He's annoying. Drives me nuts.

He doesn't think before he speaks sometimes.

Sometimes he is repetitive.

He can be disrespectful, but the same time, you don't want someone who hesitates, you don't want someone who's going to be afraid to say what he thinks either.

Wish he didn't Twitter so much.

Those concerns were closely connected to worries about his lack of humility: he "makes petty comments unnecessarily about trivial things, and then I put his ego because it seems like sometimes it's too big, therefore he comments. I feel like it's an evil cycle for him."

It the end, Trump's style and shameless self-promotion were helpful weapons in the culture war. In the end, the women excused his braggadocio campaign stump speech because they think it helps him get around the unfair media coverage.

If he didn't toot [his own horn], who would?

True.

I agree with you.

That's true.

The media's not going to do that, at least not the liberal media.

This allowed him to be more successful than other politicians who are "too reserved" to lead this way: "When you have someone that's more soft-spoken that doesn't toot his own horn, the media's going to bash him either way."

And you might think watching Donald Trump making offensive and lewd remarks about women might pause these social conservatives, but not for a second. They were quick to steer condemnation away from Trump and there was no erosion in their support.

> I mean in the past Bill Clinton. I think he—I mean that was degrading to women and that's another example of [Trump] speaking what he's thinking but I'm neutral. I mean like I said, he doesn't actually mean anything. I'm, you know, confident.

> And the thing is, if that's the worst that they could find on him is that they—he said something bad, not that he did something bad as opposed to sort of like what Bill Clinton did. He did something bad, you know.

> His words get him in trouble and women happen to be the issue and so again, the media or whoever is going to hone in on that issue so it just happens to be amplified.

The Evangelical GOP made a deal with the devil, and they are all-in. In their postcards to Donald Trump, they thanked him for putting the country on the right track and said they were praying for him.

Post-session postcards to Donald Trump

> Thank you for making America great again. Please continue with the action items promised at election. I like the patriotism that you are bringing back to America.

> Dear President Trump, I wanted to let you know how proud you have made me. Your love for this country stands out among other presidents—thank you so much for your salary donations—the VA is in great need of funds! Our family prays for you and your family—may God bless.

Thank you for leading our country in the right direction. You are doing a great job. It is good to see the jobs and economy grow. So good you are not allowing the USA to be disrespected.

Dear Mr. President, Thank you for your hard work. I pray that you continue in your efforts to help make America great. Always remember that your position is important because of our nation and its people not just on occupation. All of your actions and attitudes are seen. I pray grace and wisdom for you always.

You have done a great job and "We the People" truly appreciate [you] Gods [sic] Blessings to you and your family.

Thank you President Trump for leading our country in a more positive direction. I look forward to voting for you again in 2020. You have made an HUGE difference and for the better.

Thank you for rooting for our country. Thank you for the support you give to our military and police who protect our country. You [sic] strength as a leader will hopefully bring the US back to the highest standing in the world has us as a country who has gained the world's respect.

Dear Mr. President, I am grateful for the stance you've taken in our country to help make it great again. I appreciate the backbone and audacity you continually and tirelessly have. I am praying that you will continue to be surrounded by God's best and that only decisions that have Him are made.

CATHOLIC CONSERVATIVES

The debates among the conservative Catholics in this moderated group sounded a lot like the debate in the country that moved many pro-life, socially conservative, patriotic Catholics to trek to the GOP, particularly in the Midwest and Northeast. That took me to Macomb County, Michigan, to talk with a group of Catholic conservative men.[9] The participants reflected that history: seven in ten were fifty or older and held traditional blue-collar jobs in the auto industry, mechanics, and construction. But they also reflected the recent tumultuous changes in the Catholic Church.

Consequently, the dynamics among Catholics could not be more different from any other group that rallied to protect President Trump in the 2018 election and might respond very differently in a post-Trump era. Like other conservative groups, they applauded the president for appointing social conservatives to the U.S. Supreme Court. But the Catholics were the only economic populists in the GOP base, and they cheered louder than all the others Trump's calling out of corporations that failed to invest in America and trashing trade agreements that failed to put America first.

The conservative Catholics were the most fractured group and literally fell into a brawl that had to be mediated by the moderator. They were deeply divided by their brands of Catholicism, one aligned with Pope Francis and the other with Fox News. The differences played out in the open and heated disagreement flared on immigration, multiculturalism, guns, regulation, the environment and climate change, the special prosecutor, and 2020.

THE GOP'S LONELY ECONOMIC POPULISTS

The conservative Catholic GOP described an economy where jobs don't pay like they did in the past, CEOs are greedy, and trade agreements are killing American jobs. That description of the economy sounds more familiar as a Democratic critique of the economy, but Democrats were not seen as battling for the working class in their world.

The conservative Catholics pushed back when the moderator played a video of Donald Trump touting job growth, stock market gains, and tax cuts at a campaign rally. They just refuted his assertions: these were not good-paying jobs and those new jobs don't pay what they used to.

> Some of the stuff is very positive. Speaking with [North] Korea is
> a fantastic achievement. 300,000 jobs back, though—if you're
> out there looking for jobs, what you're finding are not very
> good-paying jobs. And that's part of the problem. Those are part of
> the numbers and there are jobs out there that younger people need
> to start off with. But I was laid off from a good job eight years ago,
> and the jobs and the stuff that's coming back is a lot of the jobs

that I was finding. They were $9, $10 an hour, and that was with zero benefits. And that's where a lot of those numbers are coming from.

They sounded so much like voters I listened to in groups two years into the Obama presidency when they watched President Obama talk about the number of jobs that had been created, his saving of the auto industry, and the dependable recovery.

Like then, the Catholics focused on wages and the cost of living, especially the cost of insurance.

I'm concerned with the costs of living as opposed to the wage increases. I just think it's getting way too out of hand. Back in the 80s, $4 got you so much more than what 12 dollars nowadays will get you. And there's so much more back then.

I was talking to my mother about this the other week. We didn't—they didn't have to deal with high water bills, high utilities, cell phones, multiple cell phone bills, the higher car insurance. Just on and on and on. We'll bundle for internet and cable—it's just how it stacks up.

Just insurance in general, car insurance. We have the highest rates of any state in the union.

Health insurance is the same.

They pointed out that they had not received pay raises in many years and that the new jobs paid less than before.

When they heard the phrase "CEOs of large companies," they blurted out "very greedy" and said they received "outrageous" bonuses, even when they ran their companies into bankruptcy. One man recalled in detail the employment history and compensation of Bob Nardelli from General Electric to Home Depot to Chrysler, bewildered how someone could fail up so spectacularly.

When it came to trade, they were Trump's first audience for renegotiating NAFTA, "the biggest mistake out of the Clinton Administration." They were relieved that Trump was the first leader to get serious about trade agreements that had taken such a toll.

That is where their unity ended.

Half the group praised Donald Trump for fighting back against the liberal Democrats attacking their values. They were the most enthusiastic about Donald Trump and his policies. They sounded like base Republicans where Trump and Fox News are the defining dimension. They half sounded like they had Fox-crafted talking points ready when they needed to come to Trump's defense on everything from the Mueller investigation and immigration to Trump's treatment of women and kneeling NFL athletes. They were the ones who said the ugliest things about immigrants, people of different races and religions, and multiculturalism. They did not just disagree with Democrats and President Obama, they said they were evil: "I think that the Obama administration that was, it was the devil kind of party."

The Fox Catholic half reacted with enthusiasm to Trump's rallies and embraced the Fox News facts on issue after issue in his defense, and my moderator had to hold these Fox News Catholics back when they disagreed with their fellow Catholics in the group.

The other half, who might have been inspired by Pope Francis and his brand of Catholicism, expressed great concern about the level of social division in the country. The resulting partisan polarization had seeped down to their communities, workplaces, social media feeds, and even their families. And they faulted both parties for the polarization, though they wished President Trump would be more respectful and less divisive.

They condemned President Trump for his treatment of women and doubted he was a good role model.

They were open to centrist compromises on immigration, the environment, and gun control, most of all on the environment. The duty to be good stewards of the globe was raised early in the discussion.

> I think our greatest threat is potentially the environment. If we're not careful with it, and if you don't protect the environment, then you don't have life on the planet.

> So it is a vitally important topic. So you gotta protect the trees and the water and the things that you actually need to exist on this planet. And without that, it's the end of mankind.

They were united by their agreement on abortion and working-class economic populism, but both blocs argued bravely against the other's arguments and facts. The moderator had to intervene in each, as the Fox Catholics in particular were not used to this argument among Trump voters.

THE ARGUMENT OVER IMMIGRATION AND MULTICULTURALISM

For many Catholic conservatives, Trump's getting tough on immigration was the major reason for supporting him and one of his biggest accomplishments as president.

This was the only group in which people's complaints about immigration centered on unfair competition with American contractors and workers for jobs. "Statistically, they go get jobs we don't get, but it's stereotyping that they will work for less wages," said one man who "just got outbid out of a roof deal a week ago because of Mexican undocumented people did the roof $1,000 cheaper, but they wanted to use my workman's comp because they didn't have it." Several had read a story on social media that "refugees get funding for starting businesses here in the U.S.," and complained, "us Americans that already live here, born and raised here, don't get the opportunity." That is one reason it was so important to them that immigrants come here legally:

> There's paperwork and we know about some of them. The other ones, we have no idea about. There's a big difference.

> And they take jobs away from us. That's just one piece of it, and create crimes and other things.

But legal immigration, the child-separation policy, and multiculturalism were flash points in these groups. The Fox News Catholic conservatives were uncomfortable with the growing diversity in the country, wanted less immigration period, and repeated the Fox lines about child separation at the border. They were responsible for most of the ugliest quotes about immigrants and people of different races and faiths in this GOP research. One man explained that Colin Kaepernick's girlfriend had instructed him to kneel during the national anthem, and if you do your research and "find out the nationality she is, she's Muslim."

But the Pope Francis Catholics pushed back to defend legal immigrants, a vision of a multicultural America as a country of immigrants, and even advocated against Trump's child-separation immigration policy. When asked about the threats facing our country, one of these men said we were threatened by "too much immigration" and suggested we "export them all"; he immediately received pushback from another man, who said, "Illegal immigration. Immigration is good. We're [a country founded on] immigration."

The separated families were top of mind for these Trump-conflicted Catholics: "Everybody's concern[ed] with the families being torn apart and the children not being with their maternal parents and being displaced and the concern over how they're gonna resolve it."

After I played them a video of a Catholic bishop arguing against the policy on religious grounds, the two factions sparred over whether it was moral to divide children at the border from their parents or not:

> There is a gray area with that, because you let them break the law. Other people are going to see that it's OK to break the law.

> I mean, most people are humane. So, I'm sure these people at the border that are separating these families are doing the best they can.

> Well, they didn't just decide to do this. And you knew—and they knew they were coming over here that there was a chance that this was going to happen.

> They're taking them until they know what's going on and these parents are, do they have any kind of diseases, stuff like that.

> I totally understand what he was coming across with. And I consider it kidnapping. You know, to take a child away from a mother or father, whoever and put them somewhere where they're isolated away from their parents. That's just cruelty. I mean, the parents don't know where the kids are. The kids are crying because they don't know where the parents are. And like I say it's, if you did it it'd be kidnapping.

Well, they do it here. I mean there are so many parents that are incarcerated for breaking the law, and their kids go to foster care.

The two factions also had a heated exchange over whether the child-separation policy was "discriminatory" because "Canada is another border, [but] you don't see that happening there. It's only with Mexico." The Trump-Fox Catholics rushed to respond that "that's bulls***" because "people aren't flooding across our [northern] borders illegally."

A Coca-Cola Super Bowl ad featuring "America the Beautiful" sung in different languages started a debate about the nature of the country and its future. Probably half thought it was too political, disagreed with it, and said that they should learn English; that America has changed because so many don't learn the language; that "when I was a kid we'd have one of the masses in Polish on Sunday."

> It *was* the melting pot of the world because people are not melting
> . . . they're bringing in their cultures with them and staying localized. Because in my opinion—in my opinion there is—yeah, brace yourself, people—but immigration without assimilation is tantamount to an invasion.
>
> If you're going to come to America and just—that's the whole thing I don't agree with. Is you guys come here to America and you want to change our beliefs. But you guys came in *here*.
>
> We ran into the issue with terrorism and people coming over here illegally. I say, I still think we have to be the country that accepts people—in under our laws. And assimilating is important. I don't— my family, when they came over and they had a green card and it took some time before, you know—we were all real hard-core Americans, but eventually it happened. That's what I think a lot of people are afraid of, not [happening].

A lot of this was wrapped up in not speaking English—or, as one man said, "You should speak American." These men complained they were being forced to adapt, rather than the other way around:

"Now, you're changing, telling us that we're middle-aged men and women that we have to be re-educated in a different foreign language in our homeland that we grew up as an American, our first language is English?"

But a vocal minority made an argument that America is defined and united by its immigrant history and not by the prevailing ethnicity or language of its people. "America's the melting pot of the world," one man explained. "Is anybody in here Native American?" another asked, because, "Somebody came from somewhere, another country, and you have the right to live here." Another man who "grew up in a Polish neighborhood" and attended "one of the masses in Polish on Sunday" raised his hand to push back against their opinion that "it's become a jigsaw puzzle" and not a melting pot: "I understand that culture tends to build a community together, whether it's Polish, Italian, Irish, what have you, and that's obviously going to be a part of peoples' ethnicity or whatever or their heritage." They explain that "the times are changing" and "it's never going to go back," so they might as well get used to the growing number of immigrants from Latin America and Asian countries "melting with the United States."

THE CONFLICT OVER TRUMP'S SCANDALS

After viewing a video of Trump making offensive comments about other women while campaigning, most of the Trump-Fox Catholics excused it as just men being men.

We've all done or said similar.

Oh worse. Worse.

Yes, we're not any better or any worse than him, we're males. We have it inbred in us. That's how we are. Maybe not to certain extents, give or take, but that's how we are.

Another found a way to implicate Hillary Clinton and Michelle Obama as well: "I think that works both ways. I'm sure if they dug up dirt on Hillary about her comments about men, or Michelle Obama, I'm sure they would find them."

But the majority of the men believed Trump's comments were "demeaning to anybody that's a female." Trump's comments about Heidi Cruz and Melania Trump especially offended their sensibilities as husbands.

> Well, I've been married forty-nine years, and I find that offensive.

> My wife would know I'd—never say anything like that. Not a chance.

> I think it's immature. I think it's immature at that his wife where he was at. He doesn't have to fight these kind of battles. He doesn't have to do that. And I wouldn't want to see any president doing that stuff like that. But I am just—there was no reason to attack somebody else's wife for that.

> He's not even showing respect for his own wife. That's the part I can't understand.

This was the context in which watching videos of President Trump brought out the harshest criticism of his personality. These Catholics wanted a president to be a moral leader, too: "We should be looking up to him. He's the CEO of this country. We should respect him and he should be setting an example for every other family."

THE CONFLICT OVER RUSSIA

Many in the conservative Catholic base also responded strongly to potential conclusions of the special counsel's Russia investigation. In open-ended associations, one person said that Robert Mueller had "been appointed to take care of a very important subject" and "somebody needs to find out" about what the Russians did because "we just can't let some people do things improper that affect elections."

To be sure, most Fox News Catholics had their Fox talking points about the Russia probe down!

> Had Hillary Clinton won we wouldn't have found out about all the corruption in the Department of Justice.

Most of the Democratic Party and the powers that be pushing this. I just don't see—I don't see how the Russians had any impact on me throughout any of this.

Well, to me it goes bad when Obama was president before his second election, he was caught with his microphone saying to the Russians leader, wait till I get reelected, we'll really get things accomplished. And nothing was ever brought up about that except for that day or two. And I thought Hillary had off like a whole bunch of stuff tied to the Russians as well. So, and then there was all these dealings with, was it Obama, trying to get Iran tons of money before he left the presidency. And I'm just like, where is all those investigations. I just feel like they're really trying to push Trump out of office any way they can.

And a lot of people gloss over the fact that it was Rob Rosenstein recommended to Trump that he fire Comey.

But a significant minority also took seriously a hypothetical scenario in which the special counsel indicts Trump's campaign leadership for conspiring with Russia and reports to Congress that Trump obstructed justice, saying that if there was proof, then "let the currents fall where they may. It's about accepting responsibility," including possible impeachment. That response even came to include part of the Trump-Fox conservative Catholics: "I wrote, proof, proof, proof. And indictments right now are nothing more than party politics that I'm seeing. And if proof does come up, if these people were included at some point, Donald Trump, Jr., somebody's got to pay for it, Manafort. There has got to be some jail time." They said that if this were to happen, then "the Congress needs to be honest." So, like the moderates, some in this bloc of the GOP wanted leaders to be a check on President Trump.

2018 AND BEYOND

None of these older, religiously observant, pro-life Catholic economic populists would entertain voting for a Democrat in 2018. In fact, the Trump-Fox–motivated Catholic conservatives were very eager to support

Republicans in 2018, to defend Donald Trump and his agenda. They were excited by his base strategy and are the audience for his campaign rallies. All of the Catholics approved of Trump's performance on the economy and his push for new trade agreements.

But some in the summer were less motivated by the base buttons Trump was pushing. They could not forget the other ways in which he had divided the country and failed to set a moral example. In the survey, they were less likely to strongly approve of Trump, and they were less likely to vote in the midterm by a significant amount. One in five in the survey believed there needed to be accountability after hearing possible scenarios of indictments.

In 2020, when Donald Trump is on the ballot again, some of the Catholics could peel off. Some mentioned that Governor John Kasich had accomplished a lot in Ohio but also that he "is Christian and moral." One brave soul was already prepared to say he would never vote for Trump again because "President Trump has too many personal issues and beliefs that are negative and destructive to this country." He explained that he just refused to compromise his "personal beliefs."

SECULAR CONSERVATIVES

Secular conservatives are a fifth of the GOP base. They are genuinely ideological conservatives who are mostly religiously unaffiliated or nonobservant. They are more traditional conservatives on small government, trade, and taxes and have aligned with the GOP establishment in the past.

All of them supported Trump's tax cuts, deregulation, and conservative Supreme Court picks, and most thought the economy was moving in the right direction. A sizable minority embraced President Trump and repeated the Fox News narrative about the country. But the majority were turned off by Trump's protectionist policies, the way he badgers private businesses, his tendency to overclaim, and his inability to act presidential. That led them to pull back rather than contest the current direction of the party.

President Trump used his rallies to speak to Republican base voters, but most of the secular conservative men held back after watching clips of Trump speaking on the campaign trail. They were just turned off by Trump's personality and confrontational style, so they were not as motivated as Evangelicals and Tea Party Republicans to defend Trump in the off-year elections. They were not as invested in the culture war of the Evangelicals and Tea Party supporters or as desperate to stop the Democrats from taking control. They did not have much use for the Democrats, but nor did they feel motivated to protect President Trump in the 2018 off-year. Some might support a third-party candidate in 2020, if that is an option.

WEARING THEIR GOP HAT

All the secular conservatives liked that someone with "business savvy" was "running [the] USA as a businessman as opposed to a politician." They were thrilled with the "booming" economy, noting the stock market growth and the "record low unemployment." They considered the tax cuts—which they labeled "tax reform"—and cuts to regulations on businesses huge successes.

They applauded Trump for "top-notch" nominations to the Supreme Court. They appreciated that he had nominated conservatives who will "hold up the Constitution" instead of activist judges taking power from the Congress and the states.

Most secular conservatives thought that Trump was making progress on national security, particularly with respect to North Korea. They called his summit with Kim Jong-un "a crazy big step for that country and this country."

They all believed that Trump "genuinely cared about this country" because he was selflessly "losing money" by getting involved in politics instead of staying in business. A few secular conservatives excused Trump's cockiness as an act that lets him get things done because he isn't a politician.

> I think *because* of his attitude he's able to come to the table and say, "We're going to get this shit done," and most people are like, "All right."

> I think that same style that I even find distasteful and polarizing and create doubts in my mind, are actually what are still working for him.

At the very least they said it was a good thing that Trump is "assertive."

Unfortunately for President Trump and the GOP, most of the secular conservatives wanted more than victories on policy issues: there was a strong desire for a return to conservative convictions and leadership style.

TRUMP'S LEADERSHIP STYLE

When asked to write their doubts about Donald Trump, the secular conservatives went directly to his unorthodox, unpresidential behavior and speech and did not hold back. "I really don't like Donald Trump," said one man, "I don't like his style." They called him an "egomaniac" and wished "he would just keep his mouth shut."

Trump's freewheeling, confrontational approach to communication riles up his Evangelical and Tea Party base, who said it set him apart from other politicians in a good way, but it made it hard for many secular conservatives to defend Trump's presidency: "It's phenomenal to see a business acumen in the White House, but then to see the same a**hat writing stuff on Twitter about prostitutes and this, that, and the other, it's a tough dichotomy for me to really be all-in."

The limits of Trump's appeal to secular conservatives were evident in this exchange in reaction to a video of him touting his accomplishments at a campaign rally. They felt the need to qualify their praise for the policy successes.

> **John.** I don't care about what he has to say. I don't care about where we're at right now. His term's not over, so, that he's accomplishing all this crap is ridiculous. It's short-lived right now. There's a long way to go. If he thinks he's going to run and get elected again, that's great, but I don't know, I just, I—the dude can't even say nuclear, he says "nucular," and it's so frustrating to live in a world like this now. Where people are just so ignorant and dumb.

> **Howard.** It's contrived statements. I mean, Make America Great Again was his platform like his hats, tee shirts, banner ads everywhere, and now, America is Great [is his new slogan in

2020]? Whatever the hell he said, I don't know. I mean, again, I'm very 50-50 on it because I completely agree with what John just said—it's short-lived, because he's only been in for a year and a half, pushing two, I mean, it is short-lived at this point. But also, like what has happened, has been a huge economical turn. Whether you play around with investing on your phone or your multi-millions are in the market, you've seen a positive bump. Significant.

Bill. Not this year.

Howard. Well, we did take a hit early in the year.

Bill. I mean, I think his North Korea thing was taking the victory lap too soon. They have not denuclearized. It's not an official treaty, what they did. The president doesn't have the power to make an official treaty. It's in the Constitution, it's Congress. But at the same time, he does tout his achievements with the economy, and you know, even if the stock market is out of shape because of the trade war, there's still more jobs now than there's ever been in the country.

For many, their negative reaction went far beyond campaign rally antics and tweeting to who Donald Trump is as a person: "He might know what he's doing with running the country as a business, but he's not a good human being and not somebody that kids should be looking up to. And that's kind of what I thought a president was supposed to be, was what everybody wants to be when they grow up and a good role model. And he obviously doesn't do that."

They were shockingly forceful in their disgust for Donald Trump's treatment of women. After viewing a video of Donald Trump disrespecting women on the campaign trail, they called him "a pig man" and "sexist" and a "disgusting person." This was when some of the secular conservatives revealed just how conflicted they had been about Trump being the Republican nominee: "Wow, that's—You hear stuff like that about [women], you just go—again, I just don't understand how [he became the nominee]. He was not even close to being my first choice. Not even close." One man who ultimately voted for a third party in 2016 made a point to say that the Trump comments he found most offensive—those captured on the *Access Hollywood* tape—were not even included on this video.

Many of the secular conservatives, like the moderate Republicans, said social division is the biggest threat to the country. They blamed both the left—which is so eager to call those who disagree with them racists and has a "victim mentality"—and the right—which has some cultural views they wouldn't defend and then ceded the high ground by elevating Trump. They resented the difficulty they have had reconciling their ethics with their political choice in 2016, and that may be a real threat to their enthusiasm in 2020.

TRUMP'S POLICIES AND PRIORITIES

Most of the secular conservatives I spoke to in Denver expressed discomfort with some of Trump's signature executive actions and use of the bully pulpit. That included Trump's policies on issues like trade, where he diverged from the conservative orthodoxy, and the way he enjoyed telling private businesses how they should behave, which offended their libertarian sensibilities.

Most of these secular conservatives disagreed with Trump's imposition of tariffs and were worried about a potential trade war:

> I would say threats are still just maybe the fragility of the economy . . . with the trade war [and this] push for isolationism.

> I generally think that any tariff is a tax on the American consumer, and that bilateral trade agreements are a very good thing. And I think Donald Trump tearing up NAFTA would be disastrous for my home state or any of the southern states who rely on trade to Mexico. So many jobs rely on trade, more than the factories.

These secular conservatives were uncomfortable with NFL athletes kneeling during the national anthem because it is unpatriotic, divisive, and sets a bad example for children. But some also expressed a libertarian respect for the rights of the athletes and the owners to make their own decisions: "Personally, I think there should be great respect for the flag, but I also think it's your freedom to express your opinion. But I think owners, I think they can make their own decisions on how to discipline players and their consequences." They reminded themselves that "it's dangerous to have the government compel an individual to do something" because it is a slippery slope from standing for the flag to compelling you to do something liberals may want you to do.

A few secular conservatives wondered out loud whether Trump's favoritism and public chastisement of specific companies put the country down the road to "crony capitalism."

LIMITS ON POWER

Of all the GOP groups, the secular conservatives were the most aware of the special counsel's Russia investigation and the most likely to bring it up unprompted. Even though they thought a lot of the news coverage about the investigation was fuel for the media outrage machine sowing division on both sides, a few said that we should "wait and see" what comes out of the investigation: "We don't know what he's found. It might be nothing. It could be something. I'd rather, if there is collusion, I'd rather we find it."

Some of the secular conservatives took very seriously the possibility that Trump's campaign team and even Trump himself may have inappropriately conspired with the Russians. When the moderator presented them with a hypothetical scenario in which the special counsel indicted Donald Trump Jr. and other campaign principals and reported to Congress that President Trump had obstructed justice, some accepted the conclusion. "It's not gonna be illegitimate judging by his background record, just from what I know," said one man of Mueller and his investigation. "I'd be surprised," said another man, who then elaborated, "but if somebody broke the law, then they should be held accountable."

Some disputed whether it was possible for the president to obstruct justice or whether Trump's actions counted as high crimes or misdemeanors, but others insisted that "if they found concrete stuff on Trump, they should go with the law proceedings." One man said this would mean that Trump was not legitimately elected and so should be impeached to teach people a lesson.

> I would fully say if he went through Russian interference for getting him elected, then yeah. You know what? Like you don't deserve to be here. I mean, it wasn't the damn majority vote to begin with. I would say if that is the reality, then he should be on his way. If he got impeached for the first time, basically in the history of [America], because of [these] wrongdoings, I mean, everything we say about kids seeing him and not being the guy to follow and then they get the full circle and see like this guy really was a dips*** and this is how he went about it and he cut corners and now he's out. I mean, that might be a hell of a lesson for the United States and for all of its people in it.

Most of the GOP's secular conservatives were either conflicted or ambivalent about the Trump presidency and Trump's intensified efforts to communicate about his successes and the threats ahead. There was no sense in this group that secular conservative Republicans were motivated to vote in November to defend Donald Trump. If the special counsel made more indictments against the Trump campaign or reports on obstruction, these were the base voters most likely to be impacted.

THE MODERATES

President Trump sought to rally his party in 2018 with ever more frantic rallies to motivate the base of the party, but the moderates were pushed even further away.[10] One in four in the base are moderates, the second largest group, and they limit the likelihood that Trump's base strategy will succeed.

Many of the female moderates in the summer of 2018 indicated they might just vote for a Democrat but even more that they won't go out and vote to protect Donald Trump.

They were still Republicans because of their views on immigration and the accelerating diversity of the country, but they were so viscerally opposed to President Trump that other dynamics dominated their responses.

When my moderator showed the videos of Trump speaking to his admiring supporters, their response was universally negative. Trump touted his progress on North Korea, the economy, and the jobs numbers, or talked about appointments to the Supreme Court, but his aggressive style was so off-putting they could not embrace his progress, even on the issues on which they agreed—like the economy and immigration.

Trump argued people should vote in the midterms to defend his policies on abortion, but these are the most socially liberal part of the base. The moderates embraced gay marriage and Planned Parenthood, and wanted new laws to combat gun violence and regulations to protect the environment.

They were disgusted by Trump's treatment of women and worried about the apparent green light he gave to sexism. The threats to women's rights pushed them over the edge, and some indicated they would take to the streets and organize over *Roe v. Wade*.

This all led half of the moderates in the July survey to support a candidate different from Trump and a quarter to vote for a third-party candidate in 2020. They just didn't see "any Republicans standing up to him and trying to stop some of these things that are going through."

> I kind of feel the same way. I'm hoping that the Republican Party
> will open up their eyes and see Trump for what he is. I was a supporter
> of Trump, but I'm not so much now. I'm not going to say I'm totally
> against him, but I'm hoping that the Republican Party can reel him
> in a little bit.

One woman explained, "I just want an honest Republican who is sane and a decent human being." In the near term, some said they wouldn't vote in November to protect President Trump and some might vote for a Democrat to be a check on Trump.

Moderates were already pulling back from the Republican Party for being out of touch with their views on social issues and the role of government and for refusing to reel in Trump.

Moderate Republicans resembled Democrats in their social views. Asked what they thought about gay marriage, they said "cool," "sweet," and "whatever."

They were more than fine with Planned Parenthood. "Feel good"; "they've done a lot of good," without even a single qualification.

The moderates were supportive of abortion rights and "scared to death" that *Roe v. Wade* could be overturned. "It's not going to stop abortion," one woman said, "it's just going to stop legal abortion." The prospect that *Roe* would be successfully challenged would be "huge," and some said that this would turn them into activists: "I can't say that I have ever gotten involved in organizing . . . I would for 100% march, picket, and whatever I had to do to stop that from happening. I would beat down the doors at Congress."

Moderates were more worried about "going backwards with all the women's rights" because they believed that the president was "so chauvinistic against women." They were disgusted by a video of candidate Trump's disrespectful treatment of women. They said they loathed "the name-calling, the degrading, the grabbing them with the pussies," and they also cited his recent disrespect toward female world leaders as a problem. In 2016, his behavior toward women was "almost" disqualifying, but Hillary Clinton was so tarnished, many bottled up those feelings.

GOVERNMENT

The moderates are the only base group that supported a greater role for government.

That started with the Second Amendment, which was so defining for the Tea Party. They were deeply upset about the mass shootings and gun violence against children. One woman even said she and her husband were unsure whether to have children because they worried they could not keep them safe today. Yes, they supported the Second Amendment, but said up front there should be limits: "The right to bear arms means that you have the right to defend yourself, does not mean that you have the right to carry a gun out in the open. Does not mean that you [have] the right to carry an assault rifle."

Moderates also "don't think we do enough for our environment at all" and were concerned about the trend against environmental protections under Trump. "He's doing things that worry me about the environment, rolling back things that are important to me," said one moderate woman pessimistic about the future of the country.

The GOP base was consumed by President Obama's effort to guarantee affordable health care for all, but the moderates accepted with most voters that government should do more "in guaranteeing us that we have health care coverage."

> Everybody else in the world has it. I don't understand why we don't have it for us. I think Canadians have their own health care system, is that right? . . . Maybe they started out bumpy, I don't know, but how they got there, let's try to copy or do the same process for us.

> My friend in England has it . . . and she's got to wait sometimes a little bit, but at least she's not saddled with a huge bill that can bankrupt her.

And more in alignment with thinking outside the GOP, associations with CEOs of large businesses produced the normal negative reactions: "shady" and "greedy." The conversation moved quickly to special treatment of politicians.

> I think that goes with anything that's higher up like the president, well maybe not the president so much but maybe all of our senators that have all these benefits that are just absurd and that's our tax money.

> I was just going to touch base on like the government shutdown and all the senators being paid their paychecks and here our military people, military families were going without pay even though they were all there for us.

When the moderator asked the room why they directed the conversation this way, they explained, "I look at politicians as big CEOs of this country" and "they pick the candidate too." They went to the corrupt nexus of politicians and business that President Trump no longer spoke about.

When asked about the future of the country, moderates used words like "very sad," "worried," "less hopeful," and "unsafe." They were uncertain about the country's future because of the divisiveness produced by President Trump.

> I think not being together, being so divided. I know when Trump was elected, there was hope that he was going to bring this country together and I think this country is more divided than anything.

> Everybody's just fighting about politics . . . and you can't even have a conversation, say with a friend, without having an argument.

> It's not just that we're divided, people are willing to literally, physically fight because of difference of opinion. That's not what this country is about. This country is about being free to argue and to be free to have that difference of opinion. People want to fight for it.

The moderates alone in the GOP base blamed Trump for the polarization. When they watched his rallies, they saw a president who decided to push us as far apart as possible: "That's what I think Trump's about. He's about stirring the pot and making people [upset] and that's not how a president should be." They saw him as so polarizing that they just turned his job claims into minimum wage jobs or ones that President Obama created.

The moderates wanted strong control of immigration, but they did not accept his divisive formulation that precluded a multicultural America. When they watched the Coca-Cola ad featuring a multilingual version of "America the Beautiful," they said:

> I like it.

> It was amazingly beautiful. I lack the words.

> It showed America as a melting pot, which is what we are.

> I thought it was nicely shown, all wanting and doing the same sort of thing in their own ways.

And I think it shows . . . the people not speaking English that they are immigrants to the country and they are showing their pride for America by singing our national anthem in their own language.

UNITED BY IMMIGRATION, DIVIDED BY FOX

President Trump finished the 2018 off-year election with a venomous campaign against immigrants who murder the innocent and police officers. This is because he understood in his bones that the Republican Party had emerged as the party prepared to fight for white people who are losing standing as the country grows more immigrant and foreign and increasingly embraces its multiculturalism.

These results are clear in the 6,069 interviews I conducted with self-identified Republicans between April 2018 and the off-year election; half were conducted in the final two months.

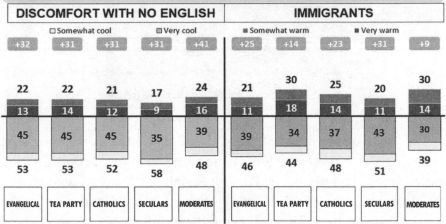

All GOP factions uncomfortable with immigration and foreignness

Please rate your feelings toward some people, organizations, and concepts, with one hundred meaning a VERY WARM, FAVORABLE feeling; zero meaning a VERY COLD, UNFAVORABLE feeling; and fifty meaning not particularly warm or cold.

DISCOMFORT WITH NO ENGLISH					IMMIGRANTS				
☐ Somewhat cool		☐ Very cool			■ Somewhat warm		■ Very warm		
+32	+31	+31	+31	+41	+25	+14	+23	+31	+9
22	22	21	17	24	21	30	25	20	30
13	14	12	9	16	11	18	14	11	14
45	45	45	35	39	39	34	37	43	30
53	53	52	58	48	46	44	48	51	39
EVANGELICAL	TEA PARTY	CATHOLICS	SECULARS	MODERATES	EVANGELICAL	TEA PARTY	CATHOLICS	SECULARS	MODERATES

All factions of the GOP base viewed immigration negatively, were uncomfortable with people not speaking English, and wanted leaders who look out for the interests of whites, including the conservative Catholics and ideological moderates. The moderates remain Republicans for a reason, though they are more modulated in their feelings and pushed away on other issues.

President Trump was the dominant dimension in a factor analysis of Republicans and their attitudes and values presented in the graphs below. That is a shift from the factor analysis I conducted in 2013 when hostility to President Obama was the dominant dimension. Today, Trump has reshaped his party to make himself the powerful current, along with Fox News, the NRA, and tax cuts. That was consistent with Trump's winning control from the GOP's Tea Party base that gave the party the backbone to fight against President Obama and with how he wanted to change the country.

Dimensions of GOP thinking: results from factor analysis by Catalist

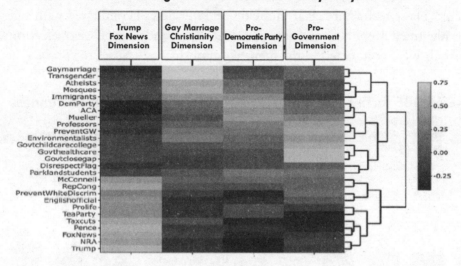

President Trump held wall-to-wall rallies in 2018 after Labor Day, annoyingly interrupted by funerals for Senator John McCain and the eleven Jewish congregants in Pittsburgh, but our focus groups showed that watching the rallies put off all of the moderates and most of the secular conservatives. The polling database of Republicans shows that secular conservatives and moderates were not part of the Fox News loop. Less than half of the former and just 30 percent of the latter viewed them favorably. But don't underestimate the powerful role Fox plays for the 58 percent of Republicans who are Trump loyalists for now: two thirds view Fox favorably, with 46 percent viewing it very favorably.

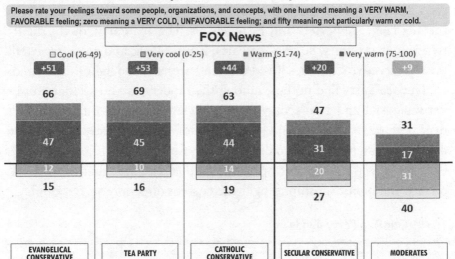

Seculars and moderates not part of Fox News loop

Please rate your feelings toward some people, organizations, and concepts, with one hundred meaning a VERY WARM, FAVORABLE feeling; zero meaning a VERY COLD, UNFAVORABLE feeling; and fifty meaning not particularly warm or cold.

FOX News

☐ Cool (26-49) ▨ Very cool (0-25) ■ Warm (51-74) ■ Very warm (75-100)

	EVANGELICAL CONSERVATIVE	TEA PARTY	CATHOLIC CONSERVATIVE	SECULAR CONSERVATIVE	MODERATES
Net	+51	+53	+44	+20	+9
Warm total	66	69	63	47	31
Very warm	47	45	44	31	17
Warm	12	10	14	20	31
Cool total	15	16	19	27	40

The second most important dimension centered on the Republicans' views on gay marriage, transgendered people, and feelings about mosques. That suggests a social conservative dimension in GOP thinking, rooted in Christianity and distrust of Islam. That was why President Trump was still getting a rise from his rallies when he mentioned President Obama's middle initial, "H," for Hussein.

That demagoguery came with a price among the moderate GOP, who were socially liberal. Many of the women have left the party over the past five years but moderates still form a quarter of the GOP base. More accept than reject the notion of most abortions being legal, and a majority view gay marriage favorably.

THE TEA PARTY VS. JOHN MCCAIN

The Republican Party had been fractured by the Tea Party takeover of the party in 2010, and the gridlock and polarization were an affront to John McCain and his supporters, who viewed bipartisanship as a virtue. The GOP was painfully divided by the Tea Party–McCain struggle that President Trump tastelessly exploited. This was a Republican Party divided over the intense partisanship that Senator McCain hated and tried to have addressed at his funeral.

What was this about? The Tea Party took on the GOP establishment that had fecklessly challenged President Obama and Obamacare. They forced government shutdowns that were hated by the GOP leadership. As a "birther" from the beginning, Trump quickly won the support of the Tea Party supporters and Evangelicals. The Tea Party fought the PC trends in the country. So, the Tea Party, Evangelicals, and, to some extent, the conservative Catholics loved the Tea Party and the fight they waged.

The Tea Party had no fans among the moderates and secular conservatives: just 1 and 2 percent respectively viewed them positively. In fact, over a third of seculars and 40 percent of the moderates disliked the movement intensely. This coalition, which formed over 40 percent of the GOP base, was ambivalent or hostile to the Tea Party that threw away civility and bipartisanship to fight the current direction of the country.

The McCain/Tea Party divide

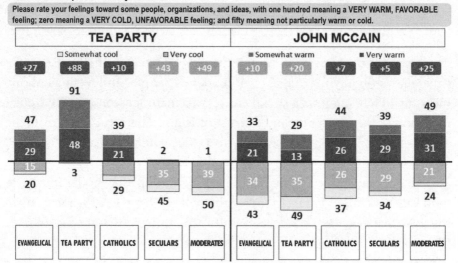

Senator McCain's hope for a return to bipartisanship and civility was on full display at his carefully staged funeral. The Tea Party, which McCain had to defeat in his own primary challenge, represented an uncompromising conservatism that must defeat the other party at all costs. Despite such a momentous funeral, just a third of Evangelicals and under 30 percent of Tea Party supporters viewed McCain favorably. The latter viewed him negatively by a margin of twenty points.

With the Robert Mueller report looming, President Trump for a week in March disparaged Senator McCain for passing a key memo to the FBI, sinking the repeal of the ACA with a thumbs down, and not thanking the White House for funeral arrangements in Washington.[11]

Senator McCain was regarded favorably by a large plurality of both conservative Catholics and secular conservatives. Moderates revered him, viewing him favorably by a two-to-one ratio. That response suggests a longing across large parts of the party for a politics that could transcend the Tea Party revolt now led by President Trump.

THE LIMITS OF TRUMP'S 2018 BASE STRATEGY

President Trump and the GOP bet everything on a base strategy, infused with Tea Party and Evangelical energy, of the high-stakes fight against immigration, and the need to protect the forgotten Americans disrespected by the PC elites and liberal media. They took their case to the country with campaign rallies and Fox News.

The verdict of my interviews was not encouraging for Republicans. President Trump drove up Tea Party and Evangelical intensity in their embrace of him and their determination to vote in the midterms. But approval of Trump for these two loyalist factions just matched the disapproval of the president among all Democrats. Critically, strong approval reached two thirds, well short of the 82 percent of all Democrats who strongly disapprove of Trump's performance in office. Yes, President Trump had pushed up the determination of the loyalists to vote, but they fall short of the 62 percent of all Democrats who showed the highest interest in voting in the off-year election.

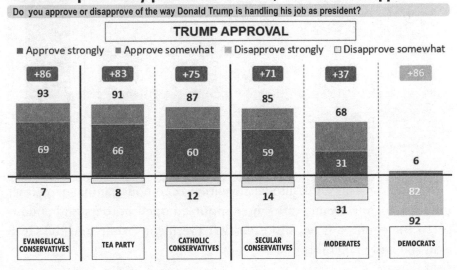

GOP Trump intensity pales before Dems; some GOP disapprove

Do you approve or disapprove of the way Donald Trump is handling his job as president?

TRUMP APPROVAL

■ Approve strongly ■ Approve somewhat ■ Disapprove strongly □ Disapprove somewhat

	EVANGELICAL CONSERVATIVES	TEA PARTY	CATHOLIC CONSERVATIVES	SECULAR CONSERVATIVES	MODERATES	DEMOCRATS
	+86	+83	+75	+71	+37	+86
Approve total	93	91	87	85	68	6
Approve strongly	69	66	60	59	31	
Approve somewhat	7	8	12	14	31	82
Disapprove total						92

Trump did own the Evangelicals and Tea Party, where over 90 percent approved his performance, more than two thirds strongly. The intensity, however, fell off to about 85 percent strong approval among Catholics and secular conservatives. And a third of moderates disapproved; just 31 percent strongly approved.

The contrasting reactions to Trump play out on our scale for voters rating their interest in the election: "10" means "extremely interested."[12] President Trump had succeeded in pushing high interest among Evangelicals to 59 percent, to 57 percent with Tea Party supporters, and to 55 percent with Catholic conservatives. Only the Evangelicals came close to the level of interest expressed by Democrats: 62 percent said they were extremely interested in the upcoming election.

Four in ten GOP base voters are secular conservatives and moderates, but only 46 percent of secular conservatives put their interest at the top of the scale and just 39 percent of moderates. Moderates and Evangelical conservatives each comprise about a quarter of the GOP base—and the turnout enthusiasm gap stood at twenty points before the election.

Trump strategy get only Evangelical/Tea Party to Dem turnout

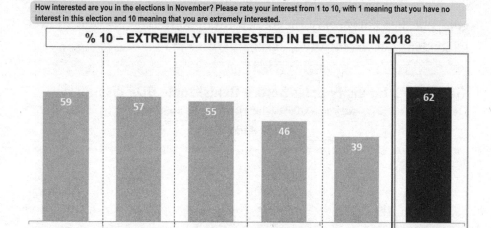

How interested are you in the elections in November? Please rate your interest from 1 to 10, with 1 meaning that you have no interest in this election and 10 meaning that you are extremely interested.

% 10 – EXTREMELY INTERESTED IN ELECTION IN 2018

Evangelical Conservatives	Tea Party	Catholic Conservatives	Secular Conservatives	Moderates	Democrats
59	57	55	46	39	62

Trump took his GOP into battle with a venomous campaign against immigrants and Democrats who supported open borders and endangered the country. It fell short and left President Trump and the GOP exposed and vulnerable.

6 THE NEW AMERICA STRIKES BACK

THE DEMOCRATS WON A SWEEPING VICTORY IN THE 2018 midterm elections. They won the highest share of the popular vote in any national election since 1946. They defeated the Republicans by 9 million votes and their 8.5-percent winning margin represents what Ron Brownstein describes as "the most emphatic repudiation of a president in modern history."[1]

The Democrats as a result picked up forty House seats—the biggest Democratic gain in House seats since Watergate, electing a record-breaking 102 women to the House, and flipping six statehouses, nearly four hundred legislative seats, and seven governors' mansions. Democrats now occupy nearly half of the fifty governors' mansions, including in all the Blue Wall states that allowed President Donald Trump to win the Electoral College. The Democrats' winning House margin exceeded that for the Republicans in the 2010 Tea Party wave election. They shifted the average vote margin by ten points, compared to President Trump's in 2016, though by fully twenty-one points in the seats that flipped to the Democrats. The enormity of this cannot be understated.

This was an unprecedented off-year election. The turnout hit 50.1 percent, up a third from 2014 and the highest since 1914. Tea Party and Evangelical Republicans raised their turnout. But that was overshadowed by the surge in activism and fund-raising catalyzed by the Women's March and response to Donald Trump's election, and carried through by progressive groups, including the Women's Voices

Women Vote Action Fund (WVWVAF) and the Voter Participation Center that I worked with.[2]

President Trump also went through what may be a realigning election. He nationalized the election around himself, producing an intense anti-Trump reaction that consolidated the Democrats and the "Rising American Electorate"—unmarried women, persons of color, and millennials—who demanded elected leaders be a check on Donald Trump. All varieties of women turned against the president. African Americans and unmarried women pushed the promise of the Rising American Electorate (RAE) to its highest off-year vote share and Democratic support. President Trump who promised to govern for the "forgotten Americans" lost a lot of white working-class and rural voters and fractured his own party. And President Trump declared war on immigrants and on multicultural America and lost.

NATIONALIZED ANTI-TRUMP VOTE

The shift toward the Democrats was produced in the first instance by an intense anti-Trump reaction among women, particularly those in the Rising American Electorate (minorities, millennials, and unmarried women) and in the suburbs, as the president nationalized the election around himself. Fully 46 percent of the country strongly disapproved of Trump—compared to only 34 percent who strongly approved. That intense negative reaction reached 84 percent with African-American women, 64 percent with millennial women, and 59 percent with unmarried women and college women.

The president's campaign raised his strong approval to 73 percent among Republicans, but that pales next to the 85 percent of Democrats who "strongly disapproved."

President Trump's personalization and nationalization of the election succeeded in raising the stakes for parts of his loyalist base, such as white working-class men: two thirds said this off-year election was much more important than prior midterms. But Trump's championing of white men proved an affront to college women and African Americans, who came to view the election as even more important than Trump's strongest base supporters did. Trump's provocations pushed Hispanics and unmarried women to the same level of urgency.

Vote urgency as high with RAE as college women & white working class men

Compared to previous midterm elections, do you think it is more important for you to vote, less important for you to vote, or about the same?

RELATIVE IMPORTANCE OF THIS MIDTERM
PRESIDENTIAL BATTLEGROUND

Less important   As important   Somewhat more important   Much more important

	Total	College Women	African American	Unmarried Women	Hispanic	White Working Class Men	White Unmarried Women	White Working Class Women	Millennial	White Millennial
	73	80	76	74	73	73	73	72	64	60
	65	68	68	67	68	68	65	63	54	47
	27	20	24	26	26	26	26	27	34	38
					27	27		28	36	40

The pro- and anti-Trump sentiment was so strong that three quarters of those voting for candidates for the House and nearly 90 percent of Senate candidate voters never considered voting for another candidate.

The top reason that Democratic House voters gave to vote *against* the Republican and *for* the Democrat across the presidential battleground was to have leaders who would be a check on President Trump. That was also the strongest reason to vote for the Democrat in the U.S. Senate elections in those contested states. So, Donald Trump succeeded in making himself the most important factor in people's vote, though not with the intended result.

Why voted against Republicans for Congress

Which THREE describe the most important reasons why you opposed the Republican candidate for Congress in your district?

Which THREE describe the most important reasons why you voted for the Democratic candidate for Congress in your district?

WHY NOT GOP FOR CONGRESS		WHY DEM FOR CONGRESS	
PRESIDENTIAL BATTLEGROUND			■ Voted Dem
THEY DON'T STAND UP TO DONALD TRUMP'S DIVISIVE BEHAVIOR AND LIES	43	THEY WILL BE CHECK ON DONALD TRUMP	35
THEY WILL BE A RUBBER-STAMP FOR DONALD TRUMP AND HIS AGENDA	32	TO PROTECT A WOMAN'S RIGHT TO CHOOSE AND LGBTQ RIGHTS	34
THE REPUBLICAN TAX CUT HELPED CORPORATIONS AND THE RICH, NOT US	31	TO MAKE THE ECONOMY WORK FOR EVERYONE, NOT JUST THE RICH & CORPORATIONS	33
THEY ARE TRYING TO CUT MEDICARE AND SOCIAL SECURITY	30	TO SAVE PROTECTIONS FOR PRE-EXISTING CONDITIONS IN HEALTH CARE LAW	32
THEY DON'T DO ENOUGH TO SHOW THEY RESPECT AND SUPPORT WOMEN	26	THEY WILL PROTECT MEDICARE AND SOCIAL SECURITY FROM CUTS	31
THEY REFUSE TO ACKNOWLEDGE CLIMATE CHANGE AND WORK FOR POLLUTERS	26	TO STOP SEPARATING IMMIGRANT PARENTS AND CHILDREN AND TO PROTECT DREAMers	29
THEY WON'T PROTECT PRE-EXISTING CONDITIONS	24	THEY SUPPORT NEW LAWS TO PROTECT AGAINST GUN VIOLENCE	18
THEY ARE OUT OF TOUCH ON THE ECONOMY	10	THEY WILL PROTECT THE RUSSIA INVESTIGATION AND THE RULE OF LAW	9

WOMEN

Democrats won not just because white college women rebelled against Trump's misogyny and disrespect of women. Nearly every possible category of women rebelled. Yes, House Democrats increased their vote margin nationally among white women with at least a four-year degree by thirteen points compared with the Clinton-Trump margin in 2016. But Democrats also pushed up their vote margin among white millennial women by eighteen points, white working-class women by thirteen points, and white unmarried women by ten points.

In fact, the white college women who were supposed to be the "fuel for this Democratic wave" played a smaller role in the Democrats' increased 2018 margin than white working-class women, because the former were 15 percent of midterm voters and the latter 25 percent.

This gender dynamic produced a House Democratic caucus that was 39 percent women. It produced a House GOP caucus that was at least 90 percent white men.

Democrats outperformed 2016 vote among all types of women

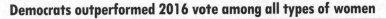

Now let me ask you about the election for Congress. Did you vote for (ROTATE) the Democratic candidate or the Republican candidate?

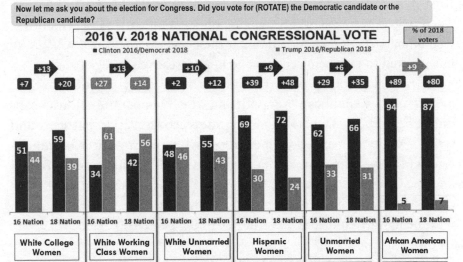

Unmarried women comprised 23 percent of the national electorate and played a decisive role in the 2018 wave. Like other women, many unmarried women decided early to oppose what was happening in the country, but some decided in the fall and as late as the final week not only to vote but also to vote out the Republicans, especially in the Rust Belt where Democrats made such big gains. We know this story because of the web panel that Democracy Corps conducted for WVWVAF, which interviewed the same respondents four times in the twelve states with competitive statewide races.[3]

African Americans too were engaged, consolidated, and played a parallel role in getting the Rising American Electorate to deliver to its full potential. Critical work done by progressive groups and, perversely, President Trump's own stance on immigration, helped dramatically move up the Democratic vote among millennials and Hispanics, though their turnout failed to keep up with the surge among other progressive groups.

The story of unmarried women voters was unique. Unmarried and white unmarried women gave the Democrats at all levels landslide numbers. Reacting to President Trump and the Women's March, many decided early to vote for Democrats by big margins, but a large proportion decided this election was very important only in September and

October and shifted to the Democrats in the final week, especially in the Rust Belt. That gave the Democrats big wins in the House and Senate. These voters were reached heavily by phone and mail. At the end of the day, unmarried women turned out at their highest level since WVWVAF has worked to put them center stage in progressive strategies.

Unmarried women were resolute in their determination to vote against the Republicans, supporting the Democratic House candidates by 68 to 31 percent in the more conservative battleground states.[4] White unmarried women, too—who are two thirds of unmarried women—helped to produce this powerful repudiation of Trump and the GOP. In 2014 and 2016, they had divided their national votes evenly between the parties, but in 2018, they supported Democrats with nearly a two-to-one margin (61 to 37 percent).

All unmarried women in big early and delivered big for House majority.

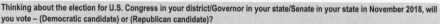

Thinking about the election for U.S. Congress in your district/Governor in your state/Senate in your state in November 2018, will you vote – (Democratic candidate) or (Republican candidate)?

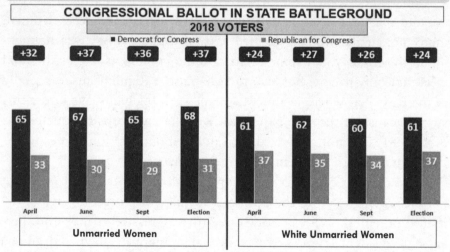

A lot happened for those strong numbers to be translated into the November wave. The RAE as a whole, particularly millennials and Hispanics, as well as unmarried women, shifted their vote margin for the Democrats by nine points in the fall in the Rust Belt states. Unmarried women supported Democrats then by 73 to 25 percent, the biggest margin of the year. The election crystallized in the Rust Belt for all the RAE groups then.

The Rising American Electorate played an even more powerful late role in the U.S. Senate contests in the Rust Belt. Between Labor Day and Election Day, the RAE pushed up its vote margin for the Democrats by seventeen points. The Democratic Senate candidates in the Rust Belt battleground states won by 67 to 30 percent. They won with the votes of unmarried women there by 72 to 21 percent.

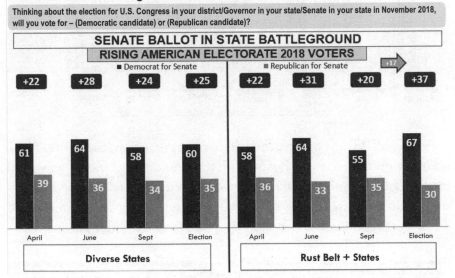

RAE delivered late surge for Senate Democrats in Rust Belt

It was hardly certain that unmarried women would turn out in large enough numbers to offset President Trump's effort to turn out his base. Unmarried women had disappointed in 2010 and 2014. But the campaign and organizational efforts of progressives began to change that. The proportion of unmarried women saying that voting in this election was *much* more important than prior midterms jumped eight points between September and the election. It jumped eight points for white unmarried women and seventeen points for white millennial women, too.

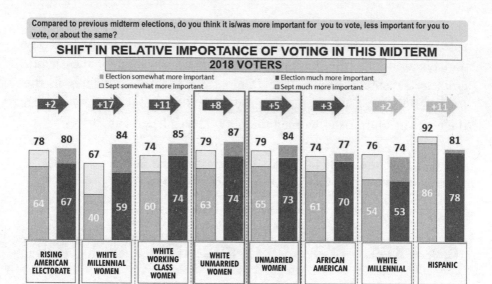

Compared to previous midterm elections, do you think it is/was more important for you to vote, less important for you to vote, or about the same?

SHIFT IN RELATIVE IMPORTANCE OF VOTING IN THIS MIDTERM
2018 VOTERS

■ Election somewhat more important ■ Election much more important
□ Sept somewhat more important □ Sept much more important

	RISING AMERICAN ELECTORATE	WHITE MILLENNIAL WOMEN	WHITE WORKING CLASS WOMEN	WHITE UNMARRIED WOMEN	UNMARRIED WOMEN	AFRICAN AMERICAN	WHITE MILLENNIAL	HISPANIC
Shift	+2	+17	+11	+8	+5	+3	+2	+11
Sept	78	67	74	79	79	74	76	92
Election	80	84	85	87	84	77	74	81
Sept much	64	40	60	63	65	61	54	86
Election much	67	59	74	74	73	70	53	78

It was not TV ads that reached these voters to get out their vote. Three quarters of unmarried women said that candidates, campaigns, and other organizations reached them with "print materials in the mail"—outpacing those indicating they saw an ad on TV by nine points—and 44 percent of unmarried women reported receiving phone calls.

These are some ways that candidates, campaigns, and other organizations try to reach people before elections. Please select all of the ways that you were contacted or received information before the election.

GOTV CONTACT METHODS

RISING AMERICAN ELECTORATE

Print materials in mail	63
Saw campaign ads on TV	53
Received phone calls	38
Received emails	32
Saw campaign ad online	31
Campaign commercial online	26
Received texts	25
Contacted by campaign to vote	16
Followed on social media	15
Visited campaign website	12
Spoke with someone at door	11
Voter participation organization	11
Contacted by friend volunteer	4
Not contacted	12

UNMARRIED WOMEN

Print materials in mail	74
Saw campaign ads on TV	65
Received phone calls	44
Received emails	38
Received texts	33
Saw campaign ad online	31
Contacted by campaign to vote	21
Campaign commercial online	17
Voter participation organization	17
Spoke with someone at door	16
Followed on social media	11
Not contacted	11
Visited campaign website	7
Contacted by friend volunteer	6

We now know from the series of interviews I conducted with the same respondents in the Rising American Electorate battleground panel that nearly half of those voters in the Rust Belt decided their vote before or during the summer. The unmarried women who decided how they would vote before the fall voted straight ticket during that period, giving nearly 75 percent of their votes to Democratic candidates for the House, Senate, and governorships.

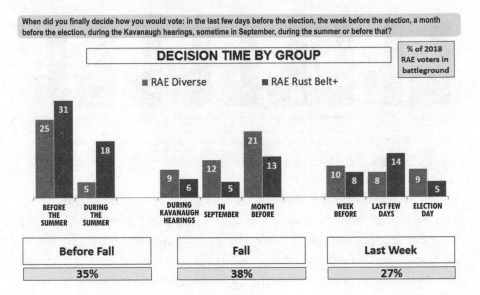

When did you finally decide how you would vote: in the last few days before the election, the week before the election, a month before the election, during the Kavanaugh hearings, sometime in September, during the summer or before that?

DECISION TIME BY GROUP

% of 2018 RAE voters in battleground

■ RAE Diverse   ■ RAE Rust Belt+

Before Fall	**Fall**	**Last Week**
35%	38%	27%

In the fall, when the Brett Kavanaugh hearings were held, over 40 percent of the Rising American Electorate in the diverse battleground states made up their minds. The unmarried women who decided then gave two thirds of their votes to Democrats in the House races but were less consolidated in the races for the Senate and for governor.

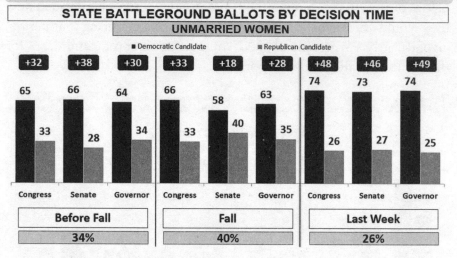

Thinking about the election for U.S. Senate/Governor in [STATE]/Congress, did you vote for—(ROTATE DEM, REP CANDIDATE)—[DEMOCRATIC CANDIDATE] or [DEMOCRATIC CANDIDATE]?

STATE BATTLEGROUND BALLOTS BY DECISION TIME

UNMARRIED WOMEN

■ Democratic Candidate   ■ Republican Candidate

	Before Fall			Fall			Last Week		
	Congress	Senate	Governor	Congress	Senate	Governor	Congress	Senate	Governor
Dem margin	+32	+38	+30	+33	+18	+28	+48	+46	+49
Democratic	65	66	64	66	58	63	74	73	74
Republican	33	28	34	33	40	35	26	27	25
	34%			**40%**			**26%**		

The last week before the election was decisive for the Rising American Electorate and the blue wave. Fully 27 percent of the RAE in the Rust Belt battleground states made their vote choices in the last week.

The unmarried women who decided in the final week gave Democrats two-to-one support in the races for the House, Senate, and governorships.

This report makes clear that there was nothing foretold in the role that unmarried women would play in 2018. Yes, these women gave Democrats landslide support and they participated at historic levels, but they responded to mobilizing events and intense campaign activity to shape the wave.

Will this shift of white women be durable? Mr. Trump is the leader of the Republican Party as it heads toward 2020. Like Mr. Trump, Senate and House Republicans were animated about white males being victimized by the PC police. The new Republican House caucus is 90 percent white men; near 40 percent of the new Democratic members are now women.

RISING AMERICAN ELECTORATE

The New America joined the battle for the country in ways that made 2018 a turning point for President Trump and the GOP. What I have called the Rising American Electorate of African Americans, Hispanics, unmarried women, and millennials was 60 percent of the voting-age population, 57 percent of those registered to vote, and 53 percent of those who voted in this off-year election. They produced unprecedented turnout and an unprecedented midterm vote for the Democrats.

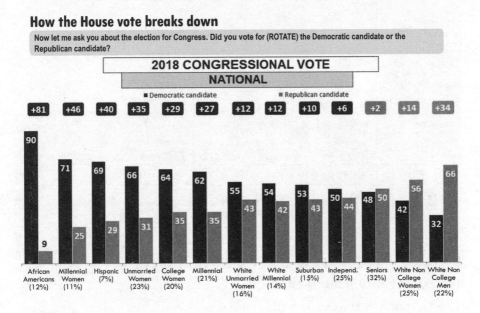

How the House vote breaks down

Now let me ask you about the election for Congress. Did you vote for (ROTATE) the Democratic candidate or the Republican candidate?

2018 CONGRESSIONAL VOTE
NATIONAL

■ Democratic candidate   ■ Republican candidate

| +81 | +46 | +40 | +35 | +29 | +27 | +12 | +12 | +10 | +6 | +2 | +14 | +34 |

	African Americans (12%)	Millennial Women (11%)	Hispanic (7%)	Unmarried Women (23%)	College Women (20%)	Millennial (21%)	White Unmarried Women (16%)	White Millennial (14%)	Suburban (15%)	Independ. (25%)	Seniors (32%)	White Non College Women (25%)	White Non College Men (22%)
Dem	90	71	69	66	64	62	55	54	53	50	48	42	32
Rep	9	25	29	31	35	35	43	42	43	44	50	56	66

Look at what they did at the ballot box in the 2018 election! African Americans gave Democrats near universal support (90 percent). Seven in ten millennial women and Hispanic voters supported Democrats, putting them at the center of the base with the two thirds of unmarried women who supported Democrats. You had to get to white unmarried women and white millennials before you got below 55 percent and double-digit leads. The suburbs were impressive but they gave the Democrats a modest ten-point win.

African Americans and unmarried women delivered their highest midterm vote share ever, thanks in no small part to the work of WVWVAF and the Voter Participation Center. Young people and Hispanics also managed to raise their share by one point each in a high-turnout midterm, but they fell back from their share in past presidential election years. Others in the New America have shown you can break that mold when the stakes are that high, and 2020 is just on the horizon.

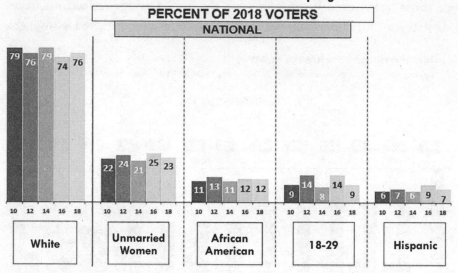

Unmarried women and African Americans showed up big!

| PERCENT OF 2018 VOTERS |
| NATIONAL |

White: 79, 76, 79, 74, 76

Unmarried Women: 22, 24, 21, 25, 23

African American: 11, 13, 11, 12, 12

18-29: 9, 14, 8, 14, 9

Hispanic: 6, 7, 6, 9, 7

(Years: 10, 12, 14, 16, 18 for each group)

MESSAGE: CORRUPT TAX DEAL FOR RICH THAT THREATENS RETIREMENT AND HEALTH CARE

The Democrats for the first time in decades ran with a clear attack on a GOP that governed for big corporations and the rich at the expense of the middle class. They exposed the corrupt tax deal that enriched the 1 percent and blew up federal deficits that put Social Security, Medicare, Medicaid, and education investments at risk. While the 1 percent loved this economy, the middle class struggled with sky-rocketing health care and prescription drug costs and the uncertainty of lost protections for preexisting conditions.

Elites, pundits, and the GOP trumpeted that this was the best economy in living memory, yet they were totally out of touch with the ordinary voter, who was living on the edge and struggling financially. The majority of voters said that their wages were not keeping up with rising costs, particularly rising health care costs. They were angry and scared about prescription drug costs. Republicans failed to understand just how "out of control" health care costs had become for working families and how they were causing them the greatest uncertainty.

The fear that Republicans would take the country back to the days when people could be denied health insurance for preexisting conditions or forced to face unbearable premiums was made real by the

Republicans' ideological assault on the Affordable Care Act, Medicare, and Medicaid. Democratic candidates' support for protections for pre-existing medical conditions was the second most important reason to vote for the Democrat for Senate in the battleground states.

Meanwhile, majorities reported that the so-called middle-class tax cut had not benefitted them personally, and, indeed, benefitted the rich and corporations at their expense. No wonder six in ten voters said Donald Trump is "self-dealing and looking out for himself"— including two thirds of independents, half strongly.

The Democrats ran against the Trump economy and opposed the Trump tax cut for the rich that threatened Medicare, Medicaid, and Social Security. That became the core content of national Democrats' closing arguments, and voters' desire for an economy for all became one of the top reasons to support them on Election Day.

In Democracy Corps's survey for WVWVAF, I asked what should be the top priorities for the new Congress. The message and mandate of the election could not be clearer. Over 70 percent said the top priority and/or near the very top of the list should be preventing Medicare, Medicaid, and Social Security from being cut. Almost 60 percent said lowering prescription drug costs should be such a priority. About 50 percent wanted to make investigating President Trump and impeachment and repealing the tax cut such a priority.

According to *The Wall Street Journal,* the Democrats' ad buys were focused predominantly on health care, tax fairness, and jobs. They were impactful in the 2018 election and in defining the mandate of the election.[5]

THE WORKING CLASS

Mr. Trump and the GOP's base were still deeply invested in the white working-class voters. Nonetheless, Democrats got their wave in part because a significant portion of male and female white working-class voters abandoned Mr. Trump and his Republican allies.

In the 2016 presidential election, the white working-class men in particular, whom Trump spoke most forcefully of as the "forgotten Americans," gave him 71 percent of their votes, with only 23 percent going to Hillary Clinton. In the 2018 off year, the Republicans won their votes with a still-impressive margin of 66 to 32 percent. And immigration continued to push these voters to the Republicans. A three-to-one balloon was deflated to two to one, still a daunting margin if Democrats are to compete everywhere.

Nonetheless, the Republicans watched their margin fall off fourteen points with white working-class men and thirteen points with women, which affected a lot of races.

Working people are no fools, and Mr. Trump had *promised* them a Republican president who would never cut Social Security, Medicare, or Medicaid; who would repeal Obamacare but provide "insurance for everybody"; who would get rid of bad trade deals and "drain the swamp," as he never tired of saying. Instead, had Trump's effort to replace Obamacare passed, it would have imposed vast cuts in retirement programs and driven up health insurance costs. His tax reforms were heavily weighted to benefit large corporations and the top 1 percent.

Working people, not just the white working class, were struggling with wages not coming close to keeping up with the rising cost of living. That is what elites had failed to understand for more than a decade. Two thirds of African Americans, unmarried women, and Hispanics said that, half with an intensity that suggests anger and resentment. Over 60 percent of white working-class women and millennials agreed they can't keep up, as well as 55 percent of white working-class men, a third with intensity. Three quarters of the white working class believed strongly that health care costs are out of control, starting with prescription drugs. And by a big margin, white working-class women (44 to 22 percent) and men (39 to 24 percent) respond warmly to "raising taxes on the rich and corporations."

Angry rejection of wages keeping up with costs

Now let me ask you some questions about the economy. Please tell me whether you agree or disagree with each statement.

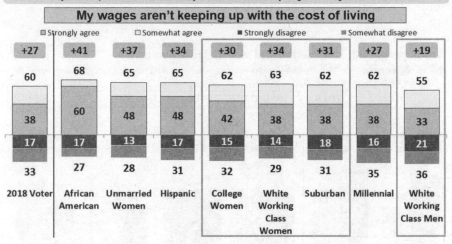

My wages aren't keeping up with the cost of living

□ Strongly agree □ Somewhat agree ■ Strongly disagree ■ Somewhat disagree

	2018 Voter	African American	Unmarried Women	Hispanic	College Women	White Working Class Women	Suburban	Millennial	White Working Class Men
	+27	+41	+37	+34	+30	+34	+31	+27	+19
	60	68	65	65	62	63	62	62	55
	38	60	48	48	42	38	38	38	33
	17	17	13	17	15	14	18	16	21
	33	27	28	31	32	29	31	35	36

So, it is no surprise that more than half of white working-class men said that Trump is "self-dealing and looking out for himself." The Democratic Senate candidates delivered that critique and romped to victory across the Midwest. The Republicans' House margin with white working-class men was cut in half in the Wisconsin, Michigan, and Ohio races, and Democratic Senate candidates won these states by double digits.

Democrats still lost white working-class men in the 2018 wave election by thirty-four points and the women by fourteen, so they have a lot of work ahead, but 10 percent of 2016 Trump voters supported Democrats in 2018, and 40 percent of moderate Republicans either voted Democratic or stayed home.

This setback will be corrosive unless a post-wave President Trump decides to acknowledge the "shellacking" and starts to actually "drain the swamp." Don't hold your breath.

RURAL GAINS

Democrats could not have picked up as many House seats as they did in 2018 without raising their share of the vote by four points in the suburbs, which have grown to encompass 50 percent of voters. Hillary Clinton had won many of these districts in 2016, so it was clear that any further shift in the Democrats' direction would prove consequential. But counter to the prevailing narrative, Democrats made their biggest gains not there, but in the rural parts of the country.

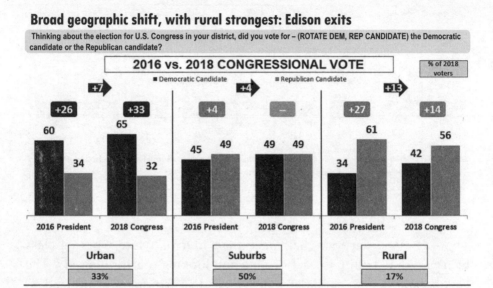

Broad geographic shift, with rural strongest: Edison exits

Thinking about the election for U.S. Congress in your district, did you vote for – (ROTATE DEM, REP CANDIDATE) the Democratic candidate or the Republican candidate?

Democrats cut the Republicans' margin in rural areas by thirteen points, according to the Edison exit poll, and by seven points in one by Catalist. Democrats still lost rural America by somewhere between fourteen and eighteen points. The top-of-the-ticket Senate candidates in more rural states received on average seventeen points less support than President Trump did in 2016, but he knocked off key Democrats by pressing his base to punish these dangerous politicians and vote a straight GOP ticket.[6] That left those Democratic officeholders exposed, with implications for the Senate.

Democrats still need to run stronger there. But it shouldn't conceal the fact that Democrats actually made progress in rural areas and pushed back against the insufferable polarization.

WAR ON IMMIGRANTS THAT TRUMP LOST

Democrats made historic gains because Mr. Trump declared war on immigrants—and on multicultural America—and lost. By sending 5,500 troops to lay barbwire at the border, warning of an immigrant invasion, and running a Willie Horton–type ad showing a Mexican who had murdered law enforcement officers, he succeeded in making immigration and the border a voting issue for his Republican base. When my poll asked voters why they had voted Republican, "open borders" was the top reason given for voting against a Democratic candidate. But it backfired among other voters.

Why voted against Democrats for Congress

Which THREE describe the most important reasons why you opposed the Democratic candidate for Congress in your district?		Which THREE describe the most important reasons why you voted for the Republican candidate for Congress in your district?	
WHY NOT DEM FOR CONGRESS		**WHY GOP FOR CONGRESS**	
PRESIDENTIAL BATTLEGROUND		■ Voted GOP	
They support open borders	45	Because the economy is growing and creating good paying jobs	44
They support Pelosi and Waters	31	To support President Trump and his agenda	39
They want to get rid of the Second Amendment	31	They support building a wall and being tough on illegal immigration	38
They will kill economic growth	26	They will protect the Second Amendment	32
They will raise taxes	26	They are pro-life and will protect religious freedom	31
They put other countries before the US	19	To support the new tax cut law	18
They want to protect Obamacare	16	They will cut spending to address the deficit	11
They will impeach Trump	16	To protect President Trump from impeachment	8

On Election Day, a stunning 54 percent of those who voted said immigrants "strengthen our country." The GOP lost the national popular vote by eight points, but Trump lost the debate over whether immigrants are a strength or a burden by twenty. Trump got more than half of Republicans to believe immigrants were a burden, but three quarters of Democrats and a large majority of independents concluded that America benefits from immigration. For the broad Rising American Electorate, immigration has become a kind of civil rights issue that produced almost identical and intense responses in support of the immigrants' role among Hispanics, African Americans, and millennials. By a two-to-one ratio, white millennials and women college graduates embraced America's immigrant future.

The idea that America is an immigrant country and that immigrants strengthen the country transcended political boundaries. It was embraced in the East and West, the metropolitan areas and the suburbs. Even in the South, it was seen to benefit, 52 percent to 38 percent. And even male and female white working-class voters were just evenly split on the issue. They showed ambivalence about immigration and a multicultural America that was not shared by the mostly white working-class Republican Party.

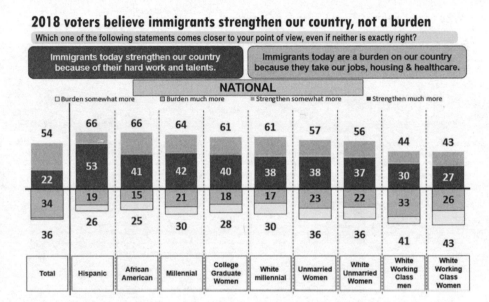

2018 voters believe immigrants strengthen our country, not a burden

Which one of the following statements comes closer to your point of view, even if neither is exactly right?

Immigrants today strengthen our country because of their hard work and talents.

Immigrants today are a burden on our country because they take our jobs, housing & healthcare.

NATIONAL

☐ Burden somewhat more   ☐ Burden much more   ▨ Strengthen somewhat more   ▪ Strengthen much more

	Total	Hispanic	African American	Millennial	College Graduate Women	White millennial	Unmarried Women	White Unmarried Women	White Working Class men	White Working Class Women
Strengthen total	54	66	66	64	61	61	57	56	44	43
Strengthen much more	22	53	41	42	40	38	38	37	30	27
Strengthen somewhat more	34	19	15	21	18	17	23	22	33	26
Burden much more	26	25	30	28	30	36	36	41	43	
Burden total	36									

For their part, the Democrats owned their diversity. They supported comprehensive immigration reform and the acceptance of Dreamers, opposed Trump's border wall, and opposed the separation of children from their families at the border. They nominated African-American candidates for governor in Georgia and Florida and fought the suppression of minority voters. When it was over, the Democrats got more votes and created a new Democratic House majority that was roughly 40 percent women, 40 percent white men, and 40 percent people of color, with eight LGBTQ members and two Muslim women.

The Republicans lost badly in the House in 2018 by running as an anti-immigrant party, while the Democrats made major gains as a self-confident diverse party, which might have the most durable impact on the character of the country.

TRUMP'S ANTI-IMMIGRANT CAMPAIGN UNITED
BUT FRACTURED THE GOP

President Trump made immigration the top reason to vote *against* Democrats among all off-year voters and succeeded in making the Democrats' support of "open borders and sanctuary cities" the top reason to oppose them in every faction of the GOP, including the moderates. That ugly campaign successfully raised hostility to immigrants and foreignness and pushed up President Trump's "strong approval" with all types of Republicans.

But critically, the divisive ultra-nationalist campaign was a step too far for some in the GOP. The 2018 campaign pushed some Republicans not to vote or to vote for Democrats, leaving the Republican Party more fractured and polarized. We know this because of the Democracy Corps and Women's Voices Women Vote Action Fund web panel in twelve contested battleground states, which interviewed the same Republican voters before and after the election, including those in the GOP who pushed back hard against the Tea Party that had dominated the party for a decade.[7]

This is a list of reasons to oppose Democrats for Congress. Which THREE describe the most important reasons why you opposed the Democratic candidate for Congress in your district?

REASONS TO VOTE AGAINST CONGRESSIONAL DEM
GOP VOTERS AMONG GOP IN STATE BATTLEGROUND

Reason	Value
For open borders	61
Kill economic growth	38
They will raise taxes	35
Support Pelosi/Waters	34
Impeach Trump	26
Other countries before US	24
Get rid of 2nd Amendment	22
Abortion on demand	21
Increase spending	20
Protect Obamacare	18

President Trump no doubt feels satisfied that he pushed up intense hostility to "immigrants to the U.S." in every faction of the party—up seven points to 43 percent with moderates, up thirteen points to 59 percent with secular conservatives, up fourteen points to 61 percent with conservative

Catholics, up fourteen points to 59 percent with Evangelicals, and up sixteen points to 52 percent with the Tea Party GOP. Before the election, all segments of the GOP were very uncomfortable with "coming into contact with people who speak little or no English." Half of every segment remained intensely negative after the election, except conservative Catholics, some of whom became uncomfortable with the anti-foreign drumbeat.

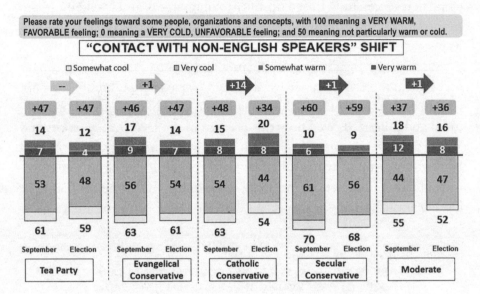

Please rate your feelings toward some people, organizations and concepts, with 100 meaning a VERY WARM, FAVORABLE feeling; 0 meaning a VERY COLD, UNFAVORABLE feeling; and 50 meaning not particularly warm or cold.

"CONTACT WITH NON-ENGLISH SPEAKERS" SHIFT

But the Trump campaign in 2018 went much further. It ended up encouraging a fervent Trump supporter and ultra-nationalist to send pipe bombs to Democratic politicians and to shoot up a synagogue in Pittsburgh. Stunningly, every segment of the GOP was less warm to the idea of "preventing discrimination against white people" in their second post-election interview. Trump's "white nationalism" had lost steam within his own party.

It would reverberate globally, with white nationalists using social media platforms to share his worries about America being invaded by Muslim terrorists. The white nationalist who murdered fifty worshippers in the New Zealand mosque in 2019 described President Trump as "a symbol of renewed white identity and common purpose."[8]

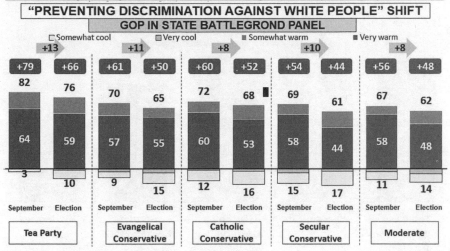

Please rate your feelings toward some people, organizations and concepts, with 100 meaning a VERY WARM, FAVORABLE feeling; 0 meaning a VERY COLD, UNFAVORABLE feeling; and 50 meaning not particularly warm or cold.

"PREVENTING DISCRIMINATION AGAINST WHITE PEOPLE" SHIFT
GOP IN STATE BATTLEGROND PANEL

President Trump successfully used his campaign rallies and Fox News to mobilize his Evangelical, Tea Party, and Catholic conservative base, and they also reached secular conservatives who got more on board with Trump at the close. About half of those groups watched a rally on TV or watch Fox News frequently. By comparison, only 26 percent of moderates watched a rally and only 18 percent watch Fox News frequently. A not inconsiderable 7 percent of Republicans attended a rally, but one quarter posted on social media, 11 percent displayed a sign, and 9 percent wore a shirt or hat. Among Evangelicals, one fifth discussed politics at church or Bible study.

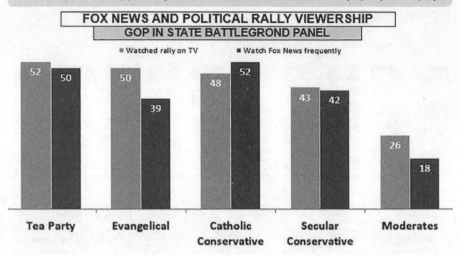

Below is a list of political activities popular among different voters. Please select all of the activities in which you participated in the past year.

FOX NEWS AND POLITICAL RALLY VIEWERSHIP
GOP IN STATE BATTLEGROND PANEL

■ Watched rally on TV   ■ Watch Fox News frequently

	Tea Party	Evangelical	Catholic Conservative	Secular Conservative	Moderates
Watched rally on TV	52	50	48	43	26
Watch Fox News frequently	50	39	52	42	18

President Trump and the Republicans' off-year campaign increased the polarization within the party on abortion and gay marriage. The Evangelical conservatives, Tea Party, and Catholic conservatives ended up much more favorable to pro-life, anti-abortion groups, while moderates and secular conservatives became much more negative.

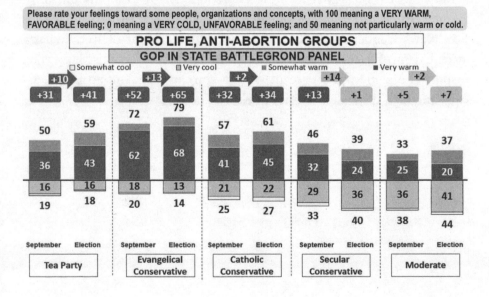

Please rate your feelings toward some people, organizations and concepts, with 100 meaning a VERY WARM, FAVORABLE feeling; 0 meaning a VERY COLD, UNFAVORABLE feeling; and 50 meaning not particularly warm or cold.

PRO LIFE, ANTI-ABORTION GROUPS
GOP IN STATE BATTLEGROND PANEL

□ Somewhat cool   □ Very cool   ■ Somewhat warm   ■ Very warm

Defections in GOP, including 40% of moderates

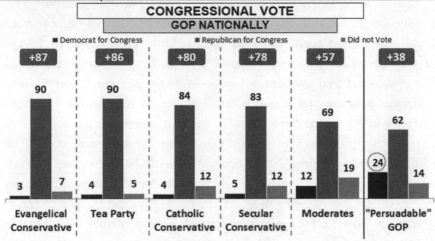

Thinking about the election for U.S. Congress in your district, did you vote for–(ROTATE DEM, REP CANDIDATE) the Democratic candidate or Republican candidate?

CONGRESSIONAL VOTE
GOP NATIONALLY

■ Democrat for Congress   ■ Republican for Congress   ■ Did not Vote

	Evangelical Conservative	Tea Party	Catholic Conservative	Secular Conservative	Moderates	"Persuadable" GOP
	+87	+86	+80	+78	+57	+38
Democrat	90	90	84	83	69	62
Republican	3	4	4	5	12	24
Did not Vote	7	5	12	12	19	14

The polarization around the Tea Party was even more dramatic and meaningful. The Tea Party symbolizes the take-no-prisoners, partisan campaign championed by President Trump. The proportion of secular conservatives viewing the Tea Party negatively jumped ten points to 55 percent and negative views of the Tea Party jumped twenty-three points with moderates. In the election week poll, over 70 percent viewed the Tea Party negatively. That gives you a view of the profound fractures in this Trump-led GOP.

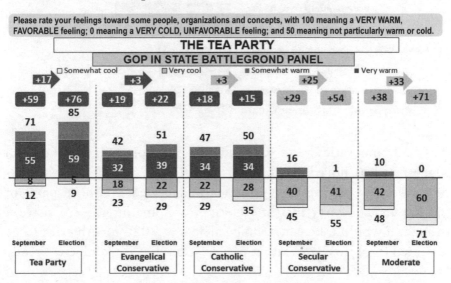

Please rate your feelings toward some people, organizations and concepts, with 100 meaning a VERY WARM, FAVORABLE feeling; 0 meaning a VERY COLD, UNFAVORABLE feeling; and 50 meaning not particularly warm or cold.

THE TEA PARTY
GOP IN STATE BATTLEGROND PANEL

□ Somewhat cool   □ Very cool   ■ Somewhat warm   ■ Very warm

Big stuff happened on Election Day. Nationally, a noticeable 12 percent of conservative Catholics and secular conservatives did not vote. Among the moderates, one quarter of the GOP, just 69 percent voted Republican, 12 percent defected to the Democrats, and 19 percent stayed home. The "persuadable GOP"—a group of targetable Republicans developed by Democracy Corps—was 40 percent larger than the moderates and may have played an even bigger role in this wave: one quarter voted for Democrats and 14 percent stayed home.

Those Republicans who considered voting for a Democrat said they were motivated "to make the economy work for everyone, not just the rich and corporations" (48 percent), to "send a message that we need decency and honesty in government" (48 percent), and to have a "check on Donald Trump" (38 percent). That sentiment has blended into the tough message to the GOP that emerged from this election.

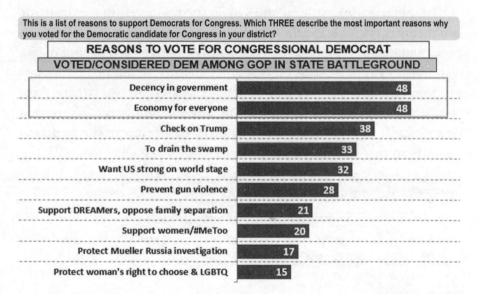

This is a list of reasons to support Democrats for Congress. Which THREE describe the most important reasons why you voted for the Democratic candidate for Congress in your district?

REASONS TO VOTE FOR CONGRESSIONAL DEMOCRAT
VOTED/CONSIDERED DEM AMONG GOP IN STATE BATTLEGROUND

Reason	Percent
Decency in government	48
Economy for everyone	48
Check on Trump	38
To drain the swamp	33
Want US strong on world stage	32
Prevent gun violence	28
Support DREAMers, oppose family separation	21
Support women/#MeToo	20
Protect Mueller Russia investigation	17
Protect woman's right to choose & LGBTQ	15

The Democratic wave exposed Mr. Trump's vulnerability and suggests a less polarized country. His divisive campaign lost parts of rural and working-class America and peeled off those parts of the Republican Party that are looking for something less divisive. I thought it would take Mr. Trump's defeat in 2020 for America to be liberated from this suffocating polarization, but it may have already begun.

7 IS THIS ALL THEY HAVE TO OFFER WORKING PEOPLE?

J. D. VANCE'S *HILLBILLY ELEGY* was on the *New York Times* bestseller list for more than two years, and deservedly, given how improbable was his struggling free of abuse from an untold number of men, broken marriages, a drug-addicted mom, family teenage pregnancies, alcoholism, violence and fatalism, and distrust and anger all around him to write this memoir at age thirty-one. Vance eventually went into the Marine Corps, then to Ohio State and Yale for his law degree, and on to Silicon Valley before moving back to Columbus, Ohio, to tip the scales a bit, as his conservative mentor David Frum urged him. He owes his life and survival to loving grandparents who protected him and believed in hard work and education.

The problem is that Republicans, conservatives, and Vance are wrong about the lessons we should take from his memoir. And they believe this powerful personal story confirms the centrality of bad personal choices and the inefficacy of government in our current troubles. Those lessons are the principal intellectual foundation of the Tea Party GOP's assault on government.

The book's cascading errors begin with the failure to appreciate how exceptional is Appalachian white history and culture and how dangerous it is to equate Vance's *hillbillies* with today's *white working class*, particularly in the industrial Rust Belt. But that is the equation Vance makes himself when he begins the memoir: "You see, I grew up poor, in the Rust Belt, in an Ohio steel town that has been hemorrhaging jobs and hope for as long as I can remember."[1]

And that equation allows conservatives and President Donald Trump to focus on coal mining, West Virginia, and Appalachia as the epicenter of America's working-class life.

The pace of Vance's cascading errors grows with his classless and benign history that erases the role of the powerful business actors who upturned timber and mineral rights and fought the coal-mining unions. They actively recruited labor from the hill counties to work in the great manufacturing centers and shaped the poor and working-class neighborhoods in the small and large cities all across the Midwest. Outside companies had long since taken over timber rights above the land and mineral rights underneath, leaving the native Appalachian whites very poor and dependent on the coal companies and company towns, who fought the United Mine Workers. Employment in the coal mines stalled during the Depression and crashed during the 1950s, falling across Appalachia to a mere 122,243—six decades before the current debate.[2]

Vance's story begins in Harlan County, where one third of the population left between 1940 and 1960 along the Hillbilly Corridor, which took people to Chicago, Detroit, and Cincinnati, but also to Dayton and small industrial cities along key riverways, like Middletown and Hamilton, built along the Great Miami River. The migrants formed "Little Kentuckys" in most of the major cities of the industrial Midwest, and Vance's family settled in Dayton and Middletown.

America's industrial infrastructure had been built by and employed mostly Catholic immigrants from Ireland, Italy, and Eastern Europe, with Protestant immigrants from Germany and Scandinavia, Jews from the Pale of Settlement (Russia), and the Chinese and Japanese playing key roles, but the United States legally ended immigration right after World War I. America's industrial leaders mobilized for World War II and the postwar boom by recruiting blacks, Mexicans, and Appalachian whites on a massive scale from the poorest rural areas of North America.

Vance's story pretty much ignores this history, the working-class battle to get its share of the pie, and the racial turmoil, riots, and struggle for civil rights that would shape the politics of America's cities.

The country invested in these workers' education, subsidized their home ownership and mobility, and they grew into America's proud middle class in the three decades after World War II. But their legs were kicked out from under them by foreign competition and ownership, technology, globalization, and trade agreements like NAFTA that undercut American jobs—all of which Vance describes as understandable: "I might have done the same."[3] He is sympathetic to company executives who didn't want to be cramped by unions. And his story makes no mention of the staggering loss of wealth, home ownership, and wage levels among working people after the 2008 financial crisis, which were front and center during his whole adult life. Stagnant wages and rising prices for health care, childcare, housing, and education are the new normal for working people.

Vance is just blind to the big developments in his short lifetime that stalled the ascent of hardworking working-class people up the socioeconomic ladder. Vance's story gives no insight into what is happening today with the white and non-white working class who dominate our cities, suburbs, and the smaller towns of the Rust Belt, which are really the epicenter of working-class life, and where life is indeed challenged.

These people are struggling and many of them are on the brink. That is why politicians and intellectuals of all stripes now are trying to figure out how to deal with the breakdown of the working-class family, men dropping out of the workforce, so many young men on an uncertain trajectory, the pathologies and inequalities that come with so many children raised by a single parent, and the opioid crisis that has taken so many lives. How much of this exceptional American problem is due to the attitudes and culture of the working class itself? How much is due to the disappearance of decently paid, secure jobs that allow working people to provide for their families and the withering of opportunities for their children and subsequent generations? And how much is due to a failure of public policy to evolve to meet the needs of the modern working family?

Vance shines a spotlight on the destructive culture in families like his that are "a hub of misery."[4] Vance's grandpa and grandma had married as teenagers and settled quickly in Middletown because his grandfather got a good job at Armco Steel, where he worked all his life. It enabled him to own a pretty big house by Appalachian standards and to live in a part of the town with neighbors almost exclusively from back home. But Vance's family was looked down on by their neighbors, who were not comfortable with the slaughtering of chickens and the openly toted guns and with seeing the drunken violence that was all too frequent.

Vance's grandparents felt guilty about leaving and abandoning the folks there and in Harlan County, Kentucky, where family remained, and went back many weekends and holidays. Vance and his grandparents were always comfortable there.

That family connection is important and unique among the various streams of migrants to the cities during World Wars I and II, as blacks went to Chicago to flee a segregated South that had attacked the recruiters promising a better life in the North. While extended family ties remained strong for African Americans, the culture of the Black Belt did not have the same kind of ongoing influence on blacks in the cities, as millions broke ties with the rural South. But the culture of rural Kentucky was ever present, including the Evangelical churches and ministers who worried about the triumph of secularism.

When they were young, everything about their poor neighborhood, Harlan County, and their family conspired to leave the Vance kids a mess, Vance wrote.[5] His mother was a drug addict for virtually his whole life, went through untold numbers of partners, and shuttled J.D. and his sister about to different towns. She had violent fights with the kids, was taken away in handcuffs by the police, and nearly got herself killed in an auto accident. She neglected her kids, Vance wrote, though at least she felt guilty about it.[6]

Increasingly, he and his sister stayed with his grandparents, whose marriage had been violent and Grandpa was an alcoholic; that had all been sorted before J.D. was born. He went to schools that were pretty modern. His grandparents demanded he get good grades, help Grandma with her chores, and get a job. He worked in a store and warehouse and took many lessons. The adults believed in hard work and the American Dream and made sure the kids had a stable place to live. Vance believes that a loving home accounts for everything good that followed.

Vance applied to attend Miami University (where I went) and Ohio State, but chose instead to enlist in the Marine Corps to show his family he could survive boot camp and learn the kind of discipline that you get only in the military. After that, he went through Ohio State in just two years and then on to Yale Law School. And that is where he came to understand the big culture clash between white working-class and meritocratic America.

And what is that white working-class culture? For Vance, it is "pessimistic" and "socially isolated" and it passes that "social isolation on to our children."[7] It is a culture in which you "blame everyone but yourself."[8] He watched his neighbors abuse food stamps, disability benefits, and Section 8 housing and saw few of his friends from the warehouse willing to take up work even when the shifts were offered.[9] Vance famously observes, "I have known many welfare queens; some were my neighbors, and all were white."[10]

So, "what goes on in the lives of real people when the industrial economy goes south [is] about reacting to bad circumstances in the worst way possible. It's about a culture that increasingly encourages social decay instead of counteracting it."[11] It is a culture in which people make bad choices and try to avoid the consequences.

If you think, as I argue, that job prospects have changed dramatically over the past decades, you might think that change would impact both the prospects and attitudes of the white working class, "But experience can be a difficult teacher, and it taught me that this story of economic insecurity is, at best, incomplete," Vance writes.[12] He is skeptical that if these workers had more job opportunities, "other parts of their lives would improve as well."[13]

Maybe Vance's hillbillies would not be helped by serious training and free education, new job opportunities, higher wages, and an upward employment ladder, less outsourcing and more American-based jobs, sustained long-term investment in building infrastructure, expanded child tax credits and income supports, food stamps, housing vouchers, nutrition programs, unpolluted rivers and air, consumer protections, early childhood programs and preschool, parenting education, sex education and family planning, affordable childcare, paid family leave after childbirth, and universal health insurance because of the persistent culture, but a lot of other working people end up with more secure families, less drug addiction, and more hope. America doesn't get the answer from Vance's story.

Nearly all the reviews of this powerful book were respectful of Vance and were sure it provided some insights for elites who needed a "genteel way" into these working-class communities where Trump ran up the score. Larry Summers tweeted, "Anyone want to understand Trump's rise or American inequality should read it."[14]

In a deeply polarized country, Jennifer Senior wrote in *The New York Times Book Review*, "Mr. Vance has inadvertently provided a civilized reference guide for an uncivilized election, and he's done so in a vocabulary intelligible to both Democrats and Republicans."[15] In *The New Yorker*, Joshua Rothman gave Vance credit for putting the spotlight on family disintegration, addiction, and domestic violence in white working-class communities and showing us how complex is the problem of poverty—he "advances the conversation."[16] With a full schedule of media punditry, Vance has emerged as "unofficial spokesman for the white working class."[17]

Well, that spokesman has an understandable and strong point of view. Many of the poor and working class lived off the dole as a life choice. They had no consciousness of their lack of industriousness. They blamed others for their plight. His mother gets no "perpetual moral get-out-of-jail-free card."[18]

And that was the starting point for nearly all the conservative reviewers. In the liberal establishment, "there's this weird refusal to deal with the poor as moral agents in their own right."[19] The liberal politicians, therefore, should "stop pretending that every problem is a structural problem, something imposed on the poor from the outside."[20] The divorce rate will not be reduced by having less economic stress, Vance concluded in an interview with Rod Dreher in *The American Conservative*.[21]

The signature liberal policies of the Great Society are no match for the deep poverty it confronted.[22] The powerful conclusion from Vance's book is that government policies are ineffective and counterproductive.

Conservative reviewers use Vance's book to show empathy for the poor, yet conclude we are totally powerless to construct any policies to change life's trajectory. Geoffrey Norman applauds Vance's writing with "affection, pity and candor," but it leaves analysts puzzled, "What, if anything, can be done?"[23] Reviewers applaud Vance's refusal "to moralize or pretend there are pat solutions to the problems he and so many other people in his circumstances have faced."[24] These "problems of family, faith and culture aren't like a Rubik's Cube," Mark Hemingway writes, "and I don't think that solutions (as most understand the term) really exist."[25]

EXPLORING WORKING-CLASS CULTURE

Joshua Rothman's *New Yorker* review reminds us that America has had this debate before: to what extent is poverty rooted in culture and norms that lead people to be more fatalistic and pessimistic, isolated from civil society, and feeling powerless to change their lot and control their destiny. The Moynihan Report in 1965 set off debate over whether poverty is determined mainly by culture or by economics, a distinction mostly ultimately rejected by those who concluded they were "entwined and equal power."[26]

I became a graduate student and professor during that debate and examined this very question. I conducted surveys and in-depth interviews in five poor neighborhoods, including a poor Appalachian community called Belmont in Hamilton, Ohio, just a few miles down the Great Miami River from Middletown, at about the time Vance's mother was approaching her teen years. I also conducted similar research in three very different poor black neighborhoods in Detroit, Philadelphia, and Atlanta and a Mexican-American neighborhood in San Jose.

Ironically, I wrote at the time that Belmont was the only community I studied where a culture of poverty played a major role in explaining attitudes and civic behavior. There is an ascendant "fatalism, personal impotence, limited time perspective, disorganization and apathy that combine to suppress any collective political urge."[27]

Vance's description of hillbilly culture was painfully accurate, but it was also isolated. It was very different from the dominant culture and attitudes in poor black neighborhoods in Atlanta, Philadelphia, and Detroit, and poor Mexican-American neighborhoods in San Jose. And importantly, its thinking and politics would be very different from those in the white working-class communities that would evolve across the Rust Belt that I would study a decade later.

How did it happen that I researched and observed these neighborhoods between 1970 and 1973 when publishing my first book, *Politics and Poverty*? I grew up acutely conscious of race and the battle for civil rights. My white Jewish family moved to Washington, D.C., for my father to take a job, and we lived in an all-black neighborhood before moving to a mostly Jewish one. When the D.C. schools were required to integrate, my whole sixth-grade class was transferred to a formerly black school where my teacher there was black. My junior class trip took us by bus across the South to New Orleans, where we witnessed separate water fountains and had arguments with the tour guide. The summer before going away to Miami University, I worked at a factory during the daytime with workers from West Virginia; blacks were segregated in the shipping department. At night I volunteered at the NAACP office on U Street and watched Martin Luther King, Jr.'s speech at the Lincoln Memorial from the organizing tent. The following summer, I would give my tickets to the Democratic Convention to the Student Nonviolent Coordinating Committee (SNCC) organizers I had worked with.

That I ended up as a pollster was pretty improbable. For my senior project as a government major in 1967, I conducted a mail survey with undergraduates at Miami University, and based on that, I was hired the following summer before starting graduate school at Harvard by Professor Ithiel de Sola Poole at MIT to analyze a survey on student housing, using new technology that allowed you to produce cross-tabulations on your desktop. Based on that, I was hired by a private research firm in Cambridge, Massachusetts, to lead a project that engaged with the poor themselves in a national evaluation of the War on Poverty for the Office of Economic Opportunity. It included an innovative leadership survey of one hundred poor neighborhoods and a survey of the poor themselves in five of them. That ended up as my Harvard Ph.D. thesis and first book.

I conducted this research in the period after urban riots convulsed most American cities, and I was looking to see whether a more radical, anti-systemic black politics was now dominant, rather than a "culture of poverty," implied in the work of Edward Banfield, Herbert Gans, and James Q. Wilson, all of whom I studied with at Harvard.[28] Wilson was my thesis adviser. In fact, I was rooting for a more developed class consciousness, given the half century of rural impoverishment, mass migration to cities, and industrialization that had shaped these communities.[29]

All these hypotheses perished before the diversity of political consciousness in these neighborhoods. My hope for a developed class consciousness fared worst of all, as black auto workers thanked Henry Ford for their five dollars a day, equal to that paid a white worker, and Kentuckians thanked Champion Paper for their parks.[30] The very different consciousness and mostly empowering politics in the black and Mexican-American neighborhoods left the culture of poverty in disrepute, too. Culture was a very large part of the story where Vance grew up. He just did not realize how exceptional it was.

The Appalachian migrants from Kentucky took up and moved into a neighborhood with some of the lowest priced housing in Hamilton. That neighborhood is intersected by the highway, river, and Peck's Addition outside city boundaries, with one-room houses made from converted chicken coops. The streets were paved, however, and the better houses had enough land for a corn patch. The migrants took up jobs at Champion Paper, Fisher Body, and Beckett Paper starting with World War II and ending by 1970, as manufacturing employment began to decline.[31]

One could hear barely a murmur of politics. Only 12 percent indicated membership in any organization. *The Hamilton Journal* found only one instance in which the community had joined together for a common cause. The only visible organization was O-Tuck—Kentuckians in Ohio providing entertainment and relief for flood and mine victims— but few from Belmont got involved. One of the leaders of the O-Tuck said, "What they have is in hand. They don't try to build up anything. They want it right now."[32]

The mayor was from Kentucky and operated a store in Belmont, though he lived on the richer West Side. He may have had a house, but his "home" was in Harlan County. Once he made his fortune, he headed home. A police officer said the Kentuckians do affect things, because they go on holidays and weekends.[33]

In the surveys, Belmont residents scored the lowest by far on trusting people in their neighborhood; on whether "the wise person lives for today and lets tomorrow take care of itself," they scored at least twenty points higher than any other neighborhood.[34] That is why the mayor took for granted how much they suspected him of having corrupt motives and how apathetic they were. You gain perspective when you see what people are thinking and doing organizationally at the same time.

Those in the Mexican-American poor community were among the most organizationally engaged: 6 percent belonged to three organizations, six times that in Belmont. These included mutual benefit societies, electoral organizations, political pressure and civil rights groups, and government-funded advisory groups. One in five belonged to fractious organizations, with very different views on how to relate to the Anglo-American mainstream.[35]

The poor neighborhood of Detroit's East Side was a more stable community, reflecting the fact that the auto industry and Ford Motors in particular recruited blacks and gave them pay equal to that of whites. Its organization and elected leaders were suspicious of the intentions of whites, suspicious of city government and the unions, and protective of its interests. It was a womb for black politicians, made possible by the three quarters of residents who were registered voters, 60 percent who voted in congressional elections, and 50 percent who voted in local ones. No other community I studied came close to this level of political participation. The funeral homes, Baptist churches, and indigenous and independent black organizations advocated for black interests, even in the UAW, which together supported liberal and political leaders. The Model Cities board listed 150 member organizations, and many got funding from the churches, the city, and the federal government.[36]

That was very different from the Summerhill area of Atlanta where black organizations and people lent support to the progressive business alliance that allowed Atlanta to offer a more accommodating response to civil rights. There were few institutions and no YMCA or political clubs in the neighborhood. Voter turnout was modest, but attitudinally, residents scored very high on receptivity to politics and a sense of personal efficacy.[37]

It could not have been more different from North Central Philadelphia and its "frenetic politics," I wrote at the time. Blacks have a prominent and early history in this city, and 22 percent in this poor neighborhood belonged to an organization, the highest among the communities studied. It had vital tenant and welfare rights organizations, large churches and church-sponsored social welfare programs, a large NAACP chapter, and Model Cities Program. It had strong citywide party electoral organizations, rooted in a neighborhood that delivered patronage for votes. This poor community had high electoral turnout and scored highest on my receptivity to politics scale.[38]

So, we are right to be in awe of the amazingly durable hillbilly culture, as Vance describes it, but his book does not offer much insight into our poor and working-class communities writ large or what kind of policies could really make a difference to their life chances and quality of life.

THE REAL WORKING-CLASS STORY

America's developing industries and cities were dominated by the influx of Irish, German, Scandinavian, Italian, Polish, Slavic, and Jewish immigrants from the late nineteenth century to 1920, when immigration to the United States was legally halted. Campaigns against Chinese and Japanese laborers were also successful in halting migration to the West Coast after the Emergency Quota Act of 1921. The cities of the Rust Belt were then shaped by immigrants who lived in homogeneous neighborhoods, usually working their way from the poorest and most crowded inner cities to the inner suburbs. The triumph of the unions in manufacturing after World War II allowed many to climb into the middle class.

In Detroit, America's fourth largest city early in the twentieth century, Catholic immigrants from Ukraine, Poland, Hungary, Romania, and Italy, as well as the Slavic states, worked in the auto plants. They were passionately pro-union and, after violent strikes, the United Automobile Workers won recognition in the big three plants by 1941; membership peaked by 1981.[39] They lived in various city neighborhoods, but began moving heavily to the white suburbs from 1970 to 1985, Macomb County among them, home to "Reagan Democrats."

Starting during the Depression and then heavily from World War II until the early 1960s, poor people began fleeing Kentucky, Tennessee, and West Virginia for Detroit, taking the Appalachian Highway. Most lived in North Corktown in 1960, though those who could afford to buy land would, by the 1980s, move to suburbs like Taylor Township.[40]

There was plenty of contemporaneous evidence that the culture in these Appalachian white communities was distinct and viewed as distinctive by other ethnic and working-class Americans at the time. While the residents' observations were full of prejudice, my polling at the time in another Appalachian community in Hamilton, Ohio, showed residents scored much higher on believing life was fated and that they were powerless compared to both poor black and Mexican-American communities. And those prejudice observations were consistent with Vance's characterization of the values and motivation that were dominant in multiple generations of his family during this very same period.

There are reasons the Appalachian white experience is exceptional and unhelpful in understanding the working-class experience and challenges.

Henry Ford bought coal mines in Appalachia and recruited Appalachian whites to come to Detroit because they were "safe," that is, much less likely to join a union—a struggle that was being violently fought in 1937 and 1941. Vance's grandfather appreciated Armco Steel in Ohio, and many of the Appalachian whites in Detroit memorialized Henry Ford. And since many viewed their work in Detroit as seasonal or temporary, they were content to accept lower wages and compete for jobs with UAW members. In any case, they resisted putting down roots and sent more money back home to Kentucky and elsewhere. And as in Hamilton, commentators wrote about their holiday exodus to Kentucky.[41]

In 1934, a Wayne State University survey asked Detroit residents, "What people in Detroit are undesirable?" The respondents ranked "poor Southern whites; hillbillies, etc." as the second most undesirable group, behind "criminals" who topped the list. Given Detroit's storied black-white history, "negroes" ranked fourth.[42]

About the same time that I conducted interviews in Hamilton, community papers' reported interviews with local residents described an Appalachian white community in the 1960s that was clannish and religious. Landlords revealed the tenants were always having plumbing problems and taking out the plumbing. A bar owner from the neighborhood noted a lot of fights: "There'd be a few throwdowns in there once or twice a week."[43] Over the next decades, most Appalachian whites came to realize they were not moving back to Kentucky, and they became part of the exodus in the 1970s and 1980s to the suburbs, to places like what others pejoratively called "Taylortucky." Again, that is prejudicial, but also a data point on hillbilly exceptionalism.

Vance and his reviewers readily equate hillbillies with the white working class, but the Appalachian white community in Detroit makes clear that equation could not be more off. I conducted my research with the "Reagan Democrats" in Macomb County, Michigan, in the mid-1980s when J.D. was born. The white working class I researched and wrote about believed in rewarding hard work, taking personal and family responsibility, owning a home with a yard, and being engaged in church, civic groups, and unions. It welcomed government that balanced corporate power with initiatives that gave working people greater security, opportunity, and mobility. They benefited when government was supportive of unions and created a system of social insurance that allowed workers to retire with security. The next generation climbed up the social and economic ladder when all had access to education.

But then what happened?

Detroit's inner city in July 1967 erupted into five days of rioting and looting that required the National Guard and U.S. paratroopers to regain control and took forty-three lives, the largest toll of any city in the country that year. Detroit was the most segregated metropolitan area in the country, and in 1971, a federal judge ordered the use of school busing to integrate the suburbs. Macomb was the center of anti-busing protests and organization. George Wallace got 66 percent of the Democratic primary vote in Macomb and Ronald Reagan 67 percent in 1984 against Walter Mondale, the candidate of organized labor.

The hardworking middle class was increasingly vulnerable as unemployment reached near 20 percent in the county, their lives threatened by a contracting auto industry and auto companies demanding givebacks, as their way of life was literally threatened by foreign imports, technology, and companies moving south. Yet Democrats seemed to care more about the blacks in Detroit and protesters on campus, more about equal rights and abortions, than about their mortgages or their kids' future. They thought blacks lacked virtue, yet the government understandably was under pressure to help minorities, while the middle-class poor footed the bill for free-spending government.

Robert Kennedy, whom I worked for in 1968, advanced a formula to win black and ethnic Catholic voters, but that formula died with him until Bill Clinton, whom I also worked for, resurrected it in 1992. Clinton was embraced early on by black voters in Detroit and elsewhere in the primary and nearly won Macomb's white voters in the general. He attacked the 1980s as a "gilded age of greed, selfishness, irresponsibility, excess and neglect," and said, "I want the jetsetters and featherbedders of corporate America to know that if you sell your companies and your workers and your country down the river, you'll get called on the carpet."[44] All the while, "millions of decent, ordinary people who worked hard, played by the rules and took responsibility for their own actions were falling behind."[45] Clinton declared those at the top must pay their fair share of taxes, but also that hardworking Americans were right to be upset about welfare, like the black ministers and most in the black community. When Clinton announced for president he promised "to end welfare as we know it." That meant new work requirements, but also major government initiatives to make work pay, including big investments in education, a higher minimum wage, a greatly expanded EITC, and health insurance for all. Clinton's offer was both "responsibility and opportunity," and that is what both white and black working people wanted and voted for in 1992.[46]

They were all dealing with the sudden retrenchment of manufacturing jobs from 1970 to the 1990s due to automation and technology, foreign competition, foreign buyouts, and shifts of companies to the non-union South. National political and business leaders embraced the North American Free Trade Agreement and China's entry into the World Trade Organization. NAFTA's passage in 1993 and China opening up for business in 2001 each produced almost immediate job losses, becoming an irresistible wave. America lost a million and a half manufacturing jobs during the 1980s, when many working-class voters turned to Ronald Reagan, but in the three decades since NAFTA and China joining the WTO, the country lost 4.5 million more. Michigan lost 182,288 manufacturing jobs.[47]

How political leaders dealt with globalization broadly and trade specifically was a big choice that accrued to the benefit of business, professional and skilled workers, and many larger cities. They turned a blind eye to China's abuses and mercantilism and did precious little to help those whose lives and communities were disrupted. And as Joseph

Stiglitz painfully pointed out in *People, Power, and Profits*, "Anybody who believes in the law of supply and demand should understand why globalization (in the absence of government programs to ameliorate its effects) hurts low-skilled workers." It reduces real wages, and "if wages don't fall, employment will."[48]

So when Macomb County voters were deciding whether to support Barack Obama in the summer of 2008, surprisingly, the candidate never brought up Detroit or black people, and he wasn't running on "black issues," like Jesse Jackson. Only a third thought he would put the interests of blacks ahead of other Americans and only a small minority thought affirmative action and blacks not taking responsibility for themselves were threats to the middle class. But they were nearly venomous in their critique of corporate CEOs, politicians, and elites of both parties who promoted global trade at the expense of American jobs and by far said "outsourcing of jobs to other countries" and "NAFTA and international trade agreements" were the biggest economic problem. They embraced the message that the middle class was "threatened by global trade, CEOs who care more about their companies than their own country and politicians who support free trade agreements backed by corporate special interests."[49]

The financial crisis of 2008 and the following Great Recession took a huge and enduring toll on working people, black and white, but so did the elites rushing to bail out the banks whose irresponsibility had led to the crash and bailing out the auto industry that had proved uncompetitive. Bank bonuses continued to be paid and nobody went to jail, while home foreclosures went on unabated. Middle-income Hispanic and black households lost over 40 percent of their wealth.[50] The new jobs after the crash paid 17 percent less, and median income did not recover for the whole decade up to 2016, when President Obama and business elites were pressing for passage and entry into the Trans-Pacific Partnership, with working people expecting to become collateral damage again.[51]

And all through these decades, the working-class family was under growing pressure. The acceptance of birth control and the sexual revolution had led to a surge of women entering the labor force starting in the 1970s and accelerating in the 1980s.[52] Family income gains were due entirely to women working more hours, even as wages stagnated.[53]

The traditional family with the male breadwinner role was increasingly under siege, particularly working-class men who struggled to find jobs that would put them on the ladder to the middle class.[54] Working women faced extraordinary stress, too, as they moved fully into the workforce with no assurance of equal pay and virtually no help with childcare and no paid family leave or guaranteed health insurance for themselves and their kids.[55]

CONFRONTING THE BUILDING CHALLENGES OF THE WORKING CLASS

Today, all of America worries about the growing dysfunction of the family, the breakdown of marriage and children raised on their own, the growing violence, and the use of drugs. Middle-size cities and small towns have lost big companies, stores, and new investment. Many expressed their anger at the political and economic elites by voting for Donald Trump.

What conservatives and Republican leaders see are people who have grown dependent on government and been failed by the War on Poverty, unemployment and disability benefits, food stamps, housing vouchers, and free health care that have created a hammock that allows people to drop out of the labor market. Vance's book suggests a dysfunctional culture has left these people and communities disabled and our medicine cabinet of policies pretty empty.

The problem with those judgments is that you have to erase a lot of history and experience with a lot of policy outcomes to get there. Working-class families and communities are in trouble, but it is fair to conclude that a lot of things contributed to it. It was not just bad choices. It was not lack of personal responsibility or a government that was clueless about how to get to a better economy and society. The country is not powerless. Voters today think others were writing the rules of the economy in ways that favored them, and they have a pretty good idea of things government can do that would make a difference.

Well, the full Republican takeover of the U.S. government gave the GOP the opportunity to address the profound problems facing the white working class who had played such a big role in Donald Trump's victory and in putting Tea Party Republicans in power in the House and Senate and in control of state governments. And they devoted 2018 to building in "work requirements" before the "able-bodied" could receive welfare benefits or food stamps, or be covered by Medicaid.[56]

In January, the Trump administration allowed states to impose work requirements, and Kentucky tried before it was blocked by the courts. In April, the administration instructed cabinet members to find areas to impose work requirements or make them more severe. And the House Republicans introduced stringent work requirements for receiving food stamps in their version of the Farm Bill. The "work requirements" remained the principal contrast between the House and Senate bills as the country went and voted.[57]

They paid no attention to the evidence that prior imposition of work requirements had no long-term effect on people staying in the labor force or on the poverty rate. Indeed, as Alvin Chang and Tara Golshan write, "It made them poorer." It ignored that half of the Supplemental Nutrition Assistance Program (SNAP) recipients already worked while they received food stamps and that three quarters worked in the year afterward. And that the people hurt are the children, who are often the reason these benefits exist.[58]

They ignored the fact that these programs exist to help people who are poor, to help them manage with wages that can't get them out of poverty, or to get health care like any other family. The reason conservatives have embraced "work requirements" is to keep lower-income and working-class Americans from becoming indolent. Is that really all they have to offer working people? What an insult. Are conservatives so bereft of ideas?

The Republicans lost dramatically in the anti-Trump wave election, but most of all, they lost across the industrial Midwest and Rust Belt, stretching from Pennsylvania to Iowa and Kansas. The repudiation of conservatives was greatest with the non-Evangelical working class who wanted more from Republicans than this anti-government trope—they didn't believe that food stamps and Medicaid led to people swinging idly in hammocks.

And for good measure, voters also retired Speaker Paul Ryan to his hammock. Republicans would do well to unlearn the lessons of *Hillbilly Elegy*.

8 HOW DID DEMOCRATS LET DONALD TRUMP WIN?

SO, HOW DID DEMOCRATS EVER let Donald Trump become president of the United States? How did they allow this Tea Party–led GOP to get total control nationally and in the majority of states? How did they let them do so much damage to the country? How did they allow the GOP to suppress every effort to use government for public benefit?

What did Democrats get wrong?

And how do they embrace a very different politics that allows them to crush the GOP electorally and lead a period of explosive change?

It begins with recognizing that Democratic leaders contributed mightily to the alienation of voters that produced successive disruptive elections that put the Republicans in power.

The spotlight turned immediately to the white working-class voters who supported Donald Trump. But Democrats didn't have a white working-class problem. They had a working-class problem. White working-class voters revolted against President Obama's bank bailout and more, but so did much of the New America that was not motivated to defend what Democrats had done on the economy and health care. Democrats lost control nationally and in the states because of an explosion of racial resentment under President Obama, but that is only part of the story. Democrats lost the confidence of voters early in the period when Democrats had control of the presidency and the U.S. Congress and most of the states. They did not pause to reflect why they got "shellacked" in 2010 or lost so many seats at all levels of government, election after election. Even a disgraced GOP conducted a postmortem after President Obama was reelected in 2012, but Democrats never took stock and changed course.

Donald Trump would not be president of the United States, of course, but for critical help from the Russians, the FBI, and the Hillary Clinton campaign's malpractice. However, the 2016 election shouldn't have been close. Clinton would have closed in 2016 with an unassailable lead if Democrats had been in touch with what was happening to ordinary Americans or showed any anger about a corrupt political system dominated by the banks, big corporations, and rich donors.

The vast majority of the country, working people, and the Democrats' electoral base were shattered by the financial crisis. They lost nearly all their wealth, and their incomes only regained precrisis levels in President Obama's last year, seven years after the 2008 crash. Jobs no longer paid what they used to and few got raises now, yet people faced daunting and skyrocketing costs for health care, prescription drugs, childcare, student debt, and housing. The great majority of working people were at their wits' end. And Obamacare mandated they have health insurance or face a fine, yet the deductibles were so high they could never afford to use it.

Meanwhile, working families were a mess. More kids were being raised by single parents. Drugs and violence were shortening life expectancy. Women were deep into the labor market, yet got no help with family leave, childcare, or equal pay. Working women were on their own.

And all Democratic presidents in living memory welcomed globalization, including expanded trade, new trade agreements, and expanded immigration, without serious consideration to its impact at home. The new trade agreements accelerated the outsourcing of American jobs and put further downward pressure on American wages. The elites thought it was worth the price or prioritized other goals. While President Obama genuinely sought comprehensive immigration reform that expanded border and workplace enforcement, candidate Hillary Clinton seemed to care only about assuring a path to citizenship for the undocumented and DACA Dreamers.

The great majority of voters were seething that CEOs had so much power, despite selling out their companies and their country. The big banks had wrecked the economy yet they inexplicably got bailed out and now seemed to call the shots. Voters watched the explosion of campaign spending over a decade by super PACs, corporations, and billionaires, and believed they had rigged the rules of the economy to work for them, not for the middle class that was struggling and on the edge.

Yet, the Democrats' campaigns in four national elections starting in 2010 called on voters to "build on the progress" and "build ladders of opportunity" for those who had not yet shared in the broad gains. President Obama's closing argument while stumping for Clinton touted the economic recovery under his leadership and argued that Hillary Clinton had the experience to build on his progress: "We've seen America turn recession into recovery. Our businesses create 15.5 million new jobs." He pumped, "Incomes are rising. Poverty is falling. Twenty million more Americans have health insurance. Those are just the facts."

Liberal economists and social scientists, progressive think tanks such as the Roosevelt Institute and the Center for American Progress, and the vast network of progressive advocacy groups advanced strong critiques of the economy and proposed bold reforms, yet only in the 2018 anti-Trump election did Democrats campaign with a passion to disrupt the status quo.

If you want to understand how out of touch Democrats were before President Trump's election in 2016, please read this sincere account by White House Senior Advisor Ben Rhodes of President Obama's thinking through what they got wrong and how Donald Trump could have been elected president of the United States:

> Along the streets of Lima (Peru) the crowds still waved as the president of the United States passed by. "What if we were wrong?" Obama said, sitting opposite me in the Beast. "Wrong about what?" I asked. For days, we had been trying to deconstruct what had happened in the recent election. Obama had complained he couldn't believe that the election was lost, rattling off the

indicators—"Five percent unemployment. Twenty million covered. Gas at two bucks a gallon. We had it all teed up!" Now he told me about a piece he had read in *The New York Times*, a column asserting that liberals had forgotten how important identity is to people, that we had embraced a message indistinguishable from John Lennon's "Imagine"—touting an empty, cosmopolitan globalism that could no longer reach people. Imagine all the people, sharing all the world. "Maybe we pushed too far," he said. "Maybe people just want to fall back into their tribe."[1]

On Election Day 2016, I asked voters in a survey for the Roosevelt Institute whether the economy had "started to get to full employment" and whether "a lot of people are finding jobs that pay more" or whether "jobs still don't pay enough to live on" and people have to "struggle to save anything." When you saw that 60 percent of those who voted believed jobs didn't pay enough to live on—and when you saw that those who strongly believed that outnumbered those with great faith in the incipient recovery by three to one—you didn't need to look very far for why Donald Trump was elected. Among people of color and unmarried women—the Democrats' so-called base—two thirds rejected President Obama's view of the economy.

On Election Day 2016, I also asked people eight years after the financial crisis whether they could handle an unexpected expense of five hundred dollars, and nearly four in ten said they could not, including a majority of unmarried women and large numbers of minorities, millennials, and the white working class. The country wasn't remotely teed up to embrace a leader who would merely tinker with the economy or political system.

Hillary Clinton campaigned with President Obama in successive closing weekends and she, too, chose not to speak to the economic stress of working-class women, many of whom were still in play late in the election, nor did she empathize with the everyday struggles of the Democrats' own electoral base of minorities, millennials, and unmarried women. These voters were looking for leaders that got it, not big posters saying, "Hope, not hate." That failure to connect diminished turnout in the big metropolitan areas that allowed Trump his tragic win.[2]

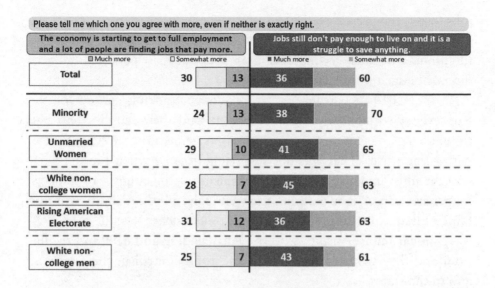

Please tell me which one you agree with more, even if neither is exactly right.				
The economy is starting to get to full employment and a lot of people are finding jobs that pay more.			**Jobs still don't pay enough to live on and it is a struggle to save anything.**	
	▣ Much more	▢ Somewhat more	■ Much more	▪ Somewhat more
Total	30	13	36	60
Minority	24	13	38	70
Unmarried Women	29	10	41	65
White non-college women	28	7	45	63
Rising American Electorate	31	12	36	63
White non-college men	25	7	43	61

Majority of unmarried women can't deal with a $500 expense

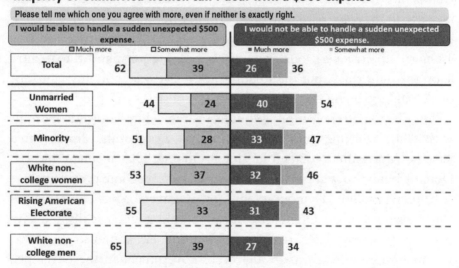

Please tell me which one you agree with more, even if neither is exactly right.				
I would be able to handle a sudden unexpected $500 expense.			**I would not be able to handle a sudden unexpected $500 expense.**	
	▣ Much more	▢ Somewhat more	■ Much more	▪ Somewhat more
Total	62	39	26	36
Unmarried Women	44	24	40	54
Minority	51	28	33	47
White non-college women	53	37	32	46
Rising American Electorate	55	33	31	43
White non-college men	65	39	27	34

Source: Democracy Corps for Roosevelt Institute, Election night survey of 2016 voters

What was the reality for most Americans during the Obama presidency? Most lost wealth and their incomes fell, particularly for those at the bottom of the ladder. Those who lost jobs when the financial crisis took its biggest toll found jobs that earned $610 less a month in salary and benefits. While the country had regained a half million manufacturing jobs by 2014, that was a fraction of the 6 million such jobs lost in the decade before the crisis. The number in minimum-wage jobs doubled between the crisis and Obama's reelection in 2012, and the number of those feeling discouraged about their personal finances did not budge up through the end of 2015.[3]

In late 2014, according to my economic tracking survey for the Roosevelt Institute, 55 percent of people said their families had had to make big changes in their buying habits at the grocery store to deal with rising prices. That was not surprising because when I asked what was the most important economic problem for the country to address, 57 percent chose "jobs that don't pay enough to live on" and "working families that can't afford childcare and student debt."[4]

A similar number picked government spending and debt and regulation, and they won out when the GOP took control in the Congress and in the states.

The president of the United States was the main messenger for the Democrats through this whole period, and Obama's consistent economic message to the country—from one year after the crash through the 2016 presidential election—was this: the recession has been transformed into a dependable recovery, our economy is creating jobs, and the country is on the right track, but the Republicans drove our economy "into the ditch" and are doing everything possible to obstruct our progress.

So, election after election, Republicans racked up landslide margins with white working-class voters, while the Democrats' discontented base failed to rally to defend President Obama. That formula allowed Donald Trump to win enough states in 2016 to become president.

Understandably, Democrats and progressives have been reluctant to criticize President Obama because his bold actions really did save America from another Great Depression and his administration was so much more effective than any other government in the developed world, where austerity reigned. Nobody wanted to say anything that diminished his presidency when it was under vicious attack then and now from a Tea Party–dominated GOP that sought to gridlock the country, impose austerity, and heighten racial resentment.

Well, the great majority of working people never heard from Democrats that this party was angry that jobs don't pay enough to live on and wages don't keep up with rising costs that put working people on the edge financially.

President Trump and the Republicans thought they had teed up an even stronger economy for the 2018 election, and they got crushed. They passed and promoted their massive tax cut, unemployment had dropped to 3.5 percent, and the economy had grown at a 3.4 percent rate in the final months before the election.[5] They shared the same view of the macro economy that put off working people. President Trump said:

> So I want to thank all of the people that are making this economy go. We have so many people working so hard. But it's booming. And veteran unemployment has reached its lowest level in nearly twenty-one years. And it's going to be better. [Applause] Going to be even be better. And that number will be better—because if you look at the various statistics, African American employment [unemployment] is the lowest level in history. Hispanic employment [unemployment] is the lowest level in history. Asian employment [unemployment] is the lowest level in history.[6]

Pundits and strategists in both parties thought President Trump's misogyny, arrogance, corruption, and divisiveness dragged him down and kept him from benefiting electorally from the economy's performance, but they had not learned anything about our economy. Trump was hurt, not helped, by his efforts to convince voters they were making economic gains.

Less than half of those who voted in 2018 endorsed the modest statement, "The economy is strong and families like mine are *beginning* to be more financially secure," while six in ten said their wages weren't keeping up with the cost of living. Two thirds of African Americans, unmarried women, and Hispanics said that, half with intensity, as did over 60 percent of millennials and white working-class women and a big majority of white working-class men, a third with intensity.

Since the financial crash and for the whole period that Obama and Trump have governed, elites just haven't understood how much working people are struggling to keep up with rising costs and how frustrated they are that those in power don't get it.

Angry rejection of wages keeping up with costs

Now let me ask you some questions about the economy. Please tell me whether you agree or disagree with each statement.

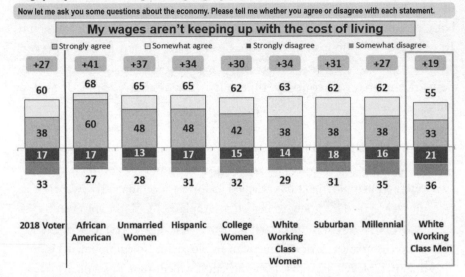

My wages aren't keeping up with the cost of living

□ Strongly agree   □ Somewhat agree   ■ Strongly disagree   ■ Somewhat disagree

	2018 Voter	African American	Unmarried Women	Hispanic	College Women	White Working Class Women	Suburban	Millennial	White Working Class Men
	+27	+41	+37	+34	+30	+34	+31	+27	+19
	60	68	65	65	62	63	62	62	55
	38	60	48	48	42	38	38	38	33
	17	17	13	17	15	14	18	16	21
	33	27	28	31	32	29	31	35	36

Most Americans now take as a given that pay increases are few and far between, and they face an endemic cost-of-living crisis. Any modest real income gains are overwhelmed by the rising and formidable costs for health care, childcare, housing, and college. Those are not discretionary expenses but critical investments where the government has provided precious little help.

CRISIS OF HEALTH CARE COSTS

It is the cost of health care that is most explosive, though. The Affordable Care Act slowed the rate of inflation but right now, those costs go up 5 percent a year. Prescription drug costs of regularly prescribed medications increased by 8.4 percent in 2017 alone.[7] That is why nine in ten say health care costs are "out of control"—three quarters with intensity. That is why health care was one of the reasons voters punished Republicans in the 2018 election.

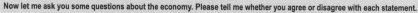

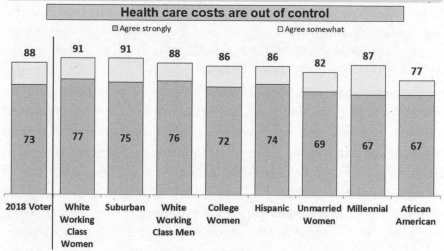

Health care costs are out of control

☐ Agree strongly   ☐ Agree somewhat

2018 Voter	White Working Class Women	Suburban	White Working Class Men	College Women	Hispanic	Unmarried Women	Millennial	African American
88	91	91	88	86	86	82	87	77
73	77	75	76	72	74	69	67	67

But in every election before 2018, working people punished Democrats on the passage and implementation of the Affordable Care Act, or Obamacare. And it was not because of government overreach. Trump voters rejected repealing it out of hand, and rarely talked about its unfair subsidies to the poor. At every point and in every state, voters have supported the expansion of Medicaid to cover more people. People were dismayed when health care reform brought impossible out-of-pocket health care costs that pushed them even closer to the edge.

Again, Democrats were not very self-critical on the implementation of the Affordable Care Act because it was under vicious ideological attack from Republicans, who were determined to make it fail. Republicans would not entertain any amendments that would allow Congress to address the problems in any new program. They opposed any increase in subsidies and fought expansion of Medicaid in the states.

Obamacare has grown more popular, but just barely. In the fall of 2018, favorable outnumbered unfavorable responses to the ACA by 47 to 42 percent, but those who hated it still outnumbered those who loved it—and that imbalance has held true from the beginning in 2010. On Election Day in 2010 and 2012, just a third viewed the program favorably, rising to just 40 percent in 2014 and 2016—all elections for which the Tea Party GOP was able to mobilize its base by promising to repeal and replace Obamacare. Only in 2018 did support rise to nearly half of the country.[8]

By contrast, Medicaid was wildly popular, viewed favorably by 58 to 19 percent, despite the GOP's efforts to shift control to the states and cut it dramatically.[9]

Support for the Affordable Care Act was dragged down by the white working class, who form 37 percent of registered voters, but also by unmarried women and millennials who were supposed to be the beneficiaries of expanded access to health care.[10] Only 20 percent of the white working class was favorable to the program through its first two years and that crept up to just a quarter by 2014. By the end of 2018, only a third viewed the ACA favorably, while 46 percent gave it the lowest possible rating.

White unmarried women who rallied to support Democrats in overwhelming numbers in the 2018 off-year election only became dependable supporters when the program was under attack from President Trump. These are single women on their own who support expansive government and who should benefit from expanding the health care safety net, yet just a third dependably supported it in the program's first five years.[11] Even in this last election with health care on the ballot, just 50 percent embraced it.

African Americans were strong supporters from the outset, but that had much more to do with the GOP labeling it "Obamacare" and Republicans' effort to destroy his legacy.

So, what is going on?

Post-Election Tracking Poll Finds Slight Uptick in ACA Favorability, Largely Driven By Democrats

As you may know a health reform bill was signed into law in 2010, known commonly as the Affordable Care Act or Obamacare. Given what you know about the health reform law, do you have a generally favorable or generally unfavorable opinion of it?

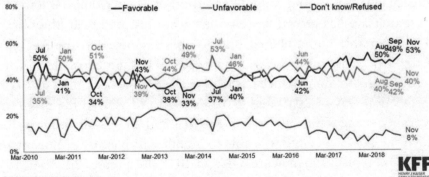

SOURCE: KFF Health Tracking Polls

It is not a great mystery. I did focus groups with white working-class independents and Democrats who voted for Trump in Macomb County, Michigan, and Donald Trump's promise to fix the health care system was the greatest hope for his presidency. They believed passionately that Obamacare had made health care less affordable. They spoke of "price hikes" and reduced coverage and fees "punishing people that can't afford it." Nearly every person in our groups struggled with how to afford their plans, co-pays, and medications. One complained the cost of health care was "cutting into a lot of peoples' income that's not growing nearly as fast as premiums." Another felt "taken advantage of" by the price hikes. Others complained of paying "outrageous" sums for coverage on the exchanges.

And the groups I did with unmarried women, African Americans, and Hispanics a year into Trump's presidency sound eerily similar. They were not getting the relief they expected and costs were unbearable.

The battle over the Affordable Care Act was transformative. Health care costs became the biggest factor impacting voters' going off a cliff financially or having some security. And it was politicized in ways I have not seen before. Voters now believed that the party you voted for would determine whether your health care costs would be "unaffordable." And perhaps most important, a big majority wanted government to play a bigger, not smaller, role in health care.

In the 2018 election, health care was issue number one and those voters voted for the Democrats by 75 to 23 percent. Going into the presidential election year, Democrats are more trusted than the Republicans on this issue by 60 to 40 percent.[12]

Health care costs

Obscene Depressing Exorbitant
Too-high Too-much Unfair
Outrageous
Ridiculous
Expensive
Unaffordable

Uttering the three words "prescription drug companies" in the working-class and college groups in December 2018 produced a reaction as personal and emotional as anything I have witnessed in my years of research. In one of the Macomb County groups, the male participants, one after the other, said: "killers," "the devil," "bad news," "drives up health care costs," "very costly." The women in Oak Creek, Wisconsin, again one after the other, said: "worst of the worst," "all money," "greedy to the tenth power."[13]

In one group in Oak Creek, the first participant said, "rapist." And the moderator responded, "That's a strong word." He pushed back, "That's the way I feel." Another said, "criminals."[14] The moderator reacted, "Another strong word. Tell me about that." This time the participant elaborated: "I feel they are poisoning people legally. I think they are killing people, legally, and they are getting away with it."

In Seattle, the first participant said, "criminal." And the moderator: "I'm sorry, what did you say?" Participant: "I mean, I have to pay for my own drugs the last twenty years with an individual plan that has a large deductible, so to me it's just ridiculous. I pay $1,000 for an antibiotic for my daughter just because I'm a small business owner and don't have insurance. It's just kind of crazy." The results can be ruinous: "When I look to the future and the medical costs that I know I'm going to have to pay every year," said one Seattle woman with a husband recovering from brain cancer, "I sometimes can't get out of bed in the morning."

Pharmaceutical drug companies

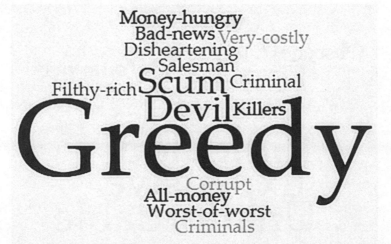

Money-hungry
Bad-news Very-costly
Disheartening
Salesman
Filthy-rich Scum Criminal
Devil Killers
Greedy
Corrupt
All-money
Worst-of-worst
Criminals

What people see are powerful companies that get doctors to push their product, spend massively on advertising to create demand, and get government to promote their interests. And consumers are left to live with the very high price. The reaction to prescription drug companies underscores how skeptical America has become of big corporations whose greed and power look just corrupt.

CEOS

CEOs of big corporations are the villain in the American story—and getting them to behave in the interest of their employees, company, and the country will be central to the Democrats' case for change.

This strong anti-corporate streak emerged from a long history of chief executives shifting production, outsourcing, and weakening unions while failing to invest in the company's competitiveness and enriching shareholders and CEOs. The anger with CEOs is fundamental and long-standing.

When I interviewed Macomb voters in the summer of 2008, their worry about candidate Barack Obama was not that he would govern for his own people, but whether he would tackle the powerful CEOs of American companies who have championed NAFTA and other trade agreements that accelerated the outsourcing of our jobs.

Globalization and technology had left all employees worried that their jobs would be disaggregated and outsourced abroad and put further downward pressure on wages. CEOs and the leaders of American business had broken a compact that had left fewer able to reach the middle class. Companies shed factory workers, who were first on the chopping block, but now outsourcing put a broader range of jobs at risk, including those of many college graduates.

And people believe CEOs and big industry used their influence over government to get a tax structure, trade agreements, and a regulatory regime that allowed them to get ever richer and make the country more and more unequal.

This is not nuanced. People are focused like a laser on CEOs, as you can see in what happened when I started testing the fairly neutral term "CEOs of large businesses." In the graph below you can see the working-class contempt in the two-to-one negative responses to the term. But CEOs had also lost the confidence of college graduates.

Negative reactions had always outweighed the positive. Just 10 percent view these deans of American capitalism with awe.

The leaders of American companies had lost millennials more than any generation and group, and they are the future. Their attitudes have been shaped by America's post-crisis policies. In 2014, negative reactions to CEOs outnumbered positive by thirty-two points: in 2018, by twenty-eight points (19 percent warm and 47 percent cool). One third of millennials give CEOs the intensely negative rating. The New America is intensely anti-corporate.

Anti-Corporate Sentiment Strong and Stable over time

Now, please rate your feelings towards some people, organizations, or concepts, with 100 meaning VERY WARM, FAVORABLE feeling; 0 meaning VERY COLD, UNFAVORABLE feeling, and 50 meaning not particularly warm or cold. State your feelings on...CEOs of Large Corporations

SHIFT FROM 2014 TO 2018

	Cool	Very cool (26<)		Warm	Very Warm (>75)	
	+24	+14	+21	+19	+13	+12
	20	27	23	27	26	27
	9	12	10	12	10	9
	29	31	30	29	24	27
	44	41	44	46	39	39
	October 2014	October 2016	September 2018	October 2014	October 2016	September 2018
	WORKING CLASS VOTERS			COLLEGE VOTERS		

In December 2018, I measured reactions to "CEOs of large corporations" for Public Citizen, and the anti-corporate pushback was as strong as I have ever seen. People told us that CEOs are overpaid, greedy, and "a lot of them are just out for themselves, not for the good of the company and their employees" (Macomb woman). They are "wealthy," "untrustworthy," "out of touch," and "don't care," according to those in the working-class groups. In Seattle, people said "overpaid" but also "entitled" and "sheltered" and having "no accountability." They especially distrust the way that corporations are able to bend the system to their will so that they can earn more profits while hurting consumers.

They know that through lobbyists and big campaign donors, "they are buying their laws, basically" (Macomb man). That is what CEOs and labor unions are able to do, according to the college men in Seattle:

> [Money and politics] reinforces and perpetuates this system that gives them more power and influences the access to campaigns and the important people running campaigns. And then there's all this shadow money that gets thrown around that is really difficult to trace, but it's almost always by self-serving corporations.

CEOs work for themselves at the expense of the country, and they use their growing wealth to influence campaigns and politicians to get government to help them enrich themselves further, without regard to what happens to other citizens.

CEOs of large corporations

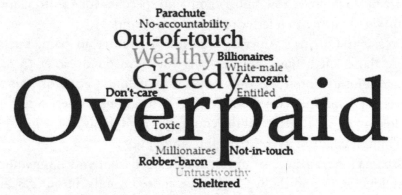

That America was angry with corporate behavior and the CEOs who led the biggest companies was utterly absent from anything Democrats have had to say during the last decade. It is why Donald Trump was able to attack Hillary Clinton for taking corporate cash for speeches and being in the pocket of Wall Street. It is why so many Trump voters even now say a "President Hillary Clinton" would mean the rich are still calling the shots:

> "She—politicians are owned by big businesses. Obama was too, they are all, they are in it for profit. I think she would not have been looking out for us, she would have been looking out for the wealthy."—moderate GOP woman, Oakland County

The Democrats' top leaders weren't seen as pushing back on corporate power or wanting government to be a check on business or the new class of oligarchs.

How were the American people left with this impression?

HILLARY CLINTON'S CAMPAIGN

Hillary Clinton fully identified with President Obama's vision of the economy and opportunity and faith in America's upward trajectory. She viewed his campaign and government as successful, and thus, stocked her campaign with his campaign consultants and those who had worked in his White House.

She believed America was dynamic, growing, making progress, and now needed an economy that truly left no one behind. Inequality had worsened, but the answer was "building ladders of opportunity," which President Obama had described in his State of the Union speech before his own reelection, in his campaign speeches for Clinton, and in his private handwritten letter to President Trump.

President Obama's America was not a country in pain, but one where those left behind were looking for a seasoned leader to make progress. And Clinton was only reluctantly willing to pull off this narrative. She lived in a cosmopolitan and professional America not very worked up about the state of the country, even if many of the groups in the Clinton coalition were struggling and angry.

Obama's refrain was so out of touch with what was happening to most Americans and the working class more broadly. In our research, "ladders of opportunity" fell far short of what real people were looking for. Incomes went down after the financial crisis, pensions lost value, and many lost their housing wealth, yet people faced dramatically rising costs for things that mattered: health care, education, housing, and childcare, which Edward Luce writes about so forcefully. People faced "vanishing" geographic and social "mobility." Billionaires spent massively to influence politicians and parked their money in the big cities, whose dynamism drew in the best talent from the smaller towns and rural areas.

Clinton's default position was Obama's refrain about America, but she invited real discussion of these issues and got close to embracing the need for change in some of her economic speeches, her convention address, and in the debates. But when the going got tough, she empowered those most wedded to Obama's vision.

My vantage point included regular meetings and exchanges with John Podesta, intended campaign chair with a long history of advising previous Democratic presidents. Early on, he pressed me for help on pushing back against Bernie Sanders's Wall Street attack and asked my reaction to Hillary's emerging stump speech. Later, I worked directly with Hillary Clinton on how to best close the primaries and was asked to react to the economic and convention speeches. And Podesta asked to email Clinton's campaign manager Robby Mook directly when he could not get him to change course at the campaign's close.

From 2015, I pushed Podesta, the other principals, and Hillary Clinton to show their discontent with the state of the economy and politics and to put forward bold economic policies, like those proposed by Joe Stiglitz and the Roosevelt Institute. Clinton was always comfortable with the policies, but her default was "build on the progress," which meant minimally disrupting the status quo.

And from the beginning, I called on her to decry the special-interest, big-money influence that was keeping government from working for the middle class. On that, I got nowhere.

But I got the opportunity to keep offering this input only because John Podesta, the speechwriters, and most of her campaign advisers agreed with me.

Early on, I chided the campaign privately for starting every economic talk with dutiful praise for President Obama's handling of the economy, and, later, for saying, "America is already great." "The New American majority," I wrote, "is looking for a president who will address the building problems"—and "not a third term of Obama."

Podesta invited me to critique Clinton's comments at an Iowa town hall that he thought was "getting there," but I was dumbfounded. "What is your core message?" I asked. You want to "build on the progress that we've made" and Republicans will "rip away the progress and turn us backwards." With some help from AutoCorrect, I said, "I think the overall message is tone-death [deaf] on what is happening in the country." Clinton "has left the change voters to Sanders."

I warned that Sanders was gaining by embracing the "level the playing field" message that I had developed with the Roosevelt Institute, which began: "Families and small businesses are struggling, yet CEOs and billionaires are using their lobbyists to rewrite the rules so government works for them." And Sanders gained on economic change by committing to "stop any new trade deals that undermine American jobs and income."

Sanders's surprising strength and the harm caused by his big money and Wall Street attacks led John Podesta and I to huddle on how Hillary could find her footing on reform. Clinton's instinctive response was to go silent and attack Sanders on guns and health care. I warned in my note on reporting a survey for the campaign reform group Every Voice: "Billionaires, corporations, and special interests buying their government is a voting issue."[15]

My survey for Every Voice in December 2015 showed a big majority and highest level of support yet for "a plan to overhaul campaign spending by getting rid of big donations and allowing only small donations to candidates, matched by taxpayer funds." You heard it right. That is with taxpayer funds, which is some measure of where voters have moved on this issue.

Hillary Clinton supported these and other bold reforms, but she was reluctant to speak out on them because of her financial support from Wall Street. I tested what would happen if Clinton were to publicize her reforms and say, "We must end secret money, unaccountable money that is corrupting our political system. On my first day in office, I'll sign an executive order to require federal contractors to disclose the money they are spending to influence politics." She committed to appoint Supreme Court justices who "value the right to vote over the right of billionaires to buy elections."

The research showed Hillary Clinton could not afford to be silent on reform. When voters heard her reform message first before her being attacked by her opponents as corrupt, a majority rallied to her reform message anyway. But when voters heard the attacks first, her message fell short of a majority and intense support fell eight points. She had to be opportunistic on reform.[16]

Reason to go on offense: more support for money reform when Democratic candidate starts the conversation

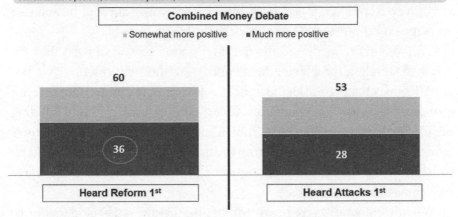

Now I am going to read you some things [Hillary Clinton / a DEMOCRATIC candidate] is saying about money and politics. Please tell me whether the statement makes you feel much more positive about Hillary Clinton / the DEMOCRATIC candidate, somewhat more positive, a little more positive, or not at all positive.

Combined Money Debate

▪ Somewhat more positive   ▪ Much more positive

60

53

36

28

Heard Reform 1st   **Heard Attacks 1st**

"LEVEL THE PLAYING FIELD" LEVELED "LADDERS OF OPPORTUNITY"

In the spring of 2016, both parties faced fateful choices, but also extraordinary opportunities to break out and offer disruptive changes to the current course of the country.

Based on the work of Joseph Stiglitz, the Roosevelt Institute developed a policy agenda to "level the playing field" and "rewrite the rules of the economy" to favor the middle class, rather than the top 1 percent. I helped evolve that agenda into a narrative and message that would be compelling in the upcoming election. It contrasted with candidate Hillary Clinton's developing message that centered on building "ladders of opportunity" for every American and building on the accomplishments of President Obama.[17]

But it was a turning point for Republicans. Donald Trump was leading the primary field and had made trade, immigration, and nationalist economics central to his conservative vision. Ted Cruz was his main competitor, and he lambasted government spending and trade deals that promoted crony capitalism.

I put this big cross-party vision battle to a test first in a large-scale, experimental web survey and then in a national phone survey.

Donald Trump's simulated "nationalist" message declared our political leaders were too incompetent, spineless, or corrupt to stand up to special interests and other countries to put American workers first. It was pitted against a Reaganesque message that asserted big government and crony capitalism stunt the economy, which requires smaller government, lower taxes, and fewer regulations to thrive. It was soon very clear Republicans led by a leader with an economic nationalist message could put the Democratic candidate at risk.

The web experiment and the national phone survey showed that the message "leveling the playing field" and "rewriting the rules" was a potential game changer for Democrats. It was dramatically stronger than an economic message that spoke of "ladders of opportunity" and "building on Obama's accomplishments," but it slayed Trump's nationalist message. Getting to this message platform allowed the Democratic candidate to be more trusted on the economy, set the economic agenda, and move base voters to get engaged.

When Democrats were heard embracing the message "ladders of opportunity," Democrats lost ground electorally and voters become less engaged.

The results were stark: 60 percent responded positively to a candidate who articulated the "level the playing field" message; 34 percent much more so. The "ladders of opportunity" message was just not compelling: 48 percent reacted positively, and only a quarter strongly.

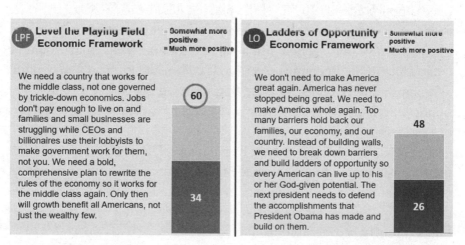

The "level the playing field, rewrite the rules" framework was embraced by the core progressive base that formed the Rising American Electorate. A stunning 83 percent of people of color supported it.

Unmarried women preferred it over the "ladders of opportunity" message by fifteen points; millennials preferred it by nineteen. It was not even a contest among the Democrats' potential base.

The "level the playing field, rewrite the rules" message allowed Democrats to more than compete for the white working class and swing voters. It was embraced by about 60 percent of independents, white unmarried women, and white working-class women. "Ladders of opportunity" was just limp with those voters. Only around 40 percent could support it. It hardly got a hearing.

And maybe most important for the fate of the country, the "level the playing field" message was uniquely powerful in a potential contest against a Republican Party led by an economic nationalist, rather than a conventional Reagan conservative. In this contest, the Democrats' message won by sixteen points overall and with a big twelve-point advantage in intensity.[18] If the contest pitted a "ladders of opportunity" candidate against a Republican running on nationalist economics, the Democrat lost any edge in intensity.

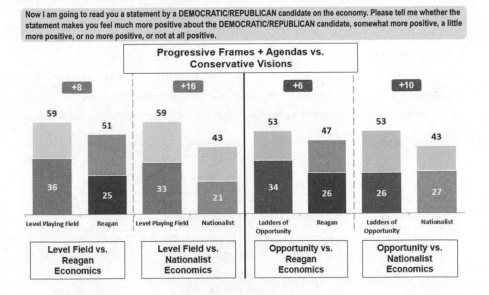

Now I am going to read you a statement by a DEMOCRATIC/REPUBLICAN candidate on the economy. Please tell me whether the statement makes you feel much more positive about the DEMOCRATIC/REPUBLICAN candidate, somewhat more positive, a little more positive, or no more positive, or not at all positive.

Progressive Frames + Agendas vs. Conservative Visions

A "level the playing field" framework also produced a chance for progressives to win the debate on which party was better on the economy—and the difference was stark. Voters who heard the "level the playing field" message gave Democrats a seven-point advantage on the economy, but when voters heard the "ladders of opportunity" message instead, the Republicans were favored by three points.

Hillary Clinton's real economic narrative left Democrats weaker on the economy—because it was not really about the state of the economy. It was about the state of society.

The 2016 election was impacted crucially by which leader's vision pushed voters to be engaged or disengaged. Hearing the "level the playing field" message increased enthusiasm among Democrats and millennials. But that enthusiasm fell when voters heard that the Democrats wanted to build "ladders of opportunity." And when the Democrat was battling the economic nationalist, enthusiasm dropped four points with Democrats and two with the Rising American Electorate (unmarried women, minorities, and millennials).

Why was the Democrats' most likely message such a disaster in the making? Because the message really was about society and sounded complacent about the economy. When asked what was convincing in the "ladders of opportunity" message, only 13 percent said it would mean help with the economy. That contrasted with the 41 percent who said that after they heard the "level the playing field" message.

The difference occurred because voters believed that the economy was rigged. And they thought it was rigged by the politicians in Washington above all, together with big corporations, lobbyists, and the wealthiest 1 percent. Voters believed this rigged economy was the result of a corrupt government that had produced an unacceptable status quo.

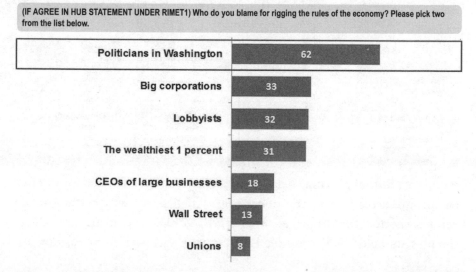

(IF AGREE IN HUB STATEMENT UNDER RIMET1) Who do you blame for rigging the rules of the economy? Please pick two from the list below.

Politicians in Washington	62
Big corporations	33
Lobbyists	32
The wealthiest 1 percent	31
CEOs of large businesses	18
Wall Street	13
Unions	8

The "level the playing field" narrative was so powerful because it began with a tough diagnosis of the current economy that left the middle class on life support while the top tier reaped all the gains. It was so powerful because it explicitly rejected trickle-down economics and challenged a political system fueled by big campaign donations that allowed CEOs and billionaires to rig the rules of the economy at the expense of the middle class and small businesses. It was so powerful because of the depth of the economic critique, the demand for political reform, and the breadth of economic changes it proposed.

CLINTON CAMPAIGN (CONTINUED)

Right before the Connecticut primary, I watched Secretary Hillary Clinton and my wife, Congresswoman Rosa DeLauro, host a café discussion with working women. Beforehand, Clinton greeted me warmly and afterward Rosa and I hung back in the holding area to allow the secretary and I to speak alone and frankly. She was really moved and disturbed by what she had heard. She recounted similar stories from women in suburban Philadelphia, Tampa, and Brooklyn. "They're in such pain. People are at their wits' end. They feel hopeless and have nobody to turn to."[19]

I said, yes, that is exactly what's happening in the country, which she acknowledged, but then said, "How do I talk about their pain without sounding like I'm criticizing President Obama and his economy? I just can't do that."

I said, "I think you can manage a different balance," and I said, "Why not use your own learning from listening to these folks as a way to talk about the economy? You are about to lock up an unassailable number of delegates, why not make that learning about the economy central to this new chapter?" I promised her a note, and worked feverishly to write it overnight.

Later, when I congratulated Clinton on the speech, via Huma Abedin, her closest confidant in every position, she wrote back, "Well you better. You inspired it!"

After that, I was asked to look at drafts of Clinton's economic speeches before and after the convention, as well as drafts of her convention acceptance speech. John Podesta had me share my emails with Jake Sullivan and Dan Schwerin and later wrote, "Take some time and try to give us a short text in her voice that uses stronger together but hits your level the playing field points." I was asked to brief Mandy Grunwald, who was managing the debate prep.

In response, I proposed a first point where "stronger together" means "everyone who works hard has an equal shot at America's promise, an equal shot at joining the middle class and a better life." But then I took my best populist shot: "We are stronger together, yet so many of our corporate and political leaders seem content to pursue their own goals, while so many hardworking people are struggling and don't have an equal shot at a better life."

The campaign's response was completely schizophrenic. After Hillary delivered her economic speech in Cleveland, I wrote John, "President Obama could have delivered this speech. It is still a 'build on the progress' speech with some cheerleading for America." And "not much populism or critique of how things went wrong or any culprits to be vanished."

The next day in North Carolina I prepared for the worst when the warm-up speakers delivered the same cheerleading message. But then, she delivered a speech I rushed to embrace. I wrote Clinton, "Madam Secretary, I loved the North Carolina speech." It was full of reforms, too.

"REWRITE THE RULES" LEVELED "BUILD ON THE PROGRESS"

The risk to Democrats in the general election was very real, and the Roosevelt Institute had Democracy Corps test a revised "rewrite the rules" message with its powerful critique of the economic status quo, yet one that closed with "stronger together." Our test pitted it against the "build on the progress" message that Hillary Clinton had embraced that also finished with "stronger together." All Democracy Corps polls were released publicly, so the goal was to get buy-in from Hillary Clinton and the campaign.

The results could not have been clearer and more instructive on how to win the election.

The candidate embracing a "rewrite the rules" message gained significant electoral ground against one with an economic nationalist vision. The "build on the progress" candidate lost ground on the vote, enthusiasm, and much more. The "rewrite the rules" candidate gained votes with the base and swing voters, and energized millennials and minority voters. Getting the message right allowed the candidate to make gains on whom to trust on the economy.

STRONGER TOGETHER ECONOMIC MESSAGES

REWRITE THE RULES	BUILD ON THE PROGRESS
We need to make our economy work for everyone, not just the rich and well-connected. Too many are wedded to the failed theory of trickle down economics. Too many CEOs move jobs overseas and prioritize short-term stock prices over long-term investments in their workers. Too many wealthy special interests are using lobbyists so the economy works for them. I have a plan to rewrite the rules of the economy so it works for everybody, not just those at the top. We must end the stranglehold of big money on our politics. We cannot allow Wall Street to wreck Main Street again and corporations and the wealthy must pay their fair share of taxes. More employees must be able to join unions. [Our trade deals must be good for working families and not encourage American companies to move jobs overseas.] And let's provide affordable childcare, paid leave and equal pay for women, make college debt-free, and make large infrastructure investments to create middle class jobs. Because we're stronger together when we grow together.	President Obama saved us from the worst economic crisis since the great depression. Thanks to his leadership and the hard work of the American people, we have created 14 million private sector jobs in past 6 and half years and the auto industry has made a strong come back. But America's economy isn't yet where we want it to be. People are working harder and longer just to keep their heads above water. The task for the next president is to build on President Obama's accomplishments to expand opportunity and break down the barriers holding too many people back. We need to give the middle class a raise and put Americans to work by investing in our infrastructure and new industries like clean energy. And let's provide affordable childcare, paid leave and equal pay for women, and make college debt-free. Because we're stronger together when we grow together.

NATIONALIST ECONOMIC MESSAGE

America doesn't win anymore. We used to be the world's greatest economy and created the biggest middle class the world has ever known. But then our politicians and the elites decided to pursue a policy of globalization. They negotiated disastrous trade deals that moved our best jobs, our wealth and our factories to Mexico and overseas. And they stopped protecting our borders so illegal immigrants take our jobs. It's time to take our country back from elites, bring back our jobs and put America first again. I will cut taxes and regulations on businesses and I will build a wall with Mexico. I will completely redo our trade deals and crack down on countries cheating on trade like China. And I will say no to the new TPP trade deal that would decimate American manufacturing. I will do for America what I have done for my businesses and make America rich again.

The "rewrite the rules" framework would have allowed Clinton to grow her vote margin by four points, while she was losing a point with the current "build on the progress" message. That was disheartening if the campaign persisted with the original strategy, but exciting if she would embrace the change. The "rewrite the rules" message pushed up her margin by seven points with college women, who were part of her current base, and by five points with swing, white working-class women.

And critically, the "rewrite the rules" approach was twelve points stronger with the anti-Trump and anti-Clinton voter who might stay home in disgust or vote for the Green Party candidate.

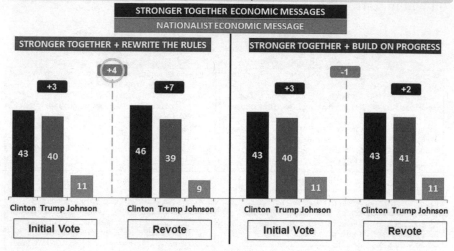

Now, thinking again about the election for President in 2016, if the election for President were held today, would you vote for— Democrat Hillary Clinton, Republican Donald Trump or Libertarian Gary Johnson?

STRONGER TOGETHER ECONOMIC MESSAGES
NATIONALIST ECONOMIC MESSAGE

STRONGER TOGETHER + REWRITE THE RULES

+4

	Clinton	Trump	Johnson		Clinton	Trump	Johnson
	+3				+7		
Initial Vote	43	40	11	Revote	46	39	9

STRONGER TOGETHER + BUILD ON PROGRESS

-1

	Clinton	Trump	Johnson		Clinton	Trump	Johnson
	+3				+2		
Initial Vote	43	40	11	Revote	43	41	11

All the respondents heard the very strong economic nationalist message, but at the end, those who heard a Democrat embracing the "rewrite the rules" critique were more likely to think the Democrat would bring growth that benefits all, help the economy, and make America stronger. That was sobering, and my public memo concluded, "We are happy to share these results in the hope of shaping this critical economic debate at the convention's close and the eve of the general election campaign. The choice could not be more consequential."

Now, I am going to again read you a list of issues and I want you to tell me whether, overall, you think (ROTATE) Hillary Clinton or Donald Trump would do a better job with each issue. If you do not know, just tell me and we'll move on.

	■ Trump Much Better		■ Clinton Much Better		Clinton-Trump
STRONGER TOGETHER + REWRITE THE RULES					
Growth that benefits everyone, not just the top	39	23	30	50	+11
Making America strong	44	31	29	46	+2
The economy	44	30	31	48	+4
Creating jobs	49	30	28	44	-5
STRONGER TOGETHER + BUILD ON PROGRESS					
Growth that benefits everyone, not just the top	41	23	31	47	+6
Making America strong	44	32	28	42	-2
The economy	44	33	30	46	+2
Creating jobs	46	31	27	43	-3

I met with John Podesta in New York and emailed Clinton: "Your economic message that you delivered in North Carolina flat out defeats" Trump's economic nationalist message. "But when you are speaking about building on the progress, none of that happens."

I had also been asked to react to a working draft of Clinton's convention speech, and it initially included a lot of cheerleading of the economy, though progressive drafts got much better. I also wrote: "The missing piece is any frustration with politicians, special interests, corporate influence that distorts government and any desire to change the role of money in politics. I [think] that is dangerous and allows Trump to look like the guy who wants to [get] rid of crony capitalism."[20]

Afterward, I wrote the campaign team, "I think the economic speech was done deftly—acknowledging Obama's progress, but not good enough, with a '!' A lot of storytelling about people's pain. There is a lot about corporate responsibility and paying their fair share." But I then added: "What's missing is any critique or discomfort with politicians too moved by special interest money to work for change."[21]

Clinton and Senator Tim Kaine headed out on their post-convention economic tour, and I wrote Podesta: "Yesterday, I'm sorry, could not have been worse on the economy. I just can't understand why you feel the need to run on progress. You are the past and Trump is change and a better life. You sound clueless in blue-collar America."

But then, they made a big turn that impacted the election. The draft economic speech included this core choice: "We have a vision for an economy and country that works for everyone, not just those at the top. Donald Trump has a vision for America that works for him and his family at the expense of everyone else."[22] That struck a chord, and Podesta had me brief Mandy Grunwald on our findings prior to the debate camp, where they worked with Clinton for a few days on how to deal with Trump in the three presidential debates in late September and early October.[23]

Clinton could not have been more on message during the three debates, and she made her biggest gains in the first and third debates on who would be better on the economy and for the middle class. She reached parity with Trump on who would do a better job on the economy. I shared the findings from the one hundred people I brought together online to watch the debates and register their responses on dial meters that I had conducted for the Women's Voices Women Vote Action Fund, and wrote her an email: "I want to congratulate you on the debate, the campaign and economic message!"[24]

That was the last America heard from Hillary Clinton on the economy.

LOSING THE ECONOMY AND CAMPAIGN

I thought Hillary Clinton was going to win this election, but I saw no evidence that the campaign had fully consolidated or excited Democrats or that voters were rushing to vote for Democrats down-ballot. The Clinton speeches and the campaign's ads hit Donald Trump for the racist and hateful things he said about various groups and his disrespect of women, but my research and experience showed that the campaign also needed to let voters know of the big economic changes and reforms Clinton's election would bring. They needed to give people hope, or at the very least, they needed to show the economic choice—the number one issue in the election.

In her book Clinton later accepted that I might have been right that attacking Trump was not enough.

My recommended economic contrast that had been tested in polls began with "We need an economy that works for everyone, not just the rich and well-connected." I hit the Republicans for supporting "trickle-down economics and more tax breaks for the richest and tax breaks for the corporations." Republicans are getting buyoffs from Wall Street and the oil companies. Well, "We need to rebuild the middle class" and "invest in families, education, and jobs with rising incomes." We must "protect Social Security by asking the rich to pay their fair share."

What a difference it made in testing to close with that economic contrast. The attack on Trump barely helped on the congressional vote with millennials and white working-class women, but it dramatically increased the vote margin for Clinton and the Democrats with millennials, white working-class women, and unmarried women.

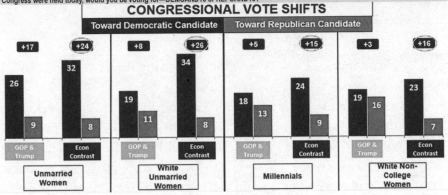

After hearing about the Republican candidates for Congress and Donald Trump, /helping the richest, not the middle class, if the election for U.S. Congress were held today, would you be voting for—DEMCAND16 or REPCAND16?

CONGRESSIONAL VOTE SHIFTS

Toward Democratic Candidate				Toward Republican Candidate			
+17	+24	+8	+26	+5	+15	+3	+16
26	32	19	34	18	24	19	23
9	8	11	8	13	9	16	7
GOP & Trump	Econ Contrast	GOP & Trump	Econ Contrast	GOP & Trump	Econ Contrast	GOP & Trump	Econ Contrast
Unmarried Women		White Unmarried Women		Millennials		White Non-College Women	

After the FBI reopened the investigation of Clinton's State Department emails and the daily release of the emails hacked by the Russians, the race got closer and the campaign decided to simply disqualify Donald Trump. The Clinton campaign ran ads on Trump's temperament, his capacity to handle the nuclear codes, and his vulgar treatment of women, which they thought would disqualify him to be president. They did not run ads on his treatment of workers and contractors. Voters did not see on the news or in Clinton's paid advertising her plans for change. She called for greater unity and opportunity for everyone after a divisive election.

This put the Democrats at growing risk, particularly with Clinton silent on the economy and her future plans. President Bill Clinton told James Carville that the campaign, maddeningly, believed Hillary "couldn't win the economy," and John Podesta told me, "Mook believes we got nothing for all that time on the economy." I now realized this was analytics, fake news, not real polling.

At Podesta's urging, I wrote to Mook on November 1:

> [James Comey] has raised the stakes in our turnout [of] our broad base. Trump will now consolidate more Republicans, and our consolidation of Democrats will stall. And that is our biggest, measurable problem: millennials are weak in the early vote, as you know, and our national polls show us getting only 79 percent of Sanders voters.

But I think there is an effective solution available to you.

The tough economic message that HRC delivered in the first and third debate, produced big gains on the economy, middle class, fighting special interests, and trust.

They are desperate to know you can bring change.

On November 3, I wrote to Mook, "Disqualifying not enough." I got no response.

President Obama campaigned for Clinton in the closing weekends, and with a big megaphone said the country could elect a president "who will build on our progress. Who will finish the job." She is "as well-prepared as anyone who ever ran" to solve the problems we have. For those "still in need of a good job or a raise" or a child who needs "a sturdier ladder out of poverty," she's your choice.

That view of the world put so many voters out of reach and gave us Donald Trump as president.

2018. AGAIN?

Everything President Donald Trump and the Republican Congress did after taking full control of the government alienated the country. They governed for their rich donors and corporations, threatened voters' health care and retirement, and made life harder for the middle class. Before the end of 2017, they had pushed the proportion of those thinking the country was on the wrong track to 75 percent.[25]

It was ugly, and I couldn't find terms strong enough in my recommended messages to describe people's sense of betrayal on affordable health care, Social Security, Medicare and Medicaid, and the GOP's promised tax cut for the 1 percent. I started with "enough politics as usual" and ended with, "I'm fed up":

The Republican Congress said, trust us, no more politics as usual but they've taken U-turn after U-turn. They said their tax cuts would be for the middle class, but their plan is more trickle-down tax cuts for the top 1 percent who should pay their fair share. They promised better, cheaper health care, but their plans would make older workers pay five times more. They promised zero cuts to Social Security, Medicare, and Medicaid, but they're pushing drastic cuts to them all. Enough politics as usual and broken promises!

Just a year from the 2016 election, and my polls found that the most powerful message in influencing choice in the midterm election was already "Donald Trump and the Republicans are wedded to trickle-down economics and tax cuts for the richest." The Democrats said trickle-down had failed and the richest needed to "pay their fair share of taxes." And the Democrats' strongest message began: "I'm fed up. Our economy and politics are rigged so they work against the hardworking middle class." Be warned, "corporate lobbyists and billionaires" are hard at work. And the message was most effective in shifting the vote to the Democrats when it was almost wholly negative. A version that was mostly positive was about 40 percent weaker in its effect.

The GOP tax cut message was pretty effective at the time, as it was described as "tax reform" and a big tax cut for "hardworking Americans and small businesses." Of course, the Republicans could not help themselves and the actual tax cut that passed Congress in December 2017 became a corporate tax cut and bonanza for the rich.

When I presented my polling results to House and Senate leaders and campaign committees, they were uncomfortable with the idea of Democratic candidates voicing that kind of anger and frustration with Washington and wanted a more positive message.

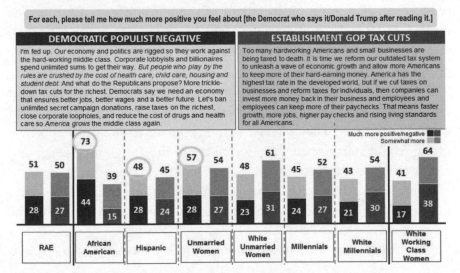

President Trump and corporate lobbyists mounted a full press and got near unanimous support from GOP House and Senate members to slash the corporate tax rate from 35 to 21 percent and other "reforms" that gave 83 percent of the benefits to the top 1 percent. That this would be seen as advantageous mainly for the rich was confirmed by President Trump's late promise to push through a tax cut for the middle class before the midterm election, even though Congress was not even in session to pass any laws at that time.

The tax cut package that passed more than doubled the standard tax deduction to $12,000 for a single person and $24,000 for a family and raised the child tax credit—so that some in the middle might see an appreciable reduction in their taxes.[26] That benefit might be offset for those in the middle class who lost tax deductions for their mortgage interest and property taxes in high-tax, mostly Democratic-controlled states.

The IRS rushed to implement the new law and President Trump urged employers to encourage employees to change their withholding in order to see immediate gains in their take-home pay in the new year. A handful of companies tried to help the president and announced they would give bonuses to all their employees. And ultimately, 80 percent of taxpyers would get some reduction in their taxes in the first year.[27]

At the same time, the macro-economy grew at an impressive 2.3 percent and unemployment fell to 4.1 percent by the end of 2017.[28] Obviously, the new tax cut played no role in producing that economic performance. But that did not stop Republicans from asserting that GOP tax cuts and reduced regulation on business had raised consumer confidence. The result was an "amazing" economy, "the best economy in the history of our country," and a "great and very vibrant economy," according to the president's statements.[29]

Progressives across the board were nervous. They weren't the least bit confident in conservatives who said people would acknowledge real gains in their pay. They weren't sure President Trump's job approval rating would start to rise. They weren't sure the anti-Trump anger and fervor would start to cool.

Some who served in the Obama administration jumped in to claim that President Obama, not President Trump, should get credit for the good economic times.[30]

The heads of at least two economic think tanks were worried and asked me for reassurance that the economic dynamics would not shift on us.

In meetings with the Democratic leadership and party committees on the House side, I was asked repeatedly, "Don't we have to acknowledge the economic progress?"

Some union leaders thought the economic attack would have to give way to other attacks on President Trump.

And right up to Election Day and even today, pundits wondered: how could President Trump oversee such a strong economy and get higher ratings on managing the economy, while his overall approval rating remains historically low? Other factors must be at play, such as his disrespect of women, the fallout from repealing Obamacare, his self-obsession and narcissism, and his extremism that has polarized the country.

The implication was that President Trump and the GOP should be helped by the economy or other issues would displace it as a voting point.

Well, what country are you living in? I responded.

Do you really think working people can be bribed with an afterthought of a tax cut for the middle class? Do you think voters who have scorned elected leaders time and again who proclaimed progress after the financial crisis would now embrace these meager gains in income and taxes?

Do you really have respect for working people if you think they would be fooled by this scam?

Do you think people who have been demanding the rich pay their fair share of taxes wouldn't notice that this huge tax bonanza was for corporations and the billionaires?

Do you think this country that is angry about CEOs and their greed wouldn't notice that this tax cut and the stock buybacks would enrich those very same people?

If you do not remember when President Obama lost successive midterm elections in 2010 and 2014 running on "build on the progress," then recall President George H. W. Bush, who declared, "The economy is humming" after many quarters of growth and lost to a Bill Clinton campaign that said, "It's the economy, stupid!"[31]

They probably didn't recall that Prime Minister John Major lost in Britain when the Tories put up billboards proclaiming, "Britain is booming" well into the economy recovery—and lost to the Labour Party.

So I genuinely was not surprised when I rushed to listen to voters in focus groups with African Americans from Detroit, working-class voters from Macomb County, and more affluent ones living in suburban Livingston County in Michigan. Those sessions were made possible by a collaboration with Randi Weingarten, president of the American Federation of Teachers, that gave us the ability to track the effect of the tax cut and perceptions of the economy through to Election Day.

Listening to real people always clears my head and would for many others, after they listened to the commonsense reactions. The Trump voters didn't bring up the tax cut as an accomplishment or even raise the subject until the moderator introduced it, though the strong economy justified their Trump vote for some. African Americans believed it was a scam to put their programs at risk, and the suburban women focused on how Trump was setting group against group. But all of them interpreted the tax cut through their experience with an economy in which jobs didn't pay enough to live on and corporations got their way with politicians.[32] Discussing it just heightened their economic distress. It highlighted the out-of-control health care costs that wiped out any benefit from it and showed that it was merely the result of a corrupt deal between politicians and businesses to enrich Donald Trump and his billionaire friends.

Most important, they knew it was unpaid for, drove up the deficit, and meant that "we will pay the piper." They volunteered that the GOP would now come after Social Security, Medicare, and Medicaid, and the government wouldn't be able to invest in education. They wrote the scripts for the ad makers—and they were angry.

How can you not trust the voters again?

Randi Weingarten and I sent a memo on our findings after the national survey that urged pundits and campaign strategists to reject all the assumptions about the tax cut and economy: they are "not producing for working and middle-class people whose wages are not keeping up with rising costs, particularly the cost of health care." They need to make clear that "this tax cut is 'rigged for the rich' at the expense of everyone else and threatens investments and retirement protection."[33]

Republicans were depending on a macro-economic breakthrough, but in April 2018 only 40 percent of the voters said, "The economy is strong and families like mine are beginning to feel more financially secure" and the percentage only got lower in the follow-up polls I conducted for Women's Voices Women Vote Action Fund in May and into the fall.[34]

Four months after the passage of the tax cut and after employers adjusted withholdings, 39 percent said it was benefiting them personally—and that number never went up during the course of the midterm campaign.

At the end of the survey in April, voters who opposed the tax cut called it a "bad deal," "scam," "for the rich," and "garbage" in their open-ended responses. When we provided a list of descriptors, the strongest by far was "rigged for the rich," followed by "time bomb for the middle class."[35]

That fit the messaging consensus among Democrats.

Branded: tax scam for the rich

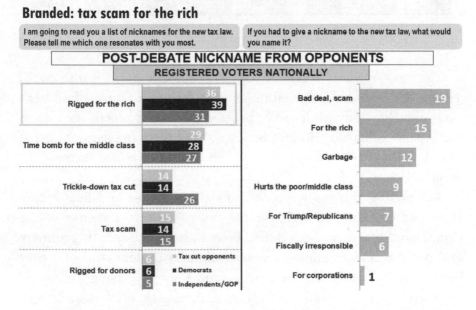

I am going to read you a list of nicknames for the new tax law. Please tell me which one resonates with you most.

If you had to give a nickname to the new tax law, what would you name it?

POST-DEBATE NICKNAME FROM OPPONENTS
REGISTERED VOTERS NATIONALLY

Rigged for the rich	36 / 39 / 31
Time bomb for the middle class	29 / 28 / 27
Trickle-down tax cut	14 / 14 / 26
Tax scam	15 / 14 / 15
Rigged for donors	6 / 6 / 5

- Tax cut opponents
- Democrats
- Independents/GOP

Bad deal, scam	19
For the rich	15
Garbage	12
Hurts the poor/middle class	9
For Trump/Republicans	7
Fiscally irresponsible	6
For corporations	1

I told progressive allies to stop worrying about the passage of the tax cut and the GOP delivering on their signature promise. The tax cut was as much a voting issue for the opponents as the proponents, and had elevated everything about the economy and politics that voters wanted to change. It made the GOP appear out of touch on wages and highlighted what they had done to health care costs. The more it was discussed, the more voters turned away from Republicans.

And that is exactly what happened when Democrats made the corrupt tax cut deal central to their message.

Democratic tax message is also stronger than GOP's top message

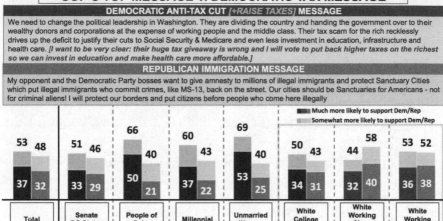

These are some things that Democrats/Republicans running for U.S. Congress and offices in (STATE) are saying. For each, please indicate whether you are much more likely, somewhat more likely, a little more likely, or no more likely to support the Democratic/Republican candidate who says that.

GOP'S TOP MESSAGE V. DEMOCRATIC TAX MESSAGE

DEMOCRATIC ANTI-TAX CUT *[+RAISE TAXES]* MESSAGE

We need to change the political leadership in Washington. They are dividing the country and handing the government over to their wealthy donors and corporations at the expense of working people and the middle class. Their tax scam for the rich recklessly drives up the deficit to justify their cuts to Social Security & Medicare and even less investment in education, infrastructure and health care. *[I want to be very clear: their huge tax giveaway is wrong and I will vote to put back higher taxes on the richest so we can invest in education and make health care more affordable.]*

REPUBLICAN IMMIGRATION MESSAGE

My opponent and the Democratic Party bosses want to give amnesty to millions of illegal immigrants and protect Sanctuary Cities which put illegal immigrants who commit crimes, like MS-13, back on the street. Our cities should be Sanctuaries for Americans - not for criminal aliens! I will protect our borders and put citizens before people who come here illegally

■■■ Much more likely to support Dem/Rep
▮▮▮ Somewhat more likely to support Dem/Rep

	Total	Senate BG States	People of Color	Millennial	Unmarried Women	White College Grads	White Working Class Women	White Working Class Men
Total top	53	51	66	60	69	50	58	53
	48	46	40	43	40	43	44	52
Bottom	37	33	50	37	53	34	32	36
	32	29	21	22	25	31	40	38

That message met voters at their real starting point in the era of Trump. The extreme polarization and breakdown of norms in American public life and politics were being exploited to benefit the rich at the expense of hardworking Americans. "Tax scam for the rich" is the branding that captured and defined the GOP's signature accomplishment.

The polling showed rising worries about wages and health care costs and declining support for the tax cut over the course of the campaign. Voters' well-developed consciousness about the economy and politics made them even angrier about a tax cut deal that they increasingly came to see as corrupt and they increasingly came to see President Trump and the GOP as enriching themselves and "self-dealing."

In September, our polling for the Women's Voices Women Vote Action Fund showed a surge in the perception among the Rising American Electorate that the Republican Party was "looking out for themselves." They were seen now just as a party for "themselves," "tax cuts," and "the richest." There was also a big jump to two thirds in the perception that Donald Trump was "self-dealing and looking out for himself." Fully 60 percent said he was "out of touch with working people."[36]

More say Trump self-dealing and looking out for himself, with intensity

For each word or phrase, please tell me whether it describes Donald Trump very well, well, not too well, or not well at all.

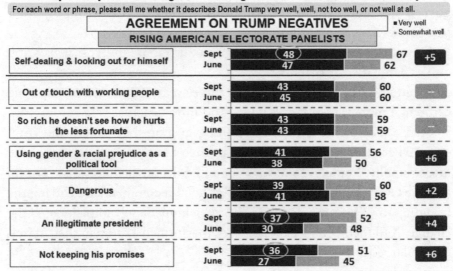

AGREEMENT ON TRUMP NEGATIVES		■ Very well
RISING AMERICAN ELECTORATE PANELISTS		▪ Somewhat well

		Very well	Somewhat well	
Self-dealing & looking out for himself	Sept	48	67	+5
	June	47	62	
Out of touch with working people	Sept	43	60	—
	June	45	60	
So rich he doesn't see how he hurts the less fortunate	Sept	43	59	—
	June	43	59	
Using gender & racial prejudice as a political tool	Sept	41	56	+6
	June	38	50	
Dangerous	Sept	39	60	+2
	June	41	58	
An illegitimate president	Sept	37	52	+4
	June	30	48	
Not keeping his promises	Sept	36	51	+6
	June	27	45	

In the fall of 2018, voters were increasingly angry about corrupt deals for wealthy corporate donors and self-dealing politicians. Something new and fundamental was happening, but would Democrats embrace the message that would get them to the blue wave? I wrote a message that explicitly hit the Republicans for saying the economy was the "greatest."

> Too many leaders divide the country and cut corrupt deals for themselves and their wealthy corporate campaign donors at the expense of working people and the middle class. The Republicans say your wages are great and it's the best economy in history. But their tax scam for the rich recklessly drives up the deficit to justify their cuts to Medicare and Medicaid and less investment in education and health care. I won't take contributions from corporations or Super PACs and the very richest must pay more in taxes so we can invest in education and make health care more affordable.

At the beginning of the 2018 election cycle, the Democrat House and Senate leaders branded their joint approach with the underwhelming "Better Deal" offer. It was a placeholder, though both House and Senate Democrats added policies that suggested they understood the kind of changes the country was looking for. That included lowering the cost of prescription drugs, addressing corporate monopolies and governance, and fighting for paid family and sick leave, among other priorities.[37]

Eventually, the Senate would get behind strong antitrust legislation and expanded voting rights.[38]

Eventually, the House focused on three areas of changed policies: big campaign money, health care costs, and infrastructure.[39]

Senate Democrats who were running in more blue-collar and rural states where Donald Trump had run strongest immediately embraced the more populist framing. Democrats had initially labeled President Trump and the GOP tax cut as a "tax scam." When I recommended evolving the branding to a "tax scam for the rich," they immediately implemented the change. And their Senate candidates outperformed Trump in their states, particularly in the Rust Belt.

It took many meetings to convince the House Democrats to move from "tax scam" to "tax scam for the rich." It may seem like a small change, but "tax scam" says only that it is deceptive. "Tax scam for the rich" says that it is a deceptive deal to enrich corporations and their wealthy donors. It says that it is probably a corrupt deal by politicians to leave a government rigged for the rich.

The House Democrats too embraced the branding and more. I watched their ad at the campaign's close and said, "Finally."[40]

GLOBALIZATION AND TRADE

Globalization has dramatically impacted the lives of working Americans, evident in the increased trade managed by the postwar trade agreements and in immigration, managed by evolving U.S. immigration laws.

While other developments also worked to produce this disruption, political leaders made choices on trade and immigration that magnified the disruption, without doing much to help those most affected by globalization. The leaders were focused on helping specific companies and American industries, not the affected communities that would provide the electoral base for Trump's GOP, like they did for so many ultra-right nationalist parties in Europe and globally. There is no excusing the racism and anti-Semitism that burst through, especially on the left, as Jonathan Freedland and E. J. Dionne wrote in their reviews of *The Nationalist Revival*. But working people, as I have argued, were right to expect their own leaders to advocate for them in the face of such changes and put their citizens before non-citizens. [41]

These changes in trade and immigration were welcomed by America's multinational businesses and in the big metropolitan areas, on the East and West coasts and in Texas, among the professional classes and college graduates and by America's growing Hispanic and foreign-born population. That all mostly overlaps with the evolving electoral base of the Democratic Party. Its national leaders negotiated separate side agreements on labor and the environment, but they were not enforced. They never seriously addressed the domestic reverberations and costs of globalization.

NAFTA was enacted under President Bill Clinton (with my support, as I was then the president's pollster, and over the very strong objections of my wife, Representative Rosa DeLauro). She was right. Obama made passage of the Trans-Pacific Partnership a consuming priority at the end of his presidency. Voters perceived—I am sure accurately—that Hillary Clinton wanted to continue in that direction.

So, on trade, Democrats were late to the party and allowed Donald Trump to win over voters who believed they were "forgotten Americans."

And most House Democrats had voted against China's entry to the WTO, and more than 70 percent of Democrats in the Senate (33 of 46) and 85 percent of Democrats in the House (160 of 188) had voted against giving Obama fast-track authority to negotiate the TPP. Democratic elected leaders voted against the Trans-Pacific Partnership because they came to perceive these trade agreements as corrupt deals negotiated in private with the full participation of corporate advisers and lobbyists to allow them to expand investment abroad and facilitate the outsourcing of jobs.[42]

The House Democratic leaders, Majority Leader Richard Gephardt and Whip David Bonior from the industrial Midwest focused on the jobs that would be lost to Mexico because of the dramatically lower wages there. So, half of House Democrats had voted against NAFTA.

But in truth, all the Democrats' national leaders had pushed for further trade deals, and none had worried very much about ongoing job losses and downward pressure on wages. These leaders and their electoral base favor the multilateral agreements that engage America in the world.

And working people had watched China join the World Trade Organization and their state-led, semi-capitalist economy rig the game and achieve parity with the United States in the global economy.[43]

Donald Trump was the first GOP presidential candidate since Pat Buchanan to wage war on the whole trade regime. Trump charged that "our trade negotiators got snookered by these smart negotiators from other countries," Joseph Stiglitz writes, when in fact, they got exactly what they wanted: trade agreements that favored the advanced countries and that "advanced corporate interests at the expense of workers in both developed and developing countries."[44]

In his delayed State of the Union in 2019, President Trump opened with his characteristic bluntness: "Another historic trade blunder was the catastrophe known as NAFTA." He rightfully pointed out that all the presidential candidates had promised to "negotiate for a better deal. But no one ever tried, until now. Our new U.S.-Mexico-Canada Agreement, the USMCA, will replace NAFTA and deliver for American workers like they haven't had delivered to in a long time." So, he called on Congress to pass it "so we can bring back our manufacturing jobs in even greater numbers, expanding American agriculture, protecting intellectual property, and ensuring that more cars are proudly stamped with the four beautiful words: Made in the USA."

As with every such Trump statement, the reality of the agreement and the state of American manufacturing looked far different.

All dislike slamming trade agreements like NAFTA, groups diverge on China & tariffs

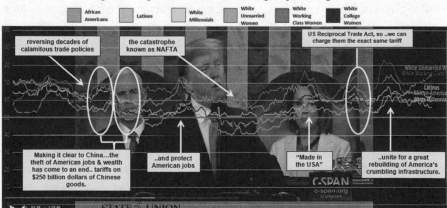

When the president made these statements, I was monitoring for the Voter Participation Center and the WVWVAF over two hundred African Americans, Hispanics, white millennials, white unmarried women, white women college graduates, and white working-class women who were pushing their cursors up or down in reaction to every word. It was clear very early on that the white working-class women's red line was pushed up to a high point on "protecting American jobs," and continued up to hit its highest point over eighty with "Made in the USA." The pink line for white unmarried women, on the edge financially and mostly working class themselves, closely shadowed the red leading the way at the top.

That was the first indicator that the president had the potential to broaden his working-class appeal, if he chose to.

What the reactions also powerfully illustrated was how much President Trump's attack on NAFTA pushed away African Americans, Hispanics, all millennials, and women college graduates. They view NAFTA favorably because Democratic presidents have embraced it and it showed an ability to work with other countries, our neighbors, and an openness to the world. It heralded mutuality important to the New America over the go-it-alone nationalism of President Trump.

In practice, the renegotiated NAFTA was crafted in secret with industry lobbyists, continued to facilitate outsourcing, put downward pressure on wages, and included a full panoply of new corporate special deals that progressive groups determined to change, and it had all the ingredients that now enflamed sentiment in the New America.

And that is exactly what I found when conducting focus groups and surveys for Public Citizen's Global Trade Watch.[45] The administration's case for the renegotiated plan was unconvincing because it was crafted by the same players and process and didn't change NAFTA very much. Critics labeled it "NAFTA 2.0."

Just learning that the renegotiated NAFTA so unashamedly benefited the pharmaceutical companies that were driving up health care costs and oil companies that already had so much power turned voters strongly against the agreement. In the focus groups, exposure to that information made participants wonder whether *all* trade agreements were corrupted and whether they should become more critical of the original NAFTA.

Simply giving people information about ways the revised agreement benefited special interests produced very serious and intense doubts about the agreement. Each was like throwing little bombs, reinforcing the bigger narrative that this was another corrupt deal that underscores how rigged are the economy and politics. The intense doubts clustered at the top—about U.S. companies able to import food that doesn't meet U.S. safety standards, the ten-year monopoly for U.S. drug companies that blocks competition from generics, and special corporate rights for oil companies to attack Mexican environmental laws.

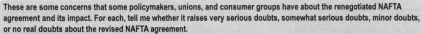

Top doubts: food safety, drug prices, corporate right environment

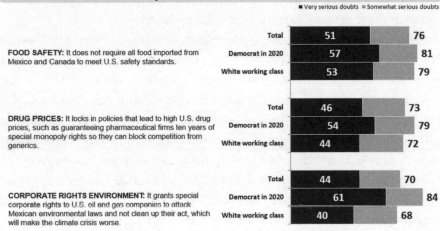

These are some concerns that some policymakers, unions, and consumer groups have about the renegotiated NAFTA agreement and its impact. For each, tell me whether it raises very serious doubts, somewhat serious doubts, minor doubts, or no real doubts about the revised NAFTA agreement.

■ Very serious doubts ■ Somewhat serious doubts

	Total	Democrat in 2020	White working class
FOOD SAFETY: It does not require all food imported from Mexico and Canada to meet U.S. safety standards.	51 / 76	57 / 81	53 / 79
DRUG PRICES: It locks in policies that lead to high U.S. drug prices, such as guaranteeing pharmaceutical firms ten years of special monopoly rights so they can block competition from generics.	46 / 73	54 / 79	44 / 72
CORPORATE RIGHTS ENVIRONMENT: It grants special corporate rights to U.S. oil and gas companies to attack Mexican environmental laws and not clean up their act, which will make the climate crisis worse.	44 / 70	61 / 84	40 / 68

This information about the agreement got the attention of every voter, but particularly the majority that would be voting Democratic for president in 2020 and the white working class. The white working-class voters were pushed back by food safety and prescription drug prices, particularly working-class women, who expressed the most intense doubts on these two issues (56 percent and 52 percent serious doubts, respectively). Even the Trump voters had trouble dealing with food safety (43 percent serious doubts) and prescription drug prices (34 percent serious doubts), though they now viewed the revised NAFTA as an important accomplishment for President Trump.

People quickly integrated their response into an anti-corporate message framework. The inclusion of the pharmaceutical provision led them to connect the dots: "Pharmaceutical shouldn't be in the NAFTA agreement" in the first place because "it just doesn't have a lot to do with the purpose of the agreement" (Macomb woman, Seattle man). "What I care about is sustaining jobs here in America," but "the lobbyists" are "throwing all of that stuff in there—they are not looking at truly protecting U.S. jobs" (Macomb man).

So, fighting to get rid of the deal for Pharma set up the integrated attack that shifted so many white working-class voters and turned the bloc of Democratic voters strongly against President Trump's agreement that he had promised would put the worker first.

Defining the agreement as another corrupt deal for the corporate lobbyists that rigged the economy raises serious doubts for half of Trump's 2020 voters and two thirds of the white working class. It angered those voting Democratic in 2020, 59 percent saying it raised serious doubts. It was the frustration with corporate influence that raised even more serious doubts for those who then opposed the renegotiated agreement after it was so tarnished.

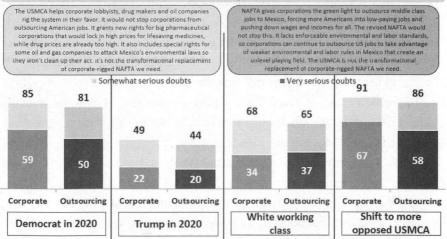

Those who become less supportive of USMCA moved by corporate power line

This is something that some labor unions, lawmakers, and consumer groups are saying about the renegotiated NAFTA agreement and how it should be changed before Congress votes on it. Does this raise very serious doubt, somewhat serious doubts, minor doubts, or no real doubts about the revised NAFTA agreement?

An engaged battle against the renegotiated NAFTA could disrupt what normally happens when the president presents a trade agreement to Congress. After this hypothetical battle, over 40 percent wanted major changes negotiated before the plan went to Congress and another 15 percent wanted Congress to oppose it period, even if that meant President Trump would have to abruptly withdraw from NAFTA. Just a third wanted to move quickly to pass it, as President Trump called for in his State of the Union Address.

That does not change the challenge Democrats face if President Trump and Republicans join the trade issue in elections ahead. The New America does not pay close attention to trade agreements, and just a small minority of the newly elected House Democrats mentioned "trade" on their websites.[46] The Democratic base of voters is pretty fond of the North American Free Trade Agreement, particularly with President Trump working so hard to withdraw from every trade agreement. Democratic presidential candidates might well defend the legacy of NAFTA and support TPP-like agreements that enhance our national security. Vice President Biden and Texas congressman Beto O'Rourke could embrace that tradition.

This time other voices could be louder. Senator Elizabeth Warren declared the new NAFTA is "stuffed with handouts that will let big drug companies lock in the high prices they charge for many drugs," gouging "seniors and anyone else who needs access to life-saving medicines."[47] The top Democrats leading on trade in both the Senate and House and Speaker Nancy Pelosi declared it must be dramatically changed.

This time President Trump's protectionist policies will push Democrats to better manage the effects of globalization and technology. His unilateral tariffs, "mindless undoing of the global rules-based system" and "reckless deglobalization," Stiglitz warns in *People, Power and Profits*, will wreak so much havoc that Democrats will be united on trade. His tariffs are pushing up prices, making American firms less competitive and "destroying jobs again."[48]

At the same time, William Galston wrote a kind of mea culpa for moderate, free-trade Democrats in *The Wall Street Journal*. The leaders of both parties dramatically misjudged how many manufacturing jobs would be lost, particularly outside the metropolitan areas, and how much China would become less autocratic and change its trade practices.

Democrats may argue for a rules-based international system that promotes American jobs, large-scale investment in people and infrastructure, and finally managing and mitigating the effects of globalization.

The forgotten Americans may well be contested by Democrats in the pivotal 2020 election.

IMMIGRATION AND MULTICULTURAL AMERICA

The escalating Republican assault on immigration has allowed the GOP some tactical victories with nontrivial consequences for the country.

President Trump's tactical victories on immigration led many to think America was moved by the same forces that propelled ultranationalist, anti-immigrant leaders and parties in Britain, France, Hungary, Poland, and Italy, even Spain and Germany. Steve Bannon's European tour was premised on the power of shared worries about white "birth rates" and streets "flipped" to mostly Arab businesses. Unfortunately for the GOP, America is on a different path.[49]

In the 2016 primary battle, immigration was the top issue for the Tea Party and base that propelled Trump into the lead and the top issue in nearly every primary down-ballot. In the general election, it was one of the top two reasons voters supported Trump in the end. It was the top issue for white working-class voters who pulled back from Democrats. Indeed, attitudes toward immigration had supplanted racial equality as the strongest correlate of switching from President Obama to vote for Trump and switching party identification to the Republicans.

When I asked independents and Democrats who voted for Trump after the 2016 election what their biggest hope was for him, it was that he would get immigration under control and deport those immigrants who were here illegally.

President Trump declared war on immigrants and refugees in the 2018 election and had some success. He made immigration the top reason to vote for him and against Democrats, yet Republicans faced grievous losses anyway, and a large majority of Americans said immigration benefits the country. Nonetheless, immigration was the top voting issue for white workers, even if support eroded from 2016 in 2018.

It is very hard for Democrats to make a full run at working-class voters who are grappling with the results of globalization without a developed position on how to manage immigration.

It is not hard to offer a comprehensive plan for managing immigration because that is precisely what the U.S. Senate passed with bipartisan support and what is now a touchstone for all Democrats who are running for president. Democrats have forgotten how they built broad support for that plan at the time.

Donald Trump's demagogic rants against immigrants and his outrageous policies have made it difficult for pro-immigration leaders to remind voters of what progressives really support. They have to condemn the Trump administration for separating children from their parents, for his attacks on the caravans as hiding Islamic terrorists, for his description of undocumented immigrants as murderers, and for his willingness to deport the Dreamers.

And when they did so, voters plausibly thought Democrats prioritized only legalizing the undocumented immigrants and getting them on a path to citizenship. In the 2016 presidential election and probably in 2018 as well, it seemed as if Democrats were interested only in immigrant rights. It seemed like Democrats might prioritize non-citizens over citizens.

That is precisely the inference Donald Trump, Fox News, and Breitbart have been intent on spotlighting.

Democrats believe America is an immigrant and multicultural country, that immigrants enrich the country, and that immigration has to be managed in ways that benefit the country and all its citizens. By making that clear in the Democrats' contrast with Trump, they both strengthen their electoral position and become more deeply associated with the country's growing diversity and multiculturalism.

America is a country shaped by increased immigration and those who are foreign born. As I wrote in chapter 6, "The New America Strikes Back," the massive growth in global migration has dramatically increased the number of immigrants, and the percent of foreign born in 2017 reached its highest percentage since 1910. Our big metropolitan areas are over 30 percent foreign born and 44.2 percent of the millennial generation are people of color.[50]

Unlike almost any other country and despite President Trump, a big majority of Americans believes immigration enriches, rather than burdens, the country. In my own surveys over the year leading into the 2018 election, voters gave an almost three-to-one positive reaction to the term "immigrants to the United States."[51]

White college-educated women are the most favorable and white working-class men the least favorable toward immigrants. In Democracy Corps's surveys in 2016 and 2018 and in my focus groups, African Americans and Hispanics expressed levels of concern about immigration that would surprise you. African Americans have come to view

Trump's attack on immigrants as a civil rights issue, so they are more pro-immigration than Hispanics. By the midterm elections, I found a quarter of Hispanics thought immigrants competed for jobs and public resources.[52]

Americans are positive about the economic effects of legalization of immigrants and see many immigrants as hardworking, but they do worry about the costs. In 2018, 34 percent believed granting legal status would lead to greater competition for public services and more than half believe it would take jobs from American citizens. Those numbers were not driven entirely by Republicans. About one in five Democrats also thought immigrants would "take jobs from U.S. citizens, as well as housing and healthcare."

President Obama led the battle for immigration reform and was fairly trusted at the time on this issue. He always began talking about it by defining "real reform." It meant "stronger border security," and his administration did in fact put "more boots on the Southern border than at any time in our history." "Real reform" also meant "establishing a responsible pathway to earned citizenship" that included "paying taxes and a meaningful penalty" for violating U.S. laws and that those who came illegally would be "going to the back of the line behind the folks trying to come here legally."

Pro-immigration advocates won majority support for comprehensive immigration reform only after the public became confident that leaders wanted to manage immigration and that they took borders and citizenship seriously. The reform that passed the U.S. Senate in 2013 increased enforcement at the border, introduced new technology to ensure lawful employment, expelled those with criminal records, and allowed a path to citizenship for those here illegally who paid a fine and back taxes and learned English. That combination allowed progressives to proudly advocate a new law that would greatly expand the number of legal immigrants and make America more culturally and economically dynamic.

By the time Hillary Clinton ran in 2016, however, the path to citizenship had moved to the center of her offer, as did concern for immigrant rights in the face of Trump's promised Muslim ban and Mexican border wall. But that is precisely what President Trump wanted.

In polling, Democrats gained electorally by affirming, "We are a nation of immigrants," a "diverse" country, enriched by each new generation of immigrants who "create our hardworking middle class and our innovative entrepreneurs." In firmly opposing President Trump and GOP efforts to reduce immigration, almost two thirds think more positively of the Democrats. When voters hear that Democrats believe America must continue to be an immigrant country and oppose the GOP effort to reduce immigration, it increases the probability of voting Democratic for Congress by 10 percent.[53]

But Democrats get even stronger and broader support—three quarters positive, and almost half strongly positive—when they embrace comprehensive immigration reform "to fix our broken immigration system." That message reflects what President Obama articulated in the past and acknowledges that the current system is not okay. Democrats want to reform immigration to promote "legal, not illegal immigration." That includes a "responsible" path to citizenship and managing immigration "so it works for our country."

If they want to reach white working-class voters, Democrats have to offer the "responsibility" part of the message, too. Half of the white working-class women react positively to the message affirming immigration, but three quarters respond that way to passing comprehensive immigration reform.

Top Democratic messages in support of Immigration

For each, please tell me how much more positive you feel about the Democrat who says it.

CELEBRATE IMMIGRANT DIVERSITY & LEGAL IMMIGRATION		COMPREHENSIVE IMMIGRATION REFORM	
America continues to be enriched by immigration, and I'm proud that we are a nation of immigrants. Each generation has brought new, responsible people that make America exceptional. They create our hardworking middle class and our innovative entrepreneurs. Our diversity and continued immigration makes us exceptional. That's why I oppose proposals to sharply reduce legal immigration.		I believe in comprehensive immigration reform to fix our broken immigration system. But we need reform that puts American citizens first and promotes legal, not illegal immigration. That means stronger enforcement at the border and work place. I want a responsible pathway to earned citizenship that includes paying taxes, learning English, and going to the back of the line. People are right to want to manage immigration so it works for our country.	

Legend: Much more positive / Somewhat more positive / A little more positive

Group	Message total	Much more positive	Somewhat more positive	A little more positive
RAE	67	25	21	21
RAE	73	23	25	25
African American	82	28	23	31
African American	77	23	28	26
Hispanic	83	29	26	28
Hispanic	76	23	30	23
Unmarried Women	69	24	23	22
Unmarried Women	72	21	30	21
White Unmarried Women	60	22	20	18
White Unmarried Women	71	23	29	19
Millennials	72	26	23	23
Millennials	68	26	22	20
White Millennials	66	24	22	20
White Millennials	62	24	21	17
White Working Class Women	50	24	13	13
White Working Class Women	73	24	22	27

It is clearly time to stop being defined by the battle against Trump's outrageous policies and being on the defense on immigration. The Democrats' positions and values win broad support and can change the country.

Passing comprehensive immigration reform would be transformative. If it became law, according to the Congressional Budget Office (CBO), it would expand the population by 10 million people in ten years and 16 million in 2033. It would allow the roughly 11.7 million undocumented residents to gain legal status and place them onto a path to citizenship after ten years. The "Dreamers," those who came to the United States as minors under age sixteen, would obtain citizenship on an accelerated basis. It would remove country-specific visa caps, a legacy of a more racist past, which limited applications from countries such as China and India. It would remove limits on family-based visas for spouses and minor children, immediately clearing up the backlog of family visas and impacting future immigration. It would create new guest worker visas for low-skilled workers in industries such as construction and hospitality. Additionally, agricultural workers who meet certain requirements could be eligible for registered provisional immigrant status within five years.[54]

Green card limits would be lifted for the highly skilled and exceptionally talented, including researchers, professors, artists, executives, athletes, and those graduates with advanced degrees in science, technology, engineering, and mathematics (STEM) from U.S. universities. The bill would introduce a point-based merit visa system that takes into account skills, employment history, and educational credentials to grant visas to between 150,000 and 250,000 immigrants a year, depending on the number of applicants and the U.S. unemployment rate. The H-1B visa program would be reformed, the cap for high-skilled workers substantially raised, and the exemptions for advanced STEM degrees increased. Finally, a start-up visa would become available to entrepreneurs abroad who wish to start a company in the United States.[55]

Rather than taxing the resources of the government, the newly legal immigrants will participate in the labor force at a higher rate and pay more taxes. According to the CBO, the new tax revenue will offset the extra costs for border protection required by the law in the first decade and in the next, will reduce the deficit by $300 billion.[56]

The passage of comprehensive immigration reform would be like the passage of the civil right acts in 1965 and 1966 in terms of settling the immigration issue. That could be true if led by a president who made the case for a multicultural America, enriched by each generation of its immigrants.

9 AFTER THE CRASH

LANDSLIDE

The year 2020 will produce a second blue wave on at least the scale of the first in 2018 and finally will crash and shatter the Republican Party that was consumed by the ill-begotten battle to stop the New America from governing. As the battle was lost, it justified suppressing democracy, dancing with tyrants, and shuttering government just to show it could be done. The GOP is the ultimate anti-government party, even when the voters repudiate it, trash the place, causing lasting damage. If the president is home alone in the White House and the government is tarnished and denuded, it is a victory, with or without the wall, that symbol of America standing against foreign penetration and foreign risks to our safety.

Unsurprisingly, my first survey of 2019, conducted during the government shutdown in January, shows those saying the country is on the wrong track rose sharply. This is a stunning start of the new year. Since Trump took office, voters have only been more pessimistic when the Republicans made their last heave to repeal Obamacare and didn't deliver.[1]

Unsurprisingly, every national leader of both parties was tarnished by the shutdown, except the new speaker, Nancy Pelosi, whose image improved sharply in her first official confrontation with President Trump.

The despair with the politicians and the shutdown, however, did not produce despair with politics. Exactly the opposite. The first national poll looking at the 2020 general election found an electorate that was even more polarized, politicized, and determined to vote at levels never seen before in my polling. Just months after the midterm election, voters looked set to finish the job. Voters on both sides put their heads down and pushed forward to join what at least the resisters believed would be the ultimate battle to settle who will lead the country. President Trump has the support of 40 percent of the country no matter what.

In my poll of 2019, 42 percent approved of his performance in the midst of the shutdown, and that has been his default number in nearly all my polls since the beginning of his presidency. The Republicans' base of the Tea Party, Evangelicals, and conservative Catholics know the president was their last hope in the war against PC thinking and a multicultural, immigrant America. If a wall with Mexico is what he wants, then get out of the way.

And the Trump base was determined to vote to defend their president in 2020. Over 80 percent put themselves at the very top of the scale on following politics, six points higher than for those voting for a generic Democrat for president. They were in the battle to the end.

But the bigger bloc of voters was determined to resist and defeat Donald Trump's Republican Party, and they were set to disrupt electoral certainties in their own way. Every group that became more Democratic in the 2018 blue wave—African Americans and Hispanics, millennials, unmarried women, and women college graduates—were even more Democratic in their voting intentions for 2020. That suggests the 2020 election could produce a historic result on an even greater historic scale.

It is clear that voters of both camps have already fully polarized and nationalized their vote for the presidential election ahead. Nine in ten of those who voted Democrat for Congress in 2018 were by January voting Democratic for president. And nine in ten of those who voted Republican for Congress a few months earlier were all-in for Trump in 2020.

Democrats prevailed by 8.6 points nationally in 2018, and in this first poll of 2019, the Democratic candidate for president was ahead by ten points, 51 to 41 percent, with 5 percent volunteering third-party candidates. (Just 3 percent were undecided in a generic presidential ballot against Trump.) That means the generic Democratic nominee could double President Obama's margin in the landslide election of 2008. With Trump's vote down from 46 to 41 percent, Democrats will not struggle to rebuild the Electoral College blue wall. Trump lost independents by nine points and a quarter of moderate Republicans.

The Democratic presidential candidate in this first survey was pushed to even bigger margins by every member of the Rising American Electorate, ahead with Hispanics by 62 to 32 percent, millennials by 64 to 26 percent, millennial women by a daunting 79 to 16 percent, unmarried women by 71 to 22 percent, and even white unmarried women, by a two-to-one margin (62 to 30 percent).

There were signs of trouble for President Trump in the white working class. He was trailing the generic Democratic candidate by only three points, 49 to 46 percent.

What was most unprecedented was the historic level of voter engagement in the first month of this election cycle. Interest usually falls back after an election and builds back over many months, not even at peak right before the election the following year. However, the percentage who said they were following the election at the highest possible level was already higher than in the last months before the 2018 midterm election that produced the highest turnout ever. The remarkable level of engagement recorded in January 2019 for registered voters already exceeded what I found in my surveys of likely voters in the 2016 presidential election.

The voters crashed my pollsters' equation for determining who is a "likely voter" in a presidential election. It showed that virtually every registered voter was a likely voter. Did programming screw up? I asked. No. The year 2020 is sure to produce a second election with historic levels of voter turnout.

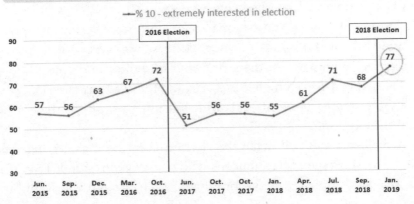

As you may know, there will be an election for President, U.S. Congress, and state and local offices next year. How interested are you in the November 2020 election? Please rate your interest from 1 to 10, with 1 meaning that you have no interest in this election and 10 meaning that you are extremely interested. You can choose any number between 1 and 10.

—% 10 - extremely interested in election

The battle for 2020 will carry forward with an even more engaged, more realigned and politicized country that will finally settle the fate of the Republican Party and liberate the New America to govern and set the country's direction. The GOP will only compete seriously nationally after a period of reckoning.

So, it will not take late into the night before people realize just how big and shattering the election of 2020 will be. It will be clear early on that Ron Brownstein's blue wall that crumbled in 2016 will look as impenetrable and "beautiful" as the one President Trump tried and failed to build on the border with Mexico. The states of Pennsylvania, Michigan, Wisconsin, and Minnesota will not be close. Nor will Maine, New Hampshire, and Virginia. Iowa will be back in the Democratic column. And when John King on CNN pulls up the rural counties on his map of western Pennsylvania as well as the map of Maine's 2nd Congressional District, it will be clear the Trump frenzy will have dimmed. The Democrats' message on issues of corruption and draining the swamp and an economy rigged against the middle class will have gotten heard.

The dynamic metropolitan areas, affluent suburbs, and women will so decisively repudiate Trump's GOP that Colorado will look like a deep blue state and North Carolina and Arizona will tip late to the Democrats.

The country will not know early whether the Democrats pick up Georgia, Florida, and Texas because Republican governors and secretaries of state, armed with new playbooks from the Koch brothers, will work passionately and creatively and without shame to disenfranchise as many black, Hispanic, and minority voters as humanly possible. In 2018, they purged about 700,000 registered voters in Florida, those who had not voted in the prior presidential election. In Georgia, the NAACP estimated the shortening of the early voting window and the closing of polling stations may have cost Stacey Abrams upwards of hundreds of thousands of votes. Both states were stolen from the Democrats, who had lost them by about fifty thousand votes.

The stakes are even higher in 2020, and the U.S. Supreme Court will give GOP state election officials wide latitude to suppress the vote and steal the election.[2]

A divided GOP will make the election even more shattering. There will be no shortage of Republicans who challenge President Trump and his Tea Party politics in the primaries, even though the Republican

National Committee will do everything possible to rig the game. Donald Trump has no shame. The anti-Trump candidates will be humiliated in the primaries against the pro-Trump forces, which are dominant, loyal, and vengeful. And you will know something unique is happening when you see the more affluent, college graduates, and independents showing up to vote in the Democratic primaries, where they are welcomed.

Republicans could very well lose Florida if John Kasich leads a third-party ticket. He would play the role of Ross Perot in 1992, whose voters were mostly disaffected Republicans, or Ralph Nader in 2000, supported mostly by disaffected Democrats. Nader won 76,000 votes in Florida.

The former Republican governor has called out the incivility, the lack of morality, the tolerance of racism and sexism, the lack of concern for the poor, and most of all, the Tea Party ethos that rejects the idea that the two political parties can work together to advance the common good. In my polls in 2018 and 2019, 10 percent of Republicans supported Kasich on a third-party ticket.[3] One third of moderate Republicans broke away to support him, and Kasich could well make inroads with observant Catholics and secular conservatives, who hate the tone of this Tea Party–dominated party.[4]

By contrast, the Democrats will be united and consolidated, substantially increasing the chances of even bigger down-ballot gains. Commentators forget how divisive the 2016 Democratic primaries between Hillary Clinton and Bernie Sanders were, when 20 percent of his voters failed to vote for Clinton in the general. President Trump has unified Democrats for now. And while the prospective nominees vary in their boldness, the Democratic base is unified in its support for bold changes, as you will see later in this chapter.

In my polls in 2019, the Democratic presidential candidate won the support of 95 percent of self-identified Democrats, who were determined to support a Democrat at every level because of the stakes. That will allow the Democrats to protect or grow their House seats and to sweep every competitive Senate race to win back control. In the states, the Democrats could net another four hundred state legislative seats in the malapportioned districts that were meant to be a firewall against such an eventuality.

This final battle has to be joined in 2020.

Donald Trump has never given up on the Tea Party–Evangelical coalition that is his base. The Trump administration every day further brands the GOP as a socially conservative, anti-immigrant, and America First party. The Republicans will go into battle as Donald Trump's party and never acknowledge the midyear repudiation of Trump and never challenge the president, even after he left them hanging during the longest government shutdown in the country's history. In my polls as the nominating began, two thirds of Republicans wanted the party to continue to move in the direction set by President Trump.[5]

After Attorney General William Barr's controlled release of the Mueller report, President Trump, in full victim mode, told Trump voters, "defend your vote" from the liberal media who have tried to steal the election from you.

The Republicans could easily nominate at some point a ticket with Vice President Mike Pence and Senator Tom Cotton running for president and vice president respectively.

Mike Pence is deeply religious and a social conservative to his bones, who as vice president has delivered the socially conservative Supreme Court President Trump promised. He has also led the administration's campaign against China, in the trade war and sanctions against Chinese companies. He called out China for "employing a whole-of-government approach, using political, economic, and military tools, as well as propaganda, to advance its influence and benefit its interests in the United States." He's accused China of Russian-like political chicanery to hurt Donald Trump, an argument the White House has unsuccessfully advanced. And he spotlighted China's plan to control 90 percent of the "world's most advanced industries." That scale of threat required that the United States and our allies demand major structural changes and refuse Chinese investment and simply choose sides.[6]

Senator Tom Cotton is one of the strongest defenders of the Donald Trump project in the Congress, including using whatever leverage is needed to build the wall, but he is a lot steelier on immigration than the president. Cotton's immigration plan reduced legal immigration, and he was one of two senators to vote against Trump's shutdown plan because it granted "amnesty" to Dreamers. Cotton was an early sponsor of legislation to bar the giant Chinese telecommunication company Huawei from operating in the United States. And when President

Trump talked about reopening discussion of America's "One China policy," Cotton agreed that Chinese leaders "need to remember that we are the world's superpower and they are not."[7]

So until there is a reckoning, the Republicans will run nationally as a party fearful of the New America and even more determined to stop them from governing. The GOP will be committed to reducing immigration and building the wall. It will promise to respect the sanctity of life and Christian values. It will be unabashedly pro-business that must be freed from regulation. It will deny the climate change scare stories so the oil and coal companies can keep us fossil fuel dependent. It will cut taxes again and slash government spending and rein in entitlements. It will promise to carry forward President Trump's economic cold war with China and trade agreements that failed to protect American jobs. America will no longer carry the weight of the world on its shoulders. "We'll not be saps. We'll put America first."

That Republican Party will be shunned by the affluent, college educated, and professionals and in the suburbs. Many Republicans will defect. Democrats will be engaged to defeat it as never before. Millennials and the generation behind them will exceed the baby boomers in their vote share, and, for them, Republicans might as well be lepers.

2020 Election Map for President and Senate

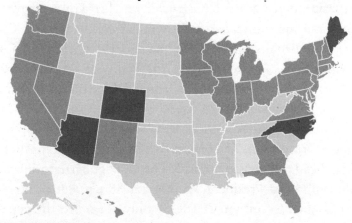

■ Democrat for President and Senate Pick-Up
■ Democrat for President
□ Republican for President
□ Republican for President and Senate Pick-Up

Will the party be so shattered that the Republican National Committee dare not conduct a postmortem as it did in 2012?

Today's Republican Party cannot be saved unless it stops being an anti-immigrant party in an immigrant country. That was obvious to all in 2012 when the party establishment and Fox News accepted that conclusion, but the GOP establishment was quickly sidelined by the dominant forces in the Republican Party that were still in full revolt against the New America. They were ultimately led by Donald Trump.

And when President Trump demanded the country in 2018 and 2019 find the money to build a thirty-foot concrete wall on the Mexican border, the president was giving the finger to those caravans of dark people hiding their Muslim terrorists ready to kill you.

This GOP can't reform itself because defeat in this battle against growing immigrants only confirms that Democrats were right. President Trump's brand of conservatism is California's: he cannot give up his fear of demography and the battle against immigrants. They are one and the same, writ large. President Trump would no more stop worrying about demography and immigrants than get on television without any clothes.

As we saw in chapter 4, "The Tea Party–Trump Decade," California's GOP faced demographic changes early on that led to the Tea Party and Trump's GOP's disastrous last battle against immigration.

The total repudiation of the GOP in California in 2018 tells you that shattering defeats don't push leaders who will reform the party to the fore, but instead leaders who will make it irrelevant. That is the term serious journalists used after the 2018 debacle. The California Republican Party "is teetering on the brink of irrelevance," Adam Nagourney wrote in *The New York Times*. Mark Barabak and Michael Finnegan's article in *The Los Angeles Times* was titled "California Republican Party Drifts Closer to Irrelevance."

President Trump got 32 percent of the vote in a state that used to elect Republicans statewide in 2016. The GOP gubernatorial candidate, who fully embraced President Trump, got 38 percent of the vote and even lost Orange County in 2018. He only got on to the general election ballot because so many Democratic candidates had divided up the first-round vote.[8] Republicans lost every statewide office, and Democrats won three quarters of the seats in the state assembly, the biggest margin in one hundred years.

The California Republicans were left with only seven House seats in the fifty-three-member delegation and lost every seat in Orange County, home of the tax revolt and Ronald Reagan. Republican registration fell to under 25 percent, below that of those with no party affiliation.[9]

Ron Brownstein was puzzled after the 2018 election on why California's Republican House incumbents didn't show any signs of independence from the president, unlike endangered House members in New Jersey, Pennsylvania, and Florida. They all voted to repeal the Affordable Care Act without a replacement in a state that had fully implemented the law. They all voted for the corporate tax cut law that raised taxes on homeowners in high-tax states like California. They all voted to allow permit holders from open-carry states to preempt California's strong gun regulations.[10]

Brownstein observed, "As the California GOP has contracted, it has generally positioned itself more overtly against these rising populations, both by maintaining [a] staunchly conservative agenda on social issues and also embracing Trump's open hostility to immigration." After the election debacle, the GOP Senate members elected a new leader who believes that "God's hand" should have a bigger say in legislating. Minority Leader Kevin McCarthy chided House Speaker Nancy Pelosi for blocking the wall.[11]

The GOP can't rescue itself because its struggle against the New America began in California and was nationalized by a Tea Party–dominated GOP that elected Donald Trump as president. The prospect of their losing only increases their certainty of a take-no-prisoners battle against a multicultural America.

The GOP can be saved only by the Democratic Party that will lead this era of reform.

HOW WILL THE DEMOCRATS RESCUE THE REPUBLICAN PARTY ON IMMIGRATION?

Republicans cannot become a nationally competitive party unless they become less toxic on immigration. Through decades of battle against immigration and the "demographic issue," the party has been deeply branded as not just anti-immigration. It is palpably racist and set against America's growing foreignness, diversity, and multiculturalism. How do you break the fever when it is the one issue that all factions of the GOP agree on and when successive electoral defeats only confirm you are right about the consequences of demographic change?

The Republicans' report after the 2012 election was on point about comprehensive immigration reform being the big federal action that could change electoral dynamics in the country. They're wrong to think this party and a Republican-led Congress could pass the reforms. So much internal blood has been shed since that the torch has been passed to the Democrats. Ironically, I believe the America adopting the U.S. Senate version of comprehensive immigration reform would prove as electorally significant for the Republicans as enactment of welfare reform was for the Democrats in 1996.

I was Bill Clinton's pollster and the guardian of his political project to modernize the Democratic Party and make it a successful national party again. The Republicans had won the White House in every election since 1964, with the exception of the election of Jimmy Carter after the Watergate scandal.

Then Governor Bill Clinton headed up the Democratic Leadership Council in the year before he announced for president. It had retained me after I had publicized my work on "Reagan Democrats" in Macomb County—offering recommendations that were not very popular in Democratic establishment circles. I argued, first, that Democrats needed to respect these working-class voters and listen to why they felt betrayed, even those who were virulently racist. Second, I observed they were open to returning to the Democrats if the party respected work and personal responsibility, and those values undergird everything the party does. Third, I reminded people they were still New Deal Democrats in their bones and embraced an economic plan that guaranteed health care for all. That showed the Democratic Party was trying to make the government work for all.[12]

However, the precondition for these voters' return was fundamentally reforming welfare, which provided cash benefits for the poor who were unable to work and their children. That was asking working families to pay taxes to subsidize other working people who chose not to work, and that was explosive. I asked myself, "How do you justify that?" Other liberal academics at the time were asking the same question, but also raising questions about the efficacy of Aid to Families with Dependent Children compared to other social insurance programs.[13]

I had written up my thinking in a series of articles in *The American Prospect*, a new liberal journal, and met with liberal academics who were looking for better ways to help the poor and working poor.[14] President Bill Clinton told people he had read three times my review of important books about this juncture by Thomas and Mary Edsall, E. J. Dionne, and Peter Brown. I argued that commentators were underestimating how open the middle class was to vote for a different kind of Democrat.

This was politically possible because southern Democratic governors, like Governor Clinton in Arkansas, passed their own progressive welfare reform that provided job training and childcare, and conditioned aid on seeking employment. Bill Clinton announced for president with a commitment to "end welfare as we know it." The goal was to make "work pay" and lift millions out of poverty. It required that the able-bodied seek work, but those jobs would now pay a higher minimum wage and a substantially enhanced earned income tax credit would raise the income of low-wage workers. And all workers had guaranteed health insurance and help with childcare.[15]

Bill Clinton could advocate this progressive welfare reform because it was strongly supported by the black clergy who were critical of the current system of Aid to Families with Dependent Children and allies in reforming it. Candidate Clinton underscored the point by giving the same speech in an inner-city black church in Detroit and at Macomb County Community College in the white suburbs.

The Democrats became a viable national party when Bill Clinton embraced progressive welfare reform that enabled him to close the margin in Macomb County in 1992 and win it in 1996. Democrats carried Macomb in every presidential election outside of 2004, until Donald Trump carried it handily in 2016.

The Republican Party, as has become clear since 2012, cannot pass immigration reform. Ask former Majority Leader Eric Cantor what price one pays for even speculating about the prospect. Ask President Marco Rubio about the price he paid for being one of the Gang of Eight in the Senate. To be frank, recall Senator John McCain who switched to enforcement first when he ran for president after coming out of the gate slowly due to his authorship of the Comprehensive Immigration Reform Act of 2007.

But what can save the Republican Party is a Democratic president passing landmark comprehensive immigration reform, with or without Republican votes, that is viewed as a juncture comparable to the passing of the civil rights laws in the 1960s. The immigration law passed by the U.S. Senate in 2013 included major funding for border security and e-verify to guarantee only those here lawfully are employed. It required that the law-abiding, undocumented immigrant pay fines, get at the back of the line to be a legal immigrant, and get on a path to citizenship. It expanded programs for short-term farm employment and visas for those graduating from universities—to greatly diminish the number of undocumented.

This law would only change the political trajectory of the country if the administration visibly worked to manage and control immigration. Citizens would feel prioritized over non-citizens. The government would have to punish employers who employed people illegally. The number of undocumented would have to fall.

Or would passage of comprehensive immigration reform simply be a pause button before the numbers of undocumented made their way to America again? Would this look like President Reagan's amnesty and President George W. Bush's expansion of legal immigration, which dramatically increased the number of immigrants, undocumented and foreign born? That is what conservatives expect.

The tentacles of bold, landmark immigration reforms will only go deep into civil society if Fox News supports them, and perhaps even the Koch brothers. That seems like an impossible lift with Lachlan taking over the Murdoch empire and cheering the ultranationalists and fanning anti-immigrant fears and worries about Muslims on its affiliates in the United States, Britain, and Australia. But the Murdoch empire has been extraordinary at adapting to political changes and leveraging elected officials to create a friendly regulatory environment. What happens when Trump's repudiation leaves them out in the cold? What happens when its own employees rebel? What happens when the network is held accountable for the domestic death toll?[16]

They will come under attack within the conservative ecosphere, but it is the only way the GOP can move away from being an anti-immigrant party in an immigrant country. Fox News has to stop amplifying Breitbart News if the party is to change.

Recall this.

President Clinton signed the welfare reform bill, or the Personal Responsibility and Work Opportunity Reconciliation Act of 1996 (PRWORA), passed by the Gingrich Congress after he had vetoed it twice. It was hardly the progressive version that included an increased minimum wage and universal health care. I was no longer in the White House then but urged Clinton to veto it a third time. The president was able to get some changes in but hardly enough. He signed it to the consternation of many in the administration, though he was able to win important improvements that affected non-citizens the following year. President Clinton felt vindicated. And near full employment covered up a lot of sins.

Amid all the scrutiny about the impact of the law, one can miss one of the biggest consequences. The issue disappeared. It is hard today to reconstruct how much political energy was devoted to it, but it just disappeared. It was no longer a voting issue.

The Democrats have to lead if there is any chance of the parties being freed from the polarization on immigration.

BECOMING RELEVANT AGAIN

At the heart of the GOP is a large bloc of Evangelicals and observant and conservative Catholics who form about 40 percent of the party and are pro-life; indeed, that is probably why they are Republicans. The fervor, at least of the Evangelicals, has pushed away the moderates in the GOP, who are socially liberal, and the secular conservatives, who don't like the Evangelical embrace of the Tea Party. This bloc has pushed away millennials and a lot of women.

The GOP cannot be relevant for these voters until it accepts the sexual revolution and today's working family, even if it doesn't become pro-choice. The GOP is still trying to defund Planned Parenthood and to fund abstinence-only sex education. It is battling to limit contraception coverage in the Affordable Care Act. And conservatives have pulled back from ways to pay for childcare because they don't want to incentivize work over caring for children and the home.[17] Donald Trump won strong support in the Evangelical and Tea Party base when he stood up for men and their breadwinner role in the traditional family.

But you cannot be relevant as a pro-family party if you are still trying to incentivize women to be homemakers and are still contesting the sexual revolution. You just cannot speak to working women who feel as if they are on their own and are demanding government do something about family and sick leave, childcare, and equal pay. Champion tax credits for the youngest children and universal pre-K. Only then would the GOP get a hearing on marriage, children with too little parenting, and young children benefiting from parenting and early socialization programs.

The Republicans will not get a hearing with millennials in the country unless the post–Donald Trump leaders accept gay marriage, which was legalized by the U.S. Supreme Court in 2014. The issue is not even a close call or even a brave one among Republicans, since more Republicans now support it than do not.[18] A presidential candidate accepting gay marriage as the law of the land and the right thing to do is a larger statement about the sexual revolution and marriage.

The final crushing Republican defeats were led by women of all classes and races, who believe women face discrimination up and down the employment ladder and receive unequal pay compared with men in similar positions. So, when the new Congress convenes in January 2021, the Democrats will reintroduce the Paycheck Fairness Bill and pass it, the same way the victorious Democrats passed the Lilly Ledbetter Fair Pay Act, the first law signed by President Obama in 2009. My wife, Rosa DeLauro, was the principal author of the law, which passed the House three times, including in March 2019. The bill lost by two votes in the Senate in 2010, failing to win the votes of Senators Susan Collins and Olympia Snowe. For the sake of the GOP, this time a number of Republican women who are U.S. senators will need to be at the White House to be handed a pen after the president signs the Paycheck Fairness Act into law.

Now for the hard part.

The GOP has to break with the oil companies and the fossil fuel industry that puts the party in the implausible position of denying climate change and withdrawing America from the battle to contest it. It associates the party with the past, with dirty coal, while leaving the green economy to the Democrats. It also means the party will get no hearing with millennials and the generation behind them and will perhaps struggle to be relevant in Florida.

The energy industry is a huge player in GOP campaigns and allied conservative institutions, in order to stop consideration of climate change or a shift to renewable energy. Yet Donald Trump has shown that the GOP can also energize and raise small-dollar donations on a large scale to free up its agenda.

And the GOP has to follow the lead of many Republican governors who fought for the expansion of Medicaid in their states. The Republican Party since the New Deal has at each point accepted or expanded or introduced market reforms that have sometimes threatened the original intent, but the battle to repeal Obamacare was sui generis and cost the GOP dearly. Health care is now nationalized and politicized, and ironically, the GOP must find ways to make the Affordable Care Act work. They own the dysfunction now, unless they are ready for some form of Medicare for all. A majority of Republicans say they support health insurance for all. Indeed, there is broad support within the GOP for the government doing more about health care, childcare, and spending on the public schools. Deconstructing government has lost its lure, as teacher strikes highlight the need for different spending priorities. Republican governors have committed to spend more on education.

This means rejecting the Tea Party's top priority of repealing the Affordable Care Act and escaping that period of the Obama presidency when the GOP set itself against government. It means transcending a period when closing down the federal government was normal.

After the repudiation of the Trump presidency and its battle against the deep state, the GOP must get back to being a party that can be trusted on national security. That means GOP leaders defending the intelligence agencies and defense department, as well as the multilateral arrangements that make us more secure, like NATO. I see no evidence that the desire to put America first and making sure you have a strong military means wanting to withdraw from America's alliances in Europe and Asia. This is not Senator Rand Paul's party.

At its core, the Republican Party will be a party that is pro-business and wants lower taxes, a party that trusts markets as more than just a "tool," as Tucker Carlson described them in his Fox News rant against the GOP. That is surely not what America is currently looking for, but its raison d'être. Some conservatives know that markets can threaten communities and family and divide the country, and they will weigh in after the deluge.[19]

But Donald Trump and Steve Bannon did open up one area—

making global trade, trade agreements, and our relationship with China work for Americans. For the president and Bannon, making America great required a crackdown on immigration and the assertion of "national sovereignty" over multilateralism,[20] and they are surely on the defensive on both of those now.[21] But it was, readers read in Bob Woodward's account of White House discussions, among Trump's very top imperatives: "you are going to bring manufacturing jobs back to the country."[22] The president believed "US trade agreements allowed cheaper foreign goods to flood into the United States, which took away jobs from American workers." Everything was "upside down" and "underwater," as evident in the huge trade deficit. He tried to sign an executive order to resign from NAFTA, until he was blocked by his aides in the White House. His philosophy: "Walk away, threaten to blow up the deal. Real power is fear."

Trump broke through the elite discourse that had ignored the effects of global trade and U.S. trade agreements on manufacturing and working people. That struck a chord with the white working class and the GOP base, who are most skeptical about trade and NAFTA.

That allowed the Trump-led GOP to make gains in 2016. But as Tucker Carlson's recent monologue on Fox News points out, this is hardly where the party stands. The congressional chamber wins support for trade agreements from Republican Senate and House members, not Democrats.

What now for the GOP? Will working people really believe the Republican Party beyond Trump will look out for them? Trump got his opening because both the Democratic and Republican parties embraced globalization and found the domestic costs acceptable. Both supported engagement with China, and promised unbelievably to punish them for currency manipulation or denying market access.

Donald Trump gave the party an opening on standing up for American manufacturing and jobs, but the Republicans are as fractured on trade as the Democrats.

Carlson's monologue on Fox News skewered the Republican Party for fetishizing markets over the development of the family and the building of communal ties. Putting aside the hypocrisy of the rant, he set off a debate among conservatives in which some challenged the austerity the GOP had imposed on the country. Some began thinking about new policies and income supports that could strengthen the working family in a "feminist age." And most of all, some began to think that it isn't enough to say, "There are wounds that policy can't solve." Republicans too have to be inventive about government. We are not powerless.[23]

THE DEATH OF THE GOP AND PROGRESSIVE HEGEMONY

When Donald Trump took leadership of the GOP counterrevolution, Americans became conscious of every disruptive trend and embraced new norms and an expanded role of government at a breathtaking pace. Donald Trump immediately politicized the New America and more who now understood the stakes. He raised their consciousness of what they believed and what tasks the government must take up with new urgency.

Democrats captured the House in 2018 and if they learned the lessons on how they let Donald Trump win, they will win the presidency and effective control of the government in 2020. Democratic beliefs have evolved dialectically in reaction to President Trump, and now demand a very different kind of governance consistent with their values.

Democrats, with near unanimity, and a large majority of the country believe we live in a profoundly unequal country where corporate power calls the shots. They want government to play a much bigger role in offsetting that power and in taking up the unfinished agenda for women and people of color. They want to move even more boldly to tackle climate change. And they want to embrace an America that is an immigrant country, inclusive, and multicultural. The country has faced deepening economic and social problems that more and more want to address and, increasingly, to use government to bring change.

On some measures, a third or more of Republicans agreed, suggesting a significant proportion of the GOP base is looking for a different kind of country. That is when you know that Democratic hegemony may be a new norm. Fully 60 percent of Democrats, a majority of independents, and a third of Republicans say the GOP is "so misguided that they threaten the nation's well-being."[24] It is the Democrats' time and perhaps their era.

- 84 percent of Democrats say immigration strengthens the country, but 42 percent of the GOP does as well, suggesting the non-Trump GOP can get an audience.

- 82 percent of Democrats say the economy favors powerful interests, and the GOP is split on whether that is true.

- Over three quarters of Democrats say, "Stricter environmental regulations are worth the cost"; over a third of Republicans do, too. Since Trump's election, the proportion of Democrats who believe government is doing too little jumped 20 points to 86 percent.

- Over 70 percent of Democrats say, and with increasing certainty, "Government should do more to help needy Americans even if it means going into debt," while less than a quarter of Republicans believe that.

- Over three quarters of Democrats—a number that rises every year—believe, "People have hard lives because government benefits don't go far enough," while 25 percent of Republicans think that is true.

- Over 80 percent of Democrats believe the "country needs to continue making changes to give blacks equal rights with whites," while over a third of the GOP agrees with that.

- Nearly three quarters of Democrats say women face "significant obstacles that still make it harder for them to get ahead of men," and a third of Republicans believe that.

Broad Support for a Democratic Agenda in the Nation

% who say...

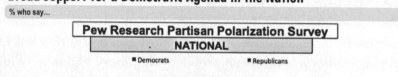

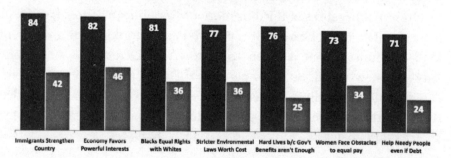

The GOP's shattering losses in 2018 may well create a mandate for reform that could grow into a new era of reform, suppressed until now by the intensity of the conservative counterrevolution.

Democrats have watched with building frustration a country where jobs don't pay enough to live on and median income has not budged in decades. The top 1 percent owns as much as the bottom 90 percent. The big money and big corporations have rigged the game.[25]

Democrats have watched with building anger the GOP hold on to power by legalizing dark money and disenfranchising millions of citizens.

People will not settle for tinkering when it comes to addressing income stagnation, inequality, taxes, fairness, corporate governance and CEO compensation, corporate abuse, investment and infrastructure, trade agreements, antitrust cases and monopolies, work and family, equal pay for women, entrenched racial disparities, early education, universal health care, climate change, and on and on. Edward Luce understates it when he says, "The center of gravity has shifted," but not when he says, "For the first time in decades, America's intellectual energy is on the left."[26]

When the Republican Party is fully defeated, the country will be freed from the decade-long effort to stop Democratic governance and governmental function. That moment will produce a new sense of possibility that will compound the intellectual energy pushing up policy innovation in this period.

The nation sees the potential for new transformative policies according to the Roosevelt Institute's report for the 2020 election, "New Rules for the 21st Century: Corporate Power, Public Power, and the Future of the American Economy."[27] It shows how out-of-control corporate power has produced a low-wage economy, inequality compounded across "generations and geographies," a "yawning racial wealth gap over the last thirty years," and "climate change that is destroying the health of our planet." Like in so many areas, the Trump presidency has proved clarifying. The economy "rewards those who have power." That is why Nell Abernathy, Darrick Hamilton, and Julie Margetta Morgan preface the Roosevelt Institute report with "the crucial need to curb corporate power and reclaim public power." The idea of getting government out of the way to strengthen the economy is so bankrupt. Their economic plan begins with empowering ordinary citizens, limiting the power of big money, attacking concentrated corporate power, banning stock buybacks, and raising taxes dramatically on corporations and the richest. That makes it possible to "revive public power." Government must make "vital investments" in infrastructure, clean energy, and emerging industries and ensure fair competition. It must create genuine public options in health care, education, and housing.

And the Democrats will not run in 2020 calling out to every aggrieved group in its potential winning coalition, as Hillary Clinton did so disastrously in 2016, unless Russian bots succeed in getting Democratic presidential candidates to sign up to support "reparations." If they succeeded, Democrats would wait longer to capture the U.S. Senate and move its agenda. That is the risk of giving in to identity politics.

Some observers looked at Stacey Abrams falling just 56,000 votes short in Georgia, and concluded Clinton was just two years too early or just not passionate enough. I faulted the Clinton campaign on many things, but not her determination to crash the glass ceiling for women. I believe her experience remains instructive.

Stacey Abrams joined a symposium with Francis Fukuyama and correctly dismissed his fear that group identity necessarily fragments the country, undermines democracy, and precludes a unified American identity. Abrams went further though, pointing to a litany of groups—"-women, Native Americans, immigrants, and LGBTQ"—that would benefit if the country understood the "barriers to entry" and the "most successful methods of fighting for inclusion." She is right that with social media "isolated cruelties are yoked into a powerful narrative of marginalization" that nationalizes these wrongs and "spurs common cause."

Yet Abrams is acutely conscious at the same time that "the current demographic and social evolution toward diversity in the United States has played out alongside a trend toward greater economic and social inequality." She knows "these parallel but distinct developments are inextricably bound together," which is why her success has such bigger implications.[28] [29] [30] The barriers to entry are not just the race-specific ones. Working people and the poor have been hurt by the broader failure of the upper classes to educate and invest and the broader power to limit access to unions and the right to vote. Black voters could not be more sophisticated about how "social and economic inequality" are woven together and the implications for politics and policy.

The Roosevelt Institute's transformative economic plan for the 2020 election powerfully underscores the problem: "Since America's founding and continuing today, our economy has been built on implicit and explicit rules that include some people and exclude others based on race." And with women facing structural obstacles, too, you get "rampant" race and gender inequality. So, reviving public power also means "actively addressing exclusions based on race and gender." Going forward, a progressive agenda must "place inclusion at the core."[31]

Every message test I conducted during the 2016 and 2018 campaigns described in chapter 8, "How Did Democrats Let Donald Trump Win?," found the same kind of sophistication and clarity in the New America of African Americans and Hispanics, single women, millennials, and college women. It got *more* engaged and *more determined* to vote for Democrats when they called out the corrupt political deals that put government to work for big corporations and big donors, rather than calling out the "barriers to inclusion" and promising "ladders of opportunity." The Democrats' multicultural base were the most frustrated and hurt by the political status quo that further enriches the top 1 percent and weakens unions; a status quo that leaves the national minimum wage frozen, that allows infrastructure to deteriorate, education spending to be slashed, leaves working families on their own and health care ever more insecure and unaffordable. These are the people who can't handle a sudden five-hundred-dollar expense and who would welcome this kind of relief.

The Democrats' electoral base understands that a Democratic Party working to weaken corporate power, expand vital investments, help the poorest, and reduce inequality will make the biggest difference for those who have lived with generations of discrimination. People of color and women will be the first beneficiaries of this inclusive approach, and they know it and act on it.

Steve Bannon, President Trump's chief strategist in the critical first year, thought he was dealing with a Democratic Party that had learned nothing from 2016. "The longer they talk about identity politics, I got 'em. I want them to talk about racism every day. If the left is focused on race and identity, and Democrats go with economic nationalism, the right can crush the Democrats on economic nationalism."[32]

But Democrats in 2018 campaigned against the corruption, self-dealing, and failure to "drain the swamp." They called for major investments in infrastructure to create American jobs. And they demanded the Republicans stop their war on the Affordable Care Act that is killing people with preexisting conditions and that makes the crisis in health care costs dramatically worse. Democrats promised to work for a government that works for all, not the special interests, and House Speaker Nancy Pelosi put forward H.R. 1, "For The People Act: bold, transformative legislation to put the power back in the hands of the people and restore the people's faith that government works for the public interest, not the special interests."[33]

Democrats in 2018 and afterward energized the New America, but also made major inroads into rural areas and with white working-class voters, too.

At the same time, most Americans have seen through Donald Trump's mad and losing battle against America's diversity and immigrant character where "social and economic inequality" are indeed fully intwined, as Stacey Abrams put it. They may not know how much New Deal programs or post–World War II housing policies discriminated against blacks and women, but they watch enough body cams or viral smartphone videos to know young black people are more at risk on the street. The legacy of segregation and discrimination, disenfranchisement, and the criminal justice system make all our economic inequalities worse.[34] So it is a good thing that about 80 percent of the Democratic base and a majority of the country also believe the job of achieving equality for women and African Americans and other people of color is unfinished.

They think that is still a priority because the Democratic Party embraces a multiculturalism that is now fully aligned with today's American creed. The political scientists John Sides, Michael Tesler, and Lynn Vavreck hit Fukuyama for failing to see how close America was to having a "creedal national identity." Fully nine in ten Americans believe accepting people of diverse racial and religious backgrounds is important to being American, far above more nationalistic and exclusive definitions, like speaking English.[35]

What if multiculturalism is no longer politically contested?

When Speaker Nancy Pelosi spoke at the London School of Economics about the state of Trump's America, which I watched from the audience as a spouse in the congressional delegation accompanying her, she decided to address the controversy around immigration. She quoted President Ronald Reagan's last speech in the White House:

> We lead the world because, unique among nations, we draw our
> people—our strength—from every country and every corner of the

world. And by doing so we continuously renew and enrich our nation. While other countries cling to the stale past, here in America we breathe life into dreams. We create the future, and the world follows us into tomorrow. Thanks to each wave of new arrivals in this land of opportunity, we're a nation forever young, forever bursting with energy and new ideas, and always on the cutting edge, always leading the world to the next frontier.[36]

The political scientists and everyone else sees the country holding yet another election where it is even more polarized—where which party you identify with supersedes all others, where one party speaks for the whites who resent the country's diversity and secularism, and where views of immigration are the strongest determination of the vote. That party has driven away millennials, suburban women, and college graduates. But what if the GOP's last heave leaves it shattered, fractured, illegitimate, and ashamed?[37]

What if the GOP is off the battlefield, figuring out how to be relevant again?

What if the politics is not linear and the past no longer predicts the future?

What happens the day after?

The year 2020 is the one hundred and tenth anniversary of the 1910 off-year elections, when a blue wave gave Democrats control of the House, captured seven Senate seats, and won three governorships. Woodrow Wilson, the president of Princeton University, ran for governor of New Jersey, swept to a surprising victory, quickly repudiated the party bosses, and introduced a corrupt-practices law to bar business and government from conspiring against the public.[38] The GOP was badly fractured then, as now, between the establishment wing led by President Taft and the progressives led by Teddy Roosevelt. Woodrow Wilson won an extraordinary victory in a three-way presidential contest and would go on to work with a Congress where progressives from both parties were the majority. In his inaugural address in front of the U.S. Capitol, the new president declared America's duty "to cleanse, to reconsider, to restore, to correct the evil" before it.[39]

After being sworn in by the chief justice, President Wilson made clear he would attack the tariff system that "makes the Government a facile instrument in the hand of private interests," including a banking and currency system suited to fifty years earlier; and an industrial system that "restricts the liberties and limits the opportunities of labor, and exploits without renewing or conserving the natural resources of the country."[40]

In this intense period, the country enacted constitutional amendments that legalized the progressive income tax and the direct election of U.S. senators, and that gave women the right to vote—all resisted by conservative forces and won after reforms advanced in the cities and states and protest movements that pressed against the doors of power. The Wilson administration won passage of the Clayton Antitrust Act to break up the big corporate monopolies and pushed the Interstate Commerce Commission, Federal Trade Commission, and Food and Drug Administration to regulate business excess and protect consumers.

They were blocked by a conservative Supreme Court from passing a forty-hour week and rights of unions—reforms that would have to wait for the election of Franklin D. Roosevelt and the New Deal in the 1930s. Progressives appreciate even more now how much racial equality was not on the agenda with Wilson or Roosevelt until new social movements to bend the arc of justice under Lyndon Baynes Johnson in the mid-1960s.

But the twentieth century's path to democratic reform began with a progressive decade after an unapologetic pro-business Republican Party refused to address the collateral pain among the poor and working class, the growing inequality, and the corruption of business and politics. They refused to open up to workers and women. It took two landslide elections in 1912 and 1936 to shatter the Republican Party, vanquish the conservatives, and create a mandate for reform.

Trump's Tea Party–Evangelical GOP can't just be defeated. It must face a repudiating, shattering defeat that frees other brands of the GOP and conservatism to breathe again, find their own Republican candidates, switch loyalties to the Democrats, or perhaps vote for an independent presidential candidate.

Because Trump's GOP fought the New America with a special ugliness, its death will give Democrats the energy and momentum to lead a new era of reform for the New America.

ACKNOWLEDGMENTS

I wrote this book because I had to.

Donald Trump becoming president of the United States was unimaginable because, to the very end, I believed that skilled and committed people would stop him. I knew a lot of working Americans might just take a chance on Trump given my own frustration with the direction of the country, but only clueless leaders and campaign malpractice would have allowed him to end up in the White House.

I felt compelled to write as quickly as possible what I believe really happened in the 2016 November election, and thankfully *The Guardian*, *The New York Times*, *Democracy Journal*, *Democratic Strategist*, and most of all, *The American Prospect* gave me the space to shout. (*The Washington Post* was first to publish my argument a year before the election.) I never wrote so fast and intently. The moment was too urgent to wait on a book. Thank you to Robert Kuttner, Harold Myerson, and Paul Starr; John Judis; and Andrew Levison.

Democrats "don't have a white working-class problem," I wrote. "They have a working-class problem." After the financial crisis that wiped out so many jobs and so much wealth and the bailout of the big banks, white working-class voters scorned the Democrats, while their own base of voters disengaged. The base declined to defend Barack Obama at the polls, even though he called on them to "build on the progress." I was pretty angry Democrats were not introspective after their deep losses down ballot in the states election after election, leading

The New York Times to headline my piece with Anna Greenberg, "Was Barack Obama Bad for Democrats?"

I jumped at the chance to write a review of *Shattered*, the first inside account of the Clinton campaign. I wrote with exasperation of the campaign's malpractice, which I got to observe fairly closely. Their failure to contest or even poll in Michigan and Wisconsin and taking for granted the discontented Bernie Sanders vote cost them the election. Hillary Clinton was hamstrung by her dogged determination to hew as closely as possible to President Obama, particularly on the economy, even when she encountered everyday people in so much pain.

I didn't believe the lazy assumption that the country wanted an Obama Third Term. The country was going to vote for a disruptor.

I knew with my history of writing about disaffected white working-class voters and "Reagan Democrats" in Macomb County, I needed to listen and write about them, too. To start, my new polls needed to better represent them. Those with some college or a high school education or less would comprise 61.5 percent of all my polls in the 2018 election cycle. And no more second-guessing who is a "likely" voter. My polls are now of registered voters, open to the kind of surge of white working-class voters that happened in 2016 and of women voters that happened in 2018.

After the 2016 election and 2018, I went to Macomb County to talk with working-class independents and Democrats who had voted for Trump. I knew they were under pressure. And I knew the elites had trouble respecting their choice, though I believed they had legitimate reasons to support him. My liberal friends would be unforgiving soon, pressing the Trump voter to regret their choice. I knew academics would soon bring back the studies on the "authoritarian personality" or start looking for nodes on the brain that make them "conservative."

My wife, Rosa DeLauro, is a member of Congress, and she chose to attend Donald Trump's inauguration; and because she is in the Democratic leadership, Rosa attended the private lunch with the president in Statuary Hall. She avoided him and never had to face shaking his hand.

So, we were in Washington for the inauguration, with its very modest crowds compared to those for President Barack Obama. The streets in Washington were pretty quiet, but not the next day, for the Women's March. The streets, shops, and cafes were overrun with people. Such energy and excitement. Our house on Capitol Hill was full of family from out of town, and our children and grandchildren and friends gathered there before joining the half million who formed a crush in all the streets. Rosa brought me and the grandkids up on the speakers' platform where we joined the women members of Congress and hugged Cecile Richards, head of Planned Parenthood, and Sister Simone Campbell, head of NETWORK and Rosa's ally in her battles for the Affordable Care Act and against the Ryan budgets.

When I woke up the next day and every day, I asked myself, *What have I done today to resist and make sure Donald Trump is repudiated?* I couldn't sleep most nights and it turns out, many millions were reacting in the same way. They got involved, gave money, attended marches, descended on town halls, rushed to airports to protect Muslim refugees.

I decided to write a book because of the resistance, most of whom were painfully uncertain how this would all turn out. I wrote it because of the opposite. I believed Donald Trump's victory was the last, desperate battle of a Tea Party–dominated Republican Party to stop an unstoppable New America from governing, and they would fail. Indeed, Trump getting the nomination confirmed the story. Trump winning the election accelerated the defeat of his party, whose battle against modernity would leave it shattered. Trump governing would make the great majority of the country newly conscious of their own values, beliefs, and priorities.

People thought I was smoking. I hope you are right.

Nobody would believe me until the country was swept by a blue wave in 2018, but not then either. I couldn't even convince James Carville. So, not until the 2020 blue wave.

I sent my book outline to Thomas Dunne, who was loyal and published nearly all my recent books. He and Stephen S. Power, executive editor at Thomas Dunne Books, came to see me at my office. Tom said he had already copyrighted a title, *RIP GOP*, which fit what I wanted to write. It was perfect.

Compelled by the moment, I got up at 4:30 most mornings and wrote for hours as a kind of therapy and relief that I was doing my part. I blew past the 70,000 words of my book contract. I met every deadline for the first time in my life. Remarkably, Stephen would send back line edits within a day or two. Something was happening there, too.

I was able to step to a new scale of research and work to influence

Acknowledgments

key players because a cadre of progressive allies were also asking themselves, *What more can I do?* And they pushed Democracy Corps into areas we could hardly have imagined.

Page Gardner created the Women's Voices Women Vote Action Fund and the Voter Participation Center to advocate for the underrepresented, which has come to encompass the rising American electorate—African Americans, Hispanics, millennials, and unmarried women, those whose values and liberties are most under threat as the GOP throws off all limits to hold on to power. With more than a little help from Ron Rosenblith, Gardner pushed her programs to be the most innovative and accountable and challenged us to do the same. Progressive donors invested more than $50 million in her efforts in 2018 alone.

Felicia Wong is president and CEO of the Roosevelt Institute, which leveraged the work of Joseph Stiglitz to elevate a bold policy agenda to rewrite the rules of the economy. She understood the big forces that would fight them and how much their policy work needed to be embedded in a narrative and employ messages that could win the public debate. She invested in a sustained, innovative, and engaged program that should have allowed a Democratic presidential candidate to win on the economy.

When President Trump and the Republicans finally passed a bold, shameless tax cut for corporations and the richest and argued they were delivering tax cuts for the middle class and the "greatest economy ever," it was Randi Weingarten, president of the American Federation of Teachers and a force of nature in the labor movement, who said, "I'm in." They backed a year-long effort to listen to the working people, the supposed beneficiaries, and expose who it really benefited. We branded it as a "tax scam for the rich" and helped campaigns win the economic and tax battle in 2018.

Lori Wallach is director of Global Trade Watch in Public Citizen and stands alone among progressive leaders, understanding how much globalization and our prevailing trade agreements have hurt working people. She bravely fights on, building coalitions finally strong enough to win, and enlisted me in the battle against TPP and to change the renegotiated NAFTA, and listened to my counterintuitive, crazy recommendations. She even made me a believer in the importance of progressives getting the trade issue right or paying a big price at the polls.

James Carville and I founded Democracy Corps nearly twenty years ago, and he pushed for Democracy Corps to conduct research with Republican base voters. It seemed like a mad idea but he asked, "What country would go to war without knowing what's going on behind enemy lines?" Steven Katzenberg gave us the seed money for the first research, and Steve Bing, who funded us for a decade, allowed us to pay for the research ourselves. That changed fundamentally when Michael Vachon, adviser to Soros Fund Management said, "This work has to happen."

William and David Harris play a special role in the progressive world that mobilized on so many fronts to confront the danger of Donald Trump. They've pressed every day, year on year for a lifetime to see an America free of child poverty. They are relentlessly effective in making progress, and more than anyone they have said, do whatever research you think is right to get a president and Congress that will do the right thing.

Nancy Zdukewicz helped direct Democracy Corps and oversaw all the research it conducted in 2016 and 2018 and coauthored the focus group reports. She assisted in getting my last book, *America Ascendant*, to press. Henry Hoglund, my project coordinator at Greenberg Research, took over the editorial direction of this book and helped me maintain the quality of the writing as I took the book in so many unexpected directions. Chad Arthur, my lead analyst at Greenberg Research, took over the book in its closing phases, but that meant bringing in our latest research, making the graphs live, and answering every last question of the copy editors. He was joined at the end by Adrian Palau-Te Jeda, my new project director, who helped get the book across the finish line.

GQR carries on, led proudly by Anna Greenberg and Jeremy Rosner, offering polling and strategy in the United States and globally. Their professionalism and ethics run deep, and they were my subcontractor for all the surveys and focus groups reported in this book. Many just noticed these changes when Anna became the pollster for presidential candidate John Hickenlooper, that my daughter (and Jeremy) had taken over the firm. Quite proud indeed.

GQR is now led by Chief Operator Officer Lindsey Reynolds, who deftly manages how we partner and maximize our shared legacy. Jade

Kish heads human relations and operations for GQR, yet takes responsibility for all my hiring. Dave Rooney is systems administrator at GQR, yet sits calmly at the vortex of my work with ready solutions, keeping my whole team integrated globally.

As with all my books, I only risked giving Rosa and my brother, Edward Greenberg, the whole book to read. Ed is a professor of political science with his own major textbooks in political science, and his comments helped me get to much greater clarity and sooner.

One observation was particularly insightful about our times: *Who is your audience?* He wrote, "Is it the people and groups that are resisting or the broader group of social and political commentators that usually engage with your work?" It was a smart and revealing question. I wrote this book in a determined frenzy and viewed Democracy Corps' clients and donors as partners and allies, resisting the Trump presidency. So, throughout the book, I wrote what "we" had concluded and done, rather than "I."

With Ed and the copy editor's help, I got back to first person, though it underscores how much Donald Trump has disrupted.

I presented the main argument of this book at a conference, "The Trap of Polarization," at the Italian Academy at Columbia University, as I was turning in the final manuscript to the publisher. I want to thank Professor Michael Walzer, who was wary of my asserting the need to "destroy" the Republican Party. Before President Trump, our democracy was secure because each party would vacate the White House when it lost an election. Would my goal encourage Trump to refuse to leave?

Actually, I never use the term "destroying" in the book. I am pressing for "shattering" electoral defeats and fractures that allow the Republican Party to be renewed and win again.

I also want to reassure Ece Temelkuran, author of *How to Lose a Country*, that America is not Turkey. Our country is indeed led by a populist ultranationalist with few self-imposed bounds. He would like nothing better than to hang out with authoritarian thugs like Vladimir Putin and Xi Jinping and with other ultranationalist populists like Benjamin Netanyahu, Victor Orban, Andrzej Duda, Jair Bolsonaro, and Rodrigo Duterte. But Donald Trump is president because he is leading the Tea Party's losing battle against the New America. His shattering losses represent the triumph of democratic forces, expanding freedom that heralds a new era of progressive reform.

Our children and their spouses—Kathryn Greenberg and Ari Zentner, Anna Greenberg and Dana Milbank, Jonathan Greenberg and Justine Gardner—each is so engaged, committed, creative, accomplished, ethical, and loving. All joined the Women's March and accept that this is my first book not dedicated to the family.

Our grandchildren—Paola Milbank, Rigby Zentner, Teo Zentner, Sadie Delicath, Jasper Delicath, and Augustus Greenberg—are part of this moment, too. They cried when Hillary lost. They stopped telling us to switch off the news. They marched and created their own signs.

This is Rosa's moment. And we all love her for being such a force of nature who will prove me right about this progressive moment. She is the chair of the Appropriations Subcommittee for Labor, Health and Human Services, Education, and Related Agencies, and line by line, thread by thread, she is restoring the social safety net. She's restoring research on gun violence. She is already calling them to account for sabotaging the Affordable Care Act, bailing out nonprofit colleges, separating children from their parents at the border, and hollowing out the Department of Labor. How many of us have fifty million views like her confrontation with Betsy DeVos? It will not be long before the next president is signing into law the bills she has fought for over so many years: equal pay for women, paid family leave, paid sick days, and an expanded young child tax cut that cuts child poverty in half. That is why one of the young, freshmen women on the House floor described her as a "feminist disruptor."

We are partners in each other's work, and I love her. Rosa lost her 103-year-old mother last year. Luisa and her husband, Theodore, were also forces of nature and partners who said, never take no for an answer.

We know.

WASHINGTON, D.C.
JULY 1, 2019

NOTES

INTRODUCTION

1. Pew Research Center, "The Partisan Divide on Political Values Grows Even Wider," October 5, 2017, http://www.people-press.org/2017/10/05/4-race-immigration-and-discrimination/, accessed July 8, 2018.

2. National web survey of eight likely Republican voters was conducted by Democracy Corps and Greenberg Quinlan Rosner on February 11–16, 2016, using a voter file sample. Likely voters were determined based on whether they voted in 2012 or had registered since and stated intention of voting in 2016. Data is among those who identify as Republicans or independents who lean Republican and vote in Republican primaries or caucuses. Margin of error for the full sample is +/-3.47 percentage points at 95 percent confidence. The five categories of Republicans are mutually exclusive categories determined by respondents' responses on ideology, religion, frequency of service attendance, strength of Tea Party support, and favorability toward the Tea Party. To ensure that the web survey accurately reflects the national Republican Party, the typologies were weighted to the average for each type from Democracy Corps's last three national surveys.

3. Fred Hiatt, "Stephen K. Bannon Has Won," *The Washington Post*, June 17, 2018; Jonathan Freedland, "Explaining Trump, Brexit and Other Expressions of Nationalism," *The New York Times Book Review*, December 18, 2018, https://www.nytimes.com/2018/12/18/books/review/john-b-judis-nationalist-revival.html, accessed May 3, 2019; E.J. Dionne, "Is There Such a Thing as Progressive Nationalism," *The American Prospect*, April 1, 2019, https://prospect.org/article/there-such-thing-progressive-nationalism, accessed April 2, 2019; John B. Judis, *The Nationalist Revival: Trade, Immigration, and the Revolt Against Globalization*, (New York: Columbia Global Reports, 2018).

4. Tara Golshan, "Trump said he wouldn't cut Medicaid, Social Security, and Medicare. His 2020 budget cuts all 3," *Vox*, March 12, 2019, https://www.vox.com/policy-and-politics/2019/3/12/18260271/trump-medicaid-social-security-medicare-budget-cuts, accessed on March 26, 2019; Paul N. Van De Water, Joel Friedman, and Sharon Parrott, "2020 Trump Budget: Disturbing Vision," Center on Budget and Policy Priorities, March 11, 2019, https://www.cbpp.org/research/federal-budget/2020-trump-budget-a-disturbing-vision, accessed on March 26, 2019.

5. Juliet Eilperin, Josh Dawsey, Seung Min Kim, "'It's way too many': As vacancies pile up in Trump Administration, Senators Grow Concerned," *The Washington Post*, February 4, 2019, https://www.washingtonpost.com/national/health-science/its-way-too-many-as-vacancies-pile

-up-in-trump-administration-senators-grow-concerned/2019/02/03/c570eb94-24b2-11e9-ad53
-824486280311_story.html?utm_term=.ef0119824f25, accessed May 3, 2019.

6. cf. http://insider.foxnews.com/2018/01/22/tomi-lahren-final-thoughts-blasting-womens
-march-linda-sarsour-mean-girls, http://www.foxnews.com/opinion/2018/01/20/womens-march
-are-watching-movement-or-just-group-therapy-for-trump-haters.html.

1 THE NEW AMERICA

1. Pew Research Center, "About Four-in-Ten of the World's Migrants Live in the U.S. or Europe,"
June 22, 2016, http://www.pewresearch.org/fact-tank/2016/06/22/about-four-in-ten-of-the
-worlds-migrants-live-in-the-u-s-or-europe/.

2. Sabrina Traverse, "U.S. Has Highest Share of Foreign-Born Since 1910, with More Coming
from Asia," *The New York Times*, September 13, 2018, https://www.nytimes.com/2018/09/13/us
/census-foreign-population.html, accessed January 12, 2019.

3. U.S. Bureau of Labor Statistics, Current Employment Statistics survey, series ID
CES3000000001, manufacturing industry, U.S. Department of Labor, extracted February 6,
2018, available at http://www.bls.gov/ces/.

4. Jonathan Freedland, "Explaining Trump, Brexit and Other Expressions of Nationalism,"
The New York Times Book Review, December 18, 2018, https://www.nytimes.com/2018/12/18
/books/review/john-b-judis-nationalist-revival.html, accessed May 3, 2019.

5. J. D. Vance would go on to found Revolution of the Rest: https://www.revolution.com
/entity/rotr/, a VC seed firm focused on investing in early stage ventures not located in New
York, Boston, or Silicon Valley.

6. Pew Research Center, "Key Findings About American Life in Urban, Suburban, and Rural
Areas," http://www.pewresearch.org/fact-tank/2018/05/22/key-findings-about-american-life-in
-urban-suburban-and-rural-areas/, accessed July 8, 2018.

7. Ibid., accessed May 22, 2018.

8. Robert Putnam and David Campbell, *American Grace* (New York: Simon & Schuster, 2012), Kindle location 1945, 331, 1500–1571; Robert P. Jones, Daniel Cox, and Juhem
Navarro-Rivera, "A Shifting Landscape," Public Religion Research Institute, February 26,
2014, p. 11. Mark J. Perry, "Stunning College Degree Gap: Women Have Earned Almost 10
Million More College Degrees Than Men Since 1982," American Enterprise Institute, May 13,
2013; Wendy Wang, Kim Parker, and Paul Taylor, "Breadwinner Moms," Pew Research Center,
May 29, 2013, p. 6; Pew Research Center analysis of Decennial Census (1960–2000) and
American Community Survey data (2008, 2010), cited in "Barely Half of U.S. Adults Are
Married—a Record Low," Pew Research Center, December 14, 2011, pp. 1–2; Leigh Gallagher,
The End of the Suburbs: Where the American Dream Is Moving (New York: Penguin Group,
2013), pp. 19, 146.

9. Survey of 2,511 adults nationwide by Pew Research Center, November 29–December 5,
2012, cited in "Modern Parenthood," Pew Research Center, March 14, 2013, pp. 9–14; "Women
in the Labor Force: A Databook," U.S. Bureau of Labor Statistics, Report 1040, February 2013,
p. 15; Wendy Wang, Kim Parker, and Paul Taylor, "Breadwinner Moms," Pew Research Center,
May 29, 2013, pp. 1, 4.

10. Data from David Autor and Melanie Wasserman, "Wayward Sons: The Emerging Gender
Gap in Labor Markets and Education," Third Way, March 2013, p. 12, presented in "Diverg-
ing Fortunes for Men and Women," *The New York Times*, March 20, 2013; Stephanie Coontz,
"How Can We Help Men? By Helping Women," *The New York Times*, January 11, 2014.

11. Stanley Greenberg, "Unlearning the Lessons of Hillbilly Elegy," *The American Prospect*,
January 8, 2019, https://prospect.org/article/unlearning-lessons-hillbilly-elegy-0, accessed January 12, 2019.

12. Survey of 2,002 adults nationwide by Pew Research Center, October 7–27, 2013, reported in "On Pay Gap, Millennial Women Near Parity—for Now," pp. 8, 29.

13. Ibid.

14. Ron Brownstein, "Millennials to Pass Baby Boomers as Largest Voter-Eligible Age Group, and What It Means," July 25, 2017, https://www.cnn.com/2017/07/25/politics/brownstein-millennials-largest-voter-group-baby-boomers/index.html; Michael Dimock, "Defining generations: Where Millennials end and Generation Z begins," Pew Research Center, January 17, 2019, https://www.pewresearch.org/fact-tank/2019/01/17/where-millennials-end-and-generation-z-begins/, accessed May 3, 2019.

15. Pew Research Center, "The Partisan Divide on Political Values Grows Even Wider," October 5, 2017, http://www.pewresearch.org/fact-tank/2018/02/13/8-facts-about-love-and-marriage/.

16. Survey of 1,821 adults with an oversample of eighteen- to thirty-three-year-olds by Pew Research Center, February 14–23, 2014, cited in "Millennials in Adulthood," Pew Research Center, March 7, 2014, p. 14; Michael Dimock, "Defining generations: Where Millennials end and Generation Z begins," Pew Research Center, January 17, 2019, https://www.pewresearch.org/fact-tank/2019/01/17/where-millennials-end-and-generation-z-begins/, accessed May 3, 2019.

17. Joe Cortright, "The Young and Restless and the Nation's Cities," City Report, City Observatory, October 2014, p. 1.

18. Kaepernick filed a grievance against the league alleging that NFL team owners worked together to keep him off the field in the wake of his kneeling protest. The NFL denied that this happened, but reached a confidential settlement with Kaepernick and another player, Eric Reid, in 2019; https://www.vox.com/identities/2018/9/6/17820158/colin-kaepernick-eric-reid-collusion-grievance-protest-settlement.

19. Cindy Boren, "Nike's Colin Kaepernick Ad Campaign Gets More Yeas Than Nays from Young People," *The Washington Post*, September 13, 2018; Jia Wertz, "Taking Risks Can Benefit Your Brand—Nike's Kaepernick Campaign Is a Perfect Example," *Forbes*, September 30, 2018.

20. James Hohmann, "'The Last Election Was a Wake-Up Call: Why GOP Leaders Are Turning on Steve King," *The Washington Post*, January 11, 2019.

21. Pew Research Center, "Americans Broadly Support Legal Status for Immigrants Brought to the US Illegally as Children," http://www.pewresearch.org/fact-tank/2018/06/18/americans-broadly-support-legal-status-for-immigrants-brought-to-the-u-s-illegally-as-children/, accessed July 8, 2018.

22. Pew Research Center, "Partisan Divide," http://www.people-press.org/2017/10/05/4-race-immigration-and-discrimination/, accessed July 8, 2018.

23. Ibid.

24. Ibid.

25. Ibid.

26. Ibid.

27. Ibid.

28. Ibid.

29. Ibid.

30. Ibid.

31. Ibid.

32. Ibid.

2 THE GOP COUNTERREVOLUTION AGAINST THE NEW AMERICA

1. Ramesh Ponnuru, "The Right's Civil Wrongs," *National Review*, June 21, 2010, https://www.nationalreview.com/2010/06/rights-civil-wrongs-ramesh-ponnuru/, accessed September 14,

2018; Matthew Yglesias, "Reagan's Race Record," *The Atlantic*, November 9, 2007, https://www
.theatlantic.com/politics/archive/2007/11/reagans-race-record/46875/, accessed September 14, 2018.

2. Yglesias, "Reagan's Race Record," *The Atlantic*.

3. USCB American Presidency Project, "Richard Nixon's Address Accepting the Presidential Nomination at the Republican National Convention in Miami Beach, Florida," August 8, 1968, http://www.presidency.ucsb.edu/ws/?pid=25968, accessed September 14, 2018; "Address to the Nation on the War in Vietnam," November 3, 1969, http://www.presidency.ucsb.edu/ws/?pid =2303, accessed September 14, 2018.

4. Associated Press, "Gravely Ill, Atwater Offers Apology," *The New York Times*, January 13, 1991, https://www.nytimes.com/1991/01/13/us/gravely-ill-atwater-offers-apology.html, accessed September 14, 2018.

5. Palin's Speech at the Republican National Convention, September 4, 2008, https://www .nytimes.com/elections/2008/president/conventions/videos/transcripts/20080903_PALIN _SPEECH.html; Alex Spillius, "Sarah Palin accuses Barack and Michelle Obama of being unpatriotic," November 19, 2010, https://www.telegraph.co.uk/news/worldnews/sarah-palin /8147673/Sarah-Palin-accuses-Barack-and-Michelle-Obama-of-being-unpatriotic.html, accessed March 26, 2019.

6. "were fine people, on both sides", President Trump's remarks at Trump Tower on Charlottesville, transcript of the question-and-answer session provided by the Federal News Service, August 15, 2017.

7. See Ari Berman, "How the 2000 Election in Florida Led to a New Wave of Voter Disenfranchisement," *The Nation*, July 28, 2015, https://www.thenation.com/article/how-the-2000 -election-in-florida-led-to-a-new-wave-of-voter-disenfranchisement/, accessed September 14, 2018.

8. Ibid.

9. Robert D. Loevy, David C. Kozak, and Kenneth N. Ciboski, eds., *The American Presidency* (Chicago: Nelson Hall, 1985), pp. 411–19.

10. Bill Moyers, *Moyers on America: A Journalist and His Times* (New York: The New Press, 2004), p. 167.

11. Jonathan Chait, "The Color of His Presidency," *New York Magazine,* April 6, 2014; Avidit Acharya, Matthrew Blackwell, and Maya Sen, "The Political Legacy of American Slavery," The Journal of Politics 78, no. 3 (July 2016): pp. 621–41, February 13, 2014.

12. Christopher H. Achen and Larry M. Bartels, *Democracy for Realists: Why Elections Do Not Produce Responsive Government* (Princeton, NJ: Princeton University Press, 2016), pp. 246–50.

13. Ibid., pp. 253–57.

14. *Griswold v. Connecticut*, 381 U.S. 479 (1965).

15. *Roe v. Wade*, 410 U.S. 113 (1973).

16. UC Santa Barbara, The American Presidency Project, "1980 Democratic Platform," http:// www.presidency.ucsb.edu/ws/index.php?pid=29607, accessed August 2, 2018.

17. UC Santa Barbara, The American Presidency Project, "1980 Republican Platform," http:// www.presidency.ucsb.edu/ws/?pid=25844, accessed September 12, 2018.

18. Ann Devroy, "Clinton Cancels Abortion Restrictions of Reagan-Bush Era," *The Washington Post*, January 23, 1993, https://www.washingtonpost.com/archive/politics/1993/01 /23/clinton-cancels-abortion-restrictions-of-reagan-bush-era/0e145a5a-0b37-4908-8c4d -44643f62b0a0/?utm_term=.3cd8d263d4b7, accessed September 14, 2018.

19. Ibid.

20. Remarks by President William J. Clinton on signing memorandums on medical research and reproductive health and an exchange with reporters given in the Roosevelt Room in the White House, January 22, 1993.

21. James C. Dobson, Focus on Family newsletter, February 2001; James Davison Hunter, *Culture Wars: The Struggle to Define America* (New York: Basic Books, 1991), pp. 112–3, 130.

22. Eric D. Gould and Esteban F. Klor, "Party Hacks and True Believers: The Effect of Party Affiliation on Political Preferences," Hebrew University of Jerusalem, 2017, https://scholars.huji.ac.il/sites/default/files/eklor/files/abortion_october_25_2015.pdf, accessed September 14, 2018.

23. William V. D'Antonio, Steven A. Tuch, and Josiah R. Baker, *Religion, Politics, and Polarization: How Religiopolitical Conflict Is Changing Congress and American Democracy*, Mitchellville, Maryland: Rowman & Littlefield Publishing Group, June 20, 2013, pp. 35, 40, 49–50.

24. Alan Cooperman, "Openly Religious, to a Point," *The Washington Post*, September 16, 2004; Tim Griffin, "What Went Wrong in 2012? The Case of the 4 Million Missing Voters," RedState, November 14, 2012; Alan Cooperman and Thomas B. Edsall, "Evangelicals Say They Led Charge for the GOP," *The Washington Post*, November 8, 2004; Bob Allen, "Miers Withdraws as Supreme Court Nominee," *Ethics Daily*, October 27, 2005.

25. Brian Faler, "Election Turnout in 2004 Was Highest Since 1968," *The Washington Post*, January 15, 2005; Stanley B. Greenberg, *The Two Americas: Our Current Political Deadlock and How to Break It* (New York: Thomas Dunne Books, 2005), pp. 321–25; Griffin, "What Went Wrong in 2012?" RedState.

26. Rosa DeLauro, *The Least Among Us: Waging the Battle for the Vulnerable* (New York: The New Press, 2017), Kindle location 1977.

27. Ibid.

28. Juliet Lapidos, "Mike Huckabee's War for Women," *The New York Times*, January 24, 2014.

29. *Burwell, et al. v. Hobby Lobby Stores, Inc.*, 573 U.S. ___ (2014).

30. National survey of 1,301 adults by NORC at the University of Chicago, March 20–September 5, 2012, cited by Tom Smith and Jaesok Son, "Trends in Public Attitudes About Sexual Morality," NORC General Social Survey 2012 final report, April 2013, p. 10; national survey of 1,001 adults by Pew Research Center, March 25–April 14, 2011, cited by Jacob Poushter in "What's Morally Acceptable? It Depends on Where in the World You Live," Pew Research Center, April 15, 2014; Robert Putnam and David Campbell, *American Grace* (New York: Simon & Schuster, 2012), Kindle location 1876.

31. Annamarya Scaccia, "What Trump's Abstinence-Only Education Budget Means for Young People," *Teen Vogue*, February 21, 2018, https://www.teenvogue.com/story/trumps-abstinence-only-education-budget-means-for-young-people, accessed September 14, 2018.

32. Joshua Linder, "The Amnesty Effect: Evidence from the 1986 Immigration Reform and Control Act," Public Purpose (Spring 2011): pp. 13–31.

33. Remarks by President Ronald Reagan at Fudan University in Shanghai, China, April 30, 1984.

34. William V. Roebuck, Jr., "The Move to Employment-Based Immigration in the Immigration Act of 1990: Towards a New Definition of Immigrant," *North Carolina Journal of International Law and Commercial Regulation*, vol. 16, & no. 3, 523 (1991), p. 524.

35. Calculations done using historical data on illegal immigration, Pew Hispanic Center, "Estimated Unauthorized Immigrant Population in the U.S. Lower in 2015 Than in 2009," May 1, 2017, http://www.pewhispanic.org/2018/09/14/facts-on-u-s-immigrants/ph_stat-portraits_foreign-born-2015_key-charts_unauthorized-pop/, accessed September 14, 2018, and Pew Hispanic Center, "Characteristic of US-Born Foreign Population," September 14, 2018, http://www.pewhispanic.org/2018/09/14/facts-on-u-s-immigrants-trend-data/, accessed September 14, 2018.

36. Ibid.

37. Ibid.

38. Ibid.

39. Steve Kornacki, *The Red and the Blue: The 1990s and the Birth of Political Tribalism*, Harper Collins, October 2, 2018, p. 157.

40. Timothy Stanley, *The Crusader: The Life and Tumultuous Times of Pat Buchanan*, Macmillan, February 14, 2012, p. 2.

41. Steve Kornacki, *The Red and the Blue*, p. 154.

42. Ibid, p.152.

43. Ibid, p.153.

44. Timothy Stanley, *The Crusader*, p. 21.

45. Southern Poverty Law Center, "In 2018, We Tracked 1,020 Hate Groups Across the U.S." February 21, 2019, accessed February 21, 2019.

46. Robert Pear, "Clinton Objects to Key Part of Welfare Bill," *The New York Times*, March 27, 1995, https://www.nytimes.com/1995/03/26/us/clinton-objects-to-key-elements-of-welfare-bill.html, accessed September 18, 2018.

47. John F. Harris and John E. Yang, "Clinton to Sign Bill Overhauling Welfare," *The Washington Post*, August 1, 1996, https://www.washingtonpost.com/wp-srv/politics/special/welfare/stories/wf080196.htm.

48. Gebe Martinez, "Learning from Proposition 187," Center for American Progress, May 5, 2010.

49. "Growth and Opportunity Project," Republican National Committee, 2013, p. 8.

50. Seung Min Kim, "Cantor Loss Kills Immigration Reform," *Politico*, June 10, 2014, https://www.politico.com/story/2014/06/2014-virginia-primary-eric-cantor-loss-immigration-reform-107697, accessed September 14, 2018.

51. Survey of 1,005 adults by United Technologies for the National Journal/Congressional Connection, June 20–23, 2013.

52. Steve Kornacki, *The Red and the Blue*, p. 294.

53. Ron Elving, "The Florida Recount Of 2000: A Nightmare That Goes On Haunting," NPR, November 12, 2018, https://www.npr.org/2018/11/12/666812854/the-florida-recount-of-2000-a-nightmare-that-goes-on-haunting, accessed April 5, 2019; Wade Payson-Denney, "So, who really won? What the Bush v. Gore studies showed," CNN, October 31, 2015, https://www.cnn.com/2015/10/31/politics/bush-gore-2000-election-results-studies/index.html, accessed April 5, 2019; Jon Schwarz, "Democrats Should Remember Al Gore Won Florida in 2000—But Lost the Presidency with a Pre-Emptive Surrender," *The Intercept*, November 10, 2018, https://theintercept.com/2018/11/10/democrats-should-remember-al-gore-won-florida-in-2000-but-lost-the-presidency-with-a-preemptive-surrender/, accessed April 5, 2019.

54. Pew Hispanic Center, "Foreign Born Population in the United States, 1850–2016," September 14, 2018, http://www.pewhispanic.org/2018/09/14/facts-on-u-s-immigrants/#fb-key-charts-population.

55. Larry M. Bartels, *Unequal Democracy: The Political Economy of the New Gilded Age-Second Edition* (Princeton, NJ: Russell Sage Foundation with Princeton University Press, 2016), p. 292.

56. Ibid., pp. 298–99.

57. U.S. Bureau of the Census, Real Median Household Income in the United States [MEHOINUSA672N], retrieved from FRED, Federal Reserve Bank of St. Louis; https://fred.stlouisfed.org/series/MEHOINUSA672N, September 14, 2018.

58. Bartels, *Unequal Democracy*, p. 300.

59. Ibid.

60. Ibid.

61. Ibid.; Emmanuel Saez, "Striking It Richer: The Evolution of Top Incomes in the United States (Updated with 2014 Preliminary Estimates)," University of California at Berkeley, June 25, 2015, https://eml.berkeley.edu/~saez/saez-UStopincomes-2014.pdf, accessed September 14, 2018.

62. Alan Blinder and Mark Zandi, "How the Great Recession Was Brought to an End," Economy.com, July 27, 2010, https://www.economy.com/mark-zandi/documents/End-of-Great-Recession.pdf, accessed September 14, 2018.

63. Ibid., pp. 296–98.

64. Frank James, National Public Radio, October 26, 2012, https://www.npr.org/sections/itsallpolitics/2012/10/26/163730734/obama-may-not-need-to-repeat-2008-support-from-white-voters-to-win, accessed September 12, 2018.

65. John Sides, "Race, Religion and Immigration in 2016: How the Debate over American Identity Shaped the Election and What It Means for a Trump Presidency," Democracy Fund Study Group, June 2017.

66. Abena Agyeman-Fisher, "Limbaugh on Obama Win: 'I Went to Bed Last Night Thinking We've Lost the Country'" NewsOne, November 7, 2012, https://newsone.com/2076846/rush-limbaugh-obama-election-2012/, accessed September 18, 2018; Ashley Elizabeth Jardina, "Demise of Dominance: Group Threat and the New Relevance of White Identity for American Politics," (PhD diss., University of Michigan, 2014), p. 138.

67. Allison Dale-Riddle and Don Kinder, *The End of Race? Obama, 2008, and Racial Politics in America"* (Yale University Press, 2012), Kindle locations 1713–1772.

68. Jardina, "Demise," pp. 89–110.

69. Ibid.

70. PRRI polls in 2012–2013 cited in Racial Attitudes graphic posted May 8, 2014, on http://publicreligion.org/research/graphic-of-the-week/racial-attitudes/.

71. Ibid.

72. Ibid.

73. Kinder, *The End of Race?*, Kindle locations 1139–1140.

74. Luke Johnson and Ryan Grim, "Is the Tea Party Racist? Ask Some Actual, Out-of-the-Closet Racists," Huffington Post, October, 24, 2013, https://www.huffingtonpost.com/2013/10/24/tea-party-racist_n_4158262.html, accessed September 14, 2018.

75. Kinder, *The End of Race?*, Kindle location 2813.

76. Ibid., Kindle location 2807, see also figure 6.2.

77. Ian Gordon and Tasneem Raja, "164 Anti-immigration Laws Passed Since 2010? A MoJo Analysis," *Mother Jones*, March/April 2012.

78. John Sides and Lynn Vavreck, *The Gamble: Choice and Chance in the 2012 Presidential Election* (Princeton, NJ: Princeton University Press, 2013), p. 208.

79. Gallup, "Immigration" time series chart, https://news.gallup.com/poll/1660/immigration.aspx, accessed September 14, 2018; Pew Research Center, "Shifting Public Views on Legal Immigration into the U.S.," June 2018, http://assets.pewresearch.org/wp-content/uploads/sites/5/2018/06/02164131/06-28-2018-Immigration-release.pdf, accessed September 18, 2018.

80. *Washington Post*–ABC News Poll, August 26–29, 2018, https://www.washingtonpost.com/politics/polling/trump-immigration-dealing-illegal/2018/09/04/540e8446-b029-11e8-8b53-50116768e499_page.html, accessed September 12, 2018.

81. This is based on findings from the first phase of research for Democracy Corps' Republican Party Project. Democracy Corps and Greenberg Quinlan Rosner conducted six focus groups among Republican partisans—divided into Evangelicals, Tea Party adherents, and moderates—between July 30 and August 1, 2013. All participants indicated that they voted only or mostly for Republican candidates and were screened on a battery of ideological and political indicators. The groups were conducted in Raleigh, North Carolina (moderate and Tea Party), Roanoke, Virginia (Tea Party and Evangelical), and Colorado Springs, Colorado (moderate and Evangelical).

82. National web survey of 800 likely Republican voters was conducted by Democracy Corps & Greenberg Quinlan Rosner on February 11–16, 2016, using a voter file sample. Likely voters were determined based on whether they voted in 2012 or had registered since and stated intention of voting in 2016. Data is among those who identify as Republicans or independents who lean Republican and vote in Republican primaries or caucuses. Margin of error for the full sample is +/-3.47 percentage points at 95 percent confidence. The five categories of Republicans are mutually exclusive categories determined by respondents' responses on ideology, religion, frequency of service attendance, strength of Tea Party support, and favorability toward the Tea Party. To ensure that the web survey accurately reflects the national Republican Party, the typologies were weighted to the average for each type from Democracy Corps's last three national surveys. http://www.democracycorps.com/attachments/article/1025/Dcorps_RPP _Web%20Survey_2.29.2016_UPDATED%20FINAL.pdf, accessed Septmeber 18, 2018.

83. These quotes and the preceding quotes are based on focus groups conducted by Democracy Corps as part of the Republican Party Project. Democracy Corps and Greenberg Quinlan Rosner conducted six focus groups among Republican partisans—divided into Evangelicals, Tea Party adherents, and moderates—between July 30 and August 1, 2013. All participants indicated that they voted only or mostly for Republican candidates and were screened on a battery of ideological and political indicators. The groups were conducted in Raleigh, North Carolina (moderate and Tea Party), Roanoke, Virigina (Tea Party and Evangelical), and Colorado Springs, Colorado (moderate and Evangelical).

3   THE GOP BATTLE AGAINST MULTICULTURALISM

1. "Here's Donald Trump's Presidential Announcement Speech," *Time,* June 16, 2015, http://time.com/3923128/donald-trump-announcement-speech/.

2. Ibid.

3. Ibid.

4. Ibid.

5. Ibid.

6. Ibid.

7. Ibid.

8. Ibid.

9. This national web survey of 800 likely Republican voters was conducted by Democracy Corps & Greenberg Quinlan Rosner on February 11–16, 2016, using a voter file sample. Likely voters were determined based on whether they voted in 2012 or had registered since and stated intention of voting in 2016. Data is among those who identify as Republicans or independents who lean Republican and vote in Republican primaries or caucuses. Margin of error for the full sample is +/-3.47 percentage points at 95 percent confidence. The five categories of Republicans are mutually exclusive categories determined by respondents' responses on ideology, religion, frequency of service attendance, strength of Tea Party support, and favorability toward the Tea Party. To ensure that the web survey accurately reflects the national Republican Party, the typologies were weighted to the average for each type from Democracy Corps's last three national surveys.

10. Ibid.

11. Ibid.

12. Ibid.

13. Ibid.

14. Moderates (31 percent) consist of: (a) liberals/moderates who are *neither* observant Catholics, *nor* Tea Party supporters, *nor* very favorable toward the Tea Party, (b) conservatives who are *neither* Evangelical Republicans *nor* observant Catholics and do *not* attend religious services more than once a week who are *neither* Tea Party supporters *nor* strongly favorable toward the Tea Party. Evangelicals (30 percent) consist of Evangelical Christians who are not moderates (see above). Tea Party (17 percent) consist of strong Tea Party supporters or those very favor-

able toward the Tea Party who are: (a) not moderates or Evangelicals (see above); (b) liberals/moderates who are not Evangelicals and are very favorable toward the Tea Party or somewhat strong Tea Party supporters. Observant Catholics (14 percent) consist of observant Catholics or Catholics who attend services more than once a week who are not moderate, Evangelical, or Tea Party (see above). Establishment (8 percent) consists of those who are not moderate, Evangelical, Tea Party, or observant Catholic (see above).

15. Democracy Corps survey of 800 likely Republican voters, February 2016.

16. Ibid.

17. Ibid.

18. Drew Magary, "What the Duck?," *GQ*, January 2014, https://www.gq.com/story/duck-dynasty-phil-robertson, accessed September 16, 2018.

19. TMZ, "Phil Robertson Publicly Bashed Gays for Years, A&E Knew All About It," December 19, 2013, http://www.tmz.com/2013/12/19/phil-robertson-2010-sermon-homosexuality-gays-homophobia-a-and-e/, accessed September 16, 2018.

20. Politico, "Full Text: Donald Trump 2016 RNC Draft Speech Transcript," July 21, 2016, https://www.politico.com/story/2016/07/full-transcript-donald-trump-nomination-acceptance-speech-at-rnc-225974.

21. Ibid.

22. Ibid.

23. Ibid.

24. Ibid.

25. Ibid.

26. Ibid.

27. Ibid.

28. Ibid.

29. Brett LoGiurato, "The Most Vicious Ad of the 2012 Campaign Blames Mitt Romney for the Death of a Steel Worker's Wife," *Business Insider*, August 7, 2012, https://www.businessinsider.com/priorities-usa-romney-ad-cancer-death-gst-steel-bain-capital-2012-8, accessed September 18, 2018.

30. Hillary Rodham Clinton, *What Happened* (New York: Simon & Schuster, 2017), Kindle location 5747–5756.

31. Ibid.

32. Jim Abrams, "Obama Signs 3 Trade Deals, Biggest Since NAFTA," NBC News, October 21, 2011, http://www.nbcnews.com/id/44989775/ns/politics-white_house/t/obama-signs-trade-deals-biggest-nafta/, accessed September 16, 2018.

33. Mutz, "Status Threat," figure 1, p. 5.

34. Rosa DeLauro, *The Least Among Us: Waging the Battle for the Vulnerable* (New York: The New Press, 2017), Kindle location 3013.

35. Ibid.

36. Donald Trump speech in Grand Rapids, Michigan, November 8, 2016, https://www.c-span.org/video/?418209-1/donald-trump-makes-final-campaign-stop-grand-rapids-michigan&start=1343; Donald Trump speech in Raleigh, North Carolina, November 7, 2016, https://www.c-span.org/video/?418210-1/donald-trump-campaigns-raleigh-north-carolina, accessed September 17, 2018.

37. Democracy Corps national survey on behalf of Public Citizen that took place October 21–24, 2016. Respondents who voted in the 2012 election or had registered since were selected from the national voter file. Likely voters were determined based on stated intention of voting the next month. Margin of error for the full sample is +/-3.27 percentage points at the 95 percent confidence level. Of the 900 respondents, 65 percent were interviewed via cell phone to accurately sample the American electorate.

38. Ibid.

39. Ibid., with data added on this question from a Democracy Corps survey done on behalf of Public Citizen, October 2017.

40. Donald Trump speech in Franklin, Tennessee, October 3, 2015, https://www.youtube.com /watch?time_continue=1&v=B7Qy3k_WMbM.

41. Jenna Johnson, "Trump Calls for 'Complete and Total Shutdown of Muslims Entering the United States,'" *The Washington Post*, December 7, 2015, https://www.washingtonpost.com /news/post-politics/wp/2015/12/07/donald-trump-calls-for-total-and-complete-shutdown-of-muslims-entering-the-united-states/?utm_term=.caf83d445190, accessed September 17, 2018.

42. John Sides, "Race, Religion and Immigration: How the Debate over American Identity Shaped the Election and What It Means for a Trump Presidency," June 2017, https://www.voter-studygroup.org/publications/2016-elections/race-religion-immigration-2016, pp. 7–11.

43. Democracy Corps National Web Survey of 800 2016 Trump Voters and GOP Base Voters. This web survey took place December 2–5, 2016, among eight hundred voters from 2016 who voted for Trump or non-Trump voters who identify as Republicans or independents who lean Republican and vote in Republican primaries or caucuses. Margin of error for the full sample is +/-3.47 percentage points at 95 percent confidence. Margin of error will be higher among subgroups.

44. Ibid.

45. Mutz, "Status Threat," pp. 5–8.

46. Ibid.

47. Ibid., figure 1, p. 5.

48. U.S. Census Bureau, "California 2000: Census 200 Profile," August 2002, https://www .census.gov/prod/2002pubs/c2kprof00-ca.pdf, accessed January 18, 2019.

49. Joel Kotkin, "The Golden State Won't Glitter for Republicans," *City Journal*, November 2, 2018, https://www.city-journal.org/california-republican-party, accessed January 18, 2019.

50. Jane Coaston, "How California Conservatives Became the Intellectual Engine of Trumpism," Vox.com, November 13, 2018, https://www.vox.com/2018/11/19/17841946 /trump-conservatism-california-gop-shapiro-midterms-2018, accessed January 17, 2019.

51. Yochai Benkler, Robert Faris, and Hal Roberts, *Network Propaganda: Manipulation, Disinformation, and Radicalization in American Politics* (New York: Oxford University Press, 2018).

52. Ibid., Kindle locations 6369–6370.

53. Ibid.

54. Ibid.

55. Ibid.

56. Ibid.

57. Joshua Green, *Devil's Bargain: Steve Bannon, Donald Trump, and the Nationalist Uprising* (New York: Penguin Press, 2017); Bob Woodward, *Fear: Trump in the White House* (New York: Simon & Schuster, 2018).

58. Jeff Zeleny and Kevin Liptak, "Trump Warns Evangelicals of 'Violence' If GOP Loses in the Midterms," CNN, August 28, 2018, https://www.cnn.com/2018/08/28/politics/trump-evangelicals -midterms/index.html, accessed September 18, 2018.

59. John T. Jost, "The End of the End of Ideology," *American Psychologist* 61, no. 7 (October 2006): 655, 661–62.

60. Peter Rentfrow, John Jost, Samuel Gosling, and Jeffrey Potter, "Statewide Differences in Personality Predict Voting Patterns in 1996–2004 U.S. Presidential Elections" in John Jost, Aaron Kay, and Hulda Thorisdottir, eds., *Social and Psychological Bases of Ideology and System Justification* (New York: Oxford University Press, 2009), Kindle locations 4570–77.

61. Rentfrow et al., "Statewide Differences in Personality," Kindle location 4305.

62. Pew Research Center, "The Partisan Divide on Political Values Grows Even Wider," October 5, 2017, http://www.people-press.org/2017/10/05/1-partisan-divides-over-political-values -widen/, accessed September 12, 2018.

63. Amber Phillips, "Is Split-Ticket Voting Officially Dead?" *The Washington Post*, November 17, 2016, https://www.washingtonpost.com/news/the-fix/wp/2016/11/17/is-split-ticket-voting-officially-dead/?utm_term=.3a609616b88c, accessed September 12, 2018.

64. Pew Research Center, "The Partisan Divide on Political Values Grows Even Wider," accessed September 17, 2018.

65. Christopher H. Achen and Larry M. Bartels, *Democracy for Realists: Why Elections Do Not Produce Responsive Government* (Princeton, NJ: Princeton University Press, 2016), p. 277.

66. Ibid., p. 268.

67. Ibid., p. 267.

4   THE TEA PARTY–TRUMP DECADE

1. Nicol Rae, "The Return of Conservative Populism; The Rise of the Tea Party and Its Impact on American Politics" (2011), APSA Annual Meeting Paper; Jamie Carson and Stephen Pettigrew, "Strategic Politicians, Partisan Roll Calls, and the Tea Party: Evaluating the 2010 Midterm Elections," *Electoral Studies* 32 (1), p. 35; Jane Mayer, *Dark Money: The Hidden History of the Billionaires Behind the Rise of the Radical Right* (New York: Doubleday, 2016), Kindle location 5073.

2. Jonathan Chait, "Anarchists of the House," *New York Magazine*, July 21, 2013, http:// nymag.com/news/features/republican-congress-2013-7/, accessed October 2, 2018.

3. Thomas Mann and Norm Ornstein, *It's Even Worse Than It Looks: How the American Constitutional System Collided with the New Politics of Extremism* (New York: Perseus, 2012), Kindle location 120.

4. Vanessa Williamson and Theda Skocpol, *The Tea Party and the Remaking of Republican Conservatism* (New York: Oxford University Press, 2012), pp. 159–61; Devin Burghart and Leonard Zeskind, "Tea Party Nationalism: A Critical Examination of the Tea Party Movement and the Size, Scope, and Focus of Its National Factions," *Institute for Research and Education of Human Rights* (2010), p. 8.

5. John C. Berg, "President Obama, the Tea Party Movement, and the Crisis of the American Political System," (April 29, 2011). Available at SSRN: https://ssrn.com/abstract=1879523 or http://dx.doi.org/10.2139/ssrn.1879523, pp. 3–4.

6. Burghart and Zeskind, "Tea Party Nationalism," p. 16.

7. Williamson and Skocpol, *The Tea Party and the Remaking*, p. 60.

8. Williamson and Skocpol, *The Tea Party and the Remaking*, pp. 37–38; Burghart and Zeskind, "Tea Party Nationalism," p. 17; Mayer, *Dark Money*, Kindle location 3420.

9. Andrew J. Perrin, Stephen J. Tepper, Neal Caren, and Sally Morris, "Political and Cultural Dimensions of Tea Party Support, 2009–2012," *The Sociological Quarterly*, August 26, 2014; Andreas Madestam, Daniel Shoag, Stan Veuger, et al., "Do Political Protests Matter? Evidence from the Tea Party Movement" (October 2013). Quarterly Journal of Economics 128(4):1633–1685, DOI: 10.1093/qje/qjt021; Michael Bailey, Jonathan Mummolo, and Hans Noel, "Tea Party Influence: A Story of Activists and Elites," *American Politics Research* (January 1, 2012). Available at SSRN: https://ssrn.com/abstract=2739254 or http://dx.doi.org/10 .2139/ssrn.2739254, June 25, 2012; Burghart and Zeskind, "Tea Party Nationalism," p. 9.

10. Burghart and Zeskind, "Tea Party Nationalism," pp. 8, 51.

11. Williamson and Skocpol, *The Tea Party and the Remaking*, p. 29.

12. Burghart and Zeskind, "Tea Party Nationalism," p. 17; Mayer, *Dark Money*, Kindle location 3471.

13. Williamson and Skocpol, *The Tea Party and the Remaking*, pp. 37–38.

14. Mayer, *Dark Money*, Kindle location 3733.

15. Willamson and Skocpol, *The Tea Party and the Remaking*, p. 78.

16. Burghart and Zeskind, "Tea Party Nationalism," p. 51.

17. Ibid., pp. 6–8, 44.

18. See Mayer, *Dark Money*, Kindle locations 197–245.

19. Ibid., Kindle location 90.

20. Ibid., Kindle locations 409–448.

21. Ben Smith, "Health Reform Foes Plan Obama's 'Waterloo,'" *Politico*, July 17, 2009, https://www.politico.com/blogs/ben-smith/2009/07/health-reform-foes-plan-obamas-waterloo-019961, accessed October 18, 2018.

22. Rae, *The Return of Conservative Populism*, p. 10.

23. Ibid., pp. 17–18.

24. Justice Anthony Kennedy opinion in re: *Citizens United v. Federal Election Commission*, 558 U.S. 310 (2010).

25. Mayer, *Dark Money*, Kindle locations 5104, 4719.

26. Williamson and Skocpol, *The Tea Party and the Remaking*, pp. 169–71, 155–60.

27. Carson and Pettigrew, "Strategic Politicians," p. 34.

28. Emily Ekins, "The Character and Economic Morality of the Tea Party," University of California Los Angeles, January 2011, SSRN-id1902394.pdf, accessed October 18, 2018.

29. Alan Abramowitz, "Partisan Polarization and the Rise of the Tea Party Movement (2011)," APSA 2011 Annual Meeting Paper. Available at SSRN: https://ssrn.com/abstract=1903153, p. 22; Ekins, "The Character."

30. Kevin Arceneaux and Stephen P. Nicholson, "Who Wants to Have a Tea Party? The Who, What, and Why of the Tea Party Movement," *Political Science*, November 2012, http://faculty2.ucmerced.edu/snicholson/Tea_Party.pdf, pp. 703–705; Ronald Rapoport, Meredith Dost, Ani-Rae Lovell, and Walter J. Stone, "Republican Factionalism and Tea Party Activists," Midwest Political Science Association Conference, April 11–14, 2013, http://citeseerx.ist.psu.edu/viewdoc/download?doi=10.1.1.673.3378&rep=rep1&type=pdf, accessed October 19, 2018.

31. Bailey, Mummolo, and Noel, "Tea Party Influence," pp. 23, 39.

32. Alan S. Blinder, *After the Music Stopped: the Financial Crisis, the Response, and the Work Ahead* (New York: Penguin Press, 2013), p.11.

33. Ibid., p. 321.

34. Ibid., pp. 171–74; Mark Blyth, *Austerity: The History of a Dangerous Idea* (New York: Oxford University Press, 2013), pp. 57–60.

35. Blinder, *After the Music Stopped*, pp. 92–97, Blyth, *Austerity*, p. 8.

36. Paul Krugman, *End This Depression Now!* (New York: W. W. Norton and Co., 2017), pp. 16–17.

37. Blinder, *After the Music Stopped*, p. 391, Krugman, *End*, p. 120.

38. Blinder, *After the Music Stopped*, p. 391.

39. Ibid, p. 8.

40. Stan Greenberg, James Carville, et al., "Despite Macro Economic Growth, 'Real Economy' Declines for Real People," Democracy Corps, March 30, 2010, http://www.democracycorps.com/wp-content/files/EconomyTrackingFINAL.pdf, accessed October 9, 2018.

41. Krugman, *End*, p. 39; Paul Krugman, "How Did Economists Get It So Wrong?," *The New York Times Magazine*, September 2, 2009, https://www.nytimes.com/2009/09/06/magazine/06Economic-t.html, accessed October 9, 2018.

42. Krugman, *End*, pp. 130–31.

43. Ibid., pp. 106, 195; Blyth, *Austerity*, pp. 4, 10.

44. Blyth, *Austerity*, pp. ix–4.
45. Krugman, *End*, p. 189.
46. Ibid., p. 188.
47. Krugman, *End*, p. 2.
48. Blinder, *After the Music Stopped*, pp. 10–11.
49. Krugman, *End*, p. 125.
50. Blinder, *After the Music Stopped*, pp. 359–360 and Krugman, *End*, pp. 192–3.
51. Robert Draper, *When the Tea Party Came to Town: Inside the U.S. House of Representatives' Most Combative, Dysfunctional, and Infuriating Term in Modern History* (New York: Simon & Schuster, 2012), p. 126.
52. Ibid., p. 127.
53. Ibid., pp. 272–76.
54. Ibid., p. 276.
55. Ibid., pp. 252–57.
56. Ibid., pp. 247–51.
57. Ibid., pp. 251–54.
58. Federal Reserve Bank of St. Louis and U.S. Office of Management and Budget, "Federal Net Outlays as Percent of Gross Domestic Product" [FYONGDA188S], retrieved from FRED, Federal Reserve Bank of St. Louis, https://fred.stlouisfed.org/series/FYONGDA188S, October 9, 2018.
59. "Slide Show: The State Budget Crisis and the Economy," Center for Budget and Policy Priorities, http://www.cbpp.org/slideshows/?fa=stateFiscalCrisis, December 19, 2011, slide 5; David Callahan, "89,000 Government Workers Have Been Laid Off Since September," Demos, January 4, 2013; Heidi Shierholz, "Six Years from Its Beginning, the Great Recession's Shadow Looms over the Labor Market," Economic Policy Institute, January 9, 2014; Gordon Lafer, "The Legislative Attack on American Wages and Labor Standards, 2011–2012," Economic Policy Institute, October 31, 2013.
60. Carolyn Barta, "Eighty-second Legislature Cuts School Funds, State Jobs," *Texas Almanac,* Texas State Historical Association; calculated based on data for 2008–2014 from the Center on Budget and Policy Priorities, accessed February 13, 2014, http://www.offthechartsblog.org/mapping-higher-ed-funding-cuts-and-tuition-hikes/.
61. Lafer, "The Legislative Attack on American Wages and Labor Standards, 2011–2012."
62. Ibid.
63. Alex Hertel-Fernandez, *State Capture: How Conservative Activists, Big Businesses and Wealthy Donors Reshaped the American States—and the Nation* (New York: Oxford University Press, 2019).
64. Nancy MacLean, *Democracy in Chains: The Deep History of the Radical Right's Stealth Plan for America* (New York: Penguin, 2017), p. xix.
65. Doris Kearns Goodwin, *The Bully Pulpit: Theodore Roosevelt, William Howard Taft, and the Golden Age of Journalism* (New York: Simon & Schuster, 2013), p. 696; Michael Wolraich, *Unreasonable Men: Theodore Roosevelt and the Republican Rebels Who Created Progressive Politics* (New York: Palgrave MacMillan, 2014), pp. 46–48.
66. Wisconsin Budget Project, "Missing Out: Recent Tax Cuts Slanted in Favor of Those with Highest Incomes," June 27, 2017, http://www.wisconsinbudgetproject.org/missing-out-recent-tax-cuts-slanted-in-favor-of-those-with-highest-incomes, accessed October 18, 2018.
67. Jason Stein, Don Walker, and Patrick Marley, "Walker Signs Budget Bill, Legal Challenges Mount," *Wisconsin Sentinel-Journal*, March 3, 2011, http://archive.jsonline.com/news/statepolitics/117798133.html/, accessed October 19, 2018.
68. Molly Beck, "Conservative Study: Teachers Make $2k Less in Base Pay Than Before Act 10," *Wisconsin State Journal,* June 22, 2016, https://madison.com/wsj/news/local/govt-

and-politics/conservative-study-teachers-make-k-less-in-base-pay-than/article_4ed2349f-344d-5a61-b3f7-92270e1f5051.html, accessed October 18, 2018; David Madland and Alex Rowell, "Attacks on Public-Sector Unions Harm States: How Act 10 Has Affected Education in Wisconsin," Center for American Progress, November 17, 2015, https://www.americanprogressaction.org/issues/economy/reports/2017/11/15/169146/attacks-public-sector-unions-harm-states-act-10-affected-education-wisconsin/, accessed October 18, 2018.

69. Douglas Belkin, "Colleges, Faced with Funding Cuts, Target Tenure Trims," *The Wall Street Journal*, February 14, 2017.

70. Kimberly Hefling, "Walker Erodes College Professor Tenure," *Politico*, July 12, 2015, https://www.politico.com/story/2015/07/scott-walker-college-professor-tenure-120009, accessed October 19, 2018.

71. Mary Spicuzza, "5 Ways the Lame Duck Laws Will Change Life for Wisconsinites," *Milwaukee Journal-Sentinel*, December 14, 2018, https://www.jsonline.com/story/news/politics/2018/12/03/wisconsin-lame-duck-session-how-changes-could-affect-wisconsinites/2191148002/, accessed December 20, 2018.

72. Mayer, *Dark Money*, Kindle location 6316.

73. Todd C. Frankel, "What Happened When North Carolina Cut Taxes Like the GOP Plans to for the Country," *The Washington Post*, December 3, 2017, https://www.washingtonpost.com/business/economy/what-happened-when-north-carolina-cut-taxes-like-the-gop-plans-to-for-the-country/2017/12/03/1b8ead74-d859-11e7-a841-2066faf731ef_story.html?utm_term=.b7dc78662c40, accessed October 18, 2018.

74. Michael Leachman, "North Carolina's Deep Tax Cuts Impeding Adequate School Funding," Center for Budget and Policy Priorities, May 10, 2018, https://www.cbpp.org/blog/north-carolinas-deep-tax-cuts-impeding-adequate-school-funding, accessed October 18, 2018; "Cuts to North Carolina's Higher Education System Jeopardize Our Economic Future," Center for Budget and Policy Priorities, https://www.cbpp.org/sites/default/files/atoms/files/sfp_highered_nc.pdf, accessed October 18, 2018; "North Carolina Tax Cap Threatens Funding for Public Services," Center for Budget and Policy Priorities, https://www.cbpp.org/blog/north-carolina-tax-cap-threatens-funding-for-public-services, accessed October 18, 2018; *Charlotte News-Observer* editorial board, "NC Is Spending Millions on Private School Vouchers—But Has No Idea If They Work," June 12, 2018, https://www.newsobserver.com/opinion/editorials/article213016279.html, accessed October 18, 2018.

75. Tara Golshan, "North Carolina Wrote the Playbook Wisconsin and Michigan Are Using to Undermine Democracy," Vox.com, December 5, 2018, https://www.vox.com/policy-and-politics/2018/12/5/18125544/north-carolina-power-grab-wisconsin-michigan-lame-duck, accessed December 27, 2018.

76. John Judis, "Sam Brownback's Conservative Utopia in Kansas Has Become Hell," *The New Republic*, September 29, 2014, https://newrepublic.com/article/119574/sam-brownbacks-conservative-utopia-kansas-has-become-hell, accessed October 19, 2018.

77. Annual State of the State address by Governor Sam Brownback to a joint session of the Kansas State Legislature at the State House Chamber in Topeka, Kansas, January 15, 2014.

78. John Gramlich, "In Kansas, Governor Sam Brownback Drives a Rightward Shift," *Stateline*, Pew Charitable Trusts, January 25, 2012.

79. Institute on Economic and Tax Policy, "Tax Plans Put Kansas on Road Away from Fair & Adequate Tax Reform," March 2012, Senate Plan, https://itep.org/wp-content/uploads/KSWrongRoad.pdf, accessed October 18, 2018; Patrick Caldwell, "What's the Matter with Sam Brownback?" *Mother Jones*, September 25, 2014, https://www.motherjones.com/politics/2014/09/sam-brownback-kansas-paul-davis/, accessed March 29, 2019.

80. Tim Carpenter, "Study: Kansas Cuts K-12 Education Funding by Fourth—Most in Nation," *The Topeka Capital-Journal*, September 12, 2013, https://www.cjonline.com/news

/education/2013-09-12/study-kansas-cuts-k-12-education-funding-fourth-most-nation, accessed October 18, 2018.

81. *Gannon v. Kansas*, Kansas State Supreme Court, No. 109,335, http://www.kscourts.org/Cases-and-Opinions/Opinions/SupCt/2014/20140307/109335.pdf, accessed October 18, 2018; Brad Cooper, "Gov. Sam Brownback Is Cutting Aid to Kansas Schools by $44.5 Million," *The Kansas City Star*, February 5, 2015, https://www.kansascity.com/news/politics-government/article9376751.html, accessed October 18, 2018.

82. Adam Nagourney and Shaila Dewan, "Republican Governors Buck Party Line on Raising Taxes," *The New York Times*, January 24, 2015; Max Ehrenfreund, "Kansas Lawmakers Want the Poor to Pay for Tax Cuts for the Rich," *The Washington Post*, April 21, 2015.

83. Trip Gabriel, "Pennsylvania Governor Faces an Uphill Battle for a Second Term," *The New York Times*, May 10, 2014; "Under Gov. Tom Corbett, 'Pennsylvania Ranks 49th in Job Creation,'" PolitiFact.com, July 15, 2014.

84. John Bebow, "Michigan Gives More Tax Breaks Than It Collects for Schools, Government," The Center for Michigan, January 23, 2018, https://www.bridgemi.com/special-report/michigan-gives-more-tax-breaks-it-collects-schools-government, accessed October 18, 2018; Stephen Henderson and Kristi Tanner, "Michigan Taxes: Businesses Pay Less, You Pay More," *Detroit Free Press,* October 5, 2014, https://www.freep.com/story/opinion/contributors/raw-data/2014/10/04/michigan-taxes-snyder/16683967/, accessed October 18, 2018; Mark Brush, "Has Public Education Funding Gone Up or Down Under Gov. Snyder's Watch?," Michigan Public Radio, October 16, 2014, http://www.michiganradio.org/post/has-public-education-funding-gone-or-down-under-gov-snyders-watch, accessed October 18, 2018.

85. Mark Binelli, "Michigan Gambled on Charter Schools. Its Children Lost," *The New York Times Magazine*, September 5, 2017, https://www.nytimes.com/2017/09/05/magazine/michigan-gambled-on-charter-schools-its-children-lost.html, accessed October 18, 2018; Marcy Wheeler, "How Rick Snyder Doomed Flint from the Start: Tax Cuts for the Ultra-Rich, Poison for the Poor," Salon.com, January 29, 2016, https://www.salon.com/2016/01/29/how_rick_snyder_doomed_flint_from_the_start_tax_cuts_for_the_ultra_rich_poison_for_the_poor/, accessed October 18, 2018; Stephen Henderson, "Betsy DeVos and the Twilight of Public Education," *Detroit Free Press*, December 3, 2016, https://www.freep.com/story/opinion/columnists/stephen-henderson/2016/12/03/betsy-devos-education-donald-trump/94728574/, accessed October 18, 2018.

86. Jarett Skorup, "A Look at Unions in Michigan, Five Years After Right-to-Work," Michigan Capitol Confidential, April 20, 2018, https://www.michigancapitolconfidential.com/a-look-at-unions-in-michigan-five-years-after-right-to-work, accessed October 18, 2018.

87. Kathleen Gray, "Snyder Tackles Most Controversial Lame-Duck Bills Passed by Lawmakers," *Detroit Free Press*, December 29, 2018, https://www.freep.com/story/news/politics/2018/12/29/snyder-signs-vetoes-lame-duck-bills/2436679002/, accessed January 1, 2019; Paul Egan and Kathleen Gray, "The Most Controversial Bills in Michigan's Lame-Duck Session," *Detroit Free Press*, December 4, 2018, https://www.freep.com/story/news/local/michigan/2018/12/04/michigan-legislature-bills-lame-duck-session/2162560002/, accessed January 1, 2019.

88. Next America survey of 1,272 adults by Princeton Survey Research Associates International for National Journal and College Board, October 14–24, 2013.

89. Ibid.

90. Rosa DeLauro, *The Least Among Us: Waging the Battle for the Vulnerable* (New York: The New Press, 2017), Kindle locations 10-217.

91. Zach Auter, "U.S. Uninsured Rate Steady at 12.2% in Fourth Quarter of 2017," Gallup, January 16, 2018, https://news.gallup.com/poll/225383/uninsured-rate-steady-fourth-quarter-2017.aspx, accessed October 19, 2018.

92. Simon Haeder and David Weimer, "You Can't Make Me Do It: State Implementation of Insurance Exchanges Under the Affordable Care Act," Public Administration Review, 73 (2013): S34–S47, doi:10.1111/puar.12065.

93. Ibid.

94. Kaiser Family Foundation, "Which States Have Approved and Pending Section 1115 Waivers?" January 2018, https://www.kff.org/medicaid/issue-brief/which-states-have-approved-and-pending-section-1115-medicaid-waivers/, accessed October 19, 2018.

95. Indiana University, "Medicaid Expansion Produces Significant Health Benefits," *Science Daily,* June 4, 2018, www.sciencedaily.com/releases/2018/06/180604172739.htm, accessed October 18, 2018.

96. Louise Norris, "Utah/Idaho/Nebraska and the ACA's Medicaid Expansion," HealthInsurance.org, November 8, 2018, https://www.healthinsurance.org/utah-medicaid/#ballot, https://www.healthinsurance.org/idaho-medicaid/#ballot, https://www.healthinsurance.org/nebraska-medicaid/#ballot, accessed December 20, 2018.

97. Kaiser Family Foundation, "Summary of the Graham-Cassidy-Heller-Johnson Amendment," September 2017, http://files.kff.org/attachment/Summary-of-Graham-Cassidy-Heller-Johnson-Amendment, accessed October 19, 2018.

98. Congressional Budget Office, "Repealing the Individual Health Insurance Mandate: An Updated Estimate," November 2017, https://www.cbo.gov/system/files?file=115th-congress-2017-2018/reports/53300-individualmandate.pdf, accessed October 17, 2018.

99. *Planned Parenthood v. Casey*, 505 U.S. 833, https://www.oyez.org/cases/1991/91-744.

100. Liam Stack, "Texas Will Require Burial of Aborted Fetuses," *The New York Times*, November 30, 2016, https://www.nytimes.com/2016/11/30/us/texas-burial-aborted-fetuses.html, accessed October 18, 2018; Cecile Richards, "The Tea Party's Attack on Women's Rights," *Politico*, November 19, 2013, https://www.politico.com/magazine/story/2013/11/the-tea-partys-attack-on-womens-rights-100062, accessed October 18, 2018; Planned Parenthood, "Texas Governor Greg Abbott Signs Two Extreme Abortion Restrictions," August 15, 2017, https://www.plannedparenthoodaction.org/pressroom/texas-governor-greg-abbott-signs-two-extreme-abortion-restrictions, accessed October 18, 2018; Manny Fernandez, "Abortion Restrictions Become Law in Texas, But Opponents Will Press the Fight," *The New York Times*, July 9, 2013, https://www.nytimes.com/2013/07/19/us/perry-signs-texas-abortion-restrictions-into-law.html, accessed October 18, 2018.

101. Samantha Allen, "Bobby Jindal's Embarrassing Abortion Obsession," The Daily Beast, September 21, 2015, https://www.thedailybeast.com/bobby-jindals-embarrassing-abortion-obsession, accessed October 18, 2018.

102. NARAL Pro Choice America, "State Laws: Kansas," https://www.prochoiceamerica.org/state-law/kansas/, accessed October 17, 2018.

103. Sean Sullivan, "Scott Walker Signs Bill to Tighten Abortion Restrictions in Wisconsin," *The Washington Post,* July 5, 2013, https://www.washingtonpost.com/news/post-politics/wp/2013/07/05/scott-walker-signs-bill-to-tighten-abortion-restrictions-in-wisconsin/?utm_term=.486240be6912; Paige Winfield Cunningham, "Wisconsin Defunds Planned Parenthood," *Washington Examiner,* February 18, 2016, https://www.washingtonexaminer.com/wisconsin-defunds-planned-parenthood; James Hohmann, "Walker Would Sign 20-week Abortion Ban," *Politico,* March 3, 2015, https://www.politico.com/story/2015/03/scott-walker-to-sign-20-week-wisconsin-abortion-ban-115726.

104. Laura Bassett, "Tom Corbett, Pennsylvania Governor, on Ultrasound Mandate: Just 'Close Your Eyes,'" The Huffington Post, March 15, 2012.

105. Population Institute, "The Divided States of Reproductive Health and Rights: A 50 State Report Card," 2017, https://www.populationinstitute.org/resources/reports/reportcard, accessed October 17, 2018.

106. Janet Reitman, "The Stealth War on Abortion: How the Tea Party and Christian Right Are Eviscerating Rights," *Rolling Stone,* January 30, 2014, https://www.rollingstone.com/politics /politics-news/the-stealth-war-on-abortion-102195/, accessed October 19, 2018.

107. Maya T. Prabhu, "States Across the South Advance Anti-Abortion 'Heartbeat' Legislation," *The Atlanta Journal-Constitution,* April 25, 2019, https://www.ajc.com/news /state--regional-govt--politics/states-across-the-south-advance-anti-abortion-heartbeat-legislation /R0QjeUfawR5FhX9biXWDoM/, accessed May 3, 2019.

108. Ibid.

109. Alex Hertel-Fernandez, *State Capture*, p. 2.

110. Ari Berman, "The Man Behind Trump's Voter Fraud Obsession," *The New York Times Magazine,* June 13, 2017, https://www.nytimes.com/2017/06/13/magazine/the-man-behind-trumps-voter-fraud-obsession.html, accessed October 18, 2018.

111. Matt Smith, "'Racial Justice Act' Repealed in North Carolina," CNN.com, June 20, 2013, https://www.cnn.com/2013/06/20/justice/north-carolina-death-penalty/index.html, accessed October 18, 2018.

112. Adam Liptak and Michael Wines, "Strict North Carolina Voter ID Law Thwarted After Supreme Court Rejects Case," *The New York Times,* May 15, 2017, https://www.nytimes. com/2017/05/15/us/politics/voter-id-laws-supreme-court-north-carolina.html, accessed October 18, 2018; Rick Hasen, "Race or Party? How Courts Should Think About Republican Efforts to Make It Harder to Vote in North Carolina and Elsewhere," *Harvard Law Review Forum,* vol. 127:58 (2014), https://harvardlawreview.org/wp-content/uploads/pdfs/forvol127_hasen.pdf; North Carolina State University, October 2013; Jonathan M. Katz, "Money, Politics, and Pollution in North Carolina," *The New Yorker,* May 7, 2014.

113. Corey Goldstone, "New Reports from Wisconsin Confirm the Harmful and Discriminatory Impact of Strict Voter Photo ID Laws," Campaign Legal Center, August 13, 2018, https://campaignlegal.org/update/new-reports-wisconsin-confirm-harmful-and-discriminatory-impact-strict-voter-photo-id-laws, accessed October 18, 2018.

114. https://www.motherjones.com/politics/2017/10/voter-suppression-wisconsin-election-2016/.

115. Scott Bauer, David Eggert, and Tom Richards, "Wisconsin, Michigan Republicans Enact Lame-Duck Limits," AP News, December 15, 2018, https://www.apnews.com/be5aa0677abf4bf-fa53f2150fd7aa4f9, accessed December 20, 2018.

116. Jerry M. Melillo, Terese (T.C.) Richmond, and Gary W. Yohe, eds., "Highlights of Climate Change Impacts in the United States: The Third National Climate Assessment," U.S. Global Change Research Program, 2014.

117. Jerry M. Melillo, Terese Richmond, and Gary W. Yohe, "Climate Change Impacts in the United States: The Third Climate Assessment," U.S. Global Change Research Program, 841(2014), pp. 7–8.

118. National survey of 1,200 adults by Greenberg Quinlan Rosner for Democracy Corps' Republican Party Project, July 10–15, 2013.

119. David Gutman, "McKinley Amendment Bars Defense Fund for Climate Change," *Charleston Gazette,* May 25, 2014; Ryan Koronowski, "House Votes to Deny Climate Science and Ties Pentagon's Hands on Climate Change," Think Progress, May 22, 2014.

120. Jamie Fuller, "Environmental Policy Is Partisan. It Wasn't Always," *The Washington Post,* June 2, 2014.

121. Rebecca Leber, "What Happens If Congress Doesn't Deliver on Obama's Climate Promises?" *The New Republic,* February 4, 2015.

122. Benjamin Bell, "Sen. Marco Rubio: Yes, I'm Ready to Be President," ABC News, May 11, 2014.

123. Paul Waldman, "Where the 2016 GOP Contenders Stand on Climate Change," *The Washington Post,* May 12, 2014.

124. Philip Bump, "Why Don't GOP Presidential Candidates Address Climate Change? Because They Want to Win," *The Washington Post*, April 22, 2015. Pope Francis, Encyclical Letter of the Holy Father Francis on Care of Our Common Home (Rome: Vatican Press, English ed., 2015); Max Ehrenfreund, "Pope Francis's Views on Climate Change Put Catholic GOP Candidates in a Bind," *The Washington Post*, June 18, 2015; Jessica Mendoza, "Why Rick Santorum Doesn't Want Pope Francis Talking About Climate Change," *The Christian Science Monitor*, June 3, 2015.

125. National Oceanic and Atmospheric Administration, "NOAA: 2017 was Third Warmest Year on Record for the Globe," https://www.noaa.gov/news/noaa-2017-was-3rd-warmest-year-on-record-for-globe; CNN, "Louisiana Flood: Worst U.S. Disaster Since Sandy," https://www.cnn.com/2016/08/18/us/louisiana-flooding/index.html; ABC News, "Hurricane Harvey Projected to Be 2nd Costliest Storm in U.S History," https://abcnews.go.com/US/hurricane-harvey-projected-2nd-costliest-storm-us-history/story?id=49565583; "Extreme Hurricanes and Wildfires Made 2017 the Most Costly Disaster Year on Record," *The Washington Post*, January 8, 2018, https://www.washingtonpost.com/news/energy-environment/wp/2018/01/08/hurricanes-wildfires-made-2017-the-most-costly-u-s-disaster-year-on-record/?utm_term=.3c63590bc891; all accessed October 19, 2018.

126. Intergovernmental Panel on Climate Change, "Global Warming of 1.5 °C: an IPCC Special Report on the Impacts of Global Warming of 1.5 °C Above Pre-Industrial Levels and Related Global Greenhouse Gas Emission Pathways, in the Context of Strengthening the Global Response to the Threat of Climate Change, Sustainable Development, and Efforts to Eradicate Poverty," published October 8, 2018.

127. John Schwartz and Nadja Popovich, "2018 Continues Warmng Trend as 4th Hottest Year Since 1880," *The New York Times*, February 7, 2019.

128. Joseph Stiglitz, *The Price of Inequality: How Today's Divided Society Endangers Our Future* (New York: Norton, 2013), p. 8; Paul Krugman, "Why We're in a New Gilded Age," *The New York Times*, May 8, 2014; Thomas Piketty, *Capital in the Twenty-First Century*, (Cambridge, MA: Harvard University Press, 2014), p. 47.

129. Piketty, *Capital in the Twenty-First Century*, pp. 292–93, 298; Krugman, "Why We're in a New Gilded Age."

130. Krugman, "Why We're in a New Gilded Age"; Lawrence Mishel and Alyssa Davis, "CEO Pay Continues to Rise as Typical Workers Are Paid Less," Economic Policy Institute, June 12, 2014.

131. Mishel and Davis, "CEO Pay Continues to Rise as Typical Workers Are Paid Less"; Gretchen Morgenson, "An Unstoppable Climb in C.E.O. Pay," *The New York Times*, June 29, 2013.

132. Theo Francis, "Many S&P CEOs Got a Raise in 2018 That Lifted Their Pay to $1 Million a Month," *The Wall Street Journal*, March 17, 2019, https://www.wsj.com/articles/many-s-p-500-ceos-got-a-raise-in-2018-that-lifted-their-pay-to-1-million-a-month-11552820400, accessed March 28, 2019.

133. Tax Foundation, "Preliminary Details and Analysis of the Tax Cuts and Jobs Act," December 18, 2017, https://taxfoundation.org/final-tax-cuts-and-jobs-act-details-analysis/, accessed December 27, 2018; Lawrence Mishel and Jessica Schider, "CEO Compensation Surged in 2017," *Economic Policy Institute*, August 16, 2018, https://www.epi.org/publication/ceo-compensation-surged-in-2017/, accessed December 28, 2018.

134. Alexander Tucciarone "U.S. Corporations Are Splurging on Stock Buybacks while Worker Wages Stagnate," Roosevelt Institute, July 31, 2018, http://rooseveltinstitute.org/new-report-us-corporations-are-splurging-stock-buybacks/, accessed May 3, 2019.

135. Stiglitz, *The Price of Inequality*, p. 28.

136. "History of Federal Individual Income Bottom and Top Bracket Rates," National Taxpayers Union, accessed August 13, 2014; Piketty, *Capital in the Twenty-first Century*, pp. 499, 508–10.

137. Jacob Hacker and Paul S. Pierson, *Winner-Take-All Politics: How Washington Made the Rich Richer* (New York: Simon & Schuster, 2010), pp. 170–71; Stiglitz, *The Price of Inequality*, pp. 131–32.

138. Stiglitz, *The Price of Inequality*, p. 47.

139. Stanley B. Greenberg, *America Ascendent: A Revolutionary Nation's Path to Addressing Its Deepest Problems and Leading the 21st Century* (New York: St. Martin's Press, 2015), p. 81.

140. Richard V. Burkhauser, Jeff Larrimore, and Kosali I. Simon, "A 'Second Opinion' on the Economic Health of the American Middle Class," National Bureau of Economic Research, Working Paper 17164, June 2011; Ron Haskins, "The Myth of the Disappearing Middle Class," *The Washington Post*, March 29, 2012; Scott Winship, "Stop Feeling Sorry for the Middle Class!" Brookings Institute, February 7, 2012, https://www.brookings.edu/opinions/stop-feeling-sorry-for-the-middle-class-theyre-doing-just-fine/; Bruce D. Meyer and James X. Sullivan, "Sorry, Mr. Biden, Most Middle Class Americans Are Better Off Now Than They Were Thirty Years Ago," Fox News, October 24, 2011.

141. Burkhauser, Larrimore, and Simon, "A 'Second Opinion,'" pp. 33–34.

142. Ibid.

143. Haskins, "The Myth of the Disappearing Middle Class."

144. Ibid.

145. Sabrina Tavernise, "Education Gap Grows Between Rich and Poor, Studies Say," *The New York Times*, February 9, 2012.

5 PRESIDENT TRUMP'S GOP IN BATTLE

1. Kevin Roose, "Cesar Sayoc's Path on Social Media: From Food Photos to Partisan Fury," *The New York Times*, October 29, 2018, https://www.nytimes.com/2018/10/27/technology/cesar-sayoc-facebook-twitter.html, accessed March 28, 2019.

2. Southern Poverty Law Center, "In 2018, We Tracked 1,020 Hate Groups Across the U.S." February 21, 2019, p. 3, accessed February 21, 2019.

3. Laurie Goodstein, "'There is still so much evil': Growing Anti-Semitism Stuns American Jews," *New York Times*, October 29, 2018, https://www.nytimes.com/2018/10/29/us/anti-semitism-attacks.html, accessed March 28, 2019; Deadly Shooting at Pittsburgh Synagogue, Anti-Defamation League, October 27, 2018, https://www.adl.org/blog/deadly-shooting-at-pittsburgh-synagogue, accessed March 28, 2019.

4. Southern Poverty Law Center, "In 2018, We Tracked 1,020 Hate Groups Across the U.S." February 21, 2019, p. 5, accessed February 21, 2019.

5. Data is derived from a combined dataset among 6,069 Republicans interviewed from April through September 2018.

6. On behalf of Women's Voices Women Vote Action Fund, Democracy Corps conducted a series of three phone surveys with accompanying web surveys among an ongoing panel of minorities, millennials, unmarried women, and white non-college-educated women (RAE+) in twelve states with governor races (ten Senate races): Arizona, Colorado, Florida, Georgia, Michigan, Minnesota, Nevada, New Mexico, Ohio, Pennsylvania, Tennessee, and Wisconsin. The phone survey of 1,000 registered voters with 66 percent cell rate was conducted September 4–10, 2018. The voter-file-matched web panel of 1,085 RAE+ registered voters was conducted August 28–September 10.

7. Democracy Corps conducted a focus group among white Republican and Republican-leaning independent women who self-identified as conservative and Evangelical in Raleigh, North Carolina, on August 10, 2018. All these women voted for Donald Trump in 2016.

8. Democracy Corps and Greenberg Research conducted a web survey of 1,200 Republicans and Republican-leaning independent registered voters nationally between August 21 and August 26, 2018.

9. Democracy Corps conducted a focus group of Republicans and Republican-leaning independent Catholic conservative and observant Catholic men who voted for Trump in 2016 from Macomb County on July 11, 2018.

10. Democracy Corps conducted a focus group on July 16, 2018, with Republicans and Republican-leaning independent white women from Oakland County, Michigan, who are ideologically moderate and don't identify as Evangelical Christian or observant Catholic. They are mostly working class. All but one third-party voter voted for Trump in 2016.

11. John Cassidy, "Donald Trump's Unhinged Obsession with 'a Man Named John McCain,'" *The New Yorker*, March 21, 2019, https://www.newyorker.com/news/our-columnists/donald-trumps-unhinged-obsession-with-a-man-named-john-mccain, accessed March 28, 2019.

12. Our polling found this 1-to-10 scale had the highest correlation with actually voting when compared with other types of election enthusiasm measures.

6 THE NEW AMERICA STRIKES BACK

1. Ron Brownstein, "Republicans Didn't Learn Anything from the Midterms," *The Atlantic*, November 29, 2018, https://www.theatlantic.com/politics/archive/2018/11/trump-cost-gop-midterms/576850/, accessed December 5, 2018; Dave Wasserman and Ally Flinn, "2018 House Popular Vote Tracker," *Cook Political Report*, https://docs.google.com/spreadsheets/d/1WxDax D5az6kdOjJncmGph37z0BPNhV1fNAH_g7IkpC0/edit#gid=0, accessed December 5, 2018; Michael McDonald, "United States Election Project," https://docs.google.com/spreadsheets/d/1 WxDaxD5az6kdOjJncmGph37z0BPNhV1fNAH_g7IkpC0/edit#gid=0, accessed December 5, 2018.

2. An election phone poll of 1,250 registered voters, including 900 in a fifteen-state battleground was conducted November 4–7, 2018, from a voter-file sample. 1,125 nationally and 800 in the battleground were voters in 2018. Two thirds of respondents were contacted on cell phones in order to accurately reflect the American electorate. Votes and vote share for key demographics were weighted to the AP VoteCast. The margin of error for the full sample is +/-2.77 and +/-3.27 in the fifteen-state presidential battleground at a 95 percent confidence interval.

3. On behalf of Women's Voices Women Vote Action Fund, Democracy Corps conducted a series of four phone surveys with accompanying web surveys among an ongoing panel of minorities, millennials, unmarried women, and white non-college-educated women (RAE+) in twelve states with governor races (10 Senate races): Arizona, Colorado, Florida, Georgia, Michigan, Minnesota, Nevada, New Mexico, Ohio, Pennsylvania, Tennessee, and Wisconsin. The phone survey of 714 registered voters with 66 percent cell rate was conducted November 4–7, 2018. The voter-file-matched web panel of 791 RAE+ registered voters was conducted November 1–14, 2018.

4. Hillary Clinton won the national popular vote by two points in 2016, but Trump won these twelve battleground states by a margin of three points. According to the exit polls, Clinton won unmarried women nationally 62 to 33 (+29) in 2016. In 2018, Democratic House candidates won unmarried women nationally 66 to 31 (+35) and won them 68 to 31 (+37) in this twelve-state battleground. White unmarried women nationally voted 55 to 43 (+12) for Democratic House candidates in 2018 after voting 48 to 46 (+2) for Hillary Clinton in 2016.

5. Mehlman, Castagnetti, Rosen, and Thomas. "A Split Decision in a Divided Nation: What the 2018 Midterms Means for Succeeding in Washington," December 5, 2018, http://mehlmancastagnetti.com/wp-content/uploads/Split-Decision-2018Midterms.pdf, accessed December 11, 2018.

6. It's about a 16.5 percent underperformance from Trump's 2016 support to the Republican Senate Margin in 2018. Note a lot of this is due to West Virginia. Calculations done from data found by J. Miles Coleman, "2018 Senate: How the 'Trump Ten' Races Compared to 2016," *Rasmussen Reports*, November 15, 2016, http://www.rasmussenreports.com/public_content

/political_commentary/commentary_by_j_miles_coleman/2018_senate_how_the_trump_ten
_races_compared_to_2016, accessed December 11, 2018.

7. Democracy Corps conducted the second in a series of two web surveys among an ongoing panel of 1,280 self-identified Republicans and Republican-leaning independents in twelve states with governor races (10 Senate races): Arizona, Colorado, Florida, Georgia, Michigan, Minnesota, Nevada, New Mexico, Ohio, Pennsylvania, Tennessee, and Wisconsin. This web survey took place November 3–16, 2018.

8. Erin Durkin, Trump claims media are blaming him for New Zealand shooting, *The Guardian*, March 18, 2019, https://www.theguardian.com/us-news/2019/mar/18/trump-claims-media-is-blaming-him-for-new-zealand-shooting, accessed March 23, 2019.

7 IS THIS ALL THEY HAVE TO OFFER WORKING PEOPLE?

1. J. D. Vance, *Hillbilly Elegy: A Memoir of a Family and Culture in Crisis* (New York: Harper-Collins, 2017), p. 1.

2. Stanley Greenberg, *Politics and Poverty: Modernization and Response in Five Poor Neighborhoods* (New York: Wiley and Sons, 1974), p. 26.

3. Vance, *Hillbilly Elegy*, p. 142.

4. Ibid., p.4.

5. Ibid., pp. 144–47.

6. Ibid., pp. 75–77.

7. Ibid., p. 4.

8. Ibid., p. 7.

9. Ibid., pp. 5–7.

10. Ibid., p. 7.

11. Ibid.

12. Ibid., p. 5.

13. Ibid.

14. Tweet by Larry H. Summers, https://twitter.com/LHSummers/status/816041644013342721, accessed 4/9/18.

15. Jennifer Senior, "In 'Hillbilly Elegy,' a Tough Love Analysis of the Poor Who Back Trump," *The New York Times*, August 10, 2016, https://www.nytimes.com/2016/08/11/books/review-in-hillbilly-elegy-a-compassionate-analysis-of-the-poor-who-love-trump.html, accessed April 12, 2018.

16. Joshua Rothman, "The Lives of Poor White People," *The New Yorker*, September 12, 2016, https://www.newyorker.com/culture/cultural-comment/the-lives-of-poor-white-people, accessed April 12, 2018.

17. Ibid.

18. Vance, *Hillbilly Elegy*, p. 232.

19. Interview with J. D. Vance by Rod Dreher, "Trump: Tribune of Poor White People," *The American Conservative*, July 22, 2016.

20. Ibid.

21. Ibid.

22. Geoffrey Norman, "Hillbilly Elegy's Unsparing Look at Those Left Behind," *The Weekly Standard*, September 4, 2016, accessed April 12, 2018.

23. Ibid.

24. Mark Hemingway, "This Blockbuster Book Explores the State of Hillbilly America," *The Federalist*, August 5, 2016, https://thefederalist.com/2016/08/05/this-blockbuster-book-explores-the-state-of-hillbilly-america/, accessed April 12, 2018.

25. Ibid.

26. Rothman, "Lives of Poor White People."

27. Greenberg, *Politics and Poverty,* pp. 75–76.

28. See for example Edward Banfield, *The Unheavenly City* (Boston: Little, Brown and Co., 1970).

29. Greenberg, *Politics and Poverty*, pp. 1–5.

30. Ibid., pp. 34–35.

31. Ibid., pp. 32–34.

32. Ibid., pp. 49–51.

33. Ibid., p. 52.

34. Ibid., pp. 208–14.

35. Ibid., pp. 43–48.

36. Ibid., pp. 53–58.

37. Ibid., pp. 59–63.

38. Ibid., pp. 64–71.

39. David E. Bonior, *Eastside Kid: A Memoir of My Youth from Detroit to Congress,* (Prospecta Press, 2014), p. 19.

40. Courtney Balestier, "In Search of the Hillbilly Highway," Metromode, Metro Detroit, November 10, 2016.

41. Ibid.; Courtney Balestier, "Beans and Dobros: Preserving What's Left of Appalachia in Detroit," Metromode, Metro Detroit, January 23, 2017.

42. Ibid.

43. Ibid.

44. Stanley Greenberg, *Middle Class Dreams: The Politics and Power of the New American Majority* (New York: Times Books, 1995), p. 213.

45. Ibid.

46. Ibid., pp. 213–14.

47. John B. Judis, "What the Left Misses About Nationalism: The perception of a common national identity is essential to democracies and to the modern welfare state," *The New York Times,* October 15, 2018, https://www.nytimes.com/2018/10/15/opinion/nationalism-trump -globalization-immigration.html, accessed May 3, 2019.

48. Joseph E. Stiglitz, *People, Power, Profits: Progressive Capitalism for an Age of Discontent,* (New York: W. W. Norton & Company, 2019), p. 82.

49. Joseph E. Stiglitz, *People, Power, Profits: Progressive Capitalism for an Age of Discontent,* (New York: W. W. Norton & Company, 2019); E.J. Dionne, "Is There Such a Thing as Progressive Nationalism," *The American Prospect,* April 1, 2019, https://prospect.org/article/there-such -thing-progressive-nationalism, accessed April 2, 2019; John B. Judis, *The Nationalist Revival: Trade, Immigration, and the Revolt Against Globalization,* (New York: Columbia Global Reports, 2018); Robert Kuttner, "Trump and China: The Art of the Desperate Deal: Will Robert Lighthizer restrain Donald Trump's impulse to take a headline-grabbing and self-defeating China deal?," *The American Prospect,* March 28, 2019, https://prospect.org/article/trump-and -china-art-desperate-deal.

50. Democracy Corps, "Back to Macomb: Reagan Democrats and Barack Obama," August 22, 2008, http://www.democracycorps.com/wp-content/files/backtomacomb082208v11 -final.pdf, accessed April 15, 2018, p. 5.

51. Rakesh Kochar and Anthony Cilluffo, "How Wealth Inequality Has Changed in the U.S. Since the Great Recession, by Race, Ethnicity and Income," Pew Research Center, November 1, 2017, http://www.pewresearch.org/fact-tank/2017/11/01/how-wealth-inequality-has-changed-in -the-u-s-since-the-great-recession-by-race-ethnicity-and-income/, accessed April 16, 2018.

52. Stanley Greenberg, *America Ascendant: A Revolutionary Nation's Path to Addressing Its Deepest Problems and Leading the 21st Century* (New York: St. Martin's Press, 2015), p. 79.

53. Ibid., pp. 129–31.

54. Ibid., pp. 131–39.

55. Ibid., pp. 119–20.

56. Ibid.

57. Alvin Chang and Tara Golshan, "The Republican Push for Welfare 'Work Requirements,' Cartoonsplained," Vox.com, July 26, 2018.

58. Ibid.

59. Ibid.; Jared Bernstein, "The Facts About Work Requirements Are Being Ignored. Here's Why," *The Washington Post*, April 16, 2018.

8 HOW DID DEMOCRATS LET DONALD TRUMP WIN?

1. Ben Rhodes, *The World as It Is: A Memoir of the Obama White House* (New York: Random House, 2018), p. xvi.

2. These graphs are derived from a survey that took place Monday, November 7, through Wednesday, November 9, 2016, among 1,300 voters or (on Monday only) those with a high stated intention of voting in 2016. In addition to a 900-voter base sample, oversamples of 200 Rising American Electorate voters (unmarried women, minorities, and millennials) and 200 battleground state voters (AZ, FL, OH, IA, NC, NV, NH, PA, VA, WI) were included. Margin of error for the full sample is +/-3.27 percentage points at the 95 percent confidence level. Of the 1,300 respondents, 65 percent were interviewed via cell phone in order to accurately sample the American electorate.

3. Annie Lowrey, "Living on Minimum Wage," *The New York Times*, June 15, 2013; "Myth and Reality: The Low-Wage Job Machine," Federal Reserve Bank of Atlanta, August 9, 2013; Steven Rattner, "The Myth of Industrial Rebound," *The New York Times*, January 25, 2014; Harold Meyerson, "The Forty-Year Slump," *The American Prospect*, November 12, 2013; Bill Marsh, "The Low Wage Americans," *The New York Times*, July 27, 2013; Kevin Drum, "The Minimum Wage in America Is Pretty Damn Low," *Mother Jones*, December 2, 2013.

4. National survey of 950 2012 voters by Greenberg Quinlan Rosner for Democracy Corps and the Roosevelt Institute, October 16–21, 2014.

5. U.S. Bureau of Economic Analysis, Real Gross Domestic Product [A191RL1Q225SBEA], retrieved from FRED, Federal Reserve Bank of St. Louis, December 26, 2018, https://fred.stlouisfed.org/series/A191RL1Q225SBEA; U.S. Bureau of Labor Statistics, Civilian Unemployment Rate [UNRATENSA], retrieved from FRED, Federal Reserve Bank of St. Louis, December 26, 2018, https://fred.stlouisfed.org/scrics/UNRATENSA.

6. Donald Trump, Remarks to Veterans, November 15, 2018.

7. Rabal Kamal and Cynthia Cox, "How Has US Spending on Healthcare Changed over Time?" Health System Tracker, Kaiser Family Foundation, https://www.healthsystemtracker.org/chart-collection/u-s-spending-healthcare-changed-time/#item-health-services-spending-growth-slowed-a-bit-in-recent-quarters_2018, accessed December 26, 2018; Leigh Purvis and Dr. Stephen Schondelmeyer, "Rx Price Watch Report: Trends in Retail Prices of Brand Name Prescription Drugs Widely Used by Older Americans: 2017 Year-End Update," AARP Public Policy Institute, https://www.aarp.org/ppi/info-2016/trends-in-retail-prices-of-drugs.html, accessed December 26, 2018.

8. On behalf of Women's Voices Women Vote Action Fund, Democracy Corps conducted a series of three phone surveys with accompanying web surveys among an ongoing panel of minorities, millennials, unmarried women, and white non-college-educated women (RAE+) in twelve states with governor races (10 Senate races): Arizona, Colorado, Florida, Georgia, Michigan, Minnesota, Nevada, New Mexico, Ohio, Pennsylvania, Tennessee, and Wisconsin. The phone survey of 1,000 registered voters with 66 percent cell rate was conducted September 4–10,

2018. The voter-file-matched web panel of 1,085 RAE+ registered voters was conducted August 28–September 10.

9. On behalf of Women's Voices Women Vote Action Fund, Democracy Corps conducted the first in a series of three 1,000 registered voter phone surveys with accompanying registered voter web surveys among an ongoing panel of minorities, millennials, unmarried women, and white non-college educated-women (RAE+) in twelve states with governor races (10 Senate race states). They include six "Diverse States"–Arizona, Colorado, Florida, Georgia, Nevada, and New Mexico–with less than 70 percent white-only populations and six "Rust Belt + States"—Michigan, Minnesota, Ohio, Pennsylvania, Wisconsin, and Tennessee—with more than 70 percent white-only populations. The phone survey of 1,000 voter-file-matched registered voters with 66 percent cell rate was conducted April 5–12, 2018. The voter-file matched web-panel of 3,140 "RAE+" registered voters was conducted April 4–16, 2018. Ideological measures in the web survey were weighted to phone-survey results to account for the bias in web panels.

10. Stephen L. Morgan and Jiwon Lee, "The White Working Class and Voter Turnout in U.S. Presidential Elections, 2004 to 2016," *Sociological Science 4* (2017): p. 664, table 2.

11. Note when I write a third, I'm giving more weight to Election Day polls, which have a much bigger sample. They are weighted down.

12. CNN 2018 exit polls, Democracy Corps September 10 phone poll and web panel.

13. On behalf of Public Citizen, Citizen Opinion conducted a series of six focus groups: two groups among white non-college-educated Trump voters who voted for Obama at least once or identify as Democrats from Macomb County, Michigan, on December 3, 2018, two among white non-college-educated Trump voters who voted for Obama at least once or identify as Democrats from Oak Creek, Wisconsin (south of Milwaukee), on December 4, and two among white college-educated non-Trump voters who voted for Democrats for Congress in 2018 from Seattle, Washington, on December 5. We spoke to the same groups of voters in the same locations on July 20, 24, and 25 in 2017, at the outset of NAFTA renegotiations.

14. This is determined by whether it was the male or female group.

15. Democracy Corps, "New Poll: In Era of Anger, Broad Support for Small Donor-Driven Reform of Campaigns," December 17, 2015, http://www.democracycorps.com/National-Surveys /new-poll-in-era-of-anger-broad-support-for-small-donor-driven-reform-of-campaigns/, accessed January 2, 2018.

16. Ibid.

17. National web survey of 1,200 likely 2016 voters conducted from April 11 through April 18, 2016. Likely voters were determined based on whether they voted in 2012 or had registered since and stated intention of voting in 2016.

18. To accurately compare the conservative visions—which include both the framework and the agenda for the economy—with the progressive alternatives, we combined the results of the progressive frameworks and progressive agendas.

19. Email from Stan Greenberg, April 24, 2016.

20. Email from Stan Greenberg, July 23, 2016.

21. Email from Stanley Greenberg, July 29, 2016.

22. Email from Stanley Greenberg, August 10, 2016.

23. Email from Stanley Greenberg, September 29, 2016.

24. Email from Stanley Greenberg, October 6, 2016.

25. Democracy Corps and Women's Voices Women's Vote Action Fund, "Change Versus More of the Same: On-Going Panel of Target Voting Groups Provides Path for Democrats in 2018," November 2, 2017, http://www.democracycorps.com/attachments/article/1077/Dcor_WV _RAE+%20Panel_Wave%202_Memo_11.2.2017_FOR%20RELEASE.pdf, accessed December 28, 2018.

26. Tax Foundation, "Preliminary Details and Analysis of the Tax Cuts and Jobs Act," Decem-

ber 18, 2017, https://taxfoundation.org/final-tax-cuts-and-jobs-act-details-analysis/, accessed December 27, 2018;

27. Howard Gleckman, "The TCJA Would Cut Taxes by an Average of $1,600 in 2018, with Most Benefits Going to Those Making $300,000-Plus," December 18, 2017, https://www
.taxpolicycenter.org/taxvox/tcja-would-cut-taxes-average-1600-2018-most-benefits-going-those-
making-300000-plus, accessed December 30, 2018.

28. Reuters, "US Economic Growth Slows in Fourth-Quarter on Surging Imports," January 26, 2018, https://www.cnbc.com/2018/01/26/gdp-q4-2017-first-reading.html, accessed January 1, 2019; U.S. Bureau of Labor Statistics, Civilian Unemployment Rate [UNRATE], retrieved from FRED, Federal Reserve Bank of St. Louis, January 1, 2019, https://fred.stlouisfed.
org/series/UNRATE.

29. Heather Long, "Trump Says U.S. Economy May Be the 'Greatest in History.' Let's Check the Record," *The Washington Post*, June 5, 2018, https://www.washingtonpost.com/news
/wonk/wp/2018/06/05/trump-says-u-s-economy-may-be-the-greatest-in-history-lets-check-the-
record/?utm_term=.13f484008621, accessed December 28, 2018; Donald J. Trump, Twitter
.com, September 20, 2018, https://twitter.com/realDonaldTrump/status/1042731410858168320,
accessed December 28, 2018.

30. https://www.marketwatch.com/story/obama-claims-ownership-of-uss-economic-recovery-
as-he-blasts-trump-2018-09-07 "By the time I left office, household income was near its all-time high, and the uninsured rate had hit an all-time low and wages were rising," he said. "I mention all this so when you hear how great the economy is doing right now, let's just remember when this recovery started.

"I'm glad it's continued, but when you hear about this economic miracle that's been going on . . . I have to kind of remind them, actually those job numbers are kind of the same as they were in 2015 and 2016."

31. Stanley Greenberg, *Dispatches from the War Room: In the Trenches with Five Extraordinary Leaders* (New York: St. Martin's Press, 2009), Kindle locations 1253–1405.

32. Democracy Corps, "The Democratic Opportunity on the Economy and Tax Cuts," April 11, 2018, http://www.democracycorps.com/attachments/article/1081/Dcor_AFT
_April%20Tax%20Poll_Memo_4.11.2018_for%20web.pdf, accessed December 30, 2018.

33. Ibid.

34. Ibid.; Democracy Corps Surveys Conducted on behalf of Women's Voices Women's Vote Action Fund, December, September, July, May 2018 surveys, http://www.democracycorps.com
/Battleground-Surveys/, accessed January 2, 2019.

35. Ibid.

36. On behalf of Women's Voices Women Vote Action Fund, Democracy Corps conducted a series of three phone surveys with accompanying web surveys among an ongoing panel of minorities, millennials, unmarried women, and white non-college-educated women (RAE+) in twelve states with governor races (10 Senate races): Arizona, Colorado, Florida, Georgia, Michigan, Minnesota, Nevada, New Mexico, Ohio, Pennsylvania, Tennessee, and Wisconsin. The phone survey of 1,000 registered voters with 66 percent cell rate was conducted September 4–10, 2018. The voter-file-matched web panel of 1,085 RAE+ registered voters was conducted August 28–September 10.

37. Senate Democrats, "A Better Deal," https://www.democrats.senate.gov/abetterdeal, accessed January 2, 2019; House Democrats, "A Better Deal: The Proposals," https://abetterdeal.
democraticleader.gov/category/the-proposals/, accessed January 2, 2019.

38. Ibid.

39. Democratic Policy and Communications Committee, "For the People," https://dpcc.house.
gov/for-the-people, accessed January 2, 2019.

40. Democratic Congressional Campaign Committee, "What Jobs Did the #GOPTaxScam"

REALLY Create?" October 3, 2018, https://www.youtube.com/watch?v=VrCNKT69Ep8, accessed January 2, 2019.

41. Jonathan Freedland, "Explaining Trump, Brexit and Other Expressions of Nationalism," *The New York Times Book Review*, December 18, 2018, https://www.nytimes.com/2018/12/18/books/review/john-b-judis-nationalist-revival.html, accessed May 3, 2019; E.J. Dionne, "Is There Such a Thing as Progressive Nationalism," *The American Prospect*, April 1, 2019, https://prospect.org/article/there-such-thing-progressive-nationalism, accessed April 2, 2019; John B. Judis, *The Nationalist Revival: Trade, Immigration, and the Revolt Against Globalization*, (New York: Columbia Global Reports, 2018).

42. Robert Kuttner, *Can Democracy Survive Global Capitalism?* (New York: W. W. Norton, Incorporated, April 2018), p.184; Tara Golshan and Dylan Scott, "The Big Divide Among 2020 Democracies over Trade—and Why It Matters," *Vox*, February 18, 2019, https://www.vox.com/policy-and-politics/2019/2/18/18215442/2020-presidential-election-trade-elizabeth-warren-bernie-sanders-kamala-harris, accessed February 26, 2019.

43. Robert Kuttner, "*Can Democracy Survive Global Capitalism?*"

44. Stiglitz, *People, Power, Profits: Progressive Capitalism for an Age of Discontent*, pp. 79-81.

45. This phone survey for Public Citizen's Global Trade Watch took place January 12–17 among 1,000 registered voters nationally. Margin of error for the full sample is +/-3.2 percentage points at the 95 percent confidence level. Of the 1,000 respondents, 67 percent were interviewed via cell phone in order to accurately sample the American electorate.

46. David Dayen, "The Biggest Question Mark for the New Congress," *The New Republic*, November 28, 2018.

47. Greg Sargent, "Democratic Focus Groups May Have Identified a Hidden Vulnerability for Trump," *The Washington Post*, February 7, 2019;

48. Freeland; Edward Luce, "Donald Trump is building a populist global club," *Financial Times*, April 11, 2019, https://www.ft.com/content/19196876-5bee-11e9-9dde-7aedca0a081a; Ishaan Tharoor, "Exposing the town crier of the West's far right," *The Washington Post*, April 1, 2019; Shaun Walker, Angela Giuffrida, and Jon Henley, "Salvini aims to forge far-right alliance ahead of European elections," *The Guardian*, April 4, 2019.

49. William H. Frey, "The Millennial Generation: A Demographic Bridge to America's Diverse Future," Brookings Institute, Metropolitan Policy Program, January 2018, https://www.brookings.edu/wp-content/uploads/2018/01/2018-jan_brookings-metro_millennials-a-demographic-bridge-to-americas-diverse-future.pdf, accessed December 27, 2018; also, Sabrina Tavernise, "U.S. Has Highest Share of Foreign-Born Since 1910, with More Coming from Asia," *The New York Times*, September 17, 2018, https://www.nytimes.com/2018/09/13/us/census-foreign-population.html.

50. *Time* series of battleground polls conducted from October 2017 through September 2018.

51. Democracy Corps, "Rising American Electorate and White Working Class Strike Back," November 27, 2018, http://www.democracycorps.com/attachments/article/1103/Dcorps_PE%20Phone_WV_Extended%20Deck_11.27.18_for%20release.pdf, accessed December 27, 2018.

52. These results are the second to be released from an innovative phone and ongoing panel research program for the Women's Voices Women Vote Action Fund to deeply understand the diversity of America and the potential to shape the electorate and outcome in 2018. It is the second in a series of three waves of 1,000 national registered-voter phone surveys with accompanying registered-voter web surveys among a panel of minorities, millennials, unmarried women, and white non-college-educated women (the RAE+), among 4,000 respondents from the first wave of web surveys and 2,454 respondents in the second wave. The national phone survey of 1,000 voter-file-matched registered voters, with 65 percent of respondents reached on cell phones, was conducted October 7–12, 2017. The voter-file matched RAE+ panel of 2,425 registered voters was conducted online October 6–18, 2017. Unless otherwise stated, the results are shown by the RAE only. Where white working-class women are displayed, the results are shown for the full RAE+ sample to accurately reflect the attitudes of these voters. Where changes from the first wave are displayed, the wave 1 responses are filtered to wave 2 respondents only.

53. "The Economic Impact of S.744, The Border Security, Economic Opportunity, and Immigration Modernization Act," Congressional Budget Office, June 2013, p. 1; Jeffrey Passel, D'Vera Cohn, and Ana Gonzalez-Barrera, "Population Decline of Unauthorized Immigrants Stalls, May Have Reversed," Pew Research Center, September, 23, 2013; U.S. Senate, The Border Security, Economic Opportunity, and Immigration Modernization Act, 113th Cong., 1st sess., 2013, S.744; American Immigration Council, "Guide to S.744: Understanding the 2013 Senate Immigration Bill," Immigration Policy Center, July 2013.

54. U.S. Senate, The Border Security, Economic Opportunity, and Immigration Modernization Act; American Immigration Council, "Guide to S.744."

55. "The Economic Impact of S.744," p. 3.

9 AFTER THE CRASH

1. This phone survey took place January 12–17 among 1,000 registered voters nationally. Margin of error for the full sample is +/-3.2 percentage points at the 95 percent confidence level. Of the 1,000 respondents, 67 percent were interviewed via cell phone in order to accurately sample the American electorate.

2. Kevin Morris and Myrna Perez, "Florida, Georgia, North Carolina Still Purging Voters at High Rates," October 1, 2019, https://www.brennancenter.org/blog/florida-georgia-north-carolina-still-purging-voters-high-rates, accessed January 18, 2019; Khushbu Shah, "'Textbook Voter Suppression': Georgia's Bitter Election a Battle Years in the Making," *The Guardian*, November 10, 2018, https://www.theguardian.com/us-news/2018/nov/10/georgia-election-recount-stacey-abrams-brian-kemp, accessed January 17, 2019.

3. Findings from a web survey of 1,200 Republican and Republican-leaning independent registered voters nationally, conducted by Democracy Corps and Greenberg Research August 21–26, 2018.

4. Democracy Corps conducted the second in a series of two web surveys among an ongoing panel of 1,280 self-identified Republicans and Republican-leaning independents in twelve states with governor races (10 Senate races): Arizona, Colorado, Florida, Georgia, Michigan, Minnesota, Nevada, New Mexico, Ohio, Pennsylvania, Tennessee, and Wisconsin. This web survey took place November 3–16, 2018.

5. Ibid.

6. Vice President Mike Pence remarks on the administration's policy toward China October 4, 2018, Hudson Institute; Josh Rogin, "Pence: It's Up to China to Avoid a Cold War," *The Washington Post*, January 27, 2019; Jason Scott, Dandan Li, and Isabel Reynolds, "Pence's Sharp China Attacks Fuel Fears of New Cold War," November 18, 2018, Bloomberg; Laurens Cerulus, "China's Ghost in Europe's Telecom Machine," *Politico*, December 11, 2017; Karen Freifeld and Eric Auchard, "U.S. Probing Huawei for Possible Iran Sanctions Violations: Source," Reuters, April 15, 2018.

7. Jeffrey Goldberg, "'Even a Shining City on a Hill Needs Walls': Senator Tom Cotton," *The Atlantic*, January 26, 2017.

8. California utilizes a "jungle primary" in which the top two vote-getters, regardless of party, face off against each other if no candidate can command a 50 percent +1 majority in the primary.

9. Adam Nagourney, "'There Isn't Hope for Us': Once Dominant, California Republicans Are on the Ropes," *The New York Times*, December 6, 2018, https://www.nytimes.com/2018/12/06/

us/california-republicans-midterms.html, accessed January 17, 2019; Mark Barabak and Michael Finnegan, "Going, Going . . . with Midterm Wipeout, California Republican Party Drifts Closer to Irrelevance," *The Los Angeles Times*, November 18, 2018, https://www.latimes.com/politics/la-me-pol-california-disappearing-republicans-20181116-story.html, accessed January 17, 2019; Ron Brownstein, "California Has Become a Crisis for Republicans," *The Atlantic*, November 22, 2018, https://www.theatlantic.com/politics/archive/2018/11/democrats-greatly-reduce-gop-california-delegation/576559/, accessed January 17, 2019.

10. Ibid.

11. Jeremy B. White, "Reeling California Republicans Elevate Social Conservative," *Politico*, January 15, 2019, https://www.politico.com/story/2019/01/15/california-republicans-social-conservative-1103040, accessed January 18, 2019; Madison Dibble, "'They'd Rather Have Open Borders Than an Open Government': McCarthy Nails Dems Over Failed Border Wall Talks," *Independent Journal Review*, January 13, 2019, https://ijr.com/mccarthy-nails-dems-over-failed-border-wall-talks/, accessed January 18, 2019.

12. Stanley Greenberg, *Dispatches from the War Room: In the Trenches with Five Extraordinary Leaders* (New York: St. Martin's Press, 1999) Kindle locations 390–462.

13. Christopher Jencks and Paul E. Peterson, eds. "Targeting Within Universalism: Politically Viable Policies to Combat Poverty in the United States," *The Urban Underclass* (Washington, D.C.: The Brookings Institution, 1991), pp. 411–36.

14. "A Politics for Our Time," in *The New Majority: Toward a Popular Progressive Politics*, edited by Skocpol Theda and Stanley B. Greenberg (New Haven, CT: Yale University Press, 1997), pp. 1–20, http://www.jstor.org/stable/j.ctt32bhnr.4.

15. Bill Clinton, "The New Covenant: Responsibility and Rebuilding the American Community," remarks delivered at Georgetown University, October 23, 1991, https://www.ibiblio.org/pub/academic/political-science/speeches/clinton.dir/c24.txtp, accessed January 17, 2019; Bill Clinton, "Announcement Speech," remarks delivered at the Old State House, Little Rock, Arkansas, October 3, 1991, http://www.4president.org/speeches/billclinton1992announcement.htm, accessed January 17, 2019.

16. Jonathan Mahler and Jim Ruttenberg, "How Rupert Murdoch's Empire of Influence Remade the World," *The New York Times Magazine*, April 3, 2019, https://www.nytimes.com/interactive/2019/04/03/magazine/rupert-murdoch-fox-news-trump.html?mtrref=www.google.com&gwh=F9A4A2E9EC5C4693BB9922AF8C040467&gwt=pay, accessed April 28, 2019.

17. Stanley Greenberg, *America Ascendant: A Revolutionary Nation's Path to Addressing Its Deepest Problems and Leading the 21st Century* (New York: St. Martin's Press, 2015), pp. 97–99.

18. Pew Research Group, "Support for Same-Sex Marriage Grows, Even Among Groups That Had Been Skeptical," June 26, 2017, http://www.people-press.org/2017/06/26/support-for-same-sex-marriage-grows-even-among-groups-that-had-been-skeptical/, accessed January 18, 2019.

19. See Stanley Greenberg, *America Ascendant*, and E. J. Dionne, *One Nation After Trump: A Guide for the Perplexed, the Disillusioned, the Desperate and the Not-Yet Deported* (New York: St. Martin's Press, 2017), for a further discussion; Tucker Carlson, "Mitt Romney Supports the Status Quo, But for Everyone Else, It's Infuriating," Fox News, January 4, 2019, https://www.foxnews.com/opinion/tucker-carlson-mitt-romney-supports-the-status-quo-but-for-everyone-else-its-infuriating, accessed January 18, 2019.

20. Secretary Mike Pompeo, "Restoring the Role of the Nation-State in the Liberal International Order," remarks delivered to the German Marshall Fund, Brussels, Belgium, December 4, 2018, https://www.state.gov/secretary/remarks/2018/12/287770.htm, accessed January 18, 2019.

21. Edward Luce, "The Double Life of Trumpian Nationalism," *Financial Times*, December 6, 2018, https://www.ft.com/content/340c8cc4-f903-11e8-af46-2022a0b02a6c, accessed January 18, 2019.

22. Bob Woodward, *Fear: Trump in the White House* (New York: Simon & Schuster, 2018), pp. 15, 154, 220–23, 275.

23. Ross Douthat, "Tucker Carlson Versus Conservatism," *The New York Times*, January 12, 2019, https://www.nytimes.com/2019/01/12/opinion/sunday/tucker-carlson-fox-news-republicans.html, accessed January 18, 2019; Jonah Goldberg, "The Free Market Is Not Just a Tool," *National Journal*, January 10, 2019, https://www.nationalreview.com/corner/the-free-market-is-not-just-a-tool/, accessed January 18, 2019.

24. Pew Research, "The Partisan Divide on Political Values Grows Even Wider," October 5, 2017, http://www.people-press.org/2017/10/05/4-race-immigration-and-discrimination/, accessed July 8, 2018; Ridley E. Dunlap, "Partisan Polarization on the Environment Grows Under Trump", *Gallup*, April 5, 2019.

25. *Navigator* no. 8 (January 2019).

26. Edward Luce, "The Clinton-Obama Era Ends as the US Democrats See a Radical New Voice," *Financial Times*, January 13, 2019.

27. Nell Abernathy, Derrick Hamilton, Julie Margetta Morgan, "New Rules for the 21st Century: Corporate Power, Public Power, and the Future of the American Economy," *Roosevelt Institute*, April 2019.

28. Stacey Abrams, "E Pluribus Unum?: Identity Politics Strengthens Democracy," *Foreign Affairs*, February 1, 2019, https://www.foreignaffairs.com/articles/2019-02-01/stacey-abrams-response-to-francis-fukuyama-identity-politics-article, accessed February 3 2019.

29. Francis Fukuyama, *Identity: The Demand for Dignity and the Politics of Resentment* (New York: Farrar, Straus and Giroux, 2018).

30. Louis Menand, "Francis Fukuyama Postpones the End of History," *The New Yorker*, September 3, 2018, https://www.newyorker.com/magazine/2018/09/03/francis-fukuyama-postpones-the-end-of-history, accessed March 24, 2019.

31. Abernathy, Hamilton, Margetta Morgan, "New Rules for the 21st Century: Corporate Power, Public Poser, and the Future of the American Economy."

32. Robert Kuttner, "Steve Bannon, Unrepentant," *The American Prospect*, August 16, 2017, https://prospect.org/article/steve-bannon-unrepentant, accessed March 24, 2019.

33. Congressional Research Service, "H.R.1-For the People Act of 2019," https://www.congress.gov/bill/116th-congress/house-bill/1, accessed March 24, 2019.

34. Ira Katznelson, "When Affirmative Action Was White; An Untold History of Racial Inequality in the Twentieth-Century America" (New York: W. W. Norton & Company, 2005).

35. John Sides, Michael Tesler, Lynn Vavreck, "Identity Politics Can Lead to Progress," *Foreign Affairs*, February 1, 2019, https://www.foreignaffairs.com/articles/2019-02-01/stacey-abrams-response-to-francis-fukuyama-identity-politics-article, p. 8, accessed February 3, 2019.

36. Ronald Reagan, Remarks at the Presentation Ceremony for the Presidential Medal of Freedom, January 19, 1989, https://www.reaganlibrary.gov/011989b, accessed April 16, 2019.

37. John Sides, Michael Tesler, Lynn Vavreck, *Identity Crisis: The 2016 Presidential Campaign and the Battle for the Meaning of America* (New Jersey: Princeton University Press, 2018).

38. New Jersey Election Law Enforcement Commission, Election White Paper, "Contribution Limits and Prohibited Contributions," October 1988, p. 9, https://elec.state.nj.us/pdffiles/white-papers/white1.pdf.

39. Woodrow Wilson, "First Inaugural Address," delivered March 4, 1913, https://www.bartleby.com/124/pres44.html.

40. Pew, "Partisan Divide," October 5, 2017, http://www.people-press.org/2017/10/05/4-race-immigration-and-discrimination/.

INDEX

Mondale, Walter, 201
Mook, Robby, 223, 235–236
Morgan, Julie Margetta, 275
Moving Michigan Forward, 98
Moyers, Bill, 27
Moynihan Report, 195
Mueller, Robert, 141, 146–147, 153, 162
Mueller report, 161, 262
multiculturalism
　and California, 67–71
　Catholic conservative voters on, 139,
　　141–143
　and Democratic Party, 65, 180, 252, 277,
　　278
　and millennials, 39
　moderate conservative voters on, 158–159
　and New America, 1, 4, 11, 17, 44, 273
　and polarization, 71–75
　and Republican Party, 42, 57, 60, 120,
　　180, 182, 258, 265, 273
　Tea Party voters on, 123
　and Trump, 51–71, 159, 166
Mulvaney, Mick, 6, 89
Mummolo, Jonathan, 83
Muslim ban, 64, 253
Mutz, Diana C., 61, 66

NAACP, 196, 199, 260
NAFTA, 14, 36, 58, 61, 63–64, 140, 152,
　191, 202–203, 219, 245–250, 272
Nagourney, Adam, 264
National Association of Manufacturers, 92
National Commission on Fiscal
　Responsibility and Reform, 87–88
Navarro, Peter, 69
New America
　as anti-corporate, 220
　characteristics and demographics, 1, 4, 6,
　　13–16, 25, 71, 72
　and consumer branding, 72
　and the economy, 207
　and health care, 207
　and message testing, 277
　and millennials, 1, 16–17
　response to 2016 presidential election,
　　8–11, 18–24
　and trade, 247, 250
　Trump's politicization of, 273
　and 2018 midterm elections, 174–175, 278
　and 2020 elections, 257, 260, 263
　and Women's Marches, 9–10
　See also Republican Party
　　counterrevolution against New America
New Deal, 28, 111, 266, 271, 278, 280
New Deal Democrats, 28, 266

"New Rules for the 21st Century"
　(Roosevelt Institute report), 275–277
New Zealand mosque shooting (2019), 120,
　184
NFL protests, 17, 72
　Catholic conservative voters on, 141
　secular conservative voters on, 152–153
　Tea Party voters on, 127–128
Nike, 17, 72
Nixon, Richard, 6, 26, 27
Noel, Hans, 83
Norman, Geoffrey, 194
Norquist, Grover, 92
North Carolina, 93–96
NRA, 8, 50, 160

Obama, Barack, 39–42
　and abortion, 37
　and birtherism, 4, 81, 162
　civilian executive branch positions under, 7
　and Clinton, Hillary, 60–61
　DACA (Deferred Action for Childhood
　　Arrivals), 14, 37, 65, 83, 208, 252, 255,
　　262
　Economic Recovery and Reinvestment
　　Act, 40
　as first African-American president, 2, 27
　immigration policy, 13
　inauguration of (2008), 9
　job approval ratings, 43
　as mixed race, 17
　nomination of Merrick Garland, 7
　post-reelection focus groups on, 44–50
　and racial polarization, 28, 41–44
　right-wing ecosystem on, 70
　and Tea Party movement, 2, 3, 26, 37,
　　39–44, 71–72, 74
　trade policy, 61–62
　and Trump, 4, 51, 52, 54, 58
　and voter party identification, 43
　Wall Street bailout (TARP), 3, 39–40, 84
Obama, Michelle, 145
Obama-Trump voters, 65, 117–120
Office of Economic Opportunity, 196
Office of Management and Budget, 6
O'Reilly, Bill, 42
Ornstein, Norman, 78
O'Rourke, Beto, 250

Palin, Sarah, 26
party identification, 27–28, 41, 43, 72, 75
Paul, Rand, 107–108, 271
Pell grants, 113, 114
Pelosi, Nancy, 49, 130, 250, 257, 265, 278
Pence, Mike, 135, 262